# CLYMER®

## MANUALS

## *YAMAHA*

### *YFZ450 & YFZ450R • 2004-2017*

# WHAT'S IN YOUR TOOLBOX?

You Tube™

# More information available at Clymer.com
### Phone: 805-498-6703

**Haynes Publishing Group**
Sparkford Nr Yeovil
Somerset BA22 7JJ England

**Haynes North America, Inc**
859 Lawrence Drive
Newbury Park
California 91320 USA

ISBN-10: 1-62092-323-8
ISBN-13: 978-1-62092-323-8
Library of Congress: 2018935723

*Author:* Mike Morlan
*Technical Illustrations:* Mitzi McCarthy
*Cover:* Mark Clifford Photography at markclifford.com
2013 YFZ450 Bert's Mega Mall, Covina, California

# Common spark plug conditions

## NORMAL
*Symptoms:* Brown to grayish-tan color and slight electrode wear. Correct heat range for engine and operating conditions.
*Recommendation:* When new spark plugs are installed, replace with plugs of the same heat range.

### WORN
*Symptoms:* Rounded electrodes with a small amount of deposits on the firing end. Normal color. Causes hard starting in damp or cold weather and poor fuel economy.
*Recommendation:* Plugs have been left in the engine too long. Replace with new plugs of the same heat range. Follow the recommended maintenance schedule.

### TOO HOT
*Symptoms:* Blistered, white insulator, eroded electrode and absence of deposits. Results in shortened plug life.
*Recommendation:* Check for the correct plug heat range, over-advanced ignition timing, lean fuel mixture, intake manifold vacuum leaks, sticking valves and insufficient engine cooling.

### CARBON DEPOSITS
*Symptoms:* Dry sooty deposits indicate a rich mixture or weak ignition. Causes misfiring, hard starting and hesitation.
*Recommendation:* Make sure the plug has the correct heat range. Check for a clogged air filter or problem in the fuel system or engine management system. Also check for ignition system problems.

### PREIGNITION
*Symptoms:* Melted electrodes. Insulators are white, but may be dirty due to misfiring or flying debris in the combustion chamber. Can lead to engine damage.
*Recommendation:* Check for the correct plug heat range, over-advanced ignition timing, lean fuel mixture, insufficient engine cooling and lack of lubrication.

### ASH DEPOSITS
*Symptoms:* Light brown deposits encrusted on the side or center electrodes or both. Derived from oil and/or fuel additives. Excessive amounts may mask the spark, causing misfiring and hesitation during acceleration.
*Recommendation:* If excessive deposits accumulate over a short time or low mileage, install new valve guide seals to prevent seepage of oil into the combustion chambers. Also try changing gasoline brands.

### HIGH SPEED GLAZING
*Symptoms:* Insulator has yellowish, glazed appearance. Indicates that combustion chamber temperatures have risen suddenly during hard acceleration. Normal deposits melt to form a conductive coating. Causes misfiring at high speeds.
*Recommendation:* Install new plugs. Consider using a colder plug if driving habits warrant.

### OIL DEPOSITS
*Symptoms:* Oily coating caused by poor oil control. Oil is leaking past worn valve guides or piston rings into the combustion chamber. Causes hard starting, misfiring and hesitation.
*Recommendation:* Correct the mechanical condition with necessary repairs and install new plugs.

### DETONATION
*Symptoms:* Insulators may be cracked or chipped. Improper gap setting techniques can also result in a fractured insulator tip. Can lead to piston damage.
*Recommendation:* Make sure the fuel anti-knock values meet engine requirements. Use care when setting the gaps on new plugs. Avoid lugging the engine.

### GAP BRIDGING
*Symptoms:* Combustion deposits lodge between the electrodes. Heavy deposits accumulate and bridge the electrode gap. The plug ceases to fire, resulting in a dead cylinder.
*Recommendation:* Locate the faulty plug and remove the deposits from between the electrodes.

### MECHANICAL DAMAGE
*Symptoms:* May be caused by a foreign object in the combustion chamber or the piston striking an incorrect reach (too long) plug. Causes a dead cylinder and could result in piston damage.
*Recommendation:* Repair the mechanical damage. Remove the foreign object from the engine and/or install the correct reach plug.

# CONTENTS

# QUICK REFERENCE DATA

## ATV INFORMATION

MODEL: _____ YEAR: _____

VIN NUMBER: _____

ENGINE SERIAL NUMBER: _____

CARBURETOR SERIAL NUMBER: _____

VEHICLE MODEL DESIGNATION: _____

KEY NUMBER: _____

## RECOMMENDED LUBRICANTS, FLUIDS AND CAPACITIES

| | |
|---|---|
| Brake fluid | DOT 4 |
| Coolant capacity | |
| Radiator and engine | |
| YFZ450 models | 1.3 L (1.37 qt.) |
| YFZ450R models | 1.25 L (1.32 qt.) |
| Reservoir | |
| YFZ450 models | 0.29 L (0.31 qt.) |
| YFZ450R models | 0.25 L (0.26 qt.) |
| Coolant mixture | 50:50 antifreeze and distilled water |
| Coolant type | Ethylene-glycol containing corrosion inhibitors for aluminum engines |
| Drive chain | Yamaha Chain and Cable Lube for O-ring chains |
| Engine oil | |
| Grade | |
| YFZ450 models | Yamalube 4, API SG, JASO MA (non-friction modified) |
| YFZ450R models | Yamalube 4 or 4-cw (cold weather), API SG or higher, JASO MA |
| Viscosity | See text for temperature/viscosity recommendations |
| YFZ450 models | SAE 5W-30, 10W-30 or 20W-40 |
| YFZ450R models | SAE 5W-30, 10W-40, 20W-50 or 5w-30 (cold weather) |
| Capacity | |
| Oil change only | |
| YFZ450 models* | 1.75 L (1.85 qt.) |
| YFZ450R models | 1.40 L (1.48 qt.) |
| Oil and filter change | |
| YFZ450 models | 1.85 L (1.96 qt.) |
| YFZ450R models | 1.45 L (1.53 qt.) |
| After disassembly (engine dry) | |
| YFZ450 models | 1.95 L (2.06 qt.) |
| YFZ450R models | 1.65 L (1.74 qt.) |
| Fuel | |
| Type | Unleaded |
| Octane | Pump octane of 91 or higher |
| Fuel tank | |
| Total capacity (including reserve) | 10 L (2.64 U.S. gal.) |
| Reserve capacity | |
| YFZ450 models | 1.9 L (0.5 gal.) |
| YFZ450R models | 3.4 L (0.9 U.S. gal.) |

*Fill oil tank with 1.55 L (1.64 qt.) of oil. Add remaining oil to crankcase.

## MAINTENANCE AND TUNE-UP SPECIFICATIONS

| | |
|---|---|
| Brake pad service limit | 1.0 mm (0.039 in.) |
| Brake pedal height (below footrest) | 11.7 mm (0.46 in.) |
| Brake pushrod nut to locknut gap | 2.2-3.2 mm (0.09-0.13 in) |
| Clutch lever free play | 8-13 mm (0.31-0.51 in.) |
| Drive chain free play | 25-35 mm (0.98-1.38 in.) |
| Idle speed | |
|   YFZ450 models | 1750-1850 rpm |
|   YFZ450R models | 1950-2050 rpm |
| Ignition timing | |
|   YFZ450 models | 7.5° BTDC @ 1800 rpm |
|   YFZ450R models | 7.5° BTDC @ 2000rpm |
| Parking brake cable length | |
|   2004-2005 models | 56-60 mm (2.2-2.4 in.) |
|   2006-on models | 47-51 mm (1.8-2.0 in.) |
| Radiator cap pressure relief | 108-137 kPa (15.6-19.8 psi) |
| Shift pedal height (above footrest) | |
|   YFZ450 models | 25.0 mm (0.98 in.) |
|   YFZ450R models | 48.0 mm (1.9 in.) |
| Spark plug | |
|   Type | CR8E (NGK) |
|   Plug gap | 0.7-0.8 mm (0.028-0.031 in.) |
| Speed limiter screw length | 12 mm (0.47 in) maximum |
| Throttle lever free play | 2-4 mm (0.08-0.16 in.) |
| Tire inflation pressure* | |
|   2004-2005 models | |
|     Front | 4.4 psi (30 kPa) |
|     Rear | 5.1 psi (35 kPa) |
|   2006-on models | |
|     Front | 4.0 psi (27.5 kPa) |
|     Rear | 4.4 psi (30 kPa) |
| Tire tread knob height (min.) | 3 mm (0.12 in.) |
| Valve clearance (cold) | |
|   Intake | 0.10-0.15 mm (0.0039-0.0059 in.) |
|   Exhaust | 0.20-0.25 mm (0.0079-0.0098 in.) |

*Tire inflation pressure is for original equipment tires. Aftermarket tires may require different inflation pressure. The use of tires other than those specified by the manufacturer may cause instability. Check tire inflation pressure when the tires are cold.

## MAINTENANCE TORQUE SPECIFICATIONS

| Item | N•m | in.-lb. | ft.-lb. |
|---|---|---|---|
| Axle hub retaining nuts (2004-2005 models) | 85 | – | 62 |
| Axle hub pinch bolts* | 21 | – | 15 |
| Chain adjuster locknut (2004-2005 models) | 16 | – | 12 |
| Coolant drain bolt | 10 | 88 | – |
| Crankcase oil drain | 20 | – | 15 |
| Drive sprocket nut | | | |
|   YFZ450 | 75 | – | 55 |
|   YFZ450R | 100 | – | 72 |
| Driven sprocket nuts | | | |
|   2004-2005 models | 55 | – | 40 |
|   2006-on models | 72 | – | 53 |
| Oil check bolt (YFZ450R models) | 7 62 | – | |
| Oil filter drain bolt | 10 | 88 | – |
| Oil filter cover bolts | 10 | 88 | – |
| Oil gallery bolt (YFZ450 models) | 10 | 88 | – |
| Oil tank drain bolt | | | |
|   YFZ450 models | 19 | – | 14 |
|   YFZ450R models | 20 | – | 15 |
| Shock absorber spring locknut (front) | | | |
|   YFZ450 models | 30 | – | 22 |
|   YFZ450R models | 50 | – | 36 |
| Shock absorber spring locknut (rear) | 44 | – | 32 |
| Spark plug | 13 | 115 | – |
| Wheel lug nuts* | 45 | – | 33 |

*Refer to text.

**CHAPTER ONE**

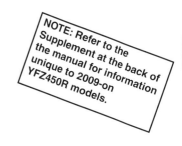

NOTE: Refer to the Supplement at the back of the manual for information unique to 2009-on YFZ450R models.

# GENERAL INFORMATION

This manual covers YFZ450 (2004-2013) and YFZ450R (2009-2012) models. For YFZ450 models the derivatives covered include: YFZ450BB Bill Balance Edition (2006-2007); YFZ450SE Special Edition (2005, 2007); YFZ450SE Special Edition II (2007); YFZ450SP Special Edition (2006, 2008) and YFZ450SP2 Special Edition II (2008).

Procedures and specifications that are unique to YFZ450R models are covered in the Supplement at the back of the manual. When working on a YFZ450R model, refer to the Supplement first. The table of contents at the front of the manual outlines the sections included in the Supplement.

## MANUAL ORGANIZATION

A shop manual is a reference tool and, as in all Clymer manuals, the chapters are thumb-tabbed for easy reference. Important items are indexed at the end of the manual. Frequently used specifications and capacities from individual chapters are summarized in the *Quick Reference Data* at the front of the manual.

During some of the procedures there will be references to headings in other chapters or sections of the manual. When a specific heading is called out in a step it is italicized as it appears in the manual. If a sub-heading is indicated as being "in this section" it is located within the same main heading. For example, the sub-heading *Gasoline* is located within the main heading *SAFETY*.

This chapter provides general information on shop safety, tool use, service fundamentals and shop supplies. **Tables 1-7** at the end of the chapter provide general vehicle, mechanical and shop information.

Chapter Two provides methods for quick and accurate diagnoses of problems. Troubleshooting procedures present typical symptoms and logical methods to pinpoint and repair a problem.

Chapter Three explains all routine maintenance.

Subsequent chapters describe specific systems, such as engine, clutch, transmission, fuel system, electrical system, cooling system, wheels, tires, drive chain, suspension, brakes and body components.

Specification tables, when applicable, are located at the end of each chapter.

## WARNINGS, CAUTIONS AND NOTES

The terms WARNING, CAUTION and NOTE have specific meanings in this manual.

A WARNING emphasizes areas where injury or even death could result from negligence. Mechanical damage may also occur. WARNINGS *are to be taken seriously*.

A CAUTION emphasizes areas where equipment damage could result. Disregarding a CAUTION could cause permanent mechanical damage, though injury is unlikely.

A NOTE provides additional information to make a step or procedure easier or clearer. Disregarding a NOTE could cause inconvenience, but would not cause equipment damage or injury.

## SAFETY

Follow these guidelines and practice common sense to safely service the ATV:

1. Do not operate the ATV in an enclosed area. The exhaust gases contain carbon monoxide, an odorless, colorless and tasteless poisonous gas. Carbon monoxide levels build quickly in small-enclosed areas and can cause unconsciousness and death in a short time. Make sure the work area is properly ventilated, or operate the ATV outside.

2. Never use gasoline or any flammable liquid to clean parts. Refer to *Gasoline* and *Parts Cleaning* in this section.

3. Never smoke or use a torch in the vicinity of flammable liquids, such as gasoline or cleaning solvent.

4. Do not remove the radiator cap or cooling system hose while the engine is hot. The cooling system is pressurized and the high temperature coolant may cause injury.

5. Dispose of and store coolant in a safe manner. Do not allow children or pets access to open containers of coolant. Animals are attracted to antifreeze.

6. Avoid contact with engine oil and other chemicals. Most are known carcinogens. Wash your hands thoroughly after coming in contact with engine oil. If possible, wear a pair of disposable gloves.

7. If welding or brazing on the ATV, remove the fuel tank and shocks to a safe distance at least 50 ft. (15 m) away.

8. Use the correct types and sizes of tools to avoid damaging fasteners.

9. Keep tools clean and in good condition. Replace or repair worn or damaged equipment.

10. When loosening a tight fastener, be guided by what would happen if the tool slips.

11. When replacing fasteners, make sure the new fasteners are the same size and strength as the originals.

12. Keep the work area clean and organized.

13. Wear eye protection *any time* the safety of your eyes is in question. This includes procedures involving drilling, grinding, hammering, compressed air and chemicals.

14. Wear the correct clothing for the job. Tie up or cover long hair so it cannot catch in moving equipment.

15. Do not carry sharp tools in clothing pockets.

16. Always have an approved fire extinguisher available. Make sure it is rated for gasoline (Class B) and electrical (Class C) fires.

17. Do not use compressed air to clean clothes, the ATV or the work area. Debris may be blown into the eyes or skin. Never direct compressed air at anyone. Do not allow children to use or play with any compressed air equipment.

18. When using compressed air to dry rotating parts, hold the part so it cannot rotate. Do not allow the force of the air to spin the part. The air jet is capable of rotating parts at extreme speeds. The part may be damaged or disintegrate, causing serious injury.

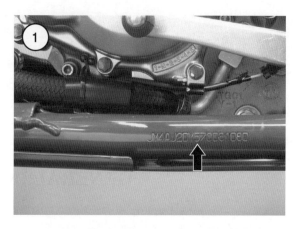

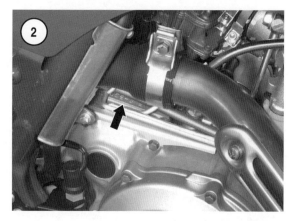

19. Do not inhale the dust created by brake pad and clutch wear. These particles may contain asbestos. In addition, some types of insulating materials and gaskets may contain asbestos. Inhaling asbestos particles is hazardous to health.

20. Never work on the ATV while someone is working under it.

21. When placing the ATV on a stand or overhead lift, make sure it is secure before walking away.

### Gasoline

Gasoline is a volatile flammable liquid and is one of the most dangerous items in the shop. Because gasoline is used so often, many people forget that it is hazardous. Only use gasoline as fuel for gasoline internal combustion engines. Keep in mind when working on an ATV, gasoline is always present in the fuel tank, fuel line and fuel body. To avoid an accident when working around the fuel system, carefully observe the following precautions:

1. *Never* use gasoline to clean parts. Refer to *Parts Cleaning* in this section.

2. When working on the fuel system, work outside or in a well-ventilated area.

3. Do not add fuel to the fuel tank or service the fuel system while the ATV is near open flames, sparks or

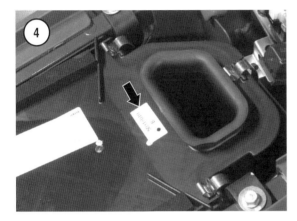

tremely flammable. To prevent chemical exposure, vapor buildup, fire and injury, observe each product's warning label and note the following:

1. Read and observe the entire product label before using any chemical. Always know what type of chemical is being used and whether it is poisonous and/or flammable.

2. Do not use more than one type of cleaning solvent at a time. If mixing chemicals is required, measure the proper amounts according to the manufacturer.

3. Work in a well-ventilated area.

4. Wear chemical-resistant gloves.

5. Wear safety glasses.

6. Wear a vapor respirator if the instructions call for it.

7. Wash hands and arms thoroughly after cleaning parts.

8. Keep chemicals away from children and pets, especially coolant. Animals are attracted to antifreeze.

9. Thoroughly clean all oil, grease and cleaner residue from any part that must be heated.

10. Use a nylon brush when cleaning parts. Metal brushes may cause a spark.

11. When using a parts washer, only use the solvent recommended by the manufacturer. Make sure the parts washer is equipped with a metal lid that will lower in case of fire.

where someone is smoking. Gasoline vapor is heavier than air, collects in low areas and is more easily ignited than liquid gasoline.

4. Allow the engine to cool completely before working on any fuel system component.

5. Do not store gasoline in glass containers. If the glass breaks, an explosion or fire may occur.

6. Immediately wipe up spilled gasoline with rags. Store the rags in a metal container with a lid until they can be properly disposed, or place them outside in a safe place for the fuel to evaporate.

7. Do not pour water onto a gasoline fire. Water spreads the fire and makes it more difficult to put out. Use a class B, BC or ABC fire extinguisher to extinguish the fire.

8. Always turn off the engine before refueling. Do not spill fuel onto the engine or exhaust system. Do not overfill the fuel tank. Leave an air space at the top of the tank to allow room for the fuel to expand due to temperature fluctuations.

## Parts Cleaning

Cleaning parts is one of the more tedious and difficult service jobs performed in the home garage. Many types of chemical cleaners and solvents are available for shop use. Most are poisonous and ex-

## Warning Labels

Most manufacturers attach information and warning labels to the ATV. These labels contain instructions that are important to safety when operating, servicing, transporting and storing the ATV. Refer to the owner's manual for the description and location of labels. Order replacement labels from the manufacturer if they are missing or damaged.

## SERIAL NUMBERS AND INFORMATION LABELS

Serial numbers are located at various locations on the machine. Record these numbers in the *Quick Reference Data* section in the front of this manual. Have these numbers available when ordering parts.

The VIN number (**Figure 1**) is located on the left side of the frame beneath the engine.

The engine serial number is stamped on a pad on the right side of the lower crankcase (**Figure 2**).

The carburetor serial number is located on the left side of the carburetor body above the float bowl (**Figure 3**).

The vehicle model designation is noted on a label attached to the air box (**Figure 4**).

A tire pressure label is affixed to the rear fender (**Figure 5**).

Record the key number (**Figure 6**) so it can be replaced if lost.

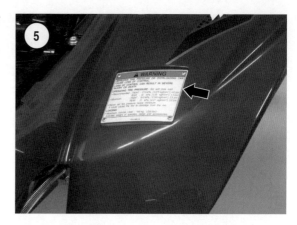

## FASTENERS

> *WARNING*
> *Do not install fasteners with a strength classification lower than what was originally installed by the manufacturer. Doing so may cause equipment failure and/or damage.*

Proper fastener selection and installation is important to ensure the ATV operates as designed and can be serviced efficiently. The choice of original equipment fasteners is not arrived at by chance. Make sure replacement fasteners meet the requirements.

### Threaded Fasteners

Threaded fasteners secure most of the components on the ATV. Most are tightened by turning them clockwise (right-hand threads). If the normal rotation of the component being tightened would loosen the fastener, it may have left-hand threads. If a left-hand threaded fastener is used, it is noted in the text.

Two dimensions are required to match the thread size of the fastener: the number of threads in a given distance and the outside diameter of the threads.

Two systems are currently used to specify threaded fastener dimensions: the U.S. Standard system and the metric system (**Figure 7**). Pay particular attention when working with unidentified fasteners; mismatching thread types can damage threads.

To ensure the fastener threads are not mismatched or cross-threaded, start all fasteners by hand. If a fastener is difficult to start or turn, determine the cause before tightening with a wrench.

Match fasteners by their length (L, **Figure 8**), diameter (D) and distance between thread crests (pitch, T). A typical metric bolt may be identified by the numbers, 8-1.25 × 130. This indicates the bolt has a diameter of 8 mm, the distance between thread crests is 1.25 mm and the length is 130 mm. Always measure bolt length as shown in L, **Figure 8** to avoid installing replacements with the wrong length.

If a number is located on the top of a metric fastener (**Figure 8**), this indicates the strength. The higher the number, the stronger the fastener is. Typically, unnumbered fasteners are the weakest.

Many screws, bolts and studs are combined with nuts to secure particular components. To indicate the

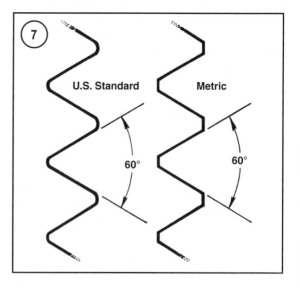

size of a nut, manufacturers specify the internal diameter and thread pitch.

The measurement across two flats on a nut or bolt indicates the wrench size.

### Torque Specifications

The materials used in the manufacture of the ATV may be subjected to uneven stresses if fasteners are

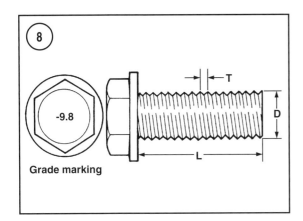

Grade marking

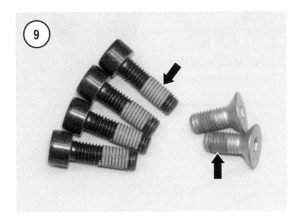

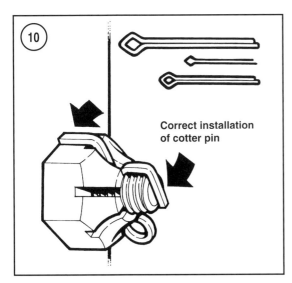

Correct installation
of cotter pin

of the fastener as described in *Threaded Fasteners* in this section. Torque specifications for specific components are at the end of the appropriate chapters. Torque wrenches are covered in *Tools* in this chapter.

### Self-Locking Fasteners

Several types of bolts, screws and nuts incorporate a system that creates interference between the two fasteners. Interference is achieved in various ways. The most common type used is the nylon insert nut and a dry adhesive coating on the threads of a bolt.

Self-locking fasteners offer greater holding strength than standard fasteners, which improves their resistance to vibration. Self-locking fasteners cannot be reused. The materials used to form the lock become distorted after the initial installation and removal. Do not replace self-locking fasteners with standard fasteners.

Some fasteners are equipped with a threadlock preapplied to the fastener threads (**Figure 9**). When replacing these fasteners, do not apply a separate threadlock. When it is necessary to reuse one of these fasteners, remove the threadlock residue from the threads. Then apply the threadlock specified in the text.

### Washers

The two basic types of washers are flat washers and lockwashers. Flat washers are simple discs with a hole to fit a screw or bolt. Lockwashers are used to prevent a fastener from working loose. Washers can be used as spacers and seals or to help distribute fastener load and prevent the fastener from damaging the component.

As with fasteners, when replacing washers make sure the replacements meet the original specifications.

### Cotter Pins

A cotter pin is a split metal pin inserted into a hole or slot to prevent a fastener from loosening. In certain applications, such as the rear axle, the fastener must be secured in this way. For these applications, a cotter pin and castellated (slotted) nut is used.

To use a cotter pin, first make sure the diameter is correct for the hole in the fastener. After correctly tightening the fastener and aligning the holes, insert the cotter pin through the hole and bend the ends over the fastener (**Figure 10**). Unless instructed to do so, never loosen a tightened fastener to align the holes. If the holes do not align, tighten the fastener just enough to achieve alignment.

not installed and tightened correctly. Improperly installed fasteners or ones that worked loose can cause extensive damage. It is essential to use an accurate torque wrench, as described in this chapter, with the torque specifications in this manual.

Specifications for torque are provided in Newton-meters (N•m), foot-pounds (ft.-lb.) and inch-pounds (in.-lb.). Refer to **Table 5** for general torque recommendations. To use **Table 5**, first determine the size

Cotter pins are available in various diameters and lengths. Measure length from the bottom of the head to the tip of the shortest pin.

### Snap Rings and E-clips

Snap rings (**Figure 11**) are circular-shaped metal retaining clips. They are required to secure parts and gears in place on parts such as shafts, pins or rods. External snap rings are used to retain items on shafts. Internal snap rings secure parts within housing bores. In some applications, in addition to securing the component(s), snap rings of varying thickness also determine endplay. These are usually called selective snap rings.

The two basic types of snap rings are machined and stamped snap rings. Machined snap rings (**Figure 12**) can be installed in either direction because both faces have sharp edges. Stamped snap rings (**Figure 13**) are manufactured with a sharp edge and round edge. When installing a stamped snap ring in a thrust application, install the sharp edge facing away from the part producing the thrust.

E-clips are used when it is not practical to use a snap ring. Remove E-clips with a flat blade screwdriver by prying between the shaft and E-clip. To install an E-clip, center it over the shaft groove and push or tap it into place.

Observe the following when installing snap rings:
1. Remove and install snap rings with snap ring pliers. Refer to *Tools* in this chapter.
2. In some applications, it may be necessary to replace snap rings after removing them.
3. Compress or expand snap rings only enough to install them. If overly expanded, they lose their retaining ability.
4. After installing a snap ring, make sure it seats completely.
5. Wear eye protection when removing and installing snap rings.

### SHOP SUPPLIES

#### Lubricants and Fluids

The following section describes the types of lubricants most often required. Make sure to follow the manufacturer's recommendations.

#### *Engine oils*

Engine oil for a four-stroke ATV engine use is classified by three standards: the American Petroleum Institute (API) service classification, the Society of Automotive Engineers (SAE) viscosity rating and

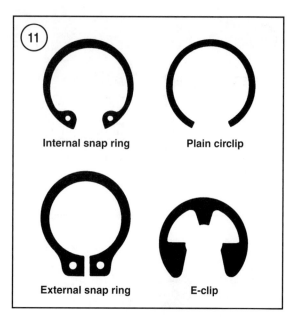

Internal snap ring      Plain circlip

External snap ring      E-clip

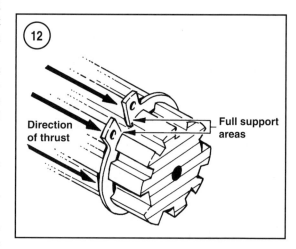

Direction of thrust      Full support areas

the Japanese Automobile Standards Organization (JASO) T 903 certification standard.

The API and SAE information is on all oil container labels. The JASO information is found on oil containers specifically for ATV use. Two letters indicate the API service classification. The number or sequence of numbers and letter (10W-40 for example) is the oil's viscosity rating. The JASO certification label identifies two separate oil classifications and a registration number to ensure the oil has passed all JASO certification standards for use in four-stroke ATV engines.

The API service classification indicates that the oil meets specific lubrication standards and is not an indication of oil quality. The first letter *S* indicates that the oil is for gasoline engines. The second letter indicates the standard the oil satisfies.

The JASO certification label identifies two separate oil classifications and a registration number to ensure the oil has passed all JASO certification stan-

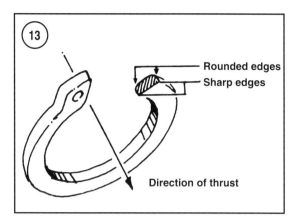

Rounded edges
Sharp edges
Direction of thrust

dards for use in four-stroke ATV engines. The classifications are: MA (high friction applications) and MB (low friction applications).

Viscosity is an indication of the oil's thickness. Thin oils have a lower number while thick oils have a higher number. Engine oils fall into the 5- to 50-weight range for single-grade oils.

Most manufacturers recommend multi-grade oil. These oils perform efficiently across a wide range of operating conditions. A W identifies multi-grade oils, which indicates the low-temperature viscosity.

Engine oils are most commonly mineral (petroleum) based; however, synthetic and semi-synthetic types are used more frequently. Always use oil with a classification recommended by the manufacturer (Chapter Three). Using oil with a different classification can cause engine damage.

### *Greases*

Grease is lubricating oil with thickening agents added to it. The National Lubricating Grease Institute (NLGI) grades grease. Grades range from No. 000 to No. 6, with No. 6 being the thickest. Typical multipurpose grease is NLGI No. 2. For specific applications, manufacturers may recommend a water-resistant grease or one with an additive, such as molybdenum disulfide ($MoS_2$).

### *Brake fluid*

> *WARNING*
> *Never put a mineral-based (petroleum) oil into the brake system. Mineral oil causes rubber parts in the system to swell and break apart, causing complete brake failure.*

Brake fluid is the hydraulic fluid used to transmit hydraulic pressure (force) to the wheel brakes. Brake fluid is classified by the Department of Transportation

(DOT). This classification appears on the fluid container. The models covered in this manual require DOT 4 brake fluid.

Each type of brake fluid has its own definite characteristics. Do not intermix different types of brake fluid; this may cause brake system failure. DOT 5 brake fluid is silicone based. DOT 5 is not compatible with other brake fluids or in systems for which it was not designed. Mixing DOT 5 fluid with other fluids may cause brake system failure. When adding brake fluid, *only* use DOT 4 brake fluid.

Brake fluid damages any plastic, painted or plated surface it contacts. Use extreme care when working with brake fluid, and remove any spills immediately with soap and water.

Hydraulic brake systems require clean and moisture free brake fluid. Never reuse brake fluid. Keep containers and reservoirs properly sealed.

### Cleaners, Degreasers and Solvents

Many chemicals are available to remove oil, grease and other residue from the ATV. Before using cleaning solvents, consider their uses and disposal methods, particularly if they are not water-soluble. Local ordinances may require special procedures for the disposal of many types of cleaning chemicals. Refer to *Parts Cleaning* in *Safety* in this chapter.

Use brake parts cleaner to clean brake system components when contact with petroleum-based products will damage seals. Brake parts cleaner leaves no residue. Use electrical contact cleaner to clean electrical connections and components without leaving any residue. Carburetor cleaner is a powerful solvent used to remove fuel deposits and varnish from fuel system components. Use this cleaner carefully; it may damage finishes.

Generally, degreasers are strong cleaners used to remove heavy accumulations of grease from engine and frame components.

Most solvents are designed to be used with a parts washing cabinet for individual component cleaning. For safety, use only nonflammable or high flash point solvents.

### Gasket Sealant

Sealants are used in combination with a gasket or seal or occasionally alone. Use extreme care when choosing a sealant different from the type originally recommended. Choose sealants based on their resistance to heat, various fluids and their sealing capabilities.

One of the most common sealants is RTV, or room temperature vulcanizing, sealant. This sealant cures at room temperature over a specific time period. This allows the repositioning of components without damaging gaskets.

Moisture in the air causes the RTV sealant to cure. Always install the tube cap as soon as possible after applying RTV sealant. RTV sealant has a limited shelf life and will not cure properly if the shelf life has expired. Keep partial tubes sealed and discard them if they have surpassed the expiration date. If there is no expiration date on a sealant tube, use a permanent marker and write the date on the tube when it is first opened. Manufacturers usually specify a shelf life of one year after a container is opened, though it is recommended to contact the sealant manufacturer to confirm shelf life.

### Removing sealant

Sealant is used on many engine gasket surfaces. When cleaning parts after disassembly, a razor blade or gasket scraper is required to remove the residue that cannot be pulled off by hand from the gasket surfaces. To avoid damaging gasket surfaces, use a gasket remover to help soften the residue before scraping.

### Applying sealant

Clean all old sealer from the mating surfaces. Then inspect the mating surfaces for damage. Remove all sealer material from blind threaded holes; it can cause inaccurate bolt torque. Spray the mating surfaces with aerosol parts cleaner, and then wipe with a lint-free cloth. Because gasket surfaces must be dry and oil-free for the sealant to adhere, be thorough when cleaning and drying the parts.

Apply sealant in a continuous bead 2-3 mm (0.08-0.12 in.) thick. Circle all the fastener holes unless otherwise specified. Do not allow any sealant to enter these holes. Note any specific chapter information showing how to apply the sealer to a specific gasket surface. Assemble and tighten the fasteners to the specified torque within the time frame recommended by the sealant manufacturer.

### Gasket Remover

Aerosol gasket remover can help remove stubborn gaskets. This product can speed up the removal process and prevent damage to the mating surface that may be caused by using a scraping tool. Most of these types of products are very caustic. Follow the gasket remover manufacturer's instructions for use.

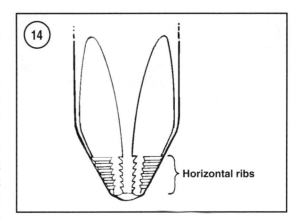

Horizontal ribs

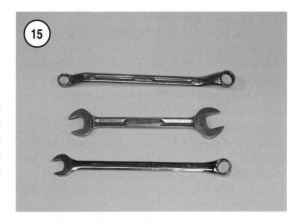

### Threadlocking Compound

*CAUTION*
*Threadlocking compounds are anaerobic and damage most plastic parts and surfaces. Use caution when using these products in areas where plastic components are located.*

A threadlocking compound is a fluid applied to the threads of fasteners. After tightening the fastener, the fluid dries and becomes solid. This makes it difficult for the fastener to work loose from vibration or heat expansion and contraction. Some threadlocking compounds also provide a seal against fluid leaks.

Before applying threadlocking compound, remove any old compound from both thread areas and clean them with aerosol parts cleaner. Use the compound sparingly. Excess fluid can run into adjoining parts.

Threadlocking compounds are available in various strengths, temperatures and repair applications.

### TOOLS

Most of the procedures in this manual can be carried out with hand tools and test equipment familiar to the home mechanic. Always use the correct tools for the

job. Keep tools organized and clean and store them in a tool chest with related tools organized together.

Quality tools are essential. The best are constructed of high-strength alloy steel. These tools are light, easy-to-use and resistant to wear. Their working surfaces are devoid of sharp edges and the tools are carefully polished. They have an easy-to-clean finish and are comfortable to use. Quality tools are a good investment.

When purchasing tools to perform the procedures covered in this manual, consider the tool's potential frequency of use. If a tool kit is just now being started, consider purchasing a tool set from a quality tool supplier. These sets are available in many tool combinations and offer substantial savings when compared to individually purchased tools. As work experience grows and tasks become more complicated, specialized tools can be added.

Some of the procedures in this manual specify special tools. In most cases, the tool is illustrated in use. In some cases it may be possible to substitute similar tools or fabricate a suitable replacement. However, at times, the specialized equipment or expertise may make it impractical for the home mechanic to perform the procedure. When necessary, such operations are identified in the text with the recommendation to have a dealership or specialist perform the task.

## Screwdrivers

The two basic types of screwdrivers are the slotted tip (flat blade) and the Phillips tip. These are available in sets that often include an assortment of tip sizes and shaft lengths.

As with all tools, use the correct screwdriver. Make sure the size of the tip conforms to the size and shape of the fastener. Use them only for driving screws. Never use a screwdriver for prying or chiseling. Repair or replace worn or damaged screwdrivers. A worn tip may damage the fastener, making it difficult to remove.

Phillips-head screws are often damaged by incorrectly fitting screwdrivers. Quality Phillips screwdrivers are manufactured with their crosshead tip machined to Phillips Screw Company specifications. Poor quality or damaged Phillips screwdrivers can back out and round over the screw head (camout). Compounding the problem of using poor quality screwdrivers are Phillips-head screws made from weak or soft materials and screws installed with air tools.

An effective alternative screwdriver for Phillips screws is the ACR Phillips II screwdriver. Horizontal anti-camout ribs on the driving faces or flutes of the screwdrivers tip (**Figure 14**) improve the driver-to-fastener grip. While designed to be used with ACR Phillips II screws, they also work well on all common Phillips screws. ACR Phillips II screwdrivers are available in different tip sizes and interchangeable bits to fit screwdriver bit holders.

Another way to prevent camout and increase the grip of a Phillips screwdriver is to apply valve grinding compound or Permatex Screw & Socket Gripper onto the screwdriver tip. After loosening/tightening the screw, clean the screw recess to prevent possible contamination.

## Wrenches

Box-end, open-end and combination wrenches (**Figure 15**) are available in a variety of types and sizes.

The number stamped on the wrench refers to the distance between the work areas. This size must match the size of the fastener head.

The box-end wrench is an excellent tool because it grips the fastener on all sides. This reduces the chance of the tool slipping. The box-end wrench is designed with either a 6- or 12-point opening. For stubborn or damaged fasteners, the 6-point provides superior holding ability by contacting the fastener across a wider area at all six edges. For general use, the 12-point works well. It allows the wrench to be removed and reinstalled without moving the handle over such a wide arc.

An open-end wrench is fast and works best in areas with limited overhead access. It contacts the fastener at only two points, and is subject to slipping under heavy force or if the tool or fastener is worn. A box-end wrench is preferred in most instances, especially when breaking loose and applying the final tightness to a fastener.

The combination wrench has a box-end on one end, and an open-end on the other. This combination makes it a convenient tool.

## Adjustable Wrenches

An adjustable wrench (**Figure 16**) can fit nearly any nut or bolt head that has clear access around its entire perimeter.

However, adjustable wrenches contact the fastener at only two points, which makes them more subject to slipping off the fastener. One jaw is adjustable and may loosen, which increases this possibility. Make certain the solid jaw is the one transmitting the force.

However, adjustable wrenches are typically used to prevent a large nut or bolt from turning while the other end is being loosened or tightened with a box-end or socket wrench.

### Socket Wrenches, Ratchets and Handles

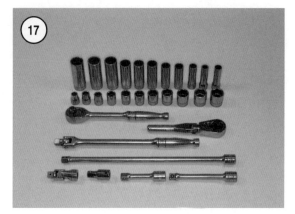

> *WARNING*
> *Do not use hand sockets with air or impact tools; they may shatter and cause injury. Always wear eye protection when using impact or air tools.*

Sockets that attach to a ratchet handle (**Figure 17**) are available with 6-point (A, **Figure 18**) or 12-point (B) openings and different drive sizes. The drive size indicates the size of the square hole that accepts the ratchet handle. The number stamped on the socket is the size of the work area and must match the fastener head.

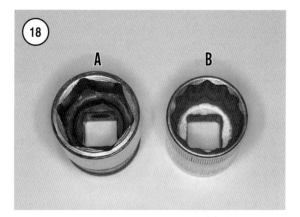

As with wrenches, a 6-point socket provides superior-holding ability, while a 12-point socket needs to be moved only half as far to reposition it on the fastener.

Sockets are designated for either hand or impact use. Impact sockets are made of a thicker material for more durability. Compare the size and wall thickness of a 19-mm hand socket (A, **Figure 19**) and the 19-mm impact socket (B). Use impact sockets when using an impact driver or air tool. Use hand sockets with hand-driven attachments.

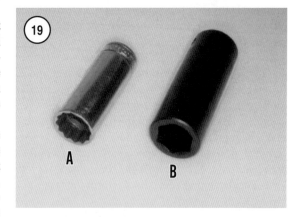

Various handles are available for sockets. The speed handle is used for fast operation. Flexible ratchet heads in varying lengths allow the socket to be turned with varying force and at odd angles. Extension bars allow the socket setup to reach difficult areas. The ratchet is the most versatile. It allows the user to install or remove the nut without removing the socket.

Sockets combined with any number of drivers make them undoubtedly the fastest, safest and most convenient tool for fastener removal and installation.

### Impact Driver

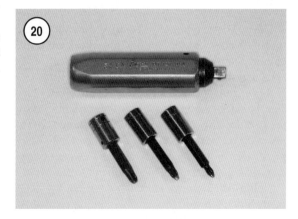

> *WARNING*
> *Do not use hand sockets with air or impact tools because they may shatter and cause injury. Always wear eye protection when using impact or air tools.*

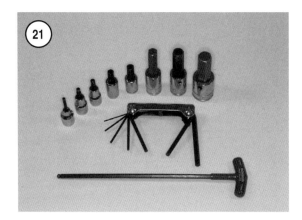

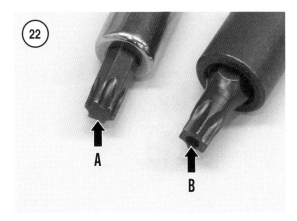

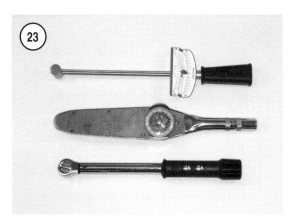

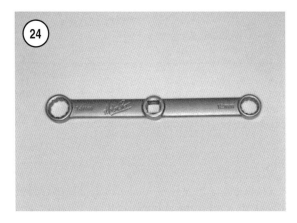

An impact driver provides extra force for removing fasteners by converting the impact of a hammer into a turning motion. This makes it possible to remove stubborn fasteners without damaging them. Impact drivers and interchangeable bits (**Figure 20**) are available from most tool suppliers. When using a socket with an impact driver, make sure the socket is designed for impact use. Refer to *Socket Wrenches, Ratchets and Handles* in this section.

### Allen Wrenches

Use Allen, or setscrew wrenches (**Figure 21**) on fasteners with hexagonal recesses in the fastener head. These wrenches are available in a L-shaped bar, socket and T-handle types. Allen bolts are sometimes called socket bolts.

### Torx Fasteners

A Torx fastener head is a 6-point star-shaped pattern (A, **Figure 22**). Torx fasteners are identified with a T and a number indicating their drive size. Torx drivers are available in L-shaped bars, sockets and T-handles. Tamper-resistant Torx fasteners are also used and have a round shaft in the center of the fastener head. Tamper-resistance Torx fasteners require a Torx bit with a hole in the center of the bit (B, **Figure 22**).

### Torque Wrenches

Use a torque wrench (**Figure 23**) with a socket, torque adapter or similar extension to tighten a fastener to a measured torque. Torque wrenches come in several drive sizes (1/4, 3/8, 1/2 and 3/4) and have various methods of reading the torque value. The drive size indicates the size of the square drive that accepts the socket, adapter or extension. Common methods of reading the torque value are the deflecting beam, the dial indicator and the audible click. When choosing a torque wrench, consider the torque range, drive size and accuracy. The torque specifications in this manual provide an indication of the range required. A torque wrench is a precision tool that must be properly cared for to remain accurate. Store torque wrenches in cases or separate padded drawers within a toolbox. Follow the manufacturer's instructions for their care and calibration.

### Torque Adapters

Torque adapters (**Figure 24**), or extensions, extend or reduce the reach of a torque wrench. Specific adapters are required to perform some of the proce-

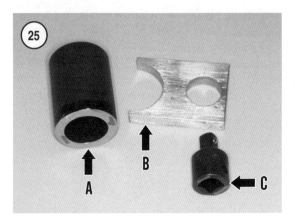

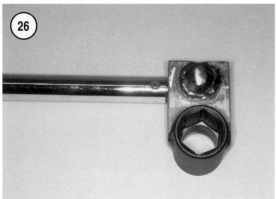

dures in this manual. These are available from the ATV manufacturer or can be fabricated by welding a socket (A, **Figure 25**) that matches the fastener onto a metal plate (B). Use another socket or extension (C, **Figure 25**) welded to the plate to attach to the torque wrench drive (**Figure 26**). The adapter shown (**Figure 27**) is used to tighten a fastener while preventing another fastener on the same shaft from turning.

If a torque adapter changes the effective lever length, the torque reading on the wrench will not equal the actual torque applied to the fastener. It is necessary to recalibrate the torque setting on the wrench to compensate for the change of lever length. When a torque adapter is used at a right angle to the drive head, calibration is not required because the lever length has not changed.

To recalculate a torque reading when using a torque adapter, use the following formula, and refer to **Figure 28**.

$$TW = \frac{TA \times L}{L + A}$$

*TW* is the torque setting or dial reading on the wrench.

*TA* is the torque specification and the actual amount of torque that will be applied to the fastener.

*A* is the amount the adapter increases (or in some cases reduces) the effective lever length as measured along the centerline of the torque wrench.

*L* is the lever length of the wrench as measured from the center of the drive to the center of the grip.

The effective lever length is the sum of *L* and *A*.

Example:

TA = 20 ft.-lb.

A = 3 in.

L = 14 in.

$$TW = \frac{20 \times 14}{14 + 3} = \frac{280}{17} = 16.5 \text{ ft.-lb.}$$

In this example, the torque wrench would be set to the recalculated torque value (TW = 16.5 ft.-lb.). When using a beam-type wrench, tighten the fastener

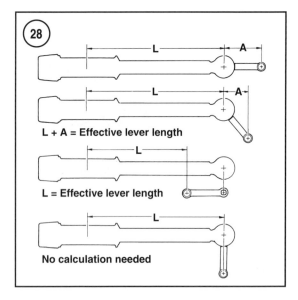

until the pointer aligns with 16.5 ft.-lb. In this example, although the torque wrench is pre set to 16.5 ft.-lb., the actual torque is 20 ft.-lb.

## Pliers

Pliers come in a wide range of types and sizes. Pliers are useful for holding, cutting, bending, and

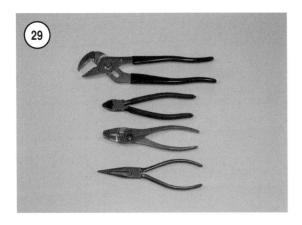

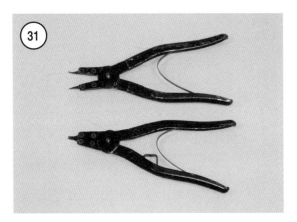

## Snap Ring Pliers

*WARNING*
*Snap rings can slip and fly off when removing and installing them. In addition, the snap ring plier's tips may break. Always wear eye protection when using snap ring pliers.*

Snap ring pliers are specialized pliers with tips that fit into the ends of snap rings to remove and install them.

Snap ring pliers (**Figure 31**) are available with a fixed action (either internal or external) or are convertible (one tool works on both internal and external snap rings). They may have fixed tips or interchangeable ones of various sizes and angles. For general use, select convertible type pliers with interchangeable tips.

## Hammers

*WARNING*
*Always wear eye protection when using hammers. Make sure the hammer face is in good condition and the handle is not cracked. Select the correct hammer for the job and make sure to strike the object squarely. Do not use the handle or the side of the hammer to strike an object.*

Various types of hammers are available to fit a number of applications. A ball-peen hammer is used to strike another tool, such as a punch or chisel. Soft-faced hammers are required when a metal object must be struck without damaging it. *Never* use a metal-faced hammer on engine and suspension components; damage will occur in most cases.

## Ignition Grounding Tool

Some test procedures in this manual require turning the engine over without starting it. Do not remove the spark plug cap(s) and crank the engine without grounding the plug cap. Doing so will damage the ignition system.

An effective way to ground the system is to fabricate the tool shown in **Figure 32** from a No. 6 screw, two washers and a length of wire with an alligator clip soldered on one end. To use the tool, insert it into the spark plug cap and attach the alligator clip to a known engine ground. A separate grounding tool is required for each spark plug cap.

This tool is safer than a spark plug or spark tester because there is no spark firing across the end of the

crimping. Do not use them to turn fasteners unless they are designed to do so. **Figure 29** and **Figure 30** show several types of pliers. Each design has a specialized function. Slip-joint pliers are general-purpose pliers used for gripping and bending. Diagonal cutting pliers are needed to cut wire and can be used to remove cotter pins. Needlenose pliers are used to hold or bend small objects. Locking pliers (**Figure 30**), sometimes called Vise Grips, hold objects tightly. They have many uses ranging from holding two parts together, to gripping the end of a broken stud. Use caution when using locking pliers; the sharp jaws will damage the objects they hold.

plug/tester to potentially ignite fuel vapor spraying from an open spark plug hole or leaking fuel component.

## MEASURING TOOLS

The ability to accurately measure components is essential to successfully service many components. Equipment is manufactured to close tolerances, and obtaining consistently accurate measurements is essential.

Each type of measuring instrument is designed to measure a dimension with a certain degree of accuracy and within a certain range. When selecting the measuring tool, make sure it is applicable to the task.

As with all tools, measuring tools provide the best results if cared for properly. Improper use can damage the tool and cause inaccurate results. If any measurement is questionable, verify the measurement using another tool. A standard gauge is usually provided with measuring tools to check accuracy and calibrate the tool if necessary.

Accurate measurements are only possible if the mechanic possesses a feel for using the tool. Heavy-handed use of measuring tools produces less accurate results. Hold the tool gently by the fingertips so the point at which the tool contacts the object is easily felt. This feel for the equipment will produce more accurate measurements and reduce the risk of damaging the tool or component. Refer to the following sections for specific measuring tools.

### Feeler Gauge

The feeler, or thickness gauge (**Figure 33**), is used for measuring the distance between two surfaces.

A feeler gauge set consists of an assortment of steel strips of graduated thickness. Each blade is marked with its thickness. Blades can be of various lengths and angles for different procedures.

A common use for a feeler gauge is to measure valve clearance. Wire (round) type gauges are used to measure spark plug gap.

### Calipers

Calipers (**Figure 34**) are excellent tools for obtaining inside, outside and depth measurements. Although not as precise as a micrometer, they allow reasonable precision, typically to within 0.05 mm (0.001 in.). Most calipers have a range up to 150 mm (6 in.).

Calipers are available in dial, vernier or digital versions. Dial calipers have a dial readout that provides convenient reading. Vernier calipers have marked

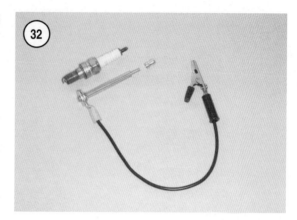

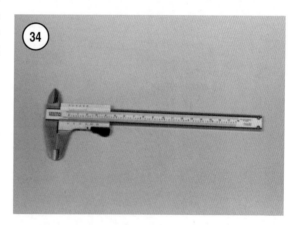

scales that must be compared to determine the measurement. The digital caliper uses a LCD to show the measurement.

Properly maintain the measuring surfaces of the caliper. There must not be any dirt or burrs between the tool and the object being measured. Never force the caliper closed around an object; close the caliper around the highest point so it can be removed with a slight drag. Some calipers require calibration. Always refer to the manufacturer's instructions when using a new or unfamiliar caliper.

To read a vernier caliper refer to **Figure 35**. The fixed scale is marked in 1 mm increments. Ten individ-

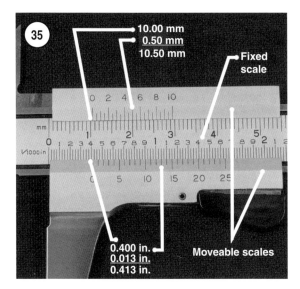

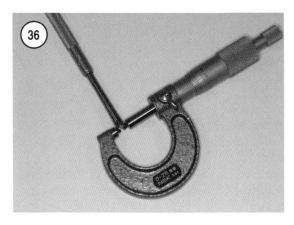

ual lines on the fixed scale equal 1 cm. The moveable scale is marked in 0.05 mm (hundredth) increments. To obtain a reading, establish the first number by the location of the 0 line on the moveable scale in relation to the first line to the left on the fixed scale. In this example, the number is 10 mm. To determine the next number, note which of the lines on the movable scale align with a mark on the fixed scale. A number of lines will seem close, but only one will align exactly. In this case, 0.50 mm is the reading to add to the first number. The result of adding 10 mm and 0.50 mm is a measurement of 10.50 mm.

## Micrometers

A micrometer (**Figure 36**) is an instrument designed for linear measurement using the decimal divisions of the inch or meter. While there are many types and styles of micrometers, most of the procedures in this manual call for an outside micrometer. The outside micrometer is used to measure the outside diameter of cylindrical forms and the thickness of materials.

A micrometer's size indicates the minimum and maximum size of a part that it can measure. The usual sizes are 0-25 mm (0-1 in.), 25-50 mm (1-2 in.), 50-75 mm (2-3 in.) and 75-100 mm (3-4 in.).

Micrometers that cover a wider range of measurements are available. These use a large frame with interchangeable anvils of various lengths. This type of micrometer offers a cost savings; however, its overall size may make it less convenient.

### Adjustment

Before using a micrometer, check its adjustment as follows.
1. Clean the anvil and spindle faces.
2A. To check a 0-1 in. or 0-25 mm micrometer:
   a. Turn the thimble until the spindle contacts the anvil. If the micrometer has a ratchet stop, use it to ensure the proper amount of pressure is applied.
   b. If the adjustment is correct, the 0 mark on the thimble will align exactly with the 0 mark on the sleeve line. If the marks do not align, the micrometer is out of adjustment.
   c. Follow the manufacturer's instructions to adjust the micrometer.
2B. To check a micrometer larger than 1 in. or 25 mm, use the standard gauge supplied by the manufacturer. A standard gauge is a steel block, disc or rod that is machined to an exact size.
   a. Place the standard gauge between the spindle and anvil and measure its outside diameter or length. If the micrometer has a ratchet stop, use it to ensure the proper amount of pressure is applied.
   b. If the adjustment is correct, the 0 mark on the thimble will align exactly with the 0 mark on the sleeve line. If the marks do not align, the micrometer is out of adjustment.
   c. Follow the manufacturer's instructions to adjust the micrometer.

### Care

Micrometers are precision instruments. They must be used and maintained with great care. Note the following:
1. Store micrometers in protective cases or separate padded drawers in a toolbox.
2. When in storage, make sure the spindle and anvil faces do not contact each other or another object. If they do, temperature changes and corrosion may damage the contact faces.
3. Do not clean a micrometer with compressed air. Dirt forced into the tool causes wear.
4. Lubricate micrometers to prevent corrosion.

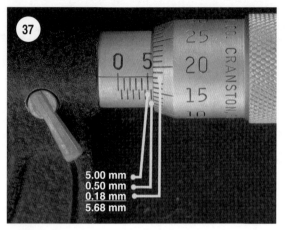

5.00 mm
0.50 mm
0.18 mm
5.68 mm

## Reading

When reading a micrometer, numbers are taken from different scales and added together.

For accurate results, properly maintain the measuring surfaces of the micrometer. There cannot be any dirt or burrs between the tool and the measured object. Never force the micrometer closed around an object. Close the micrometer around the highest point so it can be removed with a slight drag.

The standard metric micrometer is accurate to one one-hundredth of a millimeter (0.01 mm). The sleeve line is graduated in millimeter and half millimeter increments. The marks on the upper half of the sleeve line equal 1.00 mm. Each fifth mark above the sleeve line is identified with a number. The number sequence depends on the size of the micrometer. A 0-25 mm micrometer, for example, will have sleeve marks numbered 0 through 25 in 5 mm increments. This numbering sequence continues with larger micrometers. On all metric micrometers, each mark on the lower half of the sleeve equals 0.50 mm.

The tapered end of the thimble has 50 lines marked around it. Each mark equals 0.01 mm. One complete turn of the thimble aligns its 0 mark with the first line on the lower half of the sleeve line, or 0.50 mm.

When reading a metric micrometer, add the number of millimeters and half-millimeters on the sleeve line to the number of one one-hundredth millimeters on the thimble. Perform the following steps while referring to **Figure 37**.

1. Read the upper half of the sleeve line and count the number of lines visible. Each upper line equals 1 mm.
2. See if the half-millimeter line is visible on the lower sleeve line. If so, add 0.50 mm to the reading in Step 1.
3. Read the thimble mark that aligns with the sleeve line. Each thimble mark equals 0.01 mm.
4. If a thimble mark does not align exactly with the sleeve line, estimate the amount between the lines.

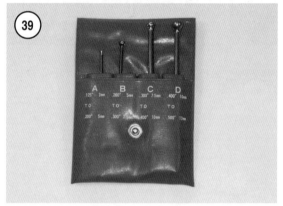

For accurate readings in two-thousandths of a millimeter (0.002 mm), use a metric vernier micrometer.
5. Add the readings from Steps 1-4.

### Telescoping and Small Hole Gauges

Use telescoping gauges (**Figure 38**) and small hole gauges (**Figure 39**) to measure bores. Neither gauge has a scale for direct readings. An outside micrometer must be used to determine the reading.

To use a telescoping gauge, select the correct size gauge for the bore. Compress the moveable post and carefully insert the gauge into the bore. Carefully move the gauge in the bore to make sure it is centered. Tighten the knurled end of the gauge to hold the moveable post in position. Remove the gauge and measure the length of the posts. Telescoping gauges are typically used to measure cylinder bores.

To use a small hole gauge, select the correct size gauge for the bore. Carefully insert the gauge into the bore. Tighten the knurled end of the gauge to carefully expand the gauge fingers to the limit within the bore. Do not overtighten the gauge; there is no built-in release. Excessive tightening can damage the bore surface and tool. Remove the gauge and measure the outside dimension with a micrometer (**Figure 36**). Small hole gauges are typically used to measure valve guides.

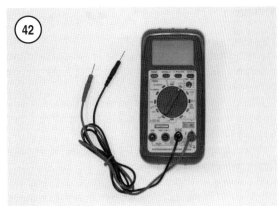

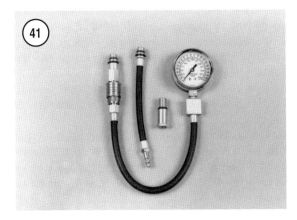

performing a compression test. An engine that does not have adequate compression cannot be properly tuned. Refer to Chapter Three.

## Multimeter

A multimeter (**Figure 42**) is an essential tool for electrical system diagnosis. The voltage function indicates the voltage applied or available to various electrical components. The ohmmeter function tests circuits for continuity, or lack of continuity, and measures the resistance of a circuit.

Some manufacturers' specifications for electrical components are based on results using a specific test meter. Results may vary if using a meter not recommend by the manufacturer. Such requirements are noted when applicable.

## Dial Indicator

A dial indicator (**Figure 40**) is a gauge with a dial face and needle used to measure variations in dimensions and movements. Measuring brake rotor runout is a typical use for a dial indicator.

Dial indicators are available in various ranges and graduations and with three types of mounting bases: magnetic, clamp or screw-in stud.

## Cylinder Bore Gauge

A cylinder bore gauge is similar to a dial indicator. These typically consist of a dial indicator, handle and different length adapters (anvils) to fit the gauge to various bore sizes. The bore gauge is used to measure bore size, taper and out-of-round. When using a bore gauge, follow the manufacturer's instructions.

## Compression Gauge

A compression gauge (**Figure 41**) measures combustion chamber (cylinder) pressure, usually in psi or kg/cm$^2$. The gauge adapter is either inserted and held in place or screwed into the spark plug hole to obtain the reading. Disable the engine so it will not start and hold the throttle in the wide-open position when

### *Ohmmeter (analog) calibration*

Each time an analog ohmmeter is used or the scale is changed, the ohmmeter must be calibrated.

Digital ohmmeters do not require calibration.

1. Make sure the meter battery is in good condition.
2. Make sure the meter probes are in good condition.
3. Touch the two probes together and observe the needle location on the ohms scale. The needle must align with the 0 mark to obtain accurate measurements.
4. If necessary, rotate the meter ohms adjust knob until the needle and 0 mark align.

## ELECTRICAL SYSTEM FUNDAMENTALS

A thorough study of the many types of electrical systems used in today's ATVs is beyond the scope of this manual. However, a basic understanding of voltage, resistance and amperage is necessary to perform diagnostic tests.

Refer to Chapter Two for troubleshooting.

## Voltage

Voltage is the electrical potential or pressure in an electrical circuit and is expressed in volts. The more pressure (voltage) in a circuit, the more work can be performed.

Direct current (DC) voltage means the electricity flows in one direction. All circuits powered by a battery are DC circuits.

Alternating current (AC) means the electricity flows in one direction momentarily and then switches to the opposite direction. Alternator output is an example of AC voltage. This voltage must be changed or rectified to direct current to operate in a battery-powered system.

## Resistance

Resistance is the opposition to the flow of electricity within a circuit or component and is measured in ohms. Resistance causes a reduction in available current and voltage.

Resistance is measured in an inactive circuit with an ohmmeter. The ohmmeter sends a small amount of current into the circuit and measures how difficult it is to push the current through the circuit.

An ohmmeter, although useful, is not always a good indicator of a circuit's actual ability under operating conditions. This is due to the low voltage (6-9 volts) that the meter uses to test the circuit. The voltage in an ignition coil secondary winding can be several thousand volts. Such high voltage can cause the coil to malfunction, even though it tests acceptable during a resistance test.

Resistance generally increases with temperature. Perform all testing with the component or circuit at room temperature. Resistance tests performed at high temperatures may indicate false resistance readings and cause the unnecessary replacement of a component.

## Amperage

Amperage is the unit of measure for the amount of current within a circuit. Current is the actual flow of electricity. The higher the current, the more work can be performed up to a given point. If the current flow exceeds the circuit or component capacity, the system will be damaged.

## SERVICE METHODS

Many of the procedures in this manual are straightforward and can be performed by anyone reasonably competent with tools. However, consider previous experience carefully before performing any operation involving complicated procedures.

1. Front, in this manual, refers to the front of the ATV. The front of any component is the end closest to the front of the ATV. The left and right sides refer to the position of the parts as viewed by the rider sitting on the seat facing forward.

2. When servicing the ATV, secure it in a safe manner.

3. Label all similar parts for location and mark all mating parts for position. If possible, photograph or draw the number and thickness of any shim as it is removed. Identify parts by placing them in sealed and labeled plastic bags. It is possible for carefully laid out parts to become disturbed, making it difficult to reassemble the components correctly without a diagram.

4. Label disconnected wires and connectors with masking tape and a marking pen. Do not rely on memory alone.

5. Protect finished surfaces from physical damage or corrosion. Keep gasoline and other chemicals off painted surfaces.

6. Use penetrating oil on frozen or tight bolts. Avoid using heat where possible. Heat can warp, melt or affect the temper of parts. Heat also damages the finish of paint and plastics. Refer to *Heating Components* in this section.

7. When a part is a press fit or requires a special tool for removal, the information or type of tool is identified in the text. Otherwise, if a part is difficult to remove or install, determine the cause before proceeding.

8. To prevent objects or debris from falling into the engine, cover all openings.

9. Read each procedure thoroughly and compare the figures to the actual components before starting the procedure. Perform the procedure in sequence.

10. Recommendations are occasionally made to refer service to a dealership or specialist. In these cases, the work can be performed more economically by the specialist than by the home mechanic.

11. The term *replace* means to discard a defective part and replace it with a new part. *Overhaul* means to remove, disassemble, inspect, measure, repair and/or replace parts as required to recondition an assembly.

12. Some operations require the use of a hydraulic press. If a press is not available, have these operations performed by a shop equipped with the necessary equipment. Do not use makeshift equipment that may damage the ATV. Do not direct high-pressure water at steering bearings, fuel hoses, wheel bearings, suspension and electrical components. The water forces the grease out of the bearings and could damage the seals.

13. Repairs are much faster and easier if the ATV is clean before starting work. Degrease the ATV with a

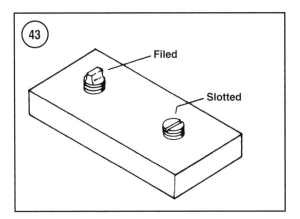

commercial degreaser; follow the directions on the container for the best results. Clean all parts with cleaning solvent.

14. If special tools are required, have them available before starting the procedure. When special tools are required, they will be described at the beginning of the procedure.

15. Make sure all shims and washers are reinstalled in the same location and position.

16. Whenever rotating parts contact a stationary part, look for a shim or washer.

17. Use new gaskets if there is any doubt about the condition of old ones.

18. If self-locking fasteners are used, replace them. Do not install standard fasteners in place of self-locking ones.

19. Use grease to hold small parts in place if they tend to fall out during assembly. Do not apply grease to electrical or brake components.

**Heating Components**

*WARNING*
*Wear protective gloves to prevent burns and injury when heating parts.*

*CAUTION*
*Do not use a welding torch when heating parts. A welding torch applies excessive heat to a small area very quickly, which can damage parts.*

A heat gun or propane torch is required to disassemble, assemble, remove and install many parts and components in this manual. Read the safety and operating information supplied by the manufacturer of the heat gun or propane torch while also noting the following:

1. Make sure the work area is clean and dry. Remove all combustible components and materials from the work area. Wipe up all grease, oil and other fluids from parts. Check for leaking or damaged fuel system components. Repair or remove these parts before beginning work.

2. Never use a flame near the battery, fuel tank, fuel lines or other flammable materials.

3. When using a heat gun, remember that the temperature can be in excess of 540° C (1000° F).

4. Have a fire extinguisher near the job.

5. Always wear protective goggles and gloves when heating parts.

6. Before heating a part installed on the ATV, check areas around the part and those *hidden* that could be damaged or possibly ignite. Do not heat surfaces than can be damaged by heat. Shield materials, such as cables and wiring, near the part or area to be heated

7. Before heating a part, read the entire procedure to make sure the required tools are available. This allows quick work while the part is at its optimum temperature.

8. The amount of heat recommended to remove or install a part is typically listed in the procedure. However, before heating parts without a specific recommendation, consider the possible effects. To avoid damaging a part, monitor the temperature with heat sticks or an infrared thermometer, if possible. Another way, though not as accurate, is to place tiny drops of water on the part. When the water starts to sizzle, the part is hot enough. Keep the heat in motion to prevent overheating.

**Removing Frozen Fasteners**

If a fastener cannot be removed, several methods may be used to loosen it. First, liberally apply penetrating oil, and let it penetrate for 10-15 minutes. Rap the fastener several times with a small hammer. Do not hit it hard enough to cause damage. Reapply the penetrating oil if necessary.

For frozen screws, apply penetrating oil as described, and then insert a screwdriver in the slot and rap the top of the screwdriver with a hammer. This loosens the rust so the screw can be removed in the normal way. If the screw head is too damaged to use this method, grip the head with locking pliers and twist it out.

If heat is required, refer to *Heating Components* in this section.

**Removing Broken Fasteners**

If the head breaks off a screw or bolt, several methods are available for removing the remaining portion. If a large portion of the remainder projects out, try gripping it with locking pliers. If the projecting portion is too small, file it to fit a wrench or cut a slot in it to fit a screwdriver (**Figure 43**).

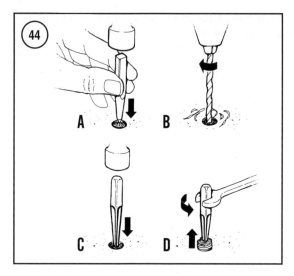

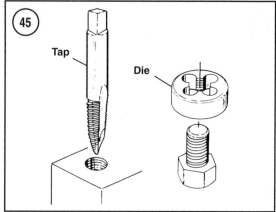

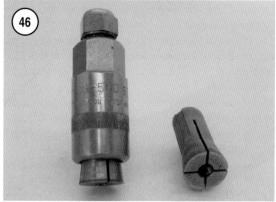

If the head breaks off flush, use a screw extractor. To do this, center punch the exact center of the screw or bolt (A, **Figure 44**), and then drill a small hole in the screw (B) and tap the extractor into the hole (C). Back the screw out with a wrench on the extractor (D, **Figure 44**).

### Repairing Damaged Threads

Occasionally, threads are stripped through carelessness or impact damage. Often the threads can be repaired by running a tap (for internal threads on nuts) or die (for external threads on bolts) through the threads (**Figure 45**). To clean or repair spark plug threads, use a spark plug tap.

If an internal thread is damaged, it may be necessary to install a Helicoil or some other type of thread insert. Follow the manufacturer's instructions when installing its insert.

If it is necessary to drill and tap a hole, refer to **Table 6** for metric tap and drill sizes.

### Stud Removal/Installation

A stud removal tool (**Figure 46**) is available from most tool suppliers. This tool makes the removal and installation of studs easier. If one is not available and the threads on the stud are not damaged, thread two nuts onto the stud and tighten them against each other. Remove the stud by turning the lower nut.
1. Measure the height of the stud above the surface.
2. Thread the stud removal tool onto the stud and tighten it, or thread two nuts onto the stud.
3. Remove the stud by turning the stud remover or the lower nut.
4. Remove any threadlocking compound from the threaded hole. Clean the threads with an aerosol parts cleaner.

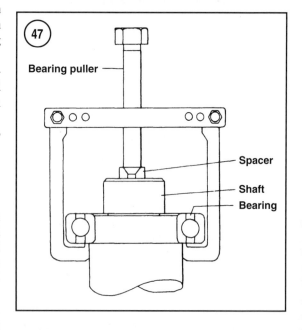

5. Install the stud removal tool onto the new stud, or thread two nuts onto the stud.
6. Apply threadlocking compound to the threads of the stud.
7. Install the stud and tighten with the stud removal tool or the top nut.

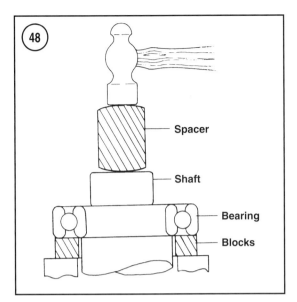

48

Spacer

Shaft

Bearing

Blocks

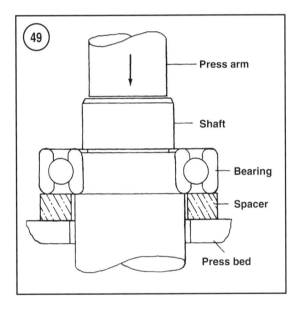

49

Press arm

Shaft

Bearing

Spacer

Press bed

8. Install the stud to the height noted in Step 1 or its torque specification.
9. Remove the stud removal tool or the two nuts.

## Removing Hoses

When removing stubborn hoses, do not exert excessive force on the hose or fitting. Remove the hose clamp and carefully insert a small screwdriver or similar blunt nose tool between the fitting and hose. Apply a spray lubricant under the hose and carefully twist the hose off the fitting. Clean the fitting of any corrosion or rubber hose material with a wire brush. Clean the inside of the hose thoroughly. Do not use any lubricant when installing the hose (new or old). The lubricant may allow the hose to come off the fitting, even with the clamp secure.

## Bearings

Bearings are precision parts, they must be maintained with proper lubrication and maintenance. If a bearing is damaged, replace it immediately. When installing a new bearing, make sure to prevent damaging it. Bearing replacement procedures are included in the individual chapters where applicable; however, use the following sections as a guideline.

Unless otherwise specified, install bearings with the manufacturer's mark or number facing outward.

### Removal

While bearings are normally removed only when damaged, there may be times when it is necessary to remove a bearing that is in good condition. However, improper bearing removal will damage the bearing and maybe the shaft or case half. Note the following when removing bearings:
1. Before removing the bearings, note the following:
   a. Refer to the bearing replacement procedure in the appropriate chapter for any special instructions.
   b. Remove any seals that interfere with bearing removal. Refer to *Seal Removal/Installation* in this section.
   c. When removing more than one bearing, identify the bearings before removing them. Refer to the bearing manufacturer's numbers on the bearing.
   d. Note and record the direction in which the bearing numbers face for proper installation.
   e. Remove any set plates or bearing retainers before removing the bearings.
2. When using a puller to remove a bearing from a shaft, make sure the shaft is not damaged. Always place a piece of metal between the end of the shaft and the puller screw. In addition, place the puller arms next to the inner bearing race. Refer to **Figure 47**.
3. When using a hammer to remove a bearing from a shaft, do not strike the hammer directly against the shaft. Instead, use a brass or aluminum rod between the hammer and shaft (**Figure 48**) and make sure to support both bearing races with wooden blocks as shown.
4. The ideal method of bearing removal is with a hydraulic press. Note the following when using a press:
   a. Always support the inner and outer bearing races with a suitable size wooden or aluminum ring (**Figure 49**). If only the outer race is supported, pressure applied against the balls and/or the inner race will damage them.

b. Always make sure the press arm (**Figure 49**) aligns with the center of the shaft. If the arm is not centered, it may damage the bearing and/or shaft.

c. The moment the shaft is free of the bearing, it will drop to the floor. Secure or hold the shaft to prevent it from falling.

d. When removing bearings from a housing, support the housing with wooden blocks to prevent damage to gasket surfaces.

5. Use a blind bearing puller to remove bearings installed in blind holes (**Figure 50**).

### Installation

1. When installing a bearing in a housing, apply pressure to the *outer* bearing race (**Figure 51**). When installing a bearing on a shaft, apply pressure to the *inner* bearing race (**Figure 52**).

2. When installing a bearing as described in Step 1, a driver is required. Never strike the bearing directly with a hammer or the bearing will be damaged. When installing a bearing, use a piece of pipe or a driver with a diameter that matches the bearing race. **Figure 53** shows the correct way to use a driver and hammer to install a bearing on a shaft.

3. Step 1 describes how to install a bearing in a housing or over a shaft. However, when installing a bearing over a shaft and into the housing at the *same time*, a tight fit will be required for both outer and inner bearing races. In this situation, install a spacer underneath the driver tool so pressure is applied evenly across both races. Refer to **Figure 54**. If the outer race is not supported, the balls push against the outer bearing race and damage it.

### Interference fit

1. Follow this procedure when installing a bearing over a shaft. When a tight fit is required, the bearing inside diameter will be smaller than the shaft. In this case, driving the bearing on the shaft using normal methods may cause bearing damage. Instead, heat the bearing before installation. Note the following:

a. Secure the shaft so it is ready for bearing installation.

b. Clean all residues from the bearing surface of the shaft. Remove burrs with a file.

c. Fill a suitable pot or beaker with clean mineral oil. Place a thermometer rated above 120° C (248° F) in the oil. Support the thermometer so it does not rest on the bottom or side of the pot.

d. Remove the bearing from its wrapper and secure it with a piece of heavy wire bent to hold

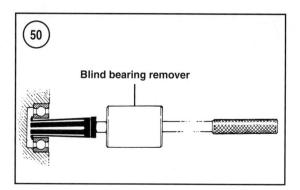

**50**

Blind bearing remover

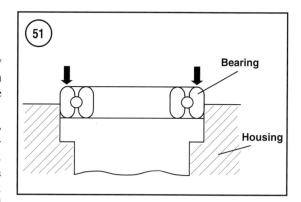

**51**

Bearing

Housing

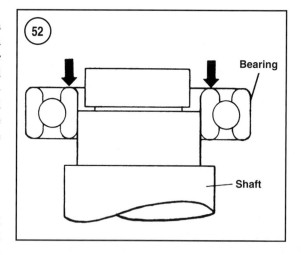

**52**

Bearing

Shaft

it in the pot. Hang the bearing in the pot so it does not touch the bottom or sides of the pot.

e. Turn the heat on and monitor the thermometer. When the oil temperature rises to approximately 120° C (248° F), remove the bearing from the pot and quickly install it. If necessary, place a socket on the inner bearing race and tap the bearing into place. As the bearing chills, it tightens on the shaft, so installation must be done quickly. Make sure the bearing is installed completely.

2. Follow this step when installing a bearing in a housing. Bearings are generally installed in a housing with a slight interference fit. Driving the bearing

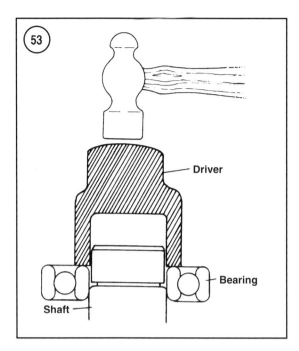

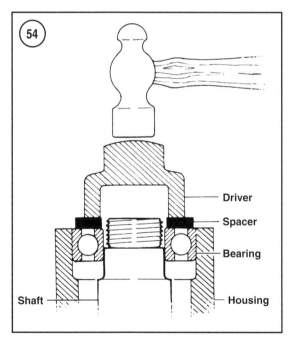

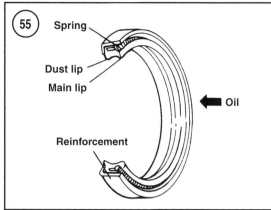

water on the housing. If the water sizzles and evaporates immediately, the temperature is correct. Heat only one housing at a time.

c. If a hot plate is used, remove the housing and place it on wooden blocks.

d. Hold the housing with the bearing side down and tap the bearing out with a suitable size socket and extension. Repeat for all bearings in the housing.

e. Before heating the bearing housing, place the new bearing in a freezer, if possible. Chilling a bearing slightly reduces its outside diameter while the heated bearing housing assembly is slightly larger due to heat expansion. This makes bearing installation easier.

f. While the housing is still hot, install the new bearing(s) into the housing. Install the bearings by hand, if possible. If necessary, lightly tap the bearing(s) into the housing with a socket placed on the outer bearing race (**Figure 51**). Do not install bearings by driving on the inner-bearing race. Install the bearing(s) until it seats completely.

### Seal Removal/Installation

Seals are used to contain oil, water, grease or combustion gases in a housing or shaft. Improper removal of a seal can damage the housing or shaft. Improper installation of the seal can damage the seal.

Before replacing a seal, identify it as a rubber or Teflon seal. Both types are used on the models covered in this manual. On a rubber seal (**Figure 55**), the body and sealing element will be made of the same material. The seal lip (element) will also be equipped with a garter spring. On a Teflon seal, the body and seal lip will be noticeably different. The outer part is normally made of rubber and the sealing lip, placed in the middle of the seal, is Teflon. A garter spring is not used.

1. Measure the installed depth of the seal.

into the housing using normal methods may damage the housing or cause bearing damage. Instead, heat the housing before the bearing is installed. Note the following:

a. Before heating the housing in this procedure, wash the housing thoroughly with detergent and water. Rinse and rewash the housing as required to remove all oil and chemicals.

b. Heat the housing to approximately 100° C (212° F) with a heat gun or on a hot plate. Monitor temperature with an infrared thermometer, heat sticks or place tiny drops of

2. Prying is generally the easiest and most effective method of removing a seal from the housing. However, always place a rag under the pry tool (**Figure 56**) to prevent damage to the housing.

3. Before installing a typical rubber seal, pack waterproof grease in the seal lips.

4. In most cases, install seals with the manufacturer's numbers or marks face out.

5. Install seals either by hand or with tools. Center the seal in its bore and attempt to install it by hand. If necessary, install the seal with a socket or bearing driver placed on the outside of the seal as shown in **Figure 57**. Drive the seal squarely into the housing until it is flush with its mounting bore. Never install a seal by hitting against the top of the seal with a hammer.

## STORAGE

Several months of non-use can cause a general deterioration of the ATV. This is especially true in areas of extreme temperature variations. This deterioration can be minimized with careful preparation for storage. A properly stored ATV is much easier to return to service.

### Storage Area Selection

When selecting a storage area, consider the following:

1. The storage area must be dry. A heated area is best, but not necessary. It should be insulated to minimize extreme temperature variations.

2. If the building has large window areas, mask them to keep sunlight off the ATV.

3. Avoid storage areas close to saltwater.

4. Consider the area's risk of fire, theft or vandalism. Check with your insurer regarding ATV coverage while in storage.

### Preparing the ATV for Storage

The amount of preparation a ATV should undergo before storage depends on the expected length of non-use, storage area conditions and personal preference. Consider the following list the minimum requirement:

1. Wash the ATV thoroughly. Make sure all dirt, mud and road debris are removed.

2. Start the engine and allow it to reach operating temperature. Drain the engine oil regardless of the riding time since the last service. Fill the engine with the recommended type and quantity of oil.

3. Fill the fuel tank completely.

4. Remove the spark plug from the cylinder head. Ground the spark plug cap to the engine. Refer to *Ignition Ground Tool* in this chapter. Pour a teaspoon

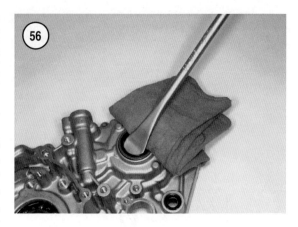

(15-20 ml) of engine oil into the cylinders. Place a rag over the openings and slowly turn the engine over to distribute the oil. Reinstall the spark plug.

5. Remove the battery. Store it in a cool, dry location. Charge the battery once a month. Refer to *Battery* in Chapter Nine for service.

6. Cover the exhaust and intake openings.

7. Apply a protective substance to the plastic and rubber components, including the tires. Make sure to follow the manufacturer's instructions for each type of product being used.

8. Rotate the tires periodically to prevent a flat spot from developing and damaging the tire.

9. Cover the ATV with old bed sheets or something similar. Do not cover it with any plastic material that will trap moisture.

### Returning the ATV to Service

The amount of service required when returning an ATV to service after storage depends on the length of non-use and storage conditions. In addition to performing the reverse of the above procedure, make sure the brakes, clutch, throttle and engine stop switch work properly before operating the ATV. Refer to Chapter Three and evaluate the service intervals to determine which areas require service.

**Table 1 GENERAL MOTORCYCLE DIMENSIONS AND WEIGHT**

|  | mm | in. |
|---|---|---|
| Ground clearance | 255 | 10.04 |
| Overall height | 1090 | 42.9 |
| Overall length | 1840 | 72.4 |
| Overall width | 1170 | 46.1 |
| Seat height |  |  |
| 2004-2005 models | 800 | 31.5 |
| 2006-on | 810 | 31.9 |
| Turning radius (min.) | 3500 | 137.8 |
| Wheelbase | 1280 | 50.4 |
| Weight (with oil and fuel) | 169 kg | 373 lb. |

**Table 2 FUEL TANK CAPACITY**

| Total (including reserve) | 10.0 L (2.6 gal.) |
|---|---|
| Reserve only | 1.9 L (0.5 gal.) |

**Table 3 CONVERSION FORMULAS**

| Multiply: | By: | To get the equivalent of: |
|---|---|---|
| Length |  |  |
| Inches | 25.4 | Millimeter |
| Inches | 2.54 | Centimeter |
| Miles | 1.609 | Kilometer |
| Feet | 0.3048 | Meter |
| Millimeter | 0.03937 | Inches |
| Centimeter | 0.3937 | Inches |
| Kilometer | 0.6214 | Mile |
| Meter | 3.281 | Feet |
| Fluid volume |  |  |
| U.S. quarts | 0.9463 | Liters |
| U.S. gallons | 3.785 | Liters |
| U.S. ounces | 29.573529 | Milliliters |
| Liters | 0.2641721 | U.S. gallons |
| Liters | 1.0566882 | U.S. quarts |
| Liters | 33.814023 | U.S. ounces |
| Milliliters | 0.033814 | U.S. ounces |
| Milliliters | 1.0 | Cubic centimeters |
| Milliliters | 0.001 | Liters |
| Torque |  |  |
| Foot-pounds | 1.3558 | Newton-meters |
| Foot-pounds | 0.138255 | Meters-kilograms |
| Inch-pounds | 0.11299 | Newton-meters |
| Newton-meters | 0.7375622 | Foot-pounds |
| Newton-meters | 8.8507 | Inch-pounds |
| Meters-kilograms | 7.2330139 | Foot-pounds |
| Volume |  |  |
| Cubic inches | 16.387064 | Cubic centimeters |
| Cubic centimeters | 0.0610237 | Cubic inches |
| Temperature |  |  |
| Fahrenheit | $(°F - 32) \times 0.556$ | Centigrade |
| Centigrade | $(°C \times 1.8) + 32$ | Fahrenheit |

(continued)

### Table 3 CONVERSION FORMULAS (continued)

| Multiply: | By: | To get the equivalent of: |
|---|---|---|
| **Weight** | | |
| Ounces | 28.3495 | Grams |
| Pounds | 0.4535924 | Kilograms |
| Grams | 0.035274 | Ounces |
| Kilograms | 2.2046224 | Pounds |
| **Pressure** | | |
| Pounds per square inch | 0.070307 | Kilograms per square centimeter |
| Kilograms per square centimeter | 14.223343 | Pounds per square inch |
| Kilopascals | 0.1450 | Pounds per square inch |
| Pounds per square inch | 6.895 | Kilopascals |
| **Speed** | | |
| Miles per hour | 1.609344 | Kilometers per hour |
| Kilometers per hour | 0.6213712 | Miles per hour |

### Table 4 TECHNICAL ABBREVIATIONS

| | |
|---|---|
| ABDC | After bottom dead center |
| ATDC | After top dead center |
| BBDC | Before bottom dead center |
| BDC | Bottom dead center |
| BTDC | Before top dead center |
| C | Celsius (Centigrade) |
| cc | Cubic centimeters |
| cid | Cubic inch displacement |
| CDI | Capacitor discharge ignition |
| cu. in. | Cubic inches |
| F | Fahrenheit |
| ft. | Feet |
| ft.-lb. | Foot-pounds |
| gal. | Gallons |
| H/A | High altitude |
| hp | Horsepower |
| in. | Inches |
| in.-lb. | Inch-pounds |
| I.D. | Inside diameter |
| kg | Kilograms |
| kgm | Kilogram meters |
| km | Kilometer |
| kPa | Kilopascals |
| L | Liter |
| m | Meter |
| MAG | Magneto |
| ml | Milliliter |
| mm | Millimeter |
| N•m | Newton-meters |
| O.D. | Outside diameter |
| oz. | Ounces |
| psi | Pounds per square inch |
| PTO | Power take off |
| pt. | Pint |
| qt. | Quart |
| rpm | Revolutions per minute |

## Table 5 METRIC, DECIMAL AND FRACTIONAL EQUIVALENTS

| mm | in. | Nearest fraction | mm | in. | Nearest fraction |
|---|---|---|---|---|---|
| 1 | 0.0394 | 1/32 | 26 | 1.0236 | 1 1/32 |
| 2 | 0.0787 | 3/32 | 27 | 1.0630 | 1 1/16 |
| 3 | 0.1181 | 1/8 | 28 | 1.1024 | 1 3/32 |
| 4 | 0.1575 | 5/32 | 29 | 1.1417 | 1 5/32 |
| 5 | 0.1969 | 3/16 | 30 | 1.1811 | 1 3/16 |
| 6 | 0.2362 | 1/4 | 31 | 1.2205 | 1 7/32 |
| 7 | 0.2756 | 9/32 | 32 | 1.2598 | 1 1/4 |
| 8 | 0.3150 | 5/16 | 33 | 1.2992 | 1 5/16 |
| 9 | 0.3543 | 11/32 | 34 | 1.3386 | 1 11/32 |
| 10 | 0.3937 | 13/32 | 35 | 1.3780 | 1 3/8 |
| 11 | 0.4331 | 7/16 | 36 | 1.4173 | 1 13/32 |
| 12 | 0.4724 | 15/32 | 37 | 1.4567 | 1 15/32 |
| 13 | 0.5118 | 1/2 | 38 | 1.4961 | 1 1/2 |
| 14 | 0.5512 | 9/16 | 39 | 1.5354 | 1 17/32 |
| 15 | 0.5906 | 19/32 | 40 | 1.5748 | 1 9/16 |
| 16 | 0.6299 | 5/8 | 41 | 1.6142 | 1 5/8 |
| 17 | 0.6693 | 21/32 | 42 | 1.6535 | 1 21/32 |
| 18 | 0.7087 | 23/32 | 43 | 1.6929 | 1 11/16 |
| 19 | 0.7480 | 3/4 | 44 | 1.7323 | 1 23/32 |
| 20 | 0.7874 | 25/32 | 45 | 1.7717 | 1 25/32 |
| 21 | 0.8268 | 13/16 | 46 | 1.8110 | 1 13/16 |
| 22 | 0.8661 | 7/8 | 47 | 1.8504 | 1 27/32 |
| 23 | 0.9055 | 29/32 | 48 | 1.8898 | 1 7/8 |
| 24 | 0.9449 | 15/16 | 49 | 1.9291 | 1 15/16 |
| 25 | 0.9843 | 31/32 | 50 | 1.9685 | 1 31/32 |

## Table 6 METRIC TAP AND DRILL SIZES

| Metric size | Drill equivalent | Decimal fraction | Nearest fraction |
|---|---|---|---|
| 3 × 0.50 | No. 39 | 0.0995 | 3/32 |
| 3 × 0.60 | 3/32 | 0.0937 | 3/32 |
| 4 × 0.70 | No. 30 | 0.1285 | 1/8 |
| 4 × 0.75 | 1/8 | 0.125 | 1/8 |
| 5 × 0.80 | No. 19 | 0.166 | 11/64 |
| 5 × 0.90 | No. 20 | 0.161 | 5/32 |
| 6 × 1.00 | No. 9 | 0.196 | 13/64 |
| 7 × 1.00 | 16/64 | 0.234 | 15/64 |
| 8 × 1.00 | J | 0.277 | 9/32 |
| 8 × 1.25 | 17/64 | 0.265 | 17/64 |
| 9 × 1.00 | 5/16 | 0.3125 | 5/16 |
| 9 × 1.25 | 5/16 | 0.3125 | 5/16 |
| 10 × 1.25 | 11/32 | 0.3437 | 11/32 |
| 10 × 1.50 | R | 0.339 | 11/32 |
| 11 × 1.50 | 3/8 | 0.375 | 3/8 |
| 12 × 1.50 | 13/32 | 0.406 | 13/32 |
| 12 × 1.75 | 13/32 | 0.406 | 13/32 |

## Table 7 GENERAL TORQUE RECOMMENDATIONS

| | N·m | ft.-lb. |
|---|---|---|
| 10 mm nut or 6 mm bolt | 6 | 4.3 |
| 12 mm nut or 8 mm bolt | 15 | 11 |
| 14 mm nut or 10 mm bolt | 30 | 22 |
| 17 mm nut or 12 mm bolt | 55 | 40 |
| 19 mm nut or14 mm bolt | 85 | 61 |
| 22 mm nut or 16 mm bolt | 130 | 94 |

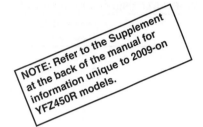
NOTE: Refer to the Supplement at the back of the manual for information unique to 2009-on YFZ450R models.

# CHAPTER TWO

# TROUBLESHOOTING

The troubleshooting procedures described in this chapter provide typical symptoms and methods for isolating the cause(s). Follow a systematic approach to isolate the problem quickly and to prevent unnecessary parts replacement. Gather as much information as possible to aid in diagnosis. Never assume anything and do not overlook the obvious. For example, make sure the stop switch is in the run position and there is fuel in the tank. An engine needs three basics to run properly: correct air/fuel mixture, compression and a spark at the correct time. If one of these is missing, the engine will not run.

Learning to recognize symptoms makes troubleshooting easier. In most cases, expensive and complicated test equipment is not needed to determine whether repairs can be performed at home. On the other hand, be realistic and do not start procedures that are beyond your experience and equipment available. If the machine requires the attention of a professional, describe symptoms and conditions accurately and fully. The more information a technician has available, the easier it is to diagnose the problem.

## STARTING THE ENGINE

When experiencing engine-starting troubles, it is easy to work out of sequence and forget basic start-ing procedures. The following sections describe the recommended starting procedures.

Before starting the engine, perform the pre-ride inspection as described in Chapter Three.

### Starting a Cold Engine

1. The machine is equipped with the following safety switches that prevent the engine from starting or running if certain conditions occur.
    a. Neutral switch. With the transmission in any position except neutral, with the clutch engaged (clutch lever out), the engine will not start.
    b. Clutch switch. With the transmission in gear, the engine will not start if the clutch is engaged (clutch lever out). If the clutch is disengaged with the transmission in gear, the engine will start.
    c. Engine stop switch (A, **Figure 1**). When moved to the off position, the switch will prevent the engine from starting, or, will stop the engine when it is running. The engine will start and run only when the switch is in the run position.
2. Shift the transmission into neutral.
3. Switch the engine stop switch to the run position.

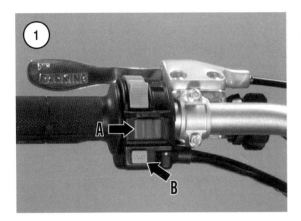

4. Turn the fuel valve lever (**Figure 2**) from the off position to the on position.

*NOTE*
*The choke knob (**Figure 3**) may be set in one of three positions: out, midway and in. Pulling out the knob enables the choke (starter enrichment circuit) on the carburetor.*

5A. If the ambient temperature is below 40° F (5° C), completely pull out the choke knob to richen the air/fuel mixture.

5B. If the ambient temperature is 30-90° F (0-30° C), pull out the choke knob to the midway position.

6. Turn the ignition switch on.

7. Check that the neutral light (**Figure 4**) comes on.

*CAUTION*
*Keep the starter button depressed until the engine is definitely started. Releasing the button too soon can cause engine kickback, which can potentially damage the starter clutch assembly.*

8. Press the starter button (B, **Figure 1**) while keeping the throttle closed. The choke system is more effective if the throttle remains completely closed during startup.

*CAUTION*
*Do not race the engine during the warm-up period. Excessive wear and potential engine damage can occur when the engine is not up to operating temperature.*

9. When the engine starts, move the choke knob to the midway position, if not originally set there. Allow the engine to warm up at an idle for one minute, or until the engine responds smoothly.

10. Push in the choke knob fully and check engine operation. The engine should accelerate cleanly. If not, return the choke knob to the midway position and allow the engine to warm up until it will accelerate cleanly with the choke pushed in fully.

**Starting a Warm Engine**

1. Shift the transmission into neutral.

2. Check that the engine stop switch is in the run position.

3. Turn the fuel valve lever (**Figure 2**) from the off position to the on position.

4. Make sure the choke knob (**Figure 3**) is fully in.

5. Turn the ignition switch on.

6. Check that the neutral light (**Figure 4**) comes on.

7. Press the starter button (B, **Figure 1**) while slightly opening the throttle.

## Starting a Flooded Engine

If the engine fails to start after several tries (particularly if the choke has been used), it is probably flooded. This occurs when too much fuel is drawn into the engine and the spark plug fails to ignite it. The smell of gasoline is often evident when the engine is flooded. Troubleshoot a flooded engine as follows:

1. Look for gasoline overflowing from the carburetor or overflow hose. If gasoline is evident, the float in the carburetor bowl is stuck. Remove and repair the float assembly as described in Chapter Eight.

2. Shift the transmission into neutral.

3. Check that the engine stop switch is in the run position.

4. Turn the fuel valve lever (**Figure 2**) from the off position to the on position.

5. Make sure the choke knob (**Figure 3**) is fully in.

6. Turn the ignition switch on.

7. Check that the neutral light (**Figure 4**) comes on.

8. Fully open the throttle, and then press the starter button (B, **Figure 1**) for 5 seconds. If the engine attempts to start, go to Step 9. If the engine does not fire, go to Step 10.

9. Vary the throttle opening until the engine runs clean.

10. If the engine does not start, wait 10 seconds and attempt to start. If engine still does not start, refer to *Engine Will Not Start* in this chapter.

## ENGINE SPARK TEST

An engine spark test will indicate whether the ignition system is providing voltage to the spark plug. It is a quick way to determine if a problem is in the electrical system or fuel system.

> *CAUTION*
> *When performing this test, the spark plug lead must be grounded before cranking the engine. If it is not, it is possible to damage the ignition components. A spark plug can be used for this test, but a spark tester (**Figure 5**) will clearly show if spark is occurring.*

1. Remove the spark plug. Inspect the spark plug by comparing its condition to the plugs shown in Chapter Three.

2. Connect the spark plug lead to the spark plug, or to a spark tester.

3. Ground the plug to bare metal on the engine (**Figure 6**). Position the plug so the firing end can be viewed.

4. Crank the engine and observe the spark. A fat, blue spark should appear at the firing end. The spark should fire consistently as the engine is cranked.

5. If the spark appears weak, or fires inconsistently, check the following areas for the cause:
   a. Fouled or improperly gapped spark plug.
   b. Defective/shorted spark plug lead and cap.
   c. Loose connection in ignition system.
   d. Dirty/shorted engine stop switch.
   e. Defective coil.
   f. Defective magneto.
   g. Defective neutral switch.
   h. Defective clutch switch.
   i. Defective CDI unit.

## ENGINE PERFORMANCE

If the engine does not operate at peak performance, the following lists of possible causes can help isolate the problem. The easiest checks for each area (fuel, ignition and engine) are listed first. Always perform the easiest checks before proceeding to steps involving component disassembly or replacement.

### Engine Will Not Start or Starts and Dies

1. Fuel system:
   a. Fuel tank near empty.
   b. Clogged or improperly installed vent in fuel tank cap.
   c. Contaminated fuel.
   d. Improper operation of the choke knob.
   e. Flooded engine.
   f. Clogged air filter.
   g. Clog in shutoff valve, fuel line or carburetor.
   h. Idle speed too low.
   i. Pilot screw misadjusted.
   j. Incorrect carburetor jet for altitude.

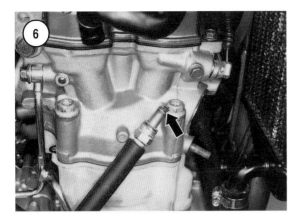

k. Carburetor float valve sticking.
l. Air leaks at intake manifold.
2. Ignition:
   a. Fouled or improperly gapped spark plug.
   b. Defective ignition coil/spark plug cap.
   c. Dirty/shorted engine stop switch.
   d. Loose connection in ignition system.
   e. Defective neutral switch.
   f. Defective clutch switch.
   g. Misadjusted or faulty throttle position sensor.
   h. Defective pickup coil.
   i. Defective CDI unit.
   j. Damaged stator coils.
3. Engine:
   a. Compression release malfunction.
   b. No valve clearance.
   c. Loose cylinder head bolts.
   d. Worn piston and/or cylinder.
   e. Leaking cylinder head gasket.
   f. Stuck or seized valve.
   g. Incorrect valve timing.

**Poor Idle and Low Speed Performance**

1. Fuel system:
   a. Improper operation of choke knob.
   b. Flooded engine.
   c. Clogged air filter.
   d. Idle speed too low.
   e. Clogged or improperly installed vent in fuel tank cap.
   f. Pilot screw misadjusted.
   g. Incorrect fuel level.
   h. Incorrect carburetor jet for altitude.
   i. Carburetor float valve sticking.
   j. Clogged carburetor jets.
   k. Loose carburetor mounting bolts.
   l. Air leaks at intake manifold.
   m. Clogged muffler.
2. Ignition:
   a. Fouled or improperly gapped spark plug.

b. Defective ignition coil/spark plug cap.
   c. Misadjusted or faulty throttle position sensor.
   d. Defective CDI unit.
   e. Defective pickup coil.
   f. Damaged stator coils.
3. Engine:
   a. Incorrect valve clearance.
   b. Low compression.
   c. Incorrect valve timing.

**Engine Lacks Power and Acceleration**

1. Fuel system:
   a. Clogged air filter.
   b. Choke lever in use.
   c. Incorrect fuel level.
   d. Incorrect carburetor jet for altitude.
   e. Clogged or improperly installed vent in fuel tank cap.
   f. Restricted fuel flow.
   g. Clogged carburetor jets.
   h. Clogged muffler.
2. Ignition:
   a. Fouled or improperly gapped spark plug.
   b. Defective ignition coil/spark plug cap.
   c. Misadjusted or faulty throttle position sensor.
   d. Defective CDI unit.
   e. Defective pickup coil.
3. Engine:
   a. Incorrect valve clearance.
   b. Loose cylinder head bolts.
   c. Worn/damaged valves.
   d. Worn cylinder and piston rings.
   e. Incorrect valve timing.
   f. Excessive oil level in crankcase.

**Poor High Speed Performance**

1. Fuel system:
   a. Clogged air filter.
   b. Choke in use.
   c. Clogged muffler.
   d. Incorrect carburetor jet for altitude.
   e. Clogged or improperly installed vent in fuel tank cap.
   f. Restricted fuel flow.
   g. Clogged carburetor jet.
2. Ignition:
   a. Misadjusted or faulty throttle position sensor.
   b. Defective CDI unit.
   c. Defective pickup coil.
3. Engine:
   a. Improper valve clearance.
   b. Worn/damaged valve springs.
   c. Worn cylinder and piston rings.

d. Incorrect valve timing.

## Engine Backfires

1. Fuel mixture too lean.
2. Air leaks into exhaust system.
3. Misadjusted or faulty throttle position sensor.
4. Defective CDI unit.

## Engine Overheating

1. Cooling system:
   a. Leak at fitting or gasket.
   b. Low coolant level.
   c. Defective radiator cap.
   d. Clogged radiators.
   e. Improper coolant mix.
   f. Damaged water pump.
   g. Clogged water passages.
   h. Collapsed coolant hoses.
2. Other causes:
   a. Clutch slip.
   b. Excessive ignition timing advance. Check for misadjusted or faulty throttle position sensor or defective CDI unit.
   c. Brakes dragging.
   d. Incorrect air/fuel mixture.
   e. Incorrect jetting for altitude.

## ENGINE NOISE

Noise is often the first indicator of something wrong with the engine. In many cases, damage can be avoided or minimized if the rider immediately stops and diagnoses the source of the noise. Any time engine noises are ignored, even when the machine seems to be running correctly, the rider risks causing more damage and possibly injury.

## Pinging During Acceleration

1. Poor quality or contaminated fuel.
2. Lean fuel mixture.
3. Excessive carbon buildup in combustion chamber.
4. Misadjusted or faulty throttle position sensor.
5. Faulty CDI unit.
6. Faulty pickup coil.

## Knocks, Ticks or Rattles

1. Loose exhaust system.
2. Loose/missing body fasteners.
3. Incorrect valve clearance.
4. Excessive connecting rod bearing clearance.

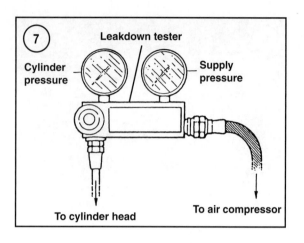

## ENGINE LEAKDOWN TEST

The condition of the piston rings and valves can be accurately checked with a leakdown tester (**Figure 7**). With both valves in the closed position, this tester is screwed into the spark plug hole and air pressure is applied to the combustion chamber. The gauge on the tester is then observed to determine the leak rate from the combustion chamber.

1. Start the engine and allow it to reach operating temperature.
2. Shut off the engine and remove the air filter assembly.
3. Secure the throttle in the wide-open position.
4. Remove the spark plug.
5. Set the piston to TDC on the compression stroke.
6. Install the leakdown tester following the manufacturer's instructions. The tester must not leak around the spark plug threads.
7. Make the test following the manufacturer's instructions for the tester. When pressure is applied to the cylinder, make sure the engine remains at TDC. If necessary, put the transmission in gear.
8. While the cylinder is under pressure, listen for air leaks at the following areas.
   a. An exhaust pipe leak indicates the exhaust valve is leaking.
   b. A leak at the carburetor indicates an intake valve is leaking.
   c. Air escaping from the crankcase breather tube points to the piston rings.
9. A leakdown rate of 10% or more indicates the engine requires repair.

## CLUTCH

The two main clutch problems are clutch slip (clutch does not fully engage) and clutch drag (clutch does not fully disengage). Incorrect clutch adjustment, a worn clutch lever or a worn release lever at the engine usually causes both of these problems.

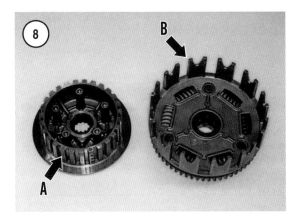

### Inspection

1. Check the clutch cable routing from the handlebar to the engine. Make sure that the cable is free when the handlebar is turned lock to lock and the ends are installed correctly.
2. With the engine off, pull and release the clutch lever. If the lever is hard to pull, or the action is rough, check for the following:
    a. Damaged cable.
    b. Incorrect cable routing.
    c. Cable not lubricated.
    d. Damaged lever and perch assembly at the handlebar.
    e. Damaged release lever at the engine.
3. If the components in Step 1 and Step 2 are good, and the lever moves without excessive roughness or binding, check the clutch lever adjustment as described in Chapter Three. Note the following:
    a. If the clutch cannot be adjusted to the specifications in Chapter Three, the clutch cable is stretched or damaged.
    b. If the clutch cable and its adjustment are good, the friction plates may be worn.

### Slip

When the clutch slips, the engine accelerates faster than what the actual forward speed indicates. Because the clutch plates are spinning against each other, excessive heat is quickly built up in the assembly. This causes plate wear, warp and spring fatigue. One or more of the following can cause the clutch to slip:

1. Clutch wear or damage.
    a. Incorrect clutch adjustment.
    b. Weak or damaged clutch springs.
    c. Loose clutch springs.
    d. Worn friction plates.
    e. Warped steel plates.
    f. Clutch release mechanism wear or damage.
2. Clutch/transmission oil:

    a. Low oil level.
    b. Oil additives.
    c. Low viscosity oil.

### Drag

When the clutch drags, the plates are not separating completely. This will cause the machine to creep or lurch forward when the transmission is put into gear. Once underway, shifting is difficult. If this condition is not corrected, it can cause transmission gear and shift fork damage due to the abnormal grinding and actions of the parts. Dragging occurs by one or more of the following:

1. Clutch wear or damage.
    a. Clutch release mechanism wear or damage.
    b. Incorrect push lever and pushrod engagement.
    c. Damaged clutch pushrod.
    d. Warped steel plates.
    e. Swollen friction plates.
    f. Warped pressure plate.
    g. Incorrect clutch spring tension.
    h. Incorrectly assembled clutch.
    i. Loose clutch nut.
    j. Burnt primary driven gear bushing.
    k. Notched clutch hub splines (A, **Figure 8**).
    l. Notched clutch housing grooves (B, **Figure 8**).
2. Clutch transmission oil:
    a. Oil level too high.
    b. Oil viscosity too high.

### Noise

Excessive clutch noise is usually caused by worn or damaged parts and is more noticeable at idle or low engine speeds. Clutch noise can be caused by the following conditions:

1. Wear on the clutch bushing or clutch housing bore. The noise is reduced or eliminated when a load is placed on the clutch housing.
2. Excessive axial play in the clutch housing.
3. Excessive friction disc-to-clutch housing clearance.
4. Excessive clutch housing-to-primary drive gear backlash.
5. Worn or damaged clutch housing and primary drive gear teeth.
6. Excessive wear in the clutch pushrod assembly.

### EXTERNAL SHIFT MECHANISM AND TRANSMISSION

Transmission problems are often difficult to distinguish from problems with the clutch and external

**⑨**                    **TRANSMISSION TROUBLESHOOTING**

| Excessive gear noise. | Check:<br>• Worn bearings.<br>• Worn or damaged gears.<br>• Excessive gear backlash. |

| Difficult shifting. | Check:<br>• Damaged gears.<br>• Damaged shift forks.<br>• Damaged shift drum.<br>• Damaged shift lever assembly.<br>• Incorrect mainshaft and countershaft engagement.<br>• Incorrect clutch disengagement. |

| Gears pop out of mesh. | Check:<br>• Worn gear or transmission spline shafts.<br>• Shift forks worn or bent.<br>• Worn dog holes in gears.<br>• Insufficient shift lever spring tension.<br>• Damaged shift lever linkage. |

| Incorrect shift lever operation. | Check:<br>• Bent shift lever.<br>• Bent or damaged shift lever shaft.<br>• Damaged shift lever linkage and gears. |

| Incorrect shifting after engine reassembly. | Check:<br>• Missing transmission shaft shims.<br>• Incorrectly installed parts.<br>• Shift forks bent during assembly.<br>• Incorrectly assembled crankcase.<br>• Incorrect clutch adjustment.<br>• Incorrectly assembled shift linkage. |

shift mechanism. Often, the symptoms may indicate a problem in one area, while the actual problem is in another area. For example, if the gears grind during shifting, the problem may be caused by a dragging clutch, not a damaged transmission. Of course, if the clutch is not repaired, the transmission will eventually become damaged too. Therefore, evaluate all of the variables that exist when the problem occurs and

always start with the easiest checks in the troubleshooting chart (**Figure 9**).

If the transmission exhibits abnormal noise or operation, drain the engine oil and check for contamination or metal particles. Examine a small quantity of oil under bright light. If a metallic cast or pieces of metal are seen, this indicates excessive wear and/ or part failure is occurring.

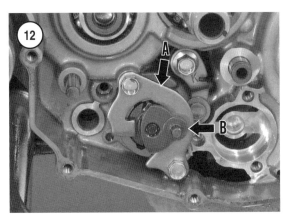

### Transmission

Note the following possible causes of transmission noise:
1. Insufficient oil level.
2. Contaminated oil.
3. Oil viscosity too low.
4. Worn or damaged transmission gear(s).
5. Excessive gear side play.
6. Worn or damaged crankshaft to transmission bearings.

### External Shift Mechanism

The external shift mechanism includes all parts related to transmission shifting that are not within the crankcase. This includes the shift pedal, shift shaft, torsion spring, shift lever, shift guide, shift drum stopper, and the stopper lever. These parts are located at the rear of the engine, behind the right crankcase cover (**Figure 10**). Refer to Chapter Six for additional views of the parts and how they are assembled. Troubleshoot as follows:

> *NOTE*
> *When shifting a constant-mesh transmission, one of the transmission shafts must be turning. Have an assistant turn a rear wheel (with chain installed), so the gears can be shifted and the action of the linkage viewed.*

1. Make sure the clutch is properly adjusted and in good condition. If the clutch is good, continue with the procedure.
2. Support the ATV with the rear wheels off the ground.
3. Remove the clutch as described in Chapter Six.
4. Turn the rear wheel and shift the transmission. Note the following:
    a. Make sure the torsion spring (A, **Figure 11**) is fitted around the pin and the shift shaft is engaged with the roller on the shift lever assembly (B).
    b. If the parts are in place, but shifting is not correct, remove and inspect the shift shaft assembly for possible damage or missing parts. Continue with the procedure, if necessary.
5. Remove the shift guide (A, **Figure 12**) and lever assembly (B), then shift the transmission at the shift drum stopper (A, **Figure 13**). Note the following:
    a. The stopper lever roller (B, **Figure 13**) is spring-loaded and should move in and out of the shift drum detents. Each detent represents a different gear selection. The raised detent is the neutral position. If the roller is not seating or staying in contact with the shift drum stopper, remove the parts and check for damage.

b. If the shift drum stopper and lever are good, and the shifting problem no longer exists, inspect the shift guide and lever assembly (**Figure 14**) for wear or damage.

c. If the shift drum stopper and lever are good, and the shifting problem still exists, continue with the procedure.

6. Check the shift drum as follows:

a. Shift the transmission into neutral (if possible) and make a mark on the crankcase that aligns with the neutral detent on the shift drum stopper.

b. While turning the rear wheel or mainshaft, turn the shift drum to change gears. Each time the shift drum moves and a new detent mark aligns with the crankcase mark, the transmission should be in another gear.

c. The transmission should shift into each gear. If the shift drum cannot be turned, or if it locks into a particular gear position, the transmission is damaged. A locked shift drum indicates a damaged shift fork, seized bearing or gear, or a damaged shift drum.

*NOTE*
*When troubleshooting the transmission, the mainshaft and center shift fork are visible through the top of the crankcase (**Figure 15**). From this view, all mainshaft gear teeth can be inspected.*

7. If necessary, disassemble the crankcase and transmission as described in Chapter Five and Chapter Seven.

8. Assemble and install all parts removed as described in the appropriate chapters.

## ELECTRICAL TESTING

Refer to Chapter Nine for electrical system test procedures. Refer to *Engine Starting System* in this chapter for troubleshooting typical starting system problems. Perform the checks before disassembling and bench testing components. When performing electrical tests, always refer to the wiring diagram at the back of the manual.

*NOTE*
*Scan the QR code or search for "Clymer Manuals Youtube Tech Tips" to see an overview on electrical troubleshooting with a wiring diagram.*

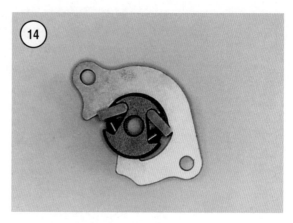

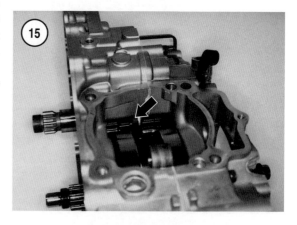

## ENGINE STARTING SYSTEM

### Starter Turns Slowly

1. Weak battery.
2. Loose or corroded battery terminals or cables.
3. Loose or corroded starter cable.
4. Worn or damaged starter.

### Starter Turns, but Does Not Crank Engine

1. Worn or damaged starter clutch.
2. Damaged teeth on starter shaft or drive gears.

### Starter Does Not Operate

If the starter does not operate, refer to **Figure 16** for troubleshooting the possible cause of the problem. If necessary, perform the starter relay switch

**(16)**

# STARTING SYSTEM TROUBLESHOOTING: STARTER WILL NOT TURN

**2**

| Check battery charge. | • Charge battery and retest.<br>• Replace battery if it will not hold a charge. |
|---|---|

| Inspect fuse. | • Replace blown fuse. |
|---|---|

| Inspect connections to battery, starter and starter relay. | • Clean and tighten connections.<br>• Test cables for shorts. |
|---|---|

| Test starter by connecting a heavy gauge wire between the positive battery terminal and starter terminal. | • If the starter does not turn, replace the starter.<br>• If the starter turns, check for a loose or damaged cable, or faulty relay switch. |
|---|---|

| Test the starter relay. The relay should make an audible click when the starter button is pressed. | • If the relay does not click, remove and bench test it. If the relay now works, test the relay's voltage and ground circuits. |
|---|---|

| Perform starter relay ground circuit test. | • Loose or dirty connector.<br>• Short in wire harness.<br>• Faulty neutral switch.<br>• Faulty circuit cutoff relay.<br>• Faulty clutch switch. |
|---|---|

| Perform starter relay voltage check. | • Loose or dirty connector.<br>• Blown fuse.<br>• Faulty ignition switch.<br>• Faulty engine stop switch.<br>• Faulty starter switch.<br>• Faulty circuit cutoff relay.<br>• Shorted wire harness. |
|---|---|

⑰                                **BRAKE TROUBLESHOOTING**

Brake fluid leaks.

Check:
• Loose or damaged line fittings.
• Worn caliper piston seals.
• Scored caliper piston or bore.
• Loose banjo bolts.
• Damaged oil line washers.
• Leaking master cylinder diaphragm.
• Leaking master cylinder secondary seal.
• Cracked master cylinder housing.
• Too high brake fluid level.
• Loose or damaged master cylinder.

Brake overheating.

Check:
• Warped brake disc.
• Incorrect brake fluid.
• Caliper piston and/or brake pads binding.
• Riding brakes during operation.

Brake chatter.

Check:
• Warped brake disc.
• Incorrect caliper alignment.
• Loose caliper mounting bolts.
• Loose front axle nut and/or clamps.
• Worn wheel bearings.
• Damaged hub.
• Restricted brake hydraulic line.
• Contaminated brake pads.

Brake locking.

Check:
• Incorrect brake fluid.
• Plugged passages in master cylinder.
• Caliper piston and/or brake pads binding.
• Warped brake disc.

Insufficient brakes.

Check:
• Air in brake lines.
• Worn brake pads.
• Low brake fluid.
• Incorrect brake fluid.
• Worn brake disc.
• Worn caliper piston seals.
• Glazed brake pads.
• Leaking primary cup seal in master cylinder.
• Contaminated brake pads and/or disc.

Brake squeal.

Check:
• Contaminated brake pads and/or disc.
• Dust or dirt collected behind brake pads.
• Loose parts.

tests (Chapter Nine) before disassembling and bench testing components.

## BRAKES

Inspect the brakes frequently and replace worn or damaged parts immediately.

When checking brake pad wear, the pads in each caliper should be squarely in contact with the disc. Uneven pad wear on one side of the disc can indicate a warped or damaged disc, caliper or pad pins.

The front and rear brake systems require DOT 4 brake fluid. Always use new fluid, from a sealed container. Refer to **Figure 17** to isolate brake problems.

## STEERING AND HANDLING

Correct steering and handling problems as soon as they are detected, because loss of control may occur. Check the following areas:
1. Tires:
   a. Incorrect/uneven air pressure.
   b. Punctured/damaged tire.
2. Wheels:
   a. Loose lug nuts.
   b. Incorrect toe in.
   c. Damaged wheel bearings.
   d. Damaged wheel.
3. Handlebars:
   a. Loose handlebars.
   b. Tight steering shaft holder.
   c. Damaged steering shaft bearing or bushing.
4. Brakes:
   a. Brake pads dragging.
   b. Misadjusted parking brake.
5. Rear axle and swing arm:
   a. Loose/damaged axle bearing holder.
   b. Loose shock absorber.
   c. Worn shock absorber bushings.
   d. Worn swing arm pivot.
   e. Bent axle.
6. Front axle:
   a. Loose wheel hub.
   b. Worn/damaged tie rods.
   c. Loose shock absorbers.
   d. Worn shock absorber bushings.
   e. Damaged wheel hub.
7. Frame:
   a. Bent/broken frame.
   b. Broken weld on frame member.
   c. Broken engine mounting bracket.

2

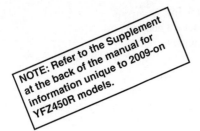

NOTE: Refer to the Supplement at the back of the manual for information unique to 2009-on YFZ450R models.

# CHAPTER THREE

# LUBRICATION AND MAINTENANCE

This chapter describes lubrication and maintenance procedures. Procedures that require more than minor disassembly or adjustment are covered in the appropriate subsequent chapter. **Tables 1-8** are at the end of this chapter.

To maximize the service life of the ATV and gain the utmost in safety and performance, it is necessary to perform periodic inspections and maintenance. Minor problems found during routine service can be corrected before they develop into major ones. A neglected ATV will be unreliable and may be dangerous to ride.

**Table 1** lists the recommended lubrication, maintenance and tune-up intervals. If the ATV is operated in extreme conditions, it may be appropriate to reduce the interval between some maintenance items.

## PRE-RIDE INSPECTION

Perform the following checks before the first ride of the day. If a component requires service, refer to the appropriate section or chapter.

1. Inspect all fuel lines and fittings for leaks.
2. Check fuel level.
3. Check engine oil level.
4. Check for proper throttle operation in all steering positions. Open the throttle all the way and release it. It should close quickly with no binding or roughness.
5. Mask sure the brake levers operate properly with no binding.
6. Check the brake fluid level in the brake reservoirs. Add DOT 4 brake fluid if necessary.
7. Check clutch operation.
8. Inspect the front and rear suspension for looseness. Turn the handlebar from side to side to check steering play. Service the steering assembly if excessive play is noted. Make sure the handlebar cables do not bind.
9. Check tire pressure.
10. Check wheel condition.
11. Check drive chain condition and adjustment.
12. Check the exhaust system for looseness or damage.
13. Check fastener tightness. Pay close attention to engine, steering and suspension fasteners.
14. Check headlight and taillight operation.
15. Make sure all switches work properly.
16. Check the air filter drain tube for contamination.
17. Start the engine, then stop it with the engine stop switch. If the engine stop switch does not operate properly, test the switch as described in Chapter Nine.

## ENGINE OIL

### Engine Oil Selection

Regular oil and filter changes contribute more to engine longevity than any other maintenance. **Table 1** lists the recommended oil and filter change intervals. Refer to **Table 3** for the specified type and quantity of engine oil. Note the interval because combustion acids, formed by gasoline and water vapor, contaminate the oil. If the ATV is operated in dusty conditions, the oil gets dirty quicker and should be changed more frequently than recommended.

**JASO CERTIFICATION LABEL**

Sales company oil code number

M001XXXXX

MA

OIL CLASSIFICATION

MA: Designed for high-friction applications
MB: Designed for low-friction applications

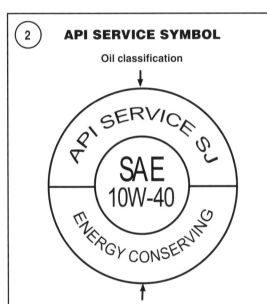

**API SERVICE SYMBOL**

Oil classification

API SERVICE SJ
SAE
10W-40
ENERGY CONSERVING

When ENERGY CONSERVING is listed in this part of the label, the oil has demonstrated energy-conserving properties in standard tests. Do not use ENERGY CONSERVING classified oil in motorcycle engines. Instead, look for this API service symbol.

API SERVICE SJ
SAE
10W-40

Oil viscosity

*WARNING*
*Prolonged contact with used engine oil may cause skin cancer. Minimize contact with the engine oil.*

*NOTE*
*There are a number of ways to discard used oil safely. The easiest way is to pour it from the drain pan into gallon plastic bleach, juice or milk containers for disposal. Some service stations and oil retailers will accept used oil for recycling. Do not discard oil in household trash or pour it onto the ground. Never add brake fluid, fork oil or any other type of petroleum-based fluid to any engine oil to be recycled.*

Oil requirements of ATV engines are different from those of automobile engines. Oils specifically designed for ATVs contain special additives to prevent premature viscosity breakdown, protect the engine from oil oxidation resulting from higher engine operating temperatures and provide lubrication qualities designed for engines operating at higher rpm. Consider the following when selecting engine oil:

1. Do not use oil with oil additives or oil with graphite or molybdenum additives. These may adversely affect clutch operation.

2. Do not use vegetable, non-detergent or castor based racing oils.

3. The Japanese Automobile Standards Organization (JASO) has established an oil classification for motorcycle engines. JASO motorcycle specific oils are identified by the JASO T 903 Standard. The JASO label (**Figure 1**) appears on the oil container and identifies the two separate motorcycle oil classifications-MA and MB. Yamaha recommends the MA classification. JASO classified oil also uses the Society of Automotive Engineers (SAE) viscosity ratings.

4. When selecting American Petroleum Institute (API) classified oil, use only a motorcycle oil with an SG or higher classification that does not display the term Energy Conserving on the oil container circular API service label (**Figure 2**).

5. Refer to **Figure 3** for ambient temperature based viscosity recommendations.

**Engine Oil Level Check**

Check the engine oil level with the dipstick cap mounted on the right side of the engine.

1. Park the ATV on level ground and set the parking brake.

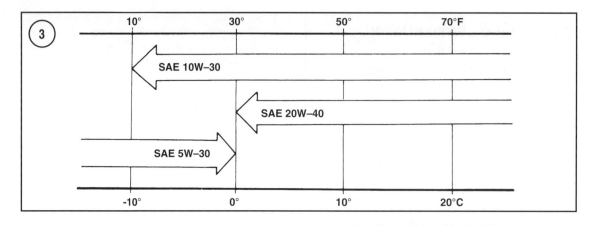

*NOTE*
*Due to the large quantity of oil con-*
*tained in the engine and oil tank, and*
*the dry sump design, the engine must*
*be run for the period specified to be*
*sure the oil in the oil tank reaches its*
*normal operating level.*

2. Start the engine. If the engine is at normal operating temperature, let it run 5 minutes. If the engine is cold, run the engine for 10 minutes.

3. Shut off the engine and let the oil drain into the crankcase for a few minutes.

4. Unscrew and remove the dipstick cap (**Figure 4**) and wipe the dipstick clean. Reinsert it onto the threads in the hole; do not screw it in. Remove the dipstick and check the oil level.

5. The level is correct when it is between the *F* and *E* dipstick lines (**Figure 5**).

6. If necessary, add the recommended type oil (**Table 3**) through the dipstick opening in the tank to correct the level.

7. Replace the dipstick O-ring if damaged.

8. Install the dipstick and tighten it securely.

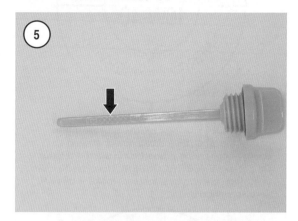

### Engine Oil and Filter Change

Always change the oil when the engine is warm. Contaminants will remain suspended in the oil and will drain more completely and quickly.

1. Park the machine on level ground and set the parking brake.

2. Remove the engine skidplate (Chapter Fifteen).

3. Wipe the area around the dipstick, and then loosen the dipstick cap (**Figure 4**).

4. Place a drain pan below the oil tank drain bolt (**Figure 6**), then remove the drain bolt. Allow the oil to drain from the oil tank.

5. Place a drain pan below the crankcase drain bolt (**Figure 7**), located by the shift lever. Remove the drain bolt and allow the oil to drain from the engine.

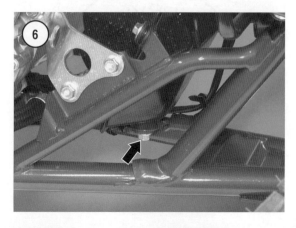

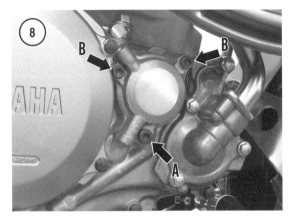

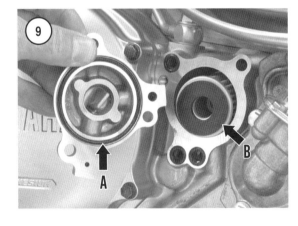

6. Remove the oil filter drain bolt (A, **Figure 8**) and allow the oil to drain.

7. Remove and replace the oil filter as follows:

    a. Remove the bolts that secure the oil filter cover (B, **Figure 8**).

    b. Remove the O-ring from the filter cover (A, **Figure 9**).

    c. Remove the oil filter (B, **Figure 9**).

    d. Remove the O-rings that seal the filter cover bolts and oil passageway (**Figure 10**).

    e. Wipe clean the filter housing and cover. Do not use compressed air to clean the housing. Debris can be blown into the passageways.

    f. Install a new O-ring onto the filter cover (A, **Figure 9**).

    g. Install new O-ring seals onto the filter cover bolts and oil passageway (**Figure 10**).

    h. Install a new oil filter into the housing.

    i. Install the cover and bolts. Tighten the cover bolts to 10 N•m (88 in.-lb.).

    j. Install the drain bolt (A, **Figure 8**). Tighten the bolt to 10 N•m (88 in.-lb.).

8. Install new sealing washers on the engine and oil tank drain bolts.

9. Install the drain bolts. Tighten the crankcase drain bolt (**Figure 7**) to 20 N•m (15 ft.-lb.). Tighten the oil tank drain bolt (**Figure 6**) to 19 N•m (14 ft.-lb.).

10. Fill the oil tank with the required quantity and weight of oil (**Table 3**).

11. Insert the dipstick and screw into place.

12. Slightly loosen the oil gallery bolt (**Figure 11**) on the cylinder head so oil circulation can be verified when the engine runs.

13. Start the engine and allow it to idle. As the engine idles, check the following:

    a. Make sure oil weeps from the oil gallery bolt within one minute. If oil is not present within this time, immediately shut off the engine and diagnose the problem. If oil is present, tighten the oil gallery bolt securely.

    b. Leaks at the drain bolts.

## AIR FILTER

A clogged air filter will decrease the efficiency and life of the engine. Never run the engine without an air filter properly installed. Dust that enters the engine can cause severe engine wear and clog carburetor jets and passages.

Service the air filter at the interval in **Table 1**. Clean the air filter more often when racing, riding in sand or in wet and muddy conditions.

### Air Box Check Hose

A check hose (**Figure 12**) is mounted in the bottom of the air box. If the check hose is filled with dirt and water, check the air box and air filter for contamination.

### Filter Element

The models covered in this manual are equipped with a foam type filter element. Follow the manufacturer's instructions if equipped with an aftermarket air filter element.

1. Remove the seat (Chapter Fifteen).
2. Disengage the spring clamps (**Figure 13**) that secure the cover to the air box. Remove the cover from the air box.
3. If necessary, wipe the inside of the air box to prevent any loose dust or dirt from falling into the intake part of the air box when removing the air filter in Step 4.
4. Remove the bolt and washer (**Figure 14**) securing the air filter to the air box. Remove the air filter (**Figure 15**).
5. Inspect the intake tract from the air box to the carburetor for dirt or other residue.

> *CAUTION*
> *To prevent air leaks and dirty air from entering the engine, make sure all connections between the carburetor, air boot and air box are sealed properly.*

6. Cover the air box opening with a clean shop rag.
7. Carefully pull the foam element off the frame (**Figure 16**).
8. Before cleaning the air filter, check it for brittleness, separation or other damage. Replace the filter if damaged or if its condition is questionable. If the air filter is in good condition, continue with Step 9.

> *WARNING*
> *Do not clean the air filter element with gasoline.*

> *CAUTION*
> *To prevent damage to the filter, do not wring or twist it during cleaning.*

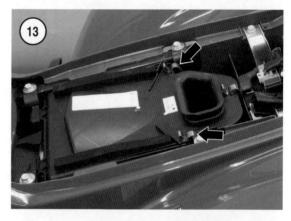

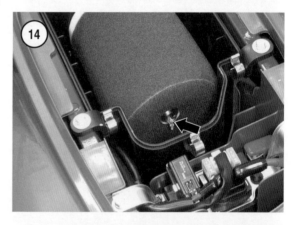

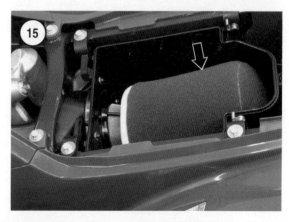

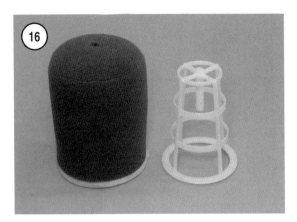

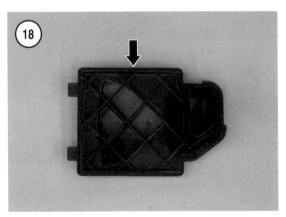

14. After cleaning the element, inspect it again. Replace the air filter if it is torn or broken in any area. Do not run the engine with a damaged element as it may allow dirt to enter the engine.
15. Set the filter aside and allow to air-dry.
16. Clean the retaining bolt and washer and dry thoroughly.

*CAUTION*
*A damp filter will not trap fine dust. Make sure the filter is completely dry before oiling it.*

*NOTE*
*Proper application of the filter oil requires squeezing oil into the filter. Nitrile gloves are recommended.*

17. Oil the filter as follows:
   a. Place the air filter into a gallon size storage bag.
   b. Pour air filter oil onto the filter to soak it completely.

*NOTE*
*Oil designed for use in foam air filters is recommended. If unavailable, clean engine oil may be used.*

   c. Gently squeeze and release the filter to soak filter oil into the filter pores. Repeat until all of the filter pores are saturated with the oil.
   d. Remove the filter from the bag and check the pores for uneven oiling. Light or dark areas on the filter indicate this. If necessary, soak the filter and squeeze it again.
   e. When the filter oiling is even, squeeze the filter a final time.
   f. Remove the air filter from the bag and inspect it for any excessive oil or uneven oiling. Remove any excessive oil from the filter with a paper towel.
18. Slide the air filter onto the frame; making sure the frame is centered properly inside the air filter.
19. Apply a coat of lithium grease to the foam-sealing surface (**Figure 17**) on the bottom of the filter. The grease will help seal the air filter against the air box.
20. Install the air filter into the air box.
21. Install the washer and retaining bolt (**Figure 14**). Tighten securely.
22. Make sure there are no gaps between the filter and the air box. If so, loosen the filter bolt and reposition the air filter.
23. Check the gasket installed in the groove in the bottom side of the air box cover (**Figure 18**). Replace the gasket if missing or damaged.
24. Install the air box cover and secure it with the spring clamps (**Figure 13**).
25. Install the seat (Chapter Fifteen).

9. Soak the air filter in a container filled with kerosene or an air filter cleaner. Gently squeeze the filter to dislodge and remove the oil and dirt from the filter pores. Swish the filter around in the cleaner a few times, then remove the air filter and set aside to air-dry.
10. Fill a clean pan with warm soapy water.
11. Submerge the filter into the cleaning solution and gently work the cleaner into the filter pores. Soak and squeeze (gently) the filter to clean it.
12. Rinse the filter under warm water while gently squeezing it.
13. Repeat the cleaning steps until there are no signs of dirt being rinsed from the filter.

## CONTROL CABLE INSPECTION AND LUBRICATION

This section describes lubrication procedures for the control cables. Clean and lubricate the throttle and clutch if cable operation is stiff. At the same time, check the cables for wear and damage or fraying that could cause the cables to bind or break. To ensure the lubricant enters the length of the cable, use a cable lubricator like the one shown in **Figure 19** and a can of cable lubricant.

> *CAUTION*
> *Do not use chain lubricant to flush and lubricate the control cables.*

1. Disconnect both clutch cable ends as described in *Clutch Cable* in Chapter Six.
2. Disconnect both throttle cable ends as described in *Throttle Cable* in Chapter Eight.

> *CAUTION*
> *Do not lubricate the throttle cable while it is attached to the carburetor. Doing so will forces debris into the TORS switch housing.*

3. Attach a cable lubricator (**Figure 19**) to one end of the cable, following the manufacturer's instructions.
4. Tie a plastic bag around the opposite cable end to catch the lubricant.
5. Fit the nozzle of the cable lubricant into the hole in the lubricator.
6. Hold a rag over the lubricator, then press and hold the button on the lubricant can. Continue until lubricant drips from the opposite end.
7. Disconnect the cable lubricator, then pull the inner cable back and forth to help distribute the lubricant.
8. Allow time for excess lubricant to drain from the cable before reconnecting it.
9. Apply a light coat of grease to the upper throttle cable ends before reconnecting them.
10. Lubricate the clutch cable ends with grease.
11. Reconnect the cables as described in the appropriate chapter.
12. Adjust the cables as described in this chapter.

## THROTTLE CABLE AND SPEED LIMITER ADJUSTMENT

> *WARNING*
> *A damaged throttle cable will prevent the engine from idling properly.*

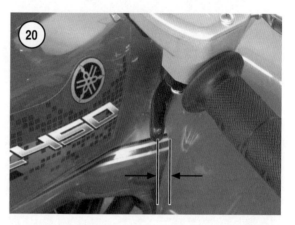

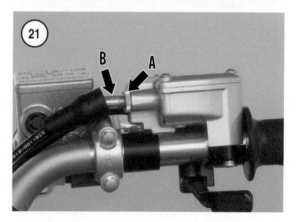

> *WARNING*
> *Do not operate the vehicle with the speed limiter screw removed from the housing. Do not exceed the 12 mm (0.47 in.) adjustment limit. If adjusting the speed limiter for a beginning rider, start and ride the vehicle yourself to determine the safe maximum speed.*

### Throttle Cable Adjustment

Cable wear and stretch affect carburetor operation. Normal amounts of cable wear and stretch can be

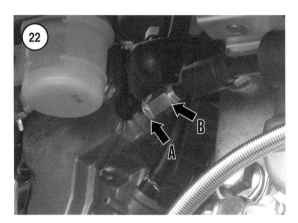

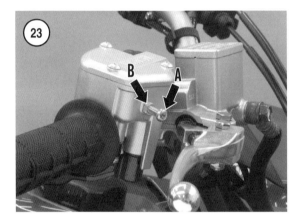

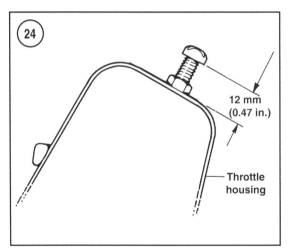

12 mm
(0.47 in.)

Throttle
housing

controlled by the free play adjustments described in this section. If the cables cannot be adjusted within their limits, the cables are excessively worn or damaged and require replacement.

Free play is the distance the throttle lever can be pushed until resistance from the throttle shaft can be felt. A throttle cable free play of 2-4 mm (0.08-0.16 in.), measured at the end of the throttle lever (**Figure 20**), is specified. Excessive cable stretch will delay throttle response. Insufficient cable free play may cause an excessively high idle.

Minor adjustments can be made at the throttle grip adjuster. Major adjustments can be made at the throttle cable adjuster on the carburetor.

1. Before adjusting the throttle cable, operate the throttle lever and make sure it opens and closes properly with the handlebar turned in different positions. If not, check the throttle cable for damage or improper routing.

2. Operate the throttle lever and measure the amount of free play travel (**Figure 20**) until the play is taken up. If the free play measurement is incorrect, perform the following.

3. At the throttle housing, loosen the throttle cable adjuster locknut (A, **Figure 21**) and turn the adjuster (B) to obtain proper free play rotation. Tighten the locknut.

4. If the adjustment cannot be corrected at the throttle housing adjuster, turn in the throttle cable adjuster (B, **Figure 21**) all the way. Slide back the rubber boot and loosen the locknut (A, **Figure 22**) at the carburetor. Turn the adjuster (B, **Figure 22**) out as required, making sure the adjuster does not thread out. Complete the adjustment by turning the adjuster at the throttle grip.

5. Tighten the locknuts and slide the rubber boots back over the cable adjusters.

6. If the throttle cable cannot be adjusted properly, the cable has stretched excessively and must be replaced.

7. Make sure the throttle lever operates freely from a fully closed to fully open position.

8. Start the engine and allow it to idle in neutral. Turn the handlebar from side to side. If the idle increases, the throttle cable is routed incorrectly or there is not enough cable free play.

**Speed Limiter Adjustment**

The throttle housing is equipped with a speed limiter (A, **Figure 23**) that can be set to prevent the rider from opening the throttle all the way. The speed limiter can be set for beginning riders or to control engine rpm when breaking in a new engine.

The speed limiter adjustment is set by varying the length of the speed limiter screw, measured from the throttle housing to the bottom of the screw head; see **Figure 24**. The standard speed limiter setting is 12 mm (0.47 in.).

1. Check throttle cable free play as described in this chapter. If necessary, adjust throttle cable free play, then continue with Step 2.

2. Loosen the locknut (B, **Figure 23**).

3. Turn the speed limiter screw (A, **Figure 23**) in or out as required. Do not exceed the 12 mm (0.47 in.) adjustment limit. Tighten the locknut (B, **Figure 23**).

## CLUTCH LEVER

Refer to **Table 1** for service intervals.

### Clutch Lever Adjustment

The clutch lever free play changes due to the clutch cable stretch, as well as clutch plate wear. Insufficient free play causes clutch slip and premature clutch plate wear. Excessive free play causes clutch drag and rough shift pedal operation.

Clutch cable adjustment is possible at the clutch lever or at the inline cable adjuster. Make minor adjustments at the clutch lever. Make major adjustments at the inline cable adjuster.

1.  Determine the clutch lever free play at the end of the clutch lever as shown in **Figure 25**. If the free play is more or less than 8-13 mm (0.31-0.51 in.), adjust the cable.

2.  Turn the clutch lever cable end adjuster (**Figure 26**) as required to obtain the specified amount of free play.

3.  If the proper amount of free play cannot be achieved by adjusting the clutch lever adjuster, the cable inline adjuster must be changed. Perform the following:

    a.  Turn the clutch lever adjuster (**Figure 26**) in all the way.

    b.  Loosen the clutch cable inline adjuster locknut (A, **Figure 27**). Turn the adjuster (B, **Figure 27**) as required to obtain the free play specified in Step 1. Tighten the locknut. If necessary, fine-tune the adjustment at the clutch lever adjuster.

4.  If the correct free play cannot be obtained, either the cable has stretched to the point that it needs to be replaced or the clutch discs are worn. Refer to Chapter Six for clutch cable and clutch service.

### Clutch Lever Pivot Bolt Lubrication

Periodically, remove the clutch lever pivot bolt and lubricate with lithium grease.

## BRAKES

This section describes routine service procedures for the front and rear disc brakes. Refer to **Table 1** for service intervals.

### Brake Pad Wear

Remove the front wheels to check brake pad wear. A small mirror helps when checking rear brake pad wear.

Inspect the brake pads for wear, scoring, grease or oil contamination, or other damage. Inspect the

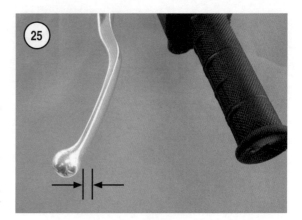

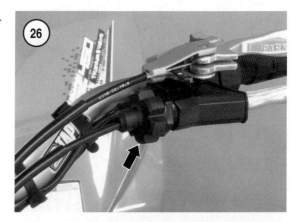

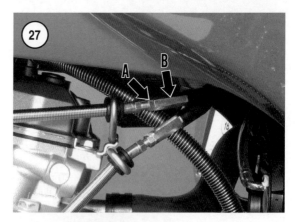

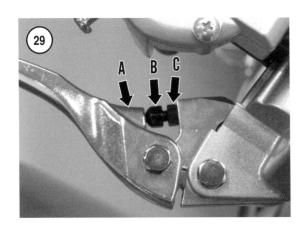

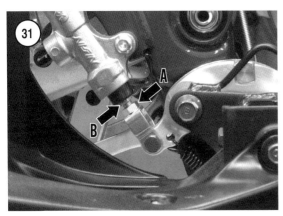

thickness of the friction material on each pad. Each brake pad is equipped with a wear groove (**Figure 28**). If any one pad on the front or rear is worn to its wear limit grooves, or measures 1.0 mm (0.039 in.) or less, replace both pads. Refer to Chapter Fourteen for brake pad service.

### Front Brake Lever Adjustment

The brake lever position is adjustable to suit rider preference. There must be zero free play when the lever boss (A, **Figure 29**) contacts the master cylinder actuator bolt (B). Otherwise, bleed the front brake as described in Chapter Fourteen.

Use the following procedure to adjust the brake lever position.
1. Push the brake lever forward.
2. Loosen the locknut (C, **Figure 29**).
3. Pull the brake lever toward the handlebar grip until the lever boss (A, **Figure 29**) just contacts the actuator bolt (B).
4. Turn the actuator bolt (B, **Figure 29**) so the lever is in the desired position.
5. Tighten the locknut (C, **Figure 29**).

### Rear Brake Pedal Height Adjustment

1. Apply the rear brake a few times and allow the pedal to come to rest. Make sure the return spring is installed and in good condition.
2. Measure the pedal height dimension as shown in **Figure 30** and compare to the specification in **Table 2**.
3. If necessary, loosen the locknut (A, **Figure 31**) and turn the pushrod (B) to adjust the pedal height. The gap between the pushrod nut and locknut must be 2.2-3.2 mm (0.09-0.13 in.).
4. Tighten the locknut and recheck the height dimension.
5. Lift the rear wheels and verify that the brake is not dragging. If so, repeat the adjustment procedure.

### Parking Brake Cable Adjustment

The parking brake cable must be properly adjusted to ensure that it fully engages and disengages.
1. Measure the cable length between the cable holder (**Figure 32**) and the centerline of the brake lever. Refer to **Table 2** for the required length.
2. If necessary, adjust the cable as follows:
   a. At the parking brake, loosen the locknut (A, **Figure 33**) and the adjuster bolt (B).
   b. On the inline cable adjuster, push back the boot and loosen the locknut (A, **Figure 34**). Turn the cable adjuster (B, **Figure 34**) until the proper length is achieved. Tighten the locknut and reposition the boot.

c. At the parking brake, turn the adjuster bolt (B, **Figure 33**) clockwise until resistance is felt. Then turn it back 1/8 turn counterclockwise. Hold the adjuster bolt in this position and tighten the locknut to 16 N•m (11 ft.-lb.). There should be no play in the cable at the handlebar lever.

3. Lift the rear wheels and verify that the brake is not dragging. If so, repeat the adjustment procedure.

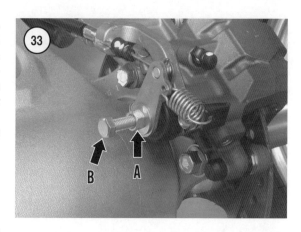

### Rear Brake Light Switch Adjustment

1. Turn the ignition switch on.
2. Depress the brake pedal and watch the brake light. The brake light should come on just before feeling pressure at the brake pedal. If necessary, adjust the rear brake light switch by performing the following.
3. To adjust the brake light switch, (**Figure 35**) hold the switch body and turn the adjusting nut. To make the light come on earlier, turn the adjusting nut and move the switch body up. Move the switch body down to delay the light coming on.
4. Check that the brake light comes on when the pedal is depressed and goes off when the pedal is released. Readjust if necessary.
5. Turn the ignition switch off.

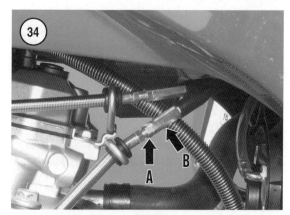

### Brake Fluid Level Inspection

> *WARNING*
> *If either reservoir is empty, or if the brake fluid level is so low that air is entering the brake system, bleed the brake system as described in Chapter Fourteen. Simply adding brake fluid to the reservoir does not restore the brake system to its full effectiveness.*

> *WARNING*
> *Use DOT 4 brake fluid. Others may vaporize and cause brake failure. Do not intermix different brands or types of brake fluid, as they may not be compatible. Do not intermix a silicone-based (DOT 5) brake fluid, as it can cause brake component damage leading to brake system failure.*

> *CAUTION*
> *Be careful when handling brake fluid. Do not spill it on painted or plastic surfaces, as it will damage them. Wash the area immediately with soap and water and rinse thoroughly.*

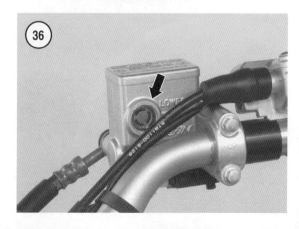

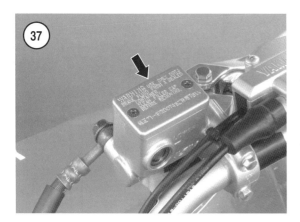

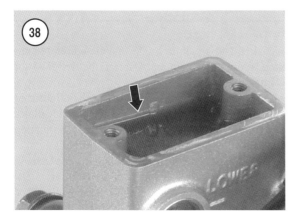

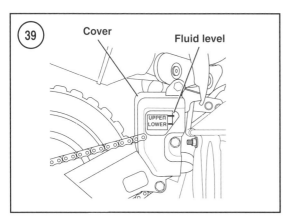

**Cover** **Fluid level**

The brake fluid level in the front and rear master cylinder reservoirs must be kept above the minimum level line. As the brake pads wear, the caliper piston moves farther out of the bore, thus causing the brake fluid level to drop in the reservoir. If the fluid level is low in either reservoir, check the brake pads as described in this section. If the pads are not worn excessively, check for loose or damaged hoses or loose fittings. If there are no visible fluid leaks, check the master cylinder bore and the brake caliper piston areas for signs of leaking brake fluid. Refer to Chapter Fourteen for brake service.

1. Park the ATV on level ground.
2. Clean the area around the reservoir cover before removing the cover to avoid contaminating the reservoir.

*CAUTION*
*Do not remove the cover on either the front or rear brake reservoirs unless the reservoirs are level.*

*CAUTION*
*When adding brake fluid to the reservoirs, inspect the reservoir diaphragm for tearing, cracks or other damage. A damaged diaphragm will allow moisture to enter the reservoir and contaminate the brake fluid.*

3A. On the front reservoir, perform the following:
    a. Turn the handlebar so the master cylinder reservoir is level.
    b. Observe the brake fluid level through the inspection window (**Figure 36**) on the master cylinder reservoir.
    c. The brake fluid level must be above the lower level line.
    d. Remove the two screws, cover (**Figure 37**) and diaphragm.
    e. Add DOT 4 brake fluid up to the upper level mark inside the reservoir (**Figure 38**).
    f. Replace the cover and diaphragm if damaged.
    g. Install the diaphragm and cover and tighten the screws securely.

3B. On the rear reservoir, perform the following:
    a. On 2004 and 2005 models, check that the brake fluid level is above the lower level mark on the reservoir (**Figure 39**). To add brake fluid, continue with the following steps.
    b. On 2006-on models, check that the brake fluid level is above the lower level mark on the reservoir (**Figure 40**). To add brake fluid, continue with the following steps.
    c. On 2004 and 2005 models, remove the cover (**Figure 39**).

d. On 2006-on models, remove the right side cover as described in Chapter Fifteen.

e. Unscrew the top cap, remove the top cap and the diaphragm.

f. Add DOT 4 brake fluid up to the upper level mark on the reservoir.

g. Replace the top cap and diaphragm. Install the cover.

### Brake Hose Replacement

Refer to Chapter Fourteen.

### Brake Fluid Change

> *WARNING*
> *Use brake fluid marked DOT 4 only. Others may vaporize and cause brake failure. Dispose of any unused fluid according to local regulations. Never reuse brake fluid. Contaminated brake fluid can cause brake failure.*

Every time a fluid reservoir cap is removed, a small amount of dirt and moisture enters the brake system. The same thing happens if a leak occurs or any part of the hydraulic system is loosened or disconnected. Dirt can clog the system and cause unnecessary wear. Water in the brake fluid can vaporize at high brake system temperatures, impairing hydraulic action and reducing stopping ability.

To maintain peak performance, change the brake fluid every year and when rebuilding a caliper or master cylinder. To change brake fluid, follow the brake bleeding procedure in Chapter Fourteen.

### Brake Lever Pivot Bolt Lubrication

Periodically, remove the brake lever pivot bolt and lubricate with lithium grease.

### DRIVE CHAIN

### Drive Chain Lubrication

> *CAUTION*
> *Not all commercial chain lubricants are recommended for use on O-ring drive chains. Read the product label to be sure it is formulated for O-ring chains. Refer to **Table 3** for the specified drive chain lube.*

Lubricate the drive chain frequently. A properly maintained drive chain will provide maximum ser-

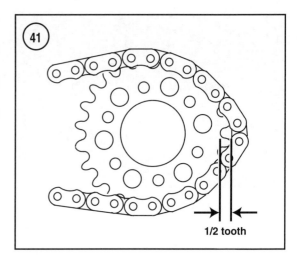

**1/2 tooth**

vice life and reliability. The manufacturer recommends Yamaha Chain and Cable Lube designed for O-ring chains.

On an O-ring type drive chain, the chain lubricant keeps the O-rings pliable and prevents the side plates and rollers from rusting. The actual chain lubrication is enclosed within the chain by the O-rings.

1. Ride the ATV a few miles to warm the drive chain. A warm chain increases lubricant penetration.

2. Park the ATV on level ground. Support the ATV securely with the rear wheels off the ground.

3. Lubricate the bottom chain run. Concentrate on getting the lubricant down between the side plates on both sides of the chain. Do not over lubricate.

4. Rotate the chain and continue lubricating until the entire chain has been lubricated.

5. Turn the rear wheels slowly and wipe off excess oil from the chain with a shop cloth. Also wipe off lubricant from the wheel and tire and rear of the ATV.

### Drive Chain Cleaning

> *CAUTION*
> *All models are equipped with an O-ring drive chain. Clean the chain with kerosene only. Solvents and gasoline cause the rubber O-rings to swell. The drive chain then becomes so stiff it cannot move or flex. If this happens, the drive chain must be replaced. High-pressure washers and steam cleaning can also damage the O-rings.*

Clean the drive chain after riding over dusty or sandy conditions.

Because all models are equipped with an endless drive chain, it is not practical to break the chain in order to clean it. This section describes how to clean the drive chain while it is mounted on the ATV.

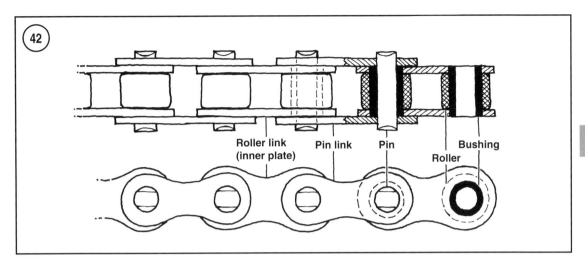

Roller link (inner plate)   Pin link   Pin   Bushing   Roller

**3**

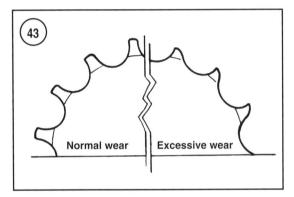

Normal wear    Excessive wear

1. Ride the ATV a few miles to warm the drive chain. A warm chain increases lubricant penetration.
2. Park the ATV on level ground. Support the ATV securely with the rear wheels off the ground.
3. Place some stiff cardboard and a drain pan underneath the drive chain.

*WARNING*
*To avoid catching your fingers between the chain and sprocket, do not rotate the rear wheels when cleaning the chain. Clean one section of the chain at a time.*

*CAUTION*
*Do not splash the kerosene when cleaning the drive chain. Make sure to keep the kerosene off the rear tires and other parts as much as possible.*

4. Soak a thick rag in kerosene, then wipe it against the section of chain that is exposed on the lower chain run. When this section of the chain is clean, turn the rear wheels to expose the next section and clean it. Repeat until all of the chain is clean. To re-

move stubborn dirt, scrub the rollers and side plates with a soft brush.
5. Turn the rear wheels slowly and wipe the drive chain dry with a thick shop cloth.
6. Clean the ATV of all kerosene residue.
7. Lubricate the drive chain as described in this section.

**Drive Chain and Sprocket Inspection**

Frequently check the chain and both sprockets for excessive wear and damage.
1. Clean the drive chain as described in this section.
2. Park the ATV on level ground. Support the ATV securely with the rear wheels off the ground.
3. Turn the rear wheels and inspect both sides of the chain for missing or damaged O-rings.
4. At the rear sprocket, pull one of the links away from the driven sprocket. If the link pulls away more than 1/2 the height of the sprocket tooth (**Figure 41**), the chain is excessively worn.
5. Inspect the inner plate chain faces (**Figure 42**). They should be polished on both sides. If they show considerable uneven wear on one side, the sprockets are not aligned properly. Severe wear requires replacement of not only the drive chain but also the drive and driven sprockets. Refer to Chapter Eleven.
6. Inspect the drive and driven sprockets for the following defects:
    a. Undercutting or sharp teeth (**Figure 43**).
    b. Broken teeth.
7. Check the drive sprocket nut and the driven sprocket nuts for looseness. If loose, tighten to the torque specified in **Table 8**.
8. If excessive chain or sprocket wear is evident, replace the drive chain and both sprockets as a complete set. If only the drive chain is replaced, the worn sprockets will cause rapid chain wear. Refer to Chapter Eleven.

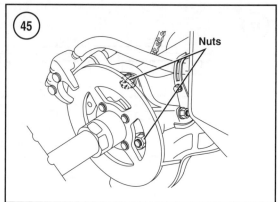

9. Inspect the drive chain slider and rollers as described in this section.

## Drive Chain Adjustment

The drive chain must have adequate play so it can adjust to the actions of the swing arm when the machine is in use. Too little play can cause the chain to become excessively tight and cause unnecessary wear to the driveline components. Too much play can cause excessive looseness and possibly cause the chain to derail.

### 2004-2005 models

1. There must be no weight on the ATV.
2. Move the ATV so the chain rotates and determine when the chain is tightest along its top length (least amount of play).
3. Measure the free play in the top length of chain (**Figure 44**). The required amount of free play is 25-35 mm (0.98-1.38 in.).
4. If necessary, adjust the chain play as follows:
   a. Loosen the axle hub nuts (**Figure 45**).
   b. Loosen the chain adjuster locknuts (**Figure 46**).
   c. Equally turn the chain adjuster bolts (**Figure 46**) until the chain play is correct. Use the adjustment marks on the hub to equally adjust the chain. If increasing chain play, push the axle forward to take the play out of the adjusters. This can also be achieved by slightly lowering the jack, allowing the wheels to force the axle against the adjusters.
   d. When free play is correct, tighten the axle hub nuts and chain adjuster locknuts to lock the setting. Tighten the axle hub nuts to 85 N•m (62 ft.-lb.). Tighten the locknuts to 16 N•m (12 ft.-lb.).
   e. Recheck the chain play. Adjust, if necessary.
5. If free play cannot be adjusted within the limits of the adjuster, the chain is excessively worn. Replace the chain as described in Chapter Eleven.

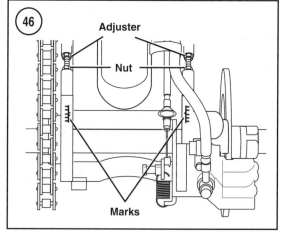

### 2006-on models

1. There must be no weight on the ATV.
2. With the transmission in neutral, move the ATV so the chain rotates and determine when the chain is tightest along its top length (least amount of play).
3. Measure the free play in the top length of chain (**Figure 44**). The required amount of free play is 25-35 mm (0.98-1.38 in.).
4. If necessary, adjust the chain play as follows:
   a. Loosen the pinch bolts at the axle hub (**Figure 47**).

#### NOTE
*The rear axle hub is eccentric shaped. Rotating the hub causes the rear axle to move forward and rearward.*

   b. Insert a rod into one of the holes in the axle hub (**Figure 48**).
   c. Make sure the transmission is in neutral.

#### NOTE
*Move the ATV slowly in the following step. The axle hub will rotate when the rod presses against a driven sprocket spoke.*

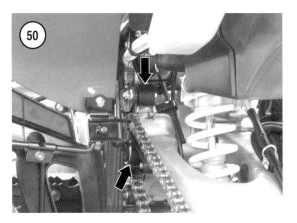

d. Move the ATV forward to loosen the drive chain, or rearward to tighten the drive chain.

e. Remove the rod and remeasure free play.

f. When free play is correct, tighten the axle hub pinch bolts to lock the setting. Tighten the bolts in the reverse sequence shown in **Figure 47** to 21 N•m (16 ft.-lb.).

5. If free play cannot be adjusted within the limits of the adjuster, the chain is excessively worn. Replace the chain as described in Chapter Eleven.

### Drive Chain Slider and Rollers Inspection

Inspect the following parts for wear or damage. The parts support the chain and protect the frame and swing arm.

1. Chain slider (**Figure 49**).

a. Inspect the upper and lower surface of the slider for wear or damage. The chain will contact the swing arm, possibly causing severe damage, if the slider is worn or missing.

b. Check the mounting bolt for tightness.

2. Chain rollers (**Figure 50**).

a. Clean and inspect the chain rollers, attached to the frame. Replace the rollers if worn or seized.

b. Check the mounting bolts for tightness.

### TIRES AND WHEELS

**Tire Pressure**

> *WARNING*
> *Tire inflation pressure is for the original equipment tires. Aftermarket tires may require different inflation pressure. The use of tires other than those specified by the manufacturer may cause instability.*

> *WARNING*
> *Always inflate tires to the correct air pressure. If the ATV is run with unequal air pressures, it may run toward one side, causing poor handling.*

> *WARNING*
> *Do not over inflate the tires as they can be permanently distorted and damaged.*

Check and adjust tire pressure to provide good traction and handling and to get the maximum life from the tire. Carry an accurate tire gauge in the ATV's tool box. The tire inflation pressures are in **Table 2**. Check tire pressure when the tires are cold.

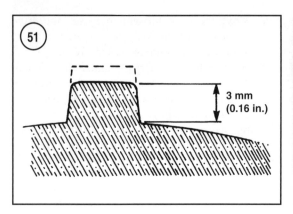

3 mm
(0.16 in.)

## Tire Inspection

> *WARNING*
> *Do not ride the ATV with damaged or*
> *excessively worn tires. Tires in these*
> *conditions can cause loss of control.*
> *Replace damaged or severely worn*
> *tires immediately.*

The tires take a lot of punishment due to the variety of terrain they are subjected to. Inspect them daily for excessive wear, cuts, abrasions or punctures. If a nail or other object in the tire is found, mark its location with a light crayon before removing it. Service the tire as described in Chapter Eleven.

To gauge tire wear, inspect the height of the tread knobs. If the average tread knob height measures 3 mm (0.12 in.) or less (**Figure 51**), replace the tire as described in Chapter Eleven.

## Wheel Inspection

Inspect the wheels for damage. Wheel damage may be sufficient to cause an air leak or knock it out of alignment. Improper wheel alignment can cause vibration and result in an unsafe riding condition.

Make sure the wheel nuts (**Figure 52**) are tightened in a crossing pattern to 45 N•m (33 ft.-lb.).

## FRONT WHEEL BEARING INSPECTION

Inspect the front wheel bearings at the front suspension interval in **Table 1**. To replace the seals and wheel bearings, refer to the service procedures in Chapter Twelve.

Check the front wheel bearings as follows:
1. Support the ATV so the front wheel is off the ground.
2. Remove the front wheel as described in Chapter Eleven.
3. Push the caliper in to push the piston into their bores. This will move the pads away from the disc.
4. Install the front wheel.

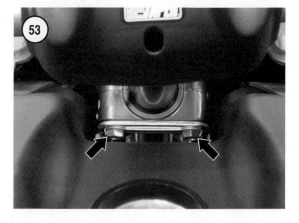

5. Spin the wheel while checking for excessive wheel bearing noise or other damage. Stop the wheel.
6. Grab the wheel at two points and rock it. There should be no play at the wheel bearings. If any movement can be seen or felt, check the wheel bearings for excessive wear or damage as described in *Front Wheel Hub* in Chapter Twelve. A faulty ball joint can also cause excessive wheel movement. Determine whether wheel movement is due to faulty bearings or ball joints.
7. Spin the wheel while applying the brake several times to reposition the pads against the disc.

## STEERING SYSTEM

### Steering System Inspection

Inspect the steering system at the interval in **Table 1**. If any of the following fasteners are loose, refer to Chapter Twelve for procedures.
1. Park the ATV on level ground and set the parking brake.
2. Inspect all components of the steering system. Repair or replace damaged components as described in Chapter Twelve.
3. Check the shock absorbers as described in *Front Suspension* in this chapter.

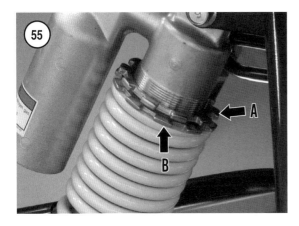

4. Remove the handlebar cover. Check that the handlebar holder bolts are tight. Refer to *Handlebar* in Chapter Twelve. Reinstall the handlebar cover.

5. Make sure the front axle nuts are tight and that all cotter pins are in place.

6. Check that the cotter pins are in place on all steering components. If any cotter pin is missing, check the nut for looseness. If necessary, refer to Chapter Twelve for procedures.

7. Check the steering shaft play as follows:
   a. Support the ATV with the front wheels off the ground.
   b. To check steering shaft radial play, move the handlebar from side to side (without attempting to move the wheels). If radial play is excessive, the upper steering bushing is probably worn or the bushing holder mounting bolts (**Figure 53**) are loose. Replace the upper bushing or tighten the bushing holder bolts as necessary.
   c. To check steering shaft thrust play, lift up and then push down on the handlebar. If there is excessive thrust play, check the lower steering shaft nut (**Figure 54**) for looseness. If the nut is tightened properly, check the lower steering shaft bearing for excessive wear or damage.
   d. If necessary, service the steering shaft as described in Chapter Twelve.

e. Lower the ATV so that all four tires are on the ground.

8. Check the steering knuckle and tie rod ends as follows:
   a. Turn the handlebar quickly from side to side. If there is appreciable looseness between the handlebar and tires, check the tie rod ends for excessive wear or damage.
   b. Service the steering knuckle and tie rods as described in Chapter Twelve.

### Toe-in Adjustment

Check the toe-in adjustment as described in *Tie Rods* in Chapter Twelve to prevent abnormal tire wear and to check for faulty steering components at the intervals specified in **Table 1**.

### FRONT SUSPENSION

### Shock Absorber Inspection

Inspect at the intervals noted in **Table 1**

1. Check the front shock absorbers for oil leaks, a bent damper rod or other damage.

2. If necessary, replace the shock absorbers as described in Chapter Twelve.

### Shock Spring Preload Adjustment

Perform the spring preload adjustment with the shock mounted on the ATV. Adjust spring preload by changing the position of the adjuster on the shock body (**Figure 55**).

1. Support the ATV with the front wheels off the ground.

2. Clean the threads on the shock body.

3. Measure the existing spring preload length. Measure the spring from end to end. Do not include the thickness of the adjuster or the spring seat. Record the measurement for reference.

4. Loosen the spring locknut (A, **Figure 55**) with a spanner wrench. If the adjuster (B, **Figure 55**) turns with the locknut, strike the locknut with a punch and hammer to break it from the locknut.

*CAUTION*
*The spring preload must be maintained within specification. If the minimum specification is exceeded, the spring may coil bind when the shock comes near full compression. This will overload and weaken the spring.*

5. Turn the adjuster to change the spring preload dimension within the limits specified in **Table 4**

or **Table 5**. Measure and record the dimension for reference. One complete turn of the adjuster moves the spring 1.5 mm (0.06 in.). Tightening the adjuster increases spring preload and loosening it decreases preload.

6. Lightly lubricate the threads on the shock body with engine oil. Then hold the adjuster and tighten the spring locknut to 30 N•m (22 ft.-lb.).

### Shock Rebound Damping

The rebound damping adjustment affects the rate of shock absorber extension after it has been compressed. This adjustment has no effect on shock compression. If rebound damping is set too low, the front wheel may bottom on subsequent bumps.

The rebound damping adjuster is located at the bottom of the shock (**Figure 56**). Refer to **Table 4** or **Table 5** for standard positions and total adjustment range. Due to production changes, the number of detent positions may vary. Verify the number of detent positions by turning the adjuster from full in to full out.

Set rebound damping as follows:

1. For the standard setting, turn the adjuster screw clockwise until it stops. This is the full hard position. Turn the adjuster screw counterclockwise the number of clicks (standard) in **Table 4** or **Table 5**. When the standard setting is set, the slit in the adjuster will align with the reference mark on the shock body.

2. Turn the adjuster as needed to obtain the desired rebound damping. To increase the rebound damping, turn the adjuster clockwise. To decrease the rebound damping, turn the adjuster counterclockwise.

3. Make sure the adjuster is located in one of the detent positions and not in between any two settings.

### Shock Compression Damping

All models are equipped with front shock absorbers that permit adjustment of compression damping. Some later models are equipped with shock absorbers that have two-stage (low/high) compression adjustment. A hex adjuster at the top of the shock absorber identifies shock absorbers equipped with two-stage compression adjustment.

#### *Single-stage compression shock absorbers*

Compression damping controls the shock absorber rate when hitting a bump. This setting has no effect on the rebound rate of the shock. The compression damping adjuster is located above the shock reservoir (**Figure 57**). Turning the adjuster clockwise increases damping (stiffens). Turning the adjuster

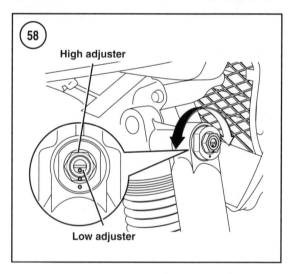

High adjuster

Low adjuster

counterclockwise decreases damping (softens). Refer to **Table 4** for the standard compression setting. Set compression damping as follows:

1. Turn the adjuster to the maximum hard position (clockwise). Do not force the adjuster beyond its normal range of travel.

2. Turn the adjuster counterclockwise so the reference punch marks align. This is the standard position.

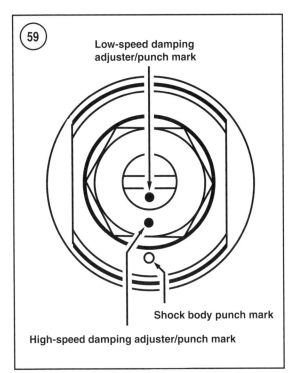

Low-speed damping adjuster/punch mark

Shock body punch mark

High-speed damping adjuster/punch mark

wise until it stops (this is the full hard position). Then turn it counterclockwise the number of turns (standard) in **Table 5**. When the standard setting is set, the high-speed damping adjuster punch mark will align with the shock body punch mark (**Figure 59**).

2. To set the low-speed adjuster to its standard setting, turn the center adjuster screw (**Figure 58**) clockwise until it stops (this is the full hard position). Then turn it counterclockwise the number of clicks (standard) in **Table 5**. When the standard setting is set, the low-speed adjuster punch mark will align with the shock body punch mark (**Figure 59**).

3. Turn the adjuster as needed to obtain the desired compression damping.

### Shock Nitrogen Pressure

Refer all nitrogen pressure adjustment to a dealership.

### Control Arm And Ball Joint Inspection

1. Support the ATV so the front wheel is off the ground.
2. Grab the wheel at two vertical points and rock it. There should be no wheel play. If any movement can be seen or felt, check the ball joints (**Figure 60**) for excessive wear or damage (Chapter Twelve). Faulty wheel bearings can cause excessive wheel movement. Determine whether wheel movement is due to faulty bearings or ball joints.
3. Remove the front wheel (Chapter Eleven).
4. Attempt to move the control arms laterally. Movement indicates worn or damaged control arm bushings. Refer to Chapter Twelve.

### Control Arm Lubrication

Lubricate the control arm bushings at the intervals in **Table 1**. Inject lithium grease into the grease fittings (**Figure 61**) on the control arms. Clean the grease fitting with a clean cloth before and after injecting grease.

### REAR SUSPENSION

### Shock Absorber Inspection

1. Remove the air box as described in Chapter Eight.
2. Check the rear shock absorber for oil leaks, a bent damper rod or other damage.
3. If necessary, replace the shock absorber as described in Chapter Thirteen.

3. Turn the adjuster as needed to obtain the desired compression damping.

### *Two-stage compression shock absorbers*

Compression damping controls the shock absorber rate when hitting a bump. This setting has no effect on the rebound rate of the shock. The shock is equipped with low- and high-speed adjusters. Both compression damping adjusters are located above the shock reservoir (**Figure 58**). Turning either adjuster clockwise increases damping (stiffens). Turning either adjuster counterclockwise decreases damping (softens). Refer to **Table 5** for the standard compression settings. Set compression damping as follows:

1. To set the high-speed adjuster to its standard setting, turn the hex-head adjuster (**Figure 58**) clock-

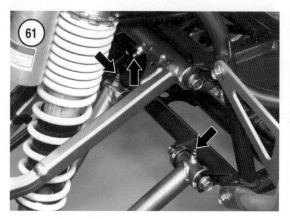

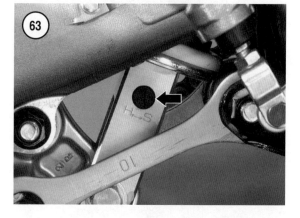

## Shock Spring Preload Adjustment

The spring preload adjustment can be performed with the shock mounted on the ATV. Adjust spring preload by changing the position of the adjuster on the shock body (**Figure 62**).

1. Remove the air box as described in Chapter Eight.
2. Support the ATV with the rear wheels off the ground.
3. Clean the threads on the shock body.
4. Measure the existing spring preload length. Measure the spring from end to end. Do not include the thickness of the adjuster or the spring seat. Record the measurement for reference.
5. Loosen the spring locknut (A, **Figure 62**) with a spanner wrench. If the adjuster turns with the locknut, strike the locknut with a punch and hammer to break it from the locknut.

> *CAUTION*
> *The spring preload must be maintained within specification. If the minimum specification is exceeded (**Table 6** or **Table 7**), the spring may coil bind when the shock comes near full compression. This will overload and weaken the spring.*

6. Turn the adjuster (B, **Figure 62**) to change the spring preload dimension within the limits specified in **Table 6** or **Table 7**. Record the measurement for reference. One complete turn of the adjuster moves the spring 1.5 mm (0.06 in.). Tightening the adjuster increases spring preload and loosening it decreases preload.
7. Lightly lubricate the threads on the shock body with engine oil. Hold the adjuster (B, **Figure 62**) and tighten the spring locknut (A) to 44 N•m (32 ft.-lb.).
8. Install the air box as described in Chapter Eight.

## Shock Rebound Damping

The rebound damping adjustment affects the rate of shock absorber extension after it has been com-

pressed. This adjustment has no effect on shock compression. If rebound damping is set too low, the rear wheels may bottom on subsequent bumps.

The rebound damping adjuster is mounted at the bottom of the shock (**Figure 63**). A clicker type adjuster is used; each click of the adjuster screw represents one adjustment or position change. Turning the adjuster one full turn changes the adjuster by eight positions. Refer to **Table 6** or **Table 7** for the standard position and adjustment range. Set rebound damping as follows:

1. For the standard setting, turn the adjuster screw clockwise until it stops (this is the full hard position). Turn the adjuster counterclockwise the number of clicks (standard) in **Table 6** or **Table 7**. When the standard setting is set, the slit in the adjuster will align with the reference mark on the shock body.
2. Turn the adjuster as needed to obtain the desired rebound damping. To increase the rebound damping, turn the adjuster clockwise. To decrease the rebound damping, turn the adjuster counterclockwise.
3. Make sure the adjuster is located in one of the detent positions and not in between any two settings.

## Shock Compression Damping

All models are equipped with a rear shock absorber that permits adjustment of compression damp-

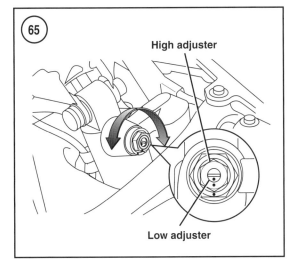

High adjuster

Low adjuster

ing. Some later models are equipped with a shock absorber that has two-stage (low/high) compression adjustment. A hex adjuster at the top of the shock absorber identifies a shock absorber equipped with a two-stage compression adjustment.

### *Single-stage compression shock absorber*

Compression damping controls the shock absorber rate when hitting a bump. This setting has no effect on the rebound rate of the shock. The compression damping adjuster is located at the top of the shock (**Figure 64**). Turning the adjuster clockwise increases damping (stiffens). Turning the adjuster counterclockwise decreases damping (softens). Refer to **Table 6** for the compression setting. Set compression damping as follows:

1. Remove the seat as described in Chapter Fifteen.
2. Turn the adjuster to the maximum hard position (clockwise). Do not force the adjuster beyond its normal range of travel.
3. Turn the adjuster counterclockwise so the reference punch marks align. This is the standard position.
4. Turn the adjuster as needed to obtain the desired compression damping.

### *Two-stage compression shock absorber*

Compression damping controls the shock absorber rate when hitting a bump. This setting has no effect on the rebound rate of the shock. The shock is equipped with low- and high-speed adjusters. Both compression-damping adjusters are located at the top of the shock (**Figure 65**). Turning either adjuster clockwise increases damping (stiffens). Turning either adjuster counterclockwise decreases damping (softens). Refer to **Table 7** for the fast and slow compression settings. Set compression damping as follows:

1. Remove the seat as described in Chapter Fifteen.
2. To set the high-speed adjuster to its standard setting, turn the hex-head adjuster (**Figure 65**) clockwise until it stops (this is the full hard position). Then turn it counterclockwise the number of turns in **Table 7** to achieve the standard damping. When the standard setting is set, the high-speed damping adjuster punch mark will align with the shock body punch mark (**Figure 59**).
3. To set the low-speed adjuster to its standard setting, turn the center adjuster screw (**Figure 65**) clockwise until it stops (this is the full hard position). Then turn it counterclockwise the number of clicks in **Table 7** to achieve the standard damping. When the standard setting is set, the low-speed adjuster punch mark will align with the shock body punch mark (**Figure 59**).
4. Turn the adjuster as needed to obtain the desired compression damping.

### Swing Arm and Linkage Inspection and Lubrication

1. Support the ATV securely.
2. Remove the rear wheels as described in Chapter Eleven.
3. Check for loose rear suspension components.
4. Check for damaged seals.
5. Check the tightness of the rear suspension fasteners.
6. Lubricate the swing arm bearings with lithium grease at the intervals specified in **Table 1**. Do not remove the bearings. Refer to Chapter Thirteen.

### BATTERY

The original equipment battery is a maintenance-free type. Maintenance-free batteries do not require periodic electrolyte inspection and water cannot be added. Refer to the *Battery* in Chapter Nine for service, testing and replacement procedures.

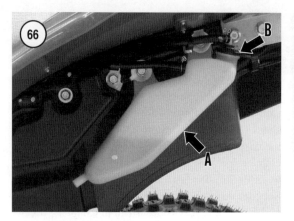

## COOLING SYSTEM

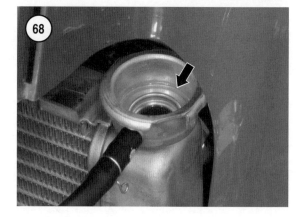

*WARNING*
*Antifreeze is toxic. Do not discharge coolant containing antifreeze into storm sewers, septic systems, or onto the ground. Place used antifreeze in the original container and dispose of it according to local regulations. Do not store coolant where it is accessible to children or pets.*

*WARNING*
*Replace the coolant in the cooling system when the engine and coolant are cold. Severe injury can occur if the system is drained while it is hot.*

*CAUTION*
*Do not allow coolant to contact painted surfaces. If contact does occur, immediately wash the surface with water.*

*CAUTION*
*Drain and flush the cooling system at the interval in **Table 1**. Refill with the specified coolant (**Table 3**). Do not reuse the old coolant, as it deteriorates with use. Do not operate the cooling system with only distilled water, even in climates where antifreeze protection is not required; doing so will promote internal engine corrosion.*

### Coolant Level

Keep the coolant level at the FULL mark on the coolant reserve tank (A, **Figure 66**).
1. Check the level with the engine at normal operating temperature and the ATV on a level surface.

2. If the level is low, remove the reservoir tank cap (B, **Figure 66**) and add coolant to the reserve tank, not to the radiator.

### Coolant Change

Drain and flush the cooling system at the interval in **Table 1**. Refill with the specified coolant (**Table 3**).
1. Park the ATV on level ground.
2. Remove the seat as described in Chapter Fifteen.
3. Remove the fuel tank cover as described in Chapter Fifteen.
4. Remove the right side cover as described in Chapter Fifteen.
5. Place a drain pan under the right side of the engine, below the water pump. Remove the drain bolt (**Figure 67**) from the bottom of the water pump.
6. As coolant begins to drain from the engine, stand to the side and slowly loosen the radiator cap so the flow from the engine increases. Be ready to reposition the drain pan.
7. Check the reserve tank (A, **Figure 66**) for remaining coolant. If coolant remains, use a syringe to extract the coolant. If dirt or other buildup is in the tank, remove the mounting bolts and wash the tank.

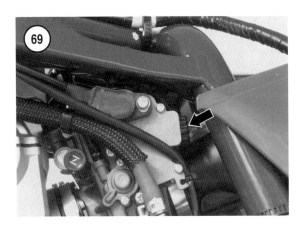

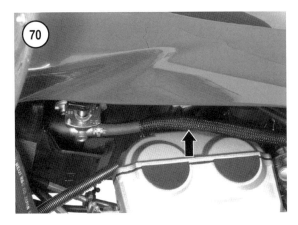

a. Remove the radiator cap and check the coolant level. If necessary, add coolant to bring the level to the bottom of the filler neck.

b. Install the radiator cap.

15. Start the engine and allow it to reach operating temperature. Shut off the engine and check the following:

a. Check for leaks at the drain plug, hoses and reserve tank.

b. Check the level in the reserve tank. If necessary, remove the cap from the reserve tank and fill it to the full mark.

16. Rinse the frame and engine where coolant was splashed.

17. Install the right side cover, fuel tank cover and seat (Chapter Fifteen).

## CARBURETOR

### Idle Speed Adjustment

Check at the intervals specified in **Table 1**.

*NOTE*
*Seat and fuel tank removal may be necessary to connect a tachometer in the following procedure.*

1. Check the air filter for cleanliness. Clean if necessary as described in this chapter.
2. Connect a shop tachometer to the engine following the manufacturer's instructions.
3. Make sure the throttle cable free play is correct. Check and adjust as described in this chapter.
4. Start and allow the engine to reach operating temperature.
5. Adjust the idle speed using the idle speed knob (**Figure 69**).
6. Adjust the idle speed to 1750-1850 rpm. Open and close the throttle a few times to make sure the idle speed returns to the rpm.
7. Turn off the engine and disconnect the tachometer.

### Pilot Screw Adjustment

The pilot screw is pre-set and adjustment is not necessary unless the carburetor has been overhauled or improperly adjusted. Refer to *Carburetor adjustment and Rejetting* in Chapter Eight.

### Fuel Hose

Inspect the fuel hose (**Figure 70**) from the fuel shutoff valve to the carburetor at the interval specified in **Table 1**. If it is cracked or starting to dete-

8. Flush the cooling system and reserve tank with clean water. Check that all water drains from the system. Applying light air pressure to the radiator can aid in purging the water passages.

9. Inspect the condition of:

a. Radiator hoses. Check for leaks, cracks and loose clamps.

b. Radiator core. Check for leaks, debris and tightness of mounting bolts.

c. Radiator fan. Check for damaged wiring and tight connections.

10. Install a new seal washer on the coolant drain bolt, then install and tighten the bolt to 10 N•m (88 in.-lb.).

11. Connect the hose to the reserve tank.

12. Fill the radiator to the bottom of the filler neck (**Figure 68**) with the specified coolant (**Table 3**). Install the radiator cap.

13. Fill the reserve tank to the full mark.

14. Start the engine and allow the coolant to circulate for about one minute. Shut off the engine and do the following:

*WARNING*
*Cover the cap with shop cloths, then open the cap slowly. Do not remove the cap until all pressure is relieved.*

riorate, replace it. Make sure the hose clamps are in place and holding securely.

## CRANKCASE BREATHER HOSES

Periodically inspect the breather hoses. Refer to Chapter Eight. Replace any cracked or deteriorated hoses. Make sure the hose clamps are in place and tight.

## SPARK PLUG

Check the spark plug at the intervals specified in **Table 1**.

### Removal

1. Raise the fuel tank as described in Chapter Eight.

*NOTE*
*The ignition coil and spark plug cap are an integral assembly.*

2. Grasp the ignition coil (**Figure 71**) as near the spark plug as possible and pull it off the plug. If it is stuck to the plug, twist it slightly to break it loose.

*CAUTION*
*Whenever the spark plug is removed, dirt around it can fall into the plug hole. This can cause engine damage.*

3. Blow away any dirt that has collected around the spark plug.
4. Remove the spark plug using a spark plug socket.

*NOTE*
*If the plug is difficult to remove, apply penetrating oil, like WD-40 or Liquid Wrench, around the base of the plug and let it soak about 10-20 minutes.*

5. Inspect the plug. Look for broken center porcelain, excessively eroded electrodes and excessive carbon or oil fouling.

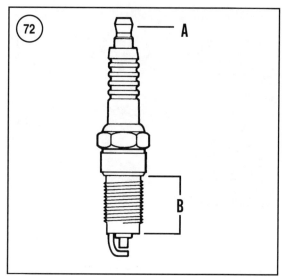

### Gap and Installation

Adjust the electrode gap on a new spark plug to ensure a reliable, consistent spark. Use a spark plug gapping tool and a wire feeler gauge.
1. If so equipped, remove the terminal nut (A, **Figure 72**) from the end of the plug.
2. Insert a wire feeler gauge between the center and side electrode of the plug (**Figure 73**). Refer to **Table 2** for gap specification. If the gap is correct, a slight drag will be felt while pulling the wire through. If there is no drag, or the gauge will not pass through,

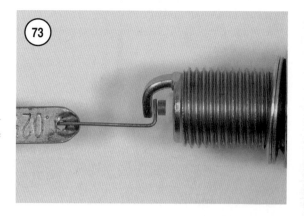

bend the side electrode with a gaping tool (**Figure 74**) to set the proper gap.
3. Apply an antiseize compound to the plug threads before installing the spark plug. Do not use engine oil on the plug threads.
4. Screw the spark plug in by hand until it seats. Very little effort should be required. If force is necessary, the plug may be cross-threaded. Unscrew it and try again.

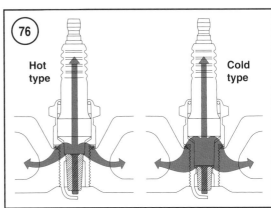

**3**

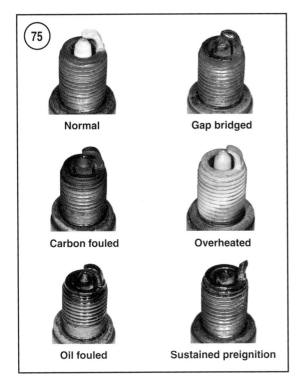

that corresponds to the jetting information desired. For example, if the main jet is in question, operate the ATV at full throttle, shut off the engine and coast to a stop.

### Heat range

Spark plugs are available in various heat ranges that are either hotter or colder than the original plugs (**Figure 76**). Select plugs of the heat range designed for the anticipated loads and operating conditions. Use of the incorrect heat range can cause the plug to foul or overheat and cause piston damage.

In general, use a hot plug for low speeds and low temperatures. Use a cold plug for high speeds, high engine loads and high temperatures. The plug should operate hot enough to burn off unwanted deposits, but not so hot that it burns itself or causes preignition. A spark plug of the correct heat range shows a light tan color on the insulator after the plug has been in service.

The reach, or length, of a plug is also important (B, **Figure 72**). A plug that is too short causes excessive carbon buildup, hard starting and plug fouling. A plug that is too long causes overheating or may contact the top of the piston. Both conditions cause engine damage.

**Table 2** lists the standard heat range spark plug.

5. Tighten the spark plug to 13 N•m (115 in.-lb.). Do not overtighten.

### Inspection

Reading a spark plug that has been in use can provide information about spark plug operation, air/fuel mixture composition and engine operating conditions (oil consumption due to wear for example). Before checking the spark plug, operate the ATV under a medium load for approximately 6 miles (10 km). Avoid prolonged idling before shutting off the engine. Remove the spark plug as described in this section. Examine the plug and compare it to the typical plugs and conditions shown in **Figure 75**.

When reading a plug to evaluate carburetor jetting, start with a new plug and operate the ATV at the load

### Normal condition

If the plug has a light tan- or gray-colored deposit and no abnormal gap wear or erosion, good engine, carburetion and ignition condition are indicated. The plug in use is of the proper heat range and may be serviced and returned to use.

### Carbon fouled

Soft, dry, sooty deposits covering the entire firing end of the plug are evidence of incomplete combustion. Even though the firing end of the plug is dry, the plug's insulation decreases. An electrical path is formed that lowers the voltage from the ignition system. Engine misfiring is a sign of carbon fouling. Carbon fouling can be caused by one or more of the following:

1. Too rich fuel mixture.
2. Spark plug heat range too cold.
3. Clogged air filter.
4. Retarded ignition timing.
5. Ignition component failure.
6. Low engine compression.
7. Prolonged idling.

### Oil fouled

The tip of an oil fouled plug has a black insulator tip, a damp oily film over the firing end and a carbon layer over the entire nose. The electrodes are not worn. An oil fouled spark plug may be cleaned in an emergency, but it is better to replace it. It is important to correct the cause of fouling before the engine is returned to service. Common causes for this condition are:

1. Incorrect carburetor jetting.
2. Low idle speed or prolonged idling.
3. Ignition component failure.
4. Spark plug heat range too cold.
5. Engine still being broken in.

### Gap bridging

A plug in this condition has a gap shorted out by combustion deposits between the electrodes. If this condition is encountered, check for an improper oil type or excessive carbon in the combustion chamber. Be sure to locate and correct the cause of this condition.

### Overheating

Badly worn electrodes and premature gap wear, along with a gray or white blistered porcelain insulator surface are signs of overheating. The most common cause for this condition is using a spark plug of the wrong heat range (too hot). If a hotter spark plug has not been installed, but the plug is overheated, consider the following causes:

1. Lean fuel mixture.
2. Ignition timing too advanced.
3. Engine lubrication system malfunction.
4. Engine vacuum leak.
5. Improper spark plug installation (too tight).
6. No spark plug gasket.

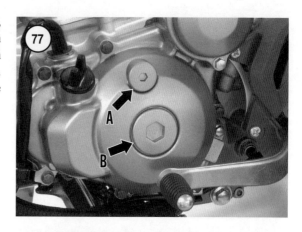

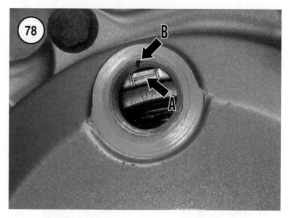

### Worn out

Corrosive gases formed by combustion and high voltage sparks have eroded the electrodes. Spark plugs in this condition require more voltage to fire under hard acceleration. Replace with a new spark plug.

### Preignition

If the electrodes are melted, preignition is almost certainly the cause. Check for carburetor mounting or intake manifold leaks and over-advanced ignition timing. It is also possible that a plug of the wrong heat range (too hot) is being used. Find the cause of the preignition before returning the engine into service.

## IGNITION TIMING INSPECTION

All models are equipped with an electronic ignition system. Ignition timing is not adjustable. Check the ignition timing to make sure all components within the ignition system are working correctly. If the ignition timing is incorrect, troubleshoot the ignition system as described in Chapter Two. Incorrect ignition timing can cause performance loss. It may also cause overheating.

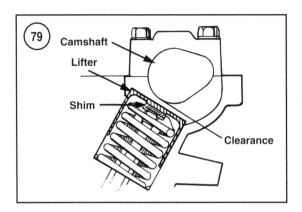

Before starting this procedure, check all electrical connections related to the ignition system. Make sure all connections are tight and free from corrosion and that all ground connections are clean and tight.

1. Start the engine and let it warm approximately 2-3 minutes. Verify the engine idle speed is within specification as described in *Carburetor* in this chapter. Shut off the engine.

*NOTE*
*Seat and fuel tank removal may be necessary to connect a timing light in the following procedure.*

2. Attach a timing light following the manufacturer's instructions.
3. Remove the timing plug from the left crankcase cover (A, **Figure 77**).
4. Run the engine at idle speed while directing the timing light into the crankcase-timing hole.
5. Timing is correct if the H mark (A, **Figure 78**) aligns with the index notch (B) in the cover.
6. If the timing mark does not align with the index notch, the timing is incorrect. Refer to Chapter Nine and test the ignition system.
7. Turn off the engine and disconnect the test equipment.
8. Install the timing plug into the crankcase cover.

## COMPRESSION TEST

A compression test checks the internal condition of the engine, including the piston rings, pistons, and head gasket. Check the compression at each tune-up, record the readings and compare them with the readings at the next tune-up. The manufacturer does not specify a standard compression pressure. However, measuring and recording the compression pressure will help spot any developing problems.

1. Before starting the compression test, make sure the following items are correct:
   a. The cylinder head bolts are tightened to the specified torque. Refer to Chapter Four.
   b. The valves are properly adjusted as described in this chapter.
   c. The battery is fully charged (Chapter Nine) to ensure proper engine cranking speed.
2. Warm the engine to normal operating temperature. Turn the engine off.
3. Remove the spark plug as described in this chapter.

*NOTE*
*A screw-in type compression gauge with a flexible adapter is required for this procedure. Before using this gauge, check the condition of the rubber gasket on the end of the adapter. This gasket must seal the spark plug hole and cylinder to ensure accurate compression readings. Replace the seal if it is cracked or starting to deteriorate.*

4. Install the tip of a compression gauge into the cylinder head following the manufacturer's instructions. Refer to *Measuring Tools* in Chapter One.

*CAUTION*
*Do not operate the starter more than absolutely necessary. When the spark plug lead is disconnected, the electronic ignition will produce the highest voltage possible and the coil may overheat and be damaged.*

5. *Open the throttle completely* and turn the engine over until there is no further rise in pressure. Maximum pressure is usually reached within 4-7 seconds. Record the pressure reading.
6. Remove the compression gauge from the cylinder.
7. Install the spark plug.
8. If the compression pressure is low based on previous readings, the low reading may be due to a valve or ring problem. To determine which, pour about a teaspoon of engine oil into the spark plug hole and repeat the procedure.
   a. If the compression increases significantly, the piston rings are probably worn.
   b. If the compression does not increase, the valves are leaking.
9. Install the spark plug.

## VALVE CLEARANCE ADJUSTMENT

The engine is equipped with three intake valves and two exhaust valves. The valves must be adjusted correctly so they will completely open and close. Valves that are out of adjustment can cause poor performance and engine damage. Valve clearance is adjusted by shimming the valve lifters, which are located under the camshafts (**Figure 79**). Whenever valve clearance is incorrect, the shim placed under the valve lifter is

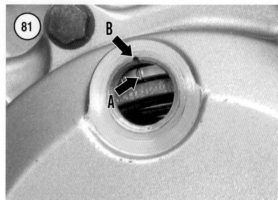

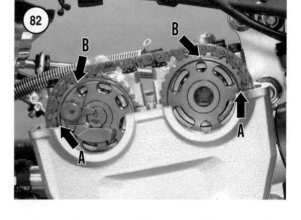

changed to bring the clearance within specification. Only one shim is used per valve. Check valve clearance when the engine temperature is cold. Check valve clearance at the interval specified in **Table 1**.

1. Remove the cylinder head cover as described in Chapter Four.

2. Remove the timing plug (A, **Figure 77**) and the flywheel nut plug (B).

3. Set the engine at TDC as follows:

    a. Fit a socket onto the flywheel nut (**Figure 80**) and turn the crankshaft counterclockwise until the I mark on the flywheel (A, **Figure 81**) aligns with the index notch (B) in the timing hole. If necessary, remove the spark plug to make turning the crankshaft easier.

*NOTE*
*Each camshaft gear has two punch marks approximately 90° apart. Use the marks located at A, **Figure 82**, and disregard the marks located at B.*

    b. Verify the engine is at TDC by checking the location of the punch marks on the camshafts. The punch marks on both camshaft sprockets must be aligned with the cylinder head surface, and at the locations shown in (A, **Figure 82**). If the punch marks are not in these exact locations, rotate the crankshaft one full turn and realign the TDC I mark. When the cams are set correctly, the cam lobes will be facing away from each other.

4. For each valve:

    a. Refer to **Table 2** for the valve clearance.

    b. Insert the correct size of flat feeler gauge between the valve lifter and cam lobe (**Figure 83**). Clearance is correct when slight resistance is felt as the gauge is inserted and withdrawn. If clearance is incorrect, use the feeler gauge to determine the actual clearance. Record the measurement for that valve.

5. If adjustment is required, refer to Chapter Four for camshaft removal.

6. To avoid errors or mixing parts, adjust the valves one at a time. Adjust the lifters that are out of adjustment as follows:

    a. Stuff a shop rag around the cam chain tunnel to prevent parts from falling into the engine.

    b. Remove the valve lifter. A magnetic tool (**Figure 84**) works well for removing the lifters.

    c. Remove the shim resting on the top of the valve (**Figure 85**).

*NOTE*
*Shims are available in 0.05 mm increments from 1.20 mm to 2.4 mm. The number on the shim surface is the thickness of the shim. For example, a 175 designation indicates the shim is 1.75 mm thick.*

7. Determine the shim size to install as follows:

    a. Refer to **Table 2** for the intake and exhaust valve clearances.

    b. Determine the difference between the specified clearance and the existing clearance.

    c. This difference is the amount that must be added (loose valve) or subtracted (tight valve) from the value of the shim removed in Step 6.

    d. For example: If the existing clearance is 0.22 mm, and the specified clearance is 0.10-0.15

10. Repeat the procedure for the remaining valves that are out of specification.

11. Install the camshaft(s) as described in Chapter Four.

12. Check valve clearance. If clearance is not correct, remove the camshaft(s) and adjust the valves that are out of specification.

13. Install the cylinder head cover as described in Chapter Four.

14. Install the timing plug (A, **Figure 77**) and the flywheel nut plug (B). Tighten the plugs securely.

### EXHAUST SYSTEM

Refer to Chapter Four for service and repair procedures.

### Inspection

Inspect the exhaust at the intervals specified in **Table 1**.

1. Inspect the exhaust system for cracks or dents that could alter performance. Refer all repairs to a dealership.

2. Check all fasteners and mounting points for loose or damaged parts. Refer to Chapter Four for torque specifications.

### Spark Arrestor Cleaning

Clean the spark arrestor at the intervals specified in **Table 1**.

> *WARNING*
> *Do not spray solvents or other combustible liquids into the muffler to remove buildup. If solvents have been used to clean the spark arrester, use compressed air to completely dry the part before installing it in the muffler. An explosion and/or fire could occur if solvents are present in the muffler.*

mm, the difference is 0.07-0.12 mm. In this example, the replacement shim should be this much thicker than the old shim.

e. Add or subtract (whichever is appropriate) the value determined in Step b to the value of the removed shim. Continuing the example, since clearance is excessive, add 0.07-0.12 mm to the size of the removed shim. Since the shims are available in increments of 0.05 mm, the shim to use would be 0.10 mm thicker than the one removed in Step 7. This would result in a valve clearance of 0.12 mm, which is within the specified range. Always round to the shim size that results in a clearance within the specification.

> *NOTE*
> *If working on a high-mileage engine, or if the removed shim shows signs of wear, measure the shim to ensure its actual dimension. Assuming a worn shim is still at its original dimension can result in a valve clearance that is not within specification.*

8. Install the new shim on the valve, and then lubricate the shim with molybdenum disulfide oil.

9. Install the valve lifter over the shim, and then lubricate the lifter with molybdenum disulfide oil.

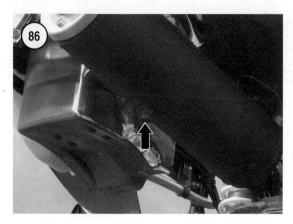

1. Park the ATV in an open area, away from combustible materials.

2. Remove the plug in the bottom of the muffler (**Figure 86**).

3. Start the engine.

4. While wearing gloves, use a rubber mallet to tap on the surface of the muffler as the engine speed is raised and lowered. Also, momentarily place a folded shop cloth over the end of the muffler to force exhaust pressure out of the plug opening.

5. When no more carbon particles are purged, stop the engine and replace the plug. Allow the muffler to cool.

6. Remove the bolt (**Figure 87**) securing the spark arrestor to the muffler.

7. Remove the spark arrestor (**Figure 88**) and brush it clean.

8. Install the spark arrestor in place.

9. Tighten the bolt (**Figure 87**) securely.

### FASTENER INSPECTION

Constant vibration can loosen many of the fasteners on the ATV. Refer to the appropriate chapters for the specified fasteners. Check the tightness of all fasteners, including:

1. Engine mounting hardware.
2. Cylinder head bracket bolts.
3. Engine crankcase covers.
4. Handlebar.
5. Gearshift lever.
6. Brake pedal and lever.
7. Exhaust system.
8. Steering and suspension components.

**Table 1 MAINTENANCE SCHEDULE\***

Every 20-40 hours.
  Clean air filter.
Initial month.
  Check valve clearance.
  Check cooling system for leaks.
  Check coolant level.
  Check spark plug.
  Change engine oil and replace oil filter.
  Check drive chain tension.
  Check the brake system.
  Check the clutch operation and lever adjustment.
  Check wheels and tires.
  Check steering and suspension system.
  Check front wheel toe-in.
  Check fastener tightness.
Initial 3 months.
  Check cooling system for leaks.
  Check coolant level.
  Check spark plug.
  Check drive chain tension.
  Check the brake system.
  Check steering and suspension system.
  Check front wheel toe-in.
  Check fastener tightness.
  Check choke operation.
  Check idle speed.
Initial 6 months and every 6 months thereafter.
  Check valve clearance.
  Check cooling system for leaks.
  Check coolant level.
  Check spark plug.
  Change engine oil and replace oil filter.
  Check drive chain tension.
  Check the brake system.
  Check the clutch operation.
  Check wheels and tires.
  Check steering and suspension system.
  Check front wheel toe-in.
  Check fastener tightness.
  Check choke operation.
  Check idle speed.
  Check crankcase breather system.
  Check exhaust system.
  Clean spark arrestor.
  Check fuel hose.
  Check front and rear suspension.
  Lubricate front and rear suspension.
Every 2 years.
  Drain and flush coolant.
  Replace coolant hoses.
  Replace seals in brake master cylinders and calipers.
Every 4 years.
  Replace brake hoses.

\*This maintenance schedule is a guide to general maintenance and lubrication intervals. Harder than normal use and operation in severe operating conditions will require more frequent attention to most maintenance items.

**Table 2 MAINTENANCE AND TUNE-UP SPECIFICATIONS**

| | |
|---|---|
| Brake pad service limit | 1.0 mm (0.039 in.) |
| Brake pedal height (below footrest) | 11.7 mm (0.46 in.) |
| Brake pushrod nut to locknut gap | 2.2-3.2 mm (0.09-0.13 in) |
| Clutch lever free play | 8-13 mm (0.31-0.51 in.) |
| Drive chain free play | 25-35 mm (0.98-1.38 in.) |

(continued)

### Table 2 MAINTENANCE AND TUNE-UP SPECIFICATIONS (continued)

| | |
|---|---|
| Idle speed | 1750-1850 rpm |
| Ignition timing | 7.5° BTDC @ 1800 rpm |
| Parking brake cable length | |
| 2004-2005 models | 56-60 mm (2.2-2.4 in.) |
| 2006-on models | 47-51 mm (1.8-2.0 in.) |
| Radiator cap pressure relief | 108-137 kPa (15.6-19.8 psi) |
| Shift pedal height | 25.0 mm (0.98 in.) |
| Spark plug | |
| Type | CR8E (NGK) |
| Plug gap | 0.7-0.8 mm (0.028-0.031 in.) |
| Speed limiter screw length | 12 mm (0.47 in) maximum |
| Throttle lever free play | 2-4 mm (0.08-0.16 in.) |
| Tire inflation pressure* | |
| 2004-2005 models | |
| Front | 4.4 psi (30 kPa) |
| Rear | 5.1 psi (35 kPa) |
| 2006-on models | |
| Front | 4.0 psi (27.5 kPa) |
| Rear | 4.4 psi (30 kPa) |
| Tire tread knob height (min.) | 3 mm (0.12 in.) |
| Valve clearance (cold) | |
| Intake | 0.10-0.15 mm (0.0039-0.0059 in.) |
| Exhaust | 0.20-0.25 mm (0.0079-0.0098 in.) |

*Tire inflation pressure is for original equipment tires. Aftermarket tires may require different inflation pressure. The use of tires other than those specified by the manufacturer may cause instability. Check tire inflation pressure when the tires are cold.

### Table 3 RECOMMENDED LUBRICANTS, FLUIDS AND CAPACITIES

| | |
|---|---|
| Brake fluid | DOT 4 |
| Cooling system | |
| Coolant capacity | |
| Radiator and engine | 1.3 L (1.37 qt.) |
| Reservoir | 0.29 L (0.31 qt.) |
| Coolant mixture | 50:50 antifreeze and distilled water |
| Coolant type | Ethylene-glycol containing corrosion inhibitors for aluminum engines |
| Drive chain | Yamaha Chain and Cable Lube for O-ring type chains |
| Engine oil | |
| Grade | Yamalube 4, API SG, JASO MA (non-friction modified) |
| Viscosity | SAE 5W-30, 10W-30 or 20W-40 See text for temperature/viscosity recommendations |
| Capacity* | |
| Oil change only | 1.75 L (1.85 qt.) |
| Oil and filter change | 1.85 L (1.96 qt.) |
| After disassembly (engine dry) | 1.95 L (2.06 qt.) |
| Fuel | |
| Type | Unleaded |
| Octane | Pump octane of 91 or higher |
| Fuel tank | |
| Capacity, including reserve | 10.0 L (2.6 gal.) |
| Reserve only | 1.9 L (0.5 gal.) |

*Fill oil tank with 1.55 L (1.64 qt.) of oil. Add remaining oil to crankcase.

## Table 4 FRONT SUSPENSION SPECIFICATIONS (2004-2006 MODELS)

| | |
|---|---|
| Front shock absorber spring preload | |
|   Standard length | 255 mm (10.04 in.) |
|   Minimum length | |
|     2004-2005 models | 245 mm (9.65 in.) |
|     2006 models | 261.5 mm (10.3 in.) |
|   Maximum length | |
|     2004-2005 models | 256.5 mm (10.10 in.) |
|     2006 models | 246.5 mm (9.7 in.) |
| Front shock rebound damping adjusting positions* | |
|   Minimum | 22 clicks out |
|   Standard | |
|     2004-2005 models | 12 clicks out |
|     2006 models | 11 clicks out |
|   Maximum | 1 click out |
| Front shock compression damping adjusting positions* | |
|   Minimum | |
|     2004-2005 models | 22 clicks out |
|     2006 models | 20 clicks out |
|   Standard | 11 clicks out |
|   Maximum | 1 click out |
| Toe-in | 2-12 mm (0.08-0.47 in.) |

*From the fully turned-in position.

## Table 5 FRONT SUSPENSION SPECIFICATIONS (2007-ON MODELS)

| | |
|---|---|
| Front shock absorber spring preload | |
|   Standard length | 255 mm (10.04 in.) |
|   Minimum length | 246.5 mm (9.7 in.) |
|   Maximum length | 261.5 mm (10.3 in.) |
| Front shock rebound damping adjusting positions* | |
|   Minimum | 20 clicks out |
|   Standard | 10 clicks out |
|   Maximum | 1 click out |
| Front shock compression damping adjusting positions* | |
|   High-speed compression damping | |
|     Minimum | 3 turns out |
|     Standard | 1 turn out |
|     Maximum | Fully turned in |
|   Low-speed compression damping | |
|     Minimum | 20 clicks out |
|     Standard | 10 clicks out |
|     Maximum | 1 click out |
| Toe-in | 2-12 mm (0.08-0.47 in.) |

*From the fully turned-in position.

## Table 6 REAR SUSPENSION SPECIFICATIONS (2004-2006 MODELS)

| | |
|---|---|
| Rear shock absorber spring preload | |
|   2004-2005 models | |
|     Standard length | 244 mm (9.61 in.) |
|     Minimum length | 237 mm (9.33 in.) |
|     Maximum length | 251 mm (9.88 in.) |

(continued)

**Table 6 REAR SUSPENSION SPECIFICATIONS (2004-2006 MODELS) (continued)**

| | |
|---|---|
| Rear shock absorber spring preload (continued) | |
| 2006 models | |
| Standard length | 257 mm (10.1 in.) |
| Minimum length | 250 mm (9.8 in.) |
| Maximum length | 264 mm (10.4 in.) |
| Rear shock rebound damping adjusting positions* | |
| Minimum | Fully out |
| Standard | |
| 2004-2005 models | 1 3/4 turns out |
| 2006 models | 1 1/4 turns out |
| Maximum | Fully turned in |
| Rear shock compression damping adjusting positions* | |
| Minimum | Fully out |
| Standard | 1 3/4 turns out |
| Maximum | Fully turned in |

*From the fully turned-in position.

**Table 7 REAR SUSPENSION SPECIFICATIONS (2007-ON MODELS)**

| | |
|---|---|
| Rear shock absorber spring preload | |
| Standard length | 257 mm (10.1 in.) |
| Minimum length | 250 mm (9.8 in.) |
| Maximum length | 264 mm (10.4 in.) |
| Rear shock rebound damping adjusting positions* | |
| Minimum | 3 turns out |
| Standard | 1 1/2 turns out |
| Maximum | Fully turned in |
| Rear shock compression damping adjusting positions* | |
| High-speed compression damping | |
| Minimum | 3 turns out |
| Standard | 2 turns out |
| Maximum | Fully turned in |
| Low-speed compression damping | |
| Minimum | 20 clicks out |
| Standard | 11 clicks out |
| Maximum | 1 click out |

*From the fully turned-in position.

**Table 8 MAINTENANCE TORQUE SPECIFICATIONS**

| Item | N•m | in.-lb. | ft.-lb. |
|---|---|---|---|
| Axle hub retaining nuts (2004-2005 models) | 85 | – | 62 |
| Axle hub pinch bolts* | 21 | – | 16 |
| Chain adjuster locknut (2004-2005 models) | 16 | – | 12 |
| Coolant drain bolt* | 10 | 88 | – |
| Crankcase oil drain bolt | 20 | – | 15 |
| Drive sprocket nut | 75 | – | 55 |
| Driven sprocket nuts | | | |
| 2004-2005 models | 55 | – | 40 |
| 2006-on models | 72 | – | 53 |
| Oil filter cover bolts | 10 | 88 | – |
| Oil filter drain bolt | 10 | 88 | – |
| Oil tank drain bolt | 19 | – | 14 |
| Oil gallery bolt | 10 | 88 | – |
| Parking brake adjuster bolt locknut | 16 | – | 11 |

(continued)

**Table 8 MAINTENANCE TORQUE SPECIFICATIONS (continued)**

| Item | N•m | in.-lb. | ft.-lb. |
|------|-----|---------|---------|
| Shift pedal clamp bolt | 12 | 106 | – |
| Shock absorber spring locknut (front) | 30 | – | 22 |
| Shock absorber spring locknut (rear) | 44 | – | 32 |
| Spark plug | 13 | 115 | – |
| Wheel lug nuts* | 45 | – | 33 |

*Refer to text.

3

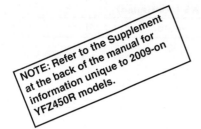
NOTE: Refer to the Supplement at the back of the manual for information unique to 2009-on YFZ450R models.

# CHAPTER FOUR

# ENGINE TOP END

This chapter provides removal, inspection and installation for the engine top end components. These include the exhaust system, cylinder head cover, cylinder head, valves, cylinder, camshafts and tensioner, piston and piston rings.

**Tables 1-5** are located at the end of this chapter.

Repairs go much faster and easier if the engine is clean before beginning the work. This is important when servicing the engine's top end. Clean the engine and surrounding area before working on the engine top end. Refer to *Parts Cleaning* in *Safety* in Chapter One. Refer to *Cleaners, Degreasers, and Solvents* in *Shop Supplies* in Chapter One.

## EXHAUST SYSTEM

### Removal/Installation

*WARNING*
*Do not remove the exhaust pipe or muffler while they are hot.*

1. Remove the fuel tank as described in Chapter Eight.
2. Remove the right foot protector as described in Chapter Fifteen.
3. Remove the engine skidplate as described in Chapter Fifteen.
4. Loosen the clamp bolt (**Figure 1**).

5. While supporting the muffler, remove the muffler mounting bolts (A, **Figure 2**), and then remove the muffler (B).

*NOTE*
*Figure 3 shows 2006-on models. On 2004 and 2005 models, the upper end of the exhaust pipe flange is retained with a bolt.*

6. On 2004-2005 models, remove the exhaust pipe flange retaining bolt and nut, then remove the exhaust pipe.
7. On 2006-on models, remove the exhaust pipe retaining nuts (A, **Figure 3**), and then remove the exhaust pipe (B).
8. If necessary, remove the heat shields from the muffler and exhaust pipe.
9. Reverse the removal steps to install the exhaust system while noting the following:
   a. Apply threadlocking compound to the heat shield mounting bolts and tighten to 7 N•m (62 in.-lb.).
   b. Install a new gasket into the exhaust port (**Figure 4**).
   c. On 2004-2005 models, tighten the exhaust pipe nut finger-tight to hold the pipe in place. Tighten the bolt to 20 N•m (15 ft.-lb.). Tighten the nut to 13 N•m (115 in.-lb.). Retighten the bolt to 24 N•m (18 ft.-lb.).

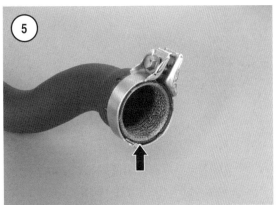

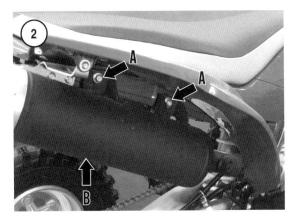

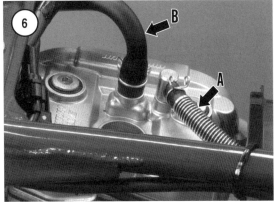

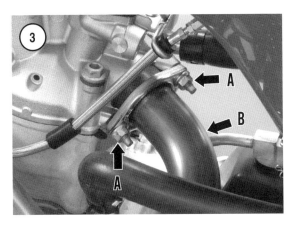

d. On 2006-on models, tighten the exhaust pipe nuts (A, **Figure 3**) finger-tight to hold the pipe in place. Tighten the nuts to 14 N•m (10 ft.-lb.).

e. Install a new gasket into the muffler pipe so the chamfered end faces out (**Figure 5**). Push in the gasket so it is 1.0-1.5 mm (0.04-0.06 in.) recessed from the end of the pipe.

f. Tighten the muffler mounting bolts to 34 N•m (25 ft.-lb.).

g. Make sure the tab on the clamp (**Figure 1**) engages a slot in the muffler pipe.

## CYLINDER HEAD COVER

### Removal

1. Remove the fuel tank as described in Chapter Eight.

2. Remove the spark plug as described in Chapter Three.

3. Detach the cylinder head breather hose (A, **Figure 6**) and oil tank breather hose (B) from the cylinder head cover.

4. Remove the cylinder head cover bolts and sealing washers (**Figure 7**).

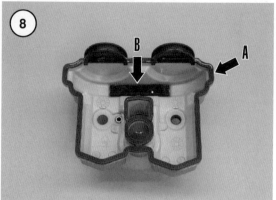

5. Remove the cylinder head cover by lightly tapping it with a soft mallet. Check that the gasket (A, Figure 8) and timing chain guide (B) are on the cover.

### Installation

1. Clean the gasket surfaces on the cylinder head and cylinder head cover, then install the gasket onto the cover.
2. Apply a small amount of Yamabond 4 or Yamabond 1215 sealant to the gasket seating surfaces on the cylinder head cover and cylinder head.
3. Place the gasket into the cover, then place the assembly onto the cylinder head. If the old gasket was leaking or is damaged, install a new gasket. Make sure the plugs (**Figure 9**) are seated in the cylinder head cutouts.
4. Check condition of the sealing washers (Figure 10) on the cover bolts. Replace if necessary.
5. Install the cover bolts and tighten to 10 N•m (88 in.-lb.).
6. Attach the cylinder head breather hose (A, Figure 6) and oil tank breather hose (B) to the cylinder head cover.
7. Install the spark plug as described in Chapter Three.
8. Install the fuel tank as described in Chapter Eight.

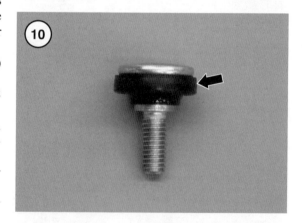

### CAMSHAFTS

The camshafts can be removed with the engine mounted in the frame.

### Removal

1. Remove the cylinder head cover as described in this chapter.
2. Remove the timing plug (A, **Figure 11**) and the flywheel nut plug (B).
3. Set the engine at TDC as follows:

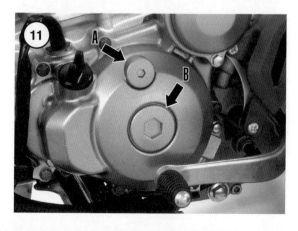

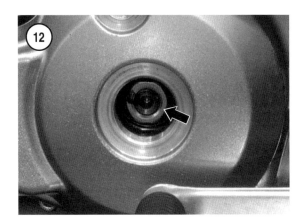

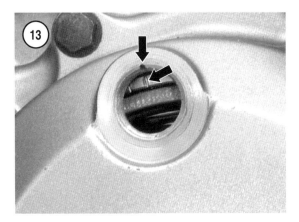

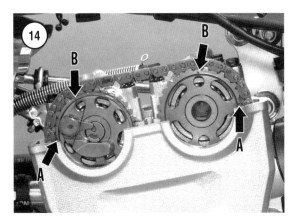

a. Fit a socket onto the flywheel nut (**Figure 12**) and turn the crankshaft counterclockwise until the I mark on the flywheel is aligned with the index notch in the timing hole (**Figure 13**). If necessary, remove the spark plug or operate the compression release to make turning the crankshaft easier.

*NOTE*
*Each camshaft gear has two punch marks approximately 90° apart. Use the marks located at A, **Figure 14**, and disregard the marks located at B.*

b. Verify the engine is at TDC by checking the location of the punch marks on the camshafts. The punch marks on both camshaft sprockets must align with the cylinder head surface, as shown in **Figure 14**. If the punch marks are not in these exact locations, rotate the crankshaft one full turn and realign the TDC I mark.

*NOTE*
*Before further disassembly, check and record the valve clearances as described in Chapter Three. Adjust incorrect clearances during the reassembly process. This will prevent removal of the camshafts a second time.*

4. Remove the cam chain tensioner as described in this chapter.
5. Remove the camshaft caps (**Figure 15**) as follows:
   a. Stuff a shop cloth into the cam chain tunnel to prevent parts or debris from falling into the engine.

*CAUTION*
*Failure to evenly loosen the camshaft cap bolts in stages can result in damage to the cylinder head, camshafts or caps.*

   b. Working in a crossing pattern, loosen the camshaft cap bolts. Loosen the bolts evenly in several stages. When the bolts are loose, remove them from the caps.
   c. Lift up on each cap, being careful not to drop the dowels (**Figure 16**). The bearing-locating clip may remain on the bearing (**Figure 17**) or to the underside of the cap.
6. Remove the camshafts as follows:
   a. Attach a length of wire to the cam chain (A, **Figure 18**). Secure the free end of the wire so the chain cannot fall into the engine when the camshafts are removed.
   b. Lift each camshaft (B, **Figure 18**) out of the cylinder head.

c. Do not disturb the valve lifters (**Figure 19**).

7. Inspect the camshafts and caps as described in this section.

8. If wear or damage is evident on the timing chain or guides, refer to *Camshaft Chain and Guides* in Chapter Five.

**Installation**

Prior to installing the camshafts, refer to Chapter Three and perform the valve clearance adjustment as needed. If the valves were reconditioned, install the original shims at this time. Valve clearance will need to be rechecked after the camshafts are installed. It may be necessary to remove the camshafts a second time to correctly set the valves.

1. Inspect the cylinder head and ensure that all surfaces are clean.

2. Make sure the engine is at TDC. If necessary, turn the crankshaft counterclockwise until the I mark on the rotor is aligned with the index mark in the timing hole (**Figure 13**).

> *NOTE*
> *The exhaust camshaft has two lobes. The intake camshaft has three lobes.*

> *NOTE*
> *Each camshaft gear has two punch marks approximately 90° apart. Use the marks located at A, **Figure 14**, and disregard the marks located at B.*

3. Install the exhaust camshaft (**Figure 20**) so the sprocket punch mark aligns with the cylinder head surface (**Figure 21**). Remove the safety wire attached to the chain after the cam is installed.

4. Repeat Step 3 for the intake camshaft. When properly installed, the cam lobes on both camshafts point out (**Figure 22**).

> *CAUTION*
> *If the punch marks are not in the correct locations with the engine at TDC, timing will be incorrect. Severe engine damage could occur if the cams are not installed properly.*

5. Verify that the engine is still at TDC. Make sure the punch marks on both camshafts align with the cylinder head surface, and at the locations shown at A, **Figure 14**. If necessary, attach the safety wire to the cam chain, then remove the camshafts and repeat Steps 2-5.

6. Fit the dowels (A, **Figure 23**) and bearing locating clips (B) into the camshaft caps. If the dowels or

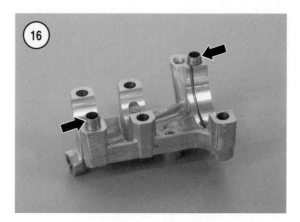

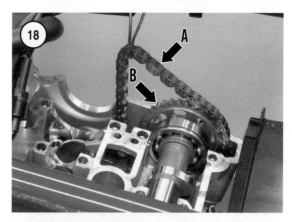

clips are a loose fit in the caps, install the parts into their respective positions on the cylinder head.

7. Place each camshaft cap assembly onto its respective camshaft. Check that the dowels and clips seat into their respective locations.

8. Bolt the camshaft caps into place as follows:

    a. Lubricate the threads of the bolts with engine oil.

    b. Insert the bolts into the caps (**Figure 15**) and finger-tighten.

> *CAUTION*
> *Failure to tighten evenly the camshaft cap bolts can result in damage to the cylinder head, camshafts or caps.*

    c. Working in a crossing pattern, tighten the cap bolts to 10 N•m (88 in.-lb.). For the intake cam, start with the center bolts and work outward. Tighten the cap bolts evenly in several stages.

9. Install the cam chain tensioner assembly as described in this chapter.

10. Remove the shop rag from the cam chain tunnel.

11. Lubricate the cam lobes, valve lifters and camshaft bearings with molybdenum disulfide oil.

12. Turn the crankshaft counterclockwise several times, and then place it at TDC. Make sure the punch marks on the camshaft sprockets align with the top edge of the cylinder head. If the camshafts are not properly aligned, disassemble the head and realign the camshaft(s).

13. Install the timing plug and the flywheel nut plug. Tighten the plugs securely.

14. Install the cylinder head cover as described in this chapter.

**Inspection**

> *CAUTION*
> *Before cleaning the camshaft caps, inspect the oil lubrication holes for contamination. Small passages and holes in the camshaft cap provide pressure lubrication for the camshaft journals. Make sure these passages and holes are clean and open. Infrequent oil and filter changes may be indicated if the camshaft cap passages are dirty.*

1. Clean the camshafts and camshaft caps in solvent and dry thoroughly. Lubricate the bearings with engine oil.

2. Inspect the cam lobes for scoring or damage. Replace the camshaft if damage is evident.

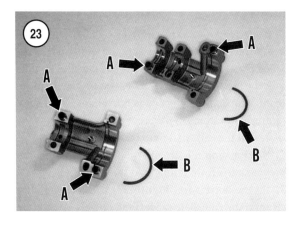

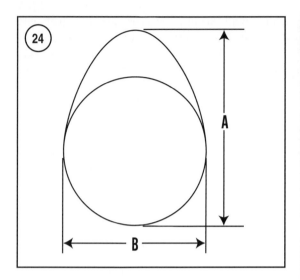

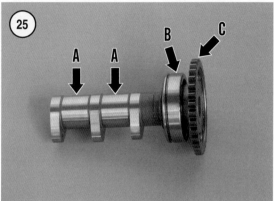

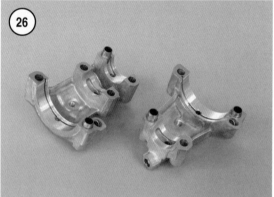

3. Measure each cam lobe height (A, **Figure 24**), then compare the measurement with **Table 2**. Replace the camshaft if it is not within specification.

4. Measure each cam base circle diameter (B, **Figure 24**) with a micrometer, then compare the measurement with **Table 2**. Replace the camshaft if it is not within specification.

5. Measure each camshaft journal diameter (A, **Figure 25**), then compare the measurement with **Table 2**. Replace the camshaft if it is not within specification.

6. Place the camshaft between lathe centers or equivalent and check runout with a dial indicator at a bearing journal. Replace the camshaft if it is not within the specification in **Table 2**.

7. Turn each camshaft bearing (B, **Figure 25**) and check for roughness and excessive play. Replace the camshaft if either condition exists.

8. Inspect the camshaft sprocket teeth (C, **Figure 25**) for wear or other damage. The profile of each tooth should be symmetrical. If the sprocket is worn, replace the camshaft, crankshaft sprocket, and cam chain as a set.

9. Inspect the camshaft caps (**Figure 26**) for stress cracks and other damage.

10. Inspect the bearing surfaces in the cylinder head (**Figure 27**) and bearing caps for wear and scoring. If damage is present, replace the cylinder head and camshaft caps as a set. To determine bearing clearance, perform the *Camshaft Bearing Clearance Measurement* procedure in this chapter.

### CAMSHAFT BEARING CLEARANCE MEASUREMENT

This section describes how to measure the bearing clearance (oil clearance) between the camshaft, the camshaft caps and cylinder head journal using Plastigage. Plastigage is a material that flattens when pressure is applied to it. The marked bands on the envelope are then used to measure the width of the flattened Plastigage. The camshafts and camshaft holder must be installed on the cylinder head when performing this procedure. Plastigage is available from automotive parts stores in different clearance ranges.

1. Install the camshaft onto the cylinder head.

2. Stuff a shop rag around the cam chain tunnel to prevent parts from falling into the engine.

3. Fit the dowels (A, **Figure 23**) and locating clips (B) into the camshaft caps. If the dowels or clips are

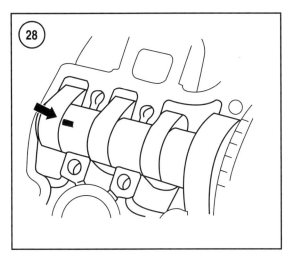

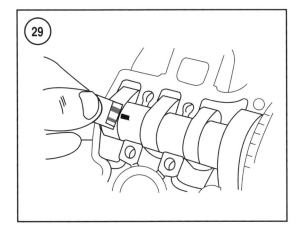

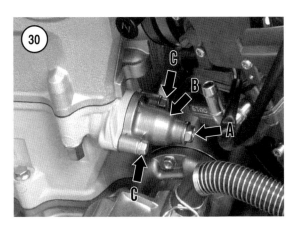

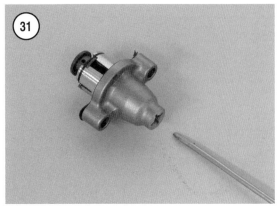

*CAUTION*
*Failure to evenly tighten and loosen the*
*camshaft cap bolts can result in dam-*
*age to the cylinder head, camshafts or*
*caps.*

7. Working in a crossing pattern, tighten the cap bolts to 10 N•m (88 in.-lb.). For the intake cam, start with the center bolts and work outward. Tighten the cap bolts evenly in several stages.

8. After the specified torque is achieved, evenly loosen the camshaft cap bolts in several stages, working in a crossing pattern. When the bolts are loose, remove them from the caps.

9. Lift the cap up, being careful not to drop the dowels and clips that are installed under each cap.

10. Using the gauge included with the Plastigage, measure the width of the Plastigage (**Figure 29**) to determine if the clearance is within the specification in **Table 2**. If necessary, replace any parts that are not within specification.

## CAM CHAIN TENSIONER

### Removal/Installation

1. Remove the bolt and washer (A, **Figure 30**) from the camshaft drive chain tensioner (B).

2. Insert a small flat blade screwdriver into the opening and engage the internal screw head. Rotate the screwdriver clockwise as far as possible. This locks the tensioner rod in the fully retracted position.

3. Remove the camshaft drive chain tensioner mounting bolts (C, **Figure 30**). Remove the tensioner assembly and gasket.

4. Inspect the tensioner assembly as described in this section.

5. Push the tensioner rod in and using a small flat blade screwdriver through the opening, rotate the screwdriver clockwise to the fully retracted position (**Figure 31**). Hold the screwdriver in this position and install the chain tensioner and a new gasket.

a loose fit in the caps, fit the parts into their respective positions on the cylinder head.

4. Place a strip of Plastigage onto the camshaft (**Figure 28**).

5. Place the camshaft cap assembly over the camshaft. Check that the dowels and clips seat into their respective locations. Do not allow the camshaft to turn while the Plastigage is between the parts.

6. Lubricate the threads of the cap bolts with engine oil. Insert the bolts into the caps and finger-tighten.

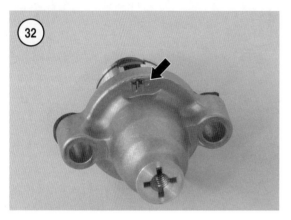

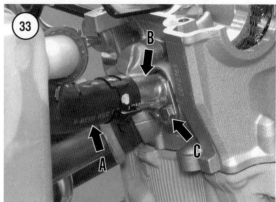

Install the tensioner so the UP mark (**Figure 32**) is toward the cylinder head.

6. Install the bolts securing the camshaft chain tensioner mounting bolts (C, **Figure 30**). Tighten the bolts to 10 N•m (88 in.-lb.).

7. Rotate the internal screw counterclockwise to release the tensioner, and then remove the screwdriver.

8. Install the bolt and washer (A, **Figure 30**) and tighten to 7 N•m (62 in.-lb.).

### Inspection

The tensioner assembly is a sealed unit and cannot be disassembled. If the unit does not function properly, replace the entire assembly. Check the spring-action of the chain tensioner as follows:

1. While holding the tensioner, slightly depress the tensioner rod. Insert a small-blade screwdriver into the opposite end of the tensioner and fully turn the rod clockwise (**Figure 31**). The tensioner rod should retract as the screwdriver is turned.

2. Release the tensioner rod and turn the screwdriver counterclockwise. The rod should fully extend. If the rod does not fully extend, or if it extends slowly, replace the unit.

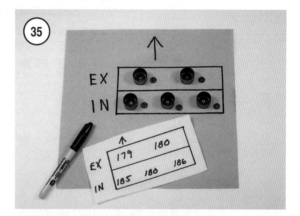

## CAM CHAIN AND GUIDE

A sprocket on the left end of the crankshaft drives the cam chain. Refer to Chapter Five for cam chain service information.

## CYLINDER HEAD

This section describes removal, inspection and installation of the cylinder head. After the cylinder head is removed, refer to the appropriate sections in this chapter for further disassembly, inspection and assembly procedures. The cylinder head can be removed with the engine mounted in the frame. If possible, perform a compression test (Chapter Three) and leakdown test (Chapter Two) prior to cylinder head removal.

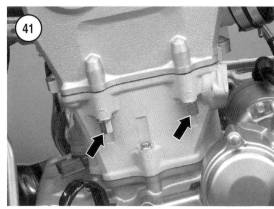

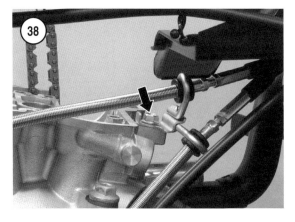

## Removal

1. Drain the coolant as described in Chapter Three.

2. Detach the radiator hose (A, **Figure 33**) from the coolant pipe (B).

3. Remove the coolant pipe retaining bolt (C, **Figure 33**), then remove the coolant pipe (B) from the cylinder head.

4. Remove the carburetor as described in Chapter Eight.

5. Remove the exhaust pipe as described in this chapter.

6. Remove the cylinder head cover, camshafts and cam chain tensioner as described in this chapter.

7. Prepare to remove the valve lifters (**Figure 34**) and shims as follows:

    a. Stuff a shop rag around the cam chain tunnel to prevent parts from falling into the engine.

    b. On a piece of cardboard, draw a guide for placing the lifters and shims as they are removed from the valves (**Figure 35**).

8. Remove each valve lifter and shim as follows:

    a. Remove the valve lifter and place it at the appropriate position on the guide (**Figure 35**). A magnetic tool (**Figure 36**) works well in removing the lifters.

    b. Remove the shim resting on the top of the valve (**Figure 37**) and place it with the matching lifter. Record the shim number for that valve position.

9. Remove the bolt securing the parking brake and clutch cable bracket (**Figure 38**).

10. Remove the bolts securing the oil tube (**Figure 39**) to the engine. Remove the oil tubes, fittings and sealing washers.

11. Remove the upper engine-mounting bolt (A, **Figure 40**).

12. Remove the bolts (B, **Figure 40**) securing the engine bracket (C), and then remove the bracket.

13. Remove the two nuts from the left side of the cylinder head (**Figure 41**).

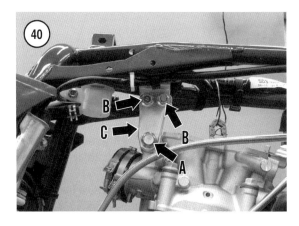

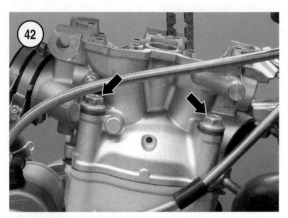

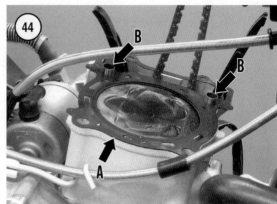

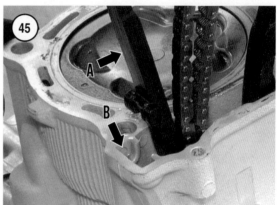

14. Remove the two bolts and washers from the right side of the cylinder head (**Figure 42**).

15. Remove the two bolts and washers from the interior of the cylinder head on the left side (**Figure 43**).

16. Loosen the cylinder head by lightly tapping around its base with a soft mallet. Lift the head from the engine while routing the cam chain out of the head.

17. Remove the head gasket (A, **Figure 44**) and the two dowels (B) from the cylinder.

18. If necessary, remove the front cam chain guide (A, **Figure 45**).

19. If necessary, remove the intake tube.

20. Secure the cam chain so it remains engaged with the crankshaft sprocket. Cover the engine openings with clean shop rags to prevent debris from entering.

21. Wash all parts in solvent and dry with compressed air. Perform the following:

   a. Check all oil passageways and the oil gallery for debris or blockage.

   b. Check the valve lifters and shims for wear or damage.

22. Inspect the cylinder head assembly as described in this section.

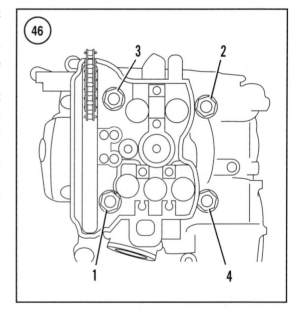

**Installation**

1. Make sure all gasket residue is removed from the mating surfaces. All cylinder head surfaces must be clean and dry.

2. Install the front cam chain guide. Seat the guide in the notch in the cylinder (B, **Figure 45**).

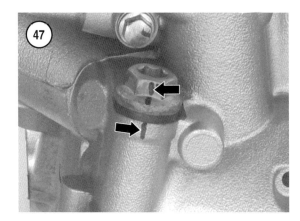

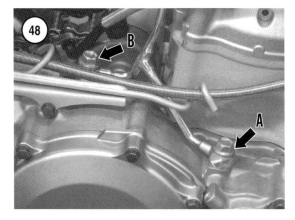

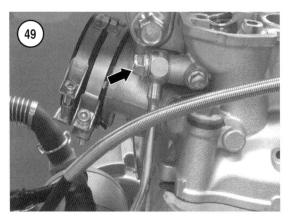

3. Insert the dowels (B, **Figure 44**) into the cylinder.

4. Install a new cylinder head gasket (A, **Figure 44**).

5. Lower the cylinder head onto the engine, routing the cam chain through the head. Keep adequate tension on the cam chain so it does not fall off the crankshaft sprocket. Secure the cam chain when the cylinder head is seated.

6. Lubricate the bolt threads and washers with molybdenum disulfide grease. Make sure each bolt has a washer. Two of the head bolts are 10 mm longer than the other two head bolts. Install the long head bolts into the left side of the cylinder, inside the head (**Figure 43**).

7. Tighten the head bolts in the following steps using the tightening sequence in **Figure 46**.

   a. In two steps, tighten the head bolts to 30 N•m (22 ft.-lb.).

   b. Remove the bolts.

   c. Lubricate the bolt threads and washers with molybdenum disulfide grease.

   d. In two steps, tighten the head bolts to 20 N•m (15 ft.-lb.).

   e. Make an alignment mark on each head bolt and the cylinder head (**Figure 47**).

   f. Following the tightening sequence, turn each head bolt 90°.

   g. Turn each head bolt another 90°. The reference mark should be 180° from the starting position.

8. Install the nuts on the left side of the cylinder head (**Figure 41**) and tighten to 10 N•m (88 in.-lb.).

9. Install the upper engine bracket and bolts. Tighten the upper engine bracket bolts (B, **Figure 40**) to 26 N•m (19 ft.-lb.). Tighten the upper engine-mounting bolt (A, **Figure 40**) to 40 N•m (29 ft.-lb.).

10. Install new sealing washers on the oil tube banjo bolts.

11. Attach the oil tube assembly to the engine. Tighten the front bolt (A, **Figure 48**) to 20 N•m (15 ft.-lb.). Tighten the upper bolt (**Figure 49**) and rear bolt (B, **Figure 48**) to 18 N•m (13 ft.-lb.).

12. Prepare to install the valve shims and lifters as follows:

   a. Stuff a shop cloth into the cam chain tunnel to prevent parts from falling into the engine.

   b. Make sure each lifter and shim (**Figure 50**) is clean and undamaged.

13. Install each valve shim and lifter set as follows:

   a. Remove the appropriate shim and lifter from the guide for the valve being adjusted.

   b. Lubricate the shims with molybdenum disulfide oil.

*NOTE*
*If the valve assembly was not recon-
ditioned or disturbed when the cylinder head was removed, reinstall the
original shim on the top of the valve. If
clearance was incorrect before the head
was removed, refer to **Valve Clearance
Adjustment** in Chapter Three to determine the correct size of shim to install.
If the valves were reconditioned, install
the original shim at this time. Recheck
the valve clearance after the camshafts
are installed. It may be necessary to
remove the camshafts a second time to
correctly set the valves.*

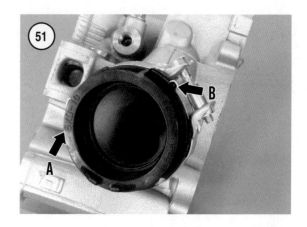

c. Place the valve lifter over the shim.
14. Remove the shop cloth from the cam chain tunnel.
15. Apply engine oil to the tops of the valve lifters.
16. Install the camshafts, cam chain tensioner and cylinder head cover as described in this chapter.
17. If removed, install the intake tube so the marked end (A, **Figure 51**) is toward the carburetor. The notch on the tube must fit around the boss on the cylinder head (**Figure 52**). Install the clamps so the notch fits over the raised edge on the tube (B, **Figure 51**).

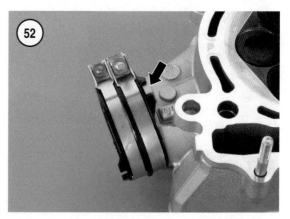

## Inspection

Before removing the valves from the cylinder head, perform a solvent test to check the valve face-to-valve seat seal.
1. Support the cylinder head with the exhaust ports facing up (**Figure 53**). Pour solvent or kerosene into the ports. Immediately check the combustion chambers for fluid leaking past the exhaust valves.
2. Repeat Step 1 for the intake valves.
3. If there is fluid leaking around one or both sets of valves, the valve(s) is not seating correctly. The following conditions will cause poor valve seating:
   a. A worn or damaged valve seat.
   b. A worn or damaged valve face.
   c. A bent valve stem.
   d. A crack in the combustion chamber.
4. Remove all gasket residue from the cylinder head mating surfaces. Do not scratch or gouge the surfaces.

*CAUTION*
*If the valves are removed from the
head, the valve seats are exposed and
can be damaged from careless cleaning. A damaged valve seat will not seal
properly.*

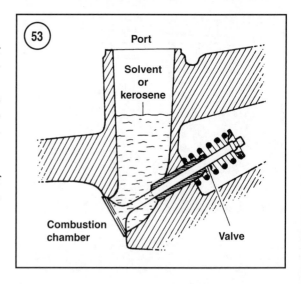

5. Remove all carbon deposits from the combustion chamber (A, **Figure 54**) and valve ports (B). Use solvent and a fine wire brush or hardwood scraper. Do not use sharp-edged tools such as screwdrivers or putty knives.
6. Inspect the spark plug hole threads. If the threads are dirty or mildly damaged, use a spark plug thread tap to clean and straighten the threads. Use kerosene or aluminum tap-cutting fluid to lubricate the threads.

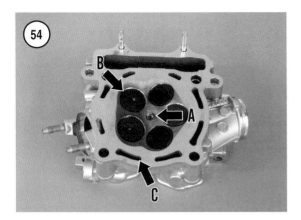

If the threads are galled, stripped or cross-threaded, install a steel thread insert (HeliCoil).

*CAUTION*
*Avoid thread damage by applying antiseize compound to the spark plug threads before installation and do not overtighten the spark plug. Refer to Chapter Three.*

7. Clean the entire cylinder head assembly in clean solvent. If the head was bead-blasted, wash the entire assembly in hot soapy water to remove all blasting grit that is lodged in crevices and threads. Clean and chase all threads to assure no grit remains. Blasting grit that remains in the head will contaminate the engine oil and damage other parts of the engine.

8. Inspect the cylinder head for cracks in the combustion chamber, water jackets (C, **Figure 54**) and exhaust port. If cracks are found, have a dealership determine if the cylinder head can be repaired. If not, replace the head.

9. Inspect the cylinder head for warp as follows:
 a. Place a machinist's straightedge across the cylinder head as shown in **Figure 55**.
 b. Attempt to insert a flat feeler gauge between the straightedge and the machined surface of the head. If clearance exists, record the measurement.
 c. Repeat Steps a and b several times, laying the straightedge both across and diagonally on the head.

10. Compare the measurements in Step 9 to the warp service limit in **Table 3**. If the clearance is not within the service limit, true the head as follows:
 a. Tape a sheet of 400-600 grit emery paper to a thick sheet of glass or surface plate.
 b. Place the head on the emery paper and move the head in a figure-eight pattern.
 c. Rotate the head at regular intervals so material is removed evenly.
 d. Check the progress often, measuring the clearance with the straightedge and feeler gauge.
 e. If warp is excessive, have a dealership determine if the cylinder head can be repaired.

## VALVES

### Tools

To remove and install the valves in this section, the following tools are required:
1. Valve spring compressor.
2. Valve lifter bore protector (**Figure 56**). This tool is used to protect the valve lifter bore when removing and installing the valves. This tool can be made from a 35 mm film container cut to fit the valve lifter bore.

### Valve Removal

Refer to **Figure 57**.
1. Remove the cylinder head, valve lifters and shims as described in this chapter.
2. Perform a solvent test on the intake and exhaust valves as described in *Inspection* in *Cylinder Head* in this chapter.
3. Install the protector (**Figure 56**) into the valve lifter bore of the valve being removed.

4. Install a valve spring compressor onto the valve assembly (**Figure 58**).
5. Tighten the valve spring compressor until the valve keepers (**Figure 59**) separate. Lift the valve keepers out through the valve spring compressor using needlenose pliers or tweezers.
6. Mark all parts during removal so that they will be installed in their same locations.
7. Loosen the valve spring compressor and remove it from the head.
8. Remove the protector from the valve lifter bore.
9. Remove the spring retainer (**Figure 60**).
10. Remove the valve spring (**Figure 61**).

11. Inspect the valve stem for sharp and flared metal around the groove (**Figure 62**) for the keepers. Remove any burrs from the valve stem before removing the valve from the head.
12. Remove the valve from the cylinder head.

13. Pull the oil seal (A, **Figure 63**) off the valve guide and discard it.
14. Remove the spring seat (B, **Figure 63**).
15. Repeat for the remaining intake and exhaust valves as necessary.

**Valve Component Inspection**

Do not intermix individual valve assemblies. Inspect one assembly at a time, repeating the procedure until each assembly is inspected.
1. Clean the valve assembly in solvent.

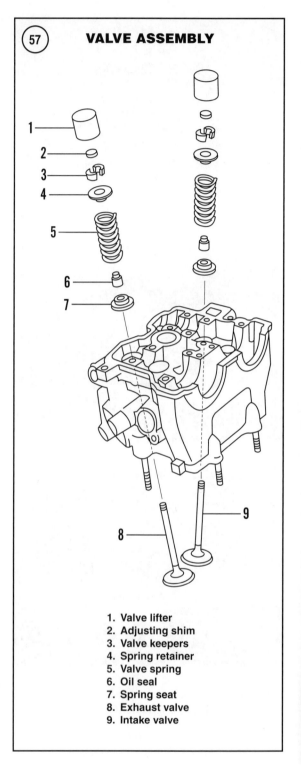

**57**    **VALVE ASSEMBLY**

1. Valve lifter
2. Adjusting shim
3. Valve keepers
4. Spring retainer
5. Valve spring
6. Oil seal
7. Spring seat
8. Exhaust valve
9. Intake valve

*not scrape the seating surface or place the valve where it could roll off the work surface.*

2. Inspect the valve head as follows:
   a. Inspect the top and perimeter of each valve (**Figure 64**). Check for burning or other damage on the top and seating surface. Replace the

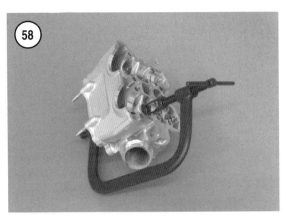

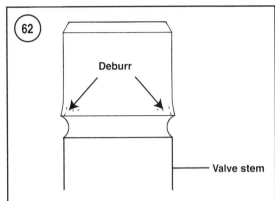

Deburr

Valve stem

4

A

B

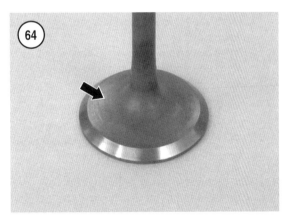

valve if damage is evident. If the valve face is uniform, with only minor wear, lap the valve face as described in this section.

b. Measure the margin thickness (**Figure 65**). Record the measurement. Replace the valve if the measurement is not within the specification in **Table 3**.

3. Inspect the valve stem for wear and roughness. Also check the end of the valve stem for mushrooming. Measure the valve stem diameter with a micrometer (**Figure 66**). Record the measurement. Replace the valve if the measurement is not within the specification in **Table 3**.

4. Place the valve in a V-block and measure runout with a dial indicator. Record the measurement. Replace the valve if the measurement is not within the specification in **Table 3**. If the valve is replaced, also replace the valve guide and oil seal.

5. Clean the valve guides so they are free of all carbon and varnish. Use solvent and a stiff, narrow, spiral brush.

6. If a small hole gauge and micrometer are available, use the following steps to measure each valve guide. If these tools are not available, perform Step 7.

   a. Measure each valve guide hole at the top, center and bottom. Record the measurements.

   b. Refer to **Table 3** to determine if the diameters are within the service limit. Replace the guide if it is not within the service limit. Refer to *Valve Guide Replacement* in this section.

   c. Subtract the valve stem measurement made in Step 3 from the largest valve guide measurement in Step 6a. Refer to **Table 3** to determine if the valve stem-to-valve guide clearance is within the service limit. If the parts are not within the service limit, replace the part(s).

7. If a small hole gauge and micrometer are not available perform the following:

   a. Insert the appropriate valve into the guide.

   b. With the valve head off the seat, rock the valve stem in the valve guide. Rock the valve in several directions, checking for any perceptible play. If movement is detected, the valve guide and/or valve are worn.

   c. Have a dealership or machine shop measure the valves and guides to determine which part(s) require replacement.

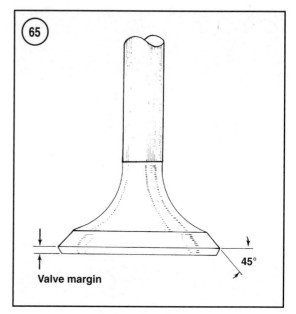

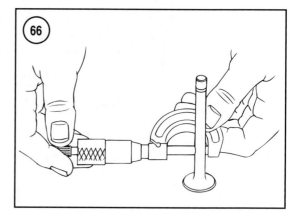

*NOTE*
*Identify the intake valve springs by their blue paint mark. Identify the exhaust valve springs by their red paint mark.*

8. Check each valve spring as follows:

   a. Check the spring for damage.

   b. Stand the spring vertically, then place a square next to the spring to check for distortion or tilt (**Figure 67**). Refer to **Table 3** to determine if the spring is within the service limit.

   c. Measure each valve spring length with a vernier caliper (**Figure 68**). Refer to **Table 3** to determine if the spring is within the service limit.

   d. Measure valve spring pressure (**Figure 69**) and compare to specifications in **Table 3**. Replace weak or damaged springs. A machine shop typically performs this procedure.

9. Inspect the valve spring seat and keepers for wear or damage.

10. Inspect the valve seats in the cylinder head to determine if they must be reconditioned.

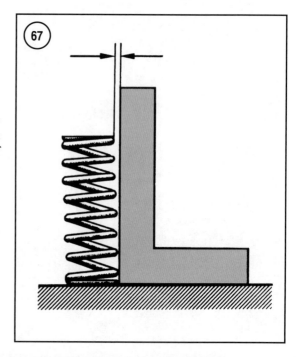

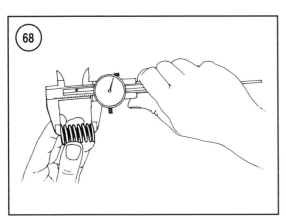

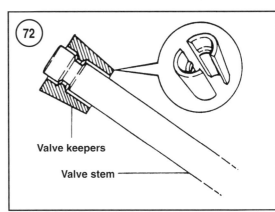

Valve keepers

Valve stem

a. Clean and dry the valve seat and valve mating area with contact cleaner.
b. Lightly coat the valve seat with Prussian Blue (gear-marking compound).
c. Install the appropriate valve into the guide, then lightly tap the valve against the seat so the compound transfers to the valve contact area.
d. Remove the valve from the guide. At several locations, measure the width of the imprint on the valve seat with a vernier caliper (**Figure 70**). Refer to **Table 3** to determine if the seat width is within the service limit. Regrind the valve seat if any width measurement exceeds the service limit. Refer to *Valve Seat Reconditioning* in this section. Always regrind a valve seat that is burned or worn.
11. Clean all residue from the valves and seats.

**Valve Installation**

Perform the following procedure for each set of valve components. All components must be clean and dry. Refer to **Figure 57**.
1. Lubricate and install a new oil seal on the valve guide.
2. Coat the valve stem with molybdenum disulfide oil.
3. Insert the appropriate valve into the cylinder head. Rotate the valve as the stem passes through the seal. Hold the valve in place.
4. Install the spring seat into the head.
5. Install the valve springs so the tightly wound coils (**Figure 71**) of the spring contact the spring seat.
6. Install the spring retainer.
7. Install a valve spring compressor over the valve assembly. Place the tool squarely over the valve head and spring seat.
8. Tighten the compressor until the spring retainer is compressed enough to install the valve keepers.
9. Insert the keepers into the groove in the valve stem (**Figure 72**).

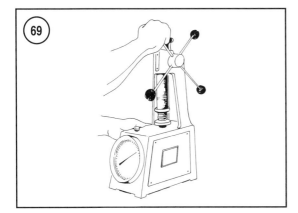

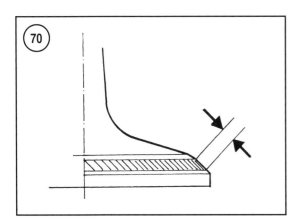

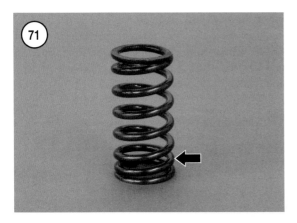

10. Relieve the pressure on the valve spring and re-move the compressor from the head.

11. Tap the end of the valve stem with a soft mallet to ensure that the keepers are seated in the valve stem groove.

12. After all the valves are installed perform a sol-vent test as described in *Inspection* in *Cylinder Head* in this chapter.

13. Install the cylinder head as described in this chapter.

## Valve Seat Reconditioning

Before reconditioning the valve seats, inspect and measure them as described in this section. The valve and seat angle is 45° (**Figure 65**). No other angles are cut above or below the valve face.

### Tools

The following tools are required:
1. Valve seat cutter (45°).
2. Vernier caliper.
3. Prussian Blue (gear-marking compound).
4. Valve-lapping tool.

### Procedure

> **CAUTION**
> *Work slowly and make light cuts during reconditioning. Excessive valve seat cutting will recede the valves into the cylinder head, which will affect valve adjustment, and may require cylinder head replacement.*

1. Install the 45° cutter onto the valve tool and light-ly cut the seat to remove roughness.

2. Measure the valve seat width in the cylinder head (**Figure 73**) with a vernier caliper. Compare the mea-surement to the specification in **Table 3**.

3. When the valve seat width is within specification, clean the valve seat and valve mating areas.

4. Lightly coat the valve seat with Prussian Blue.

5. Install the appropriate valve into the guide, then press the valve against the seat.

6. Remove the valve and evaluate where the seat has contacted the valve.

    a. The seat contact area should be in the center of the valve face area.

    b. If the seat is high on the valve face area, the valve head may not be within specification, or the seat diameter in the cylinder head is excessive.

    c. If the seat is low on the valve face area, the valve may need to be machined so it fits lower

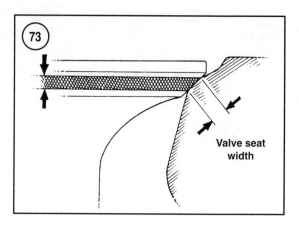

Valve seat width

in the seat. Do not continue to cut the valve seat in the cylinder head in order to accommo-date the valve. If the seat diameter is excessive, replace the cylinder head.

7. When the seat width is correct, lap the valve as described in this section.

## Valve Lapping

Valve lapping restores the seal between the seat and valve without machining. Lap valves and seats that have been inspected and are within specifica-tions or seats that have been reconditioned.

1. Lightly coat the valve face with fine-grade lap-ping compound.

2. Lubricate the valve stem, then insert the valve into the head.

3. Wet the suction cup on the lapping tool and press it onto the head of the valve (**Figure 74**).

4. Spin the stick back and forth by hand to lap the valve to the seat. Every 5 to 10 seconds, rotate the valve 180° and continue to lap the valve into the seat.

5. Frequently inspect the valve seat. Stop lapping the valve when the valve seat is smooth, even and highly polished. Identify each lapped valve so it will be installed in the correct seat during assembly.

6. Clean the valves and cylinder head in solvent and remove all lapping compound. Any abrasive remain-ing in the head will cause premature engine wear.

7. After the valves installation, perform a solvent test as described in *Inspection* in *Cylinder Head* in this chapter. If leaks are detected, remove that valve and repeat the lapping process.

## Valve Guide Replacement

### Tools

The following tools (or equivalents) are required to remove and install the valve guides:
1. Valve guide removers:

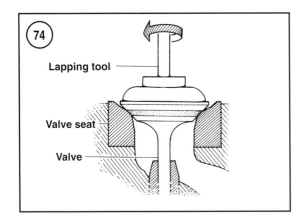

74

Lapping tool

Valve seat

Valve

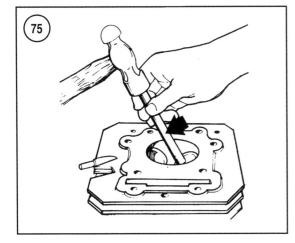

75

a. Intake 4.5 mm (0.18 in.) (part No. YM-04116/90890-04116).
b. Exhaust 5 mm (0.2 in.) (part No YM-04097/90890-04097).
2. Valve guide installers:
   a. Intake 4.5 mm (0.18 in.) (part No. YM-04117/90890-04117).
   b. Exhaust 5 mm (0.2 in.) (part No. YM-04098/90890-04098).
3. Valve guide reamers:
   a. Intake 4.5 mm (0.18 in.) (part No. YM-04118/90890-04118).
   b. Exhaust 5 mm (0.2 in.) (part No. YM-04099/90890-04099).

**Procedure**

*WARNING*
*Heating the head is required. The head will be very hot. Wear protected gloves. Read the entire procedure before attempting valve guide replacement. During some steps it will be necessary to work quickly and have the correct tools on hand.*

*CAUTION*
*Do not use a torch to heat the cylinder head. Uneven heating will warp the cylinder head.*

*NOTE*
*Before starting the installation process, place the new valve guides in a freezer. This will slightly shrink the guides and ease installation.*

1. Place the cylinder head in a shop oven or on a hot plate, set at 212-300° F (100-150° C). This will aid in removing the interference fit valve guides.
2. Remove the head from the oven or hot plate. Place the head on wooden blocks with the combustion chamber facing up.
3. Working quickly, insert the correct valve guide remover into each guide, then drive the guide out of the head (**Figure 75**). Make sure the circlip installed on the underside of the guide was removed.
4. Allow the head to cool.
5. Inspect and clean the valve guide bores.
6. Reheat the cylinder head to 212-300° F (100-150° C).
7. After heating the head, remove the head from the oven or hot plate. Place the head on wooden blocks with the combustion chamber facing down.
8. Remove the new valve guides from the freezer.
9. Install a new circlip on the underside of the valve guide.
10. Align the valve guide in the bore. Insert the correct valve guide installer into each guide and drive the guide squarely into the head until it is seated.
11. Allow the head to cool.
12. Ream each valve guide as follows:
    a. Place the head with combustion chamber facing down.
    b. Coat the valve guide and correct valve guide reamer with cutting oil.

*CAUTION*
*Make sure to keep the reamer rotating clockwise while installing and removing the tool from the guide. Rotate the tool clockwise through the entire length of the guide. Rotating the reamer in a counterclockwise direction will damage the valve guide.*

*CAUTION*
*Do not allow the reamer to tilt. Keep the tool square to the hole and apply even pressure and twisting motion during the entire operation.*

c. With a clockwise motion of the reamer, start the reamer into the guide.

4

d. Slowly work the reamer through the guide, while periodically adding cutting oil.

e. As the reamer passes into the combustion chamber, maintain the clockwise motion and work the reamer back out of the guide, and continue to add cutting oil.

f. Clean the reamed guide, then measure the inside diameter with a small hole gauge and micrometer. The measurement must be within the specifications in **Table 3**.

13. Clean the cylinder head and guides with solvent to remove all metal particles and residue. Dry the assembly with compressed air.

14. Apply engine oil to the valve guides to prevent corrosion.

15. Reface the valve seats as described in this section.

## CYLINDER

### Removal

The cylinder and piston can be removed with the engine in the frame.

1. Remove the cylinder head as described in this chapter.

2. Remove the front cam chain guide (**Figure 76**).

3. Remove the cylinder-mounting bolt (**Figure 77**).

4. Loosen the cylinder by tapping around the base.

> *CAUTION*
> *Locating dowels that remain in the underside of the cylinder may fall out during cylinder removal.*

5. Slowly remove the cylinder from the crankcase, routing the cam chain through the chain tunnel. Secure the cam chain after it passes through the cylinder.

6. Remove the base gasket (A, **Figure 78**).

7. If necessary, remove the small dowels (B, **Figure 78**).

8. Remove the O-ring (A, **Figure 79**) around the large dowel (B). If necessary, remove the large dowel.

9. Stuff a shop cloth into the crankcase to prevent entrance of small parts and debris.

10. Inspect the cylinder as described in this section.

### Inspection

1. Remove all gasket residue from the cylinder and crankcase surfaces.

2. Wash the cylinder in solvent and dry with compressed air.

3. Inspect the cylinder bore for obvious scoring or gouges. Damage may indicate replacement is required. Measure the bore and compare to the specification in **Table 4**.

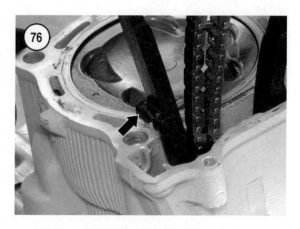

4. Inspect the overall condition of the cylinder, as well as the water jackets (**Figure 80**) for deposits.

5. Measure the cylinder for wear, taper and out of round. Measure the cylinder at three points along the bore axis (**Figure 81**). At each point, measure in line (X measurement) with the piston pin, and 90° to the pin (Y measurement). Record and identify the six measurements.

a. To determine cylinder wear, use the largest measurement recorded (X or Y) and compare it to the piston diameter to determine the piston-to-cylinder clearance. Compare the measurement to the specification in **Table 4**.

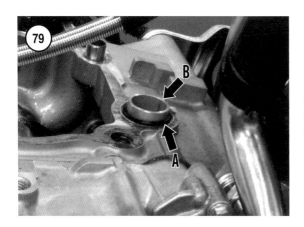

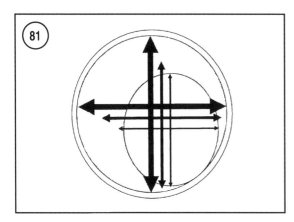

If the clearance is not within the service limit, determine whether the piston, cylinder or both require replacement.

b. To determine cylinder out of round, use the largest Y measurement and the smallest X measurement. The difference between the two is the out of round measurement. Compare the result to the service limit in **Table 4**. If the cylinder bore is not within the service limit, replace the cylinder.

c. To determine cylinder taper, use the largest X or Y measurement made at the top of the cylinder and the largest X or Y measurement made

at the bottom of the cylinder. The difference between the two is the taper measurement. Compare the result to the service limit in **Table 4**. If the cylinder bore is not within the service limit, replace the cylinder.

6. If the cylinder requires replacement, provide the dealership with the piston and rings. The cylinder cannot be bored.

> *CAUTION*
> *Excessive deglazing may damage the hardened bore. Do not remove the carbon ridge at the top of the cylinder bore. Removal of the buildup will promote oil consumption.*

7. If the cylinder is within all service limits, lightly deglaze the cylinder with a hone.

> *CAUTION*
> *Wash the cylinder as described in Step 8 in hot soapy water. Solvents will not remove the fine grit left in the cylinder. This grit will cause premature wear of the rings and cylinder.*

8. Wash the cylinder in hot soapy water to remove all residue left from the machine operations. Check the cleanliness by passing a clean, white cloth over the bore. No residue should be evident. When the cylinder is thoroughly clean and dry, lightly coat the cylinder bore with oil to prevent corrosion. Wrap the cylinder in plastic until engine reassembly.

9. Perform any service to the piston assembly as described in this chapter before installing the cylinder.

**Installation**

1. Make sure all gasket residue is removed from all mating surfaces.

2. Install a new lubricated O-ring (A, **Figure 79**) onto the large dowel (B).

3. If removed, install the small dowels (B, **Figure 78**) into the crankcase.

4. Install a new base gasket onto the crankcase.

5. Lubricate the following components with engine oil:

 a. Piston and rings.

 b. Piston pin and small end of connecting rod.

 c. Cylinder bore.

6. Support the piston so the cylinder can be lowered into place.

> *NOTE*
> *Fabricate a piston holding fixture as shown in **Figure 82**. Place this holding tool under the piston and straddling the connecting rod. This will limit piston*

*movement and prevent the piston from contacting the crankcase.*

7. Stagger the piston ring gaps on the piston as shown in **Figure 83**.

8. Lower the cylinder onto the piston, routing the cam chain and rear cam chain guide through the chain tunnel. As the piston enters the cylinder, compress each ring so it can enter the cylinder. When the bottom ring is in the cylinder, remove the holding fixture and lower the cylinder onto the crankcase. Secure the cam chain so it cannot fall into the engine.

9. Install the cylinder-mounting bolt (**Figure 77**) and tighten to 10 N•m (88 in.-lb.).

10. Install the cylinder head as described in this chapter.

## PISTON AND PISTON RINGS

### Piston Removal

1. Remove the cylinder as described in this chapter.

2. Before removing the piston, hold the rod and try to rock the piston from side to side (**Figure 84**). If rocking (not sliding) motion is detected, this indicates wear on the piston pin, pin bore, rod bushing or a combination of all three parts. Inspection will be required to determine which parts require replacement.

3. Stuff shop rags around the connecting rod and in the cam chain tunnel to prevent debris and small parts from falling into the crankcase.

4. Remove the circlips from the piston pin bore (**Figure 85**). Discard the circlips.

> *CAUTION*
> *Install new circlips during assembly.*

5. Push the piston pin out of the piston by hand. If the pin is tight, make the tool shown in **Figure 86** to remove it. Do not drive out the piston pin, as this may damage the piston pin, connecting rod or piston.

6. Lift the piston off the connecting rod.

7. Inspect the piston and piston pin as described in this section.

### Piston Inspection

1. Remove the piston rings as described in this chapter.

> *CAUTION*
> *Do not use a wire brush to clean the piston.*

2. Clean the carbon from the piston crown (**Figure 87**) using a soft scraper and solvent. Do not use tools

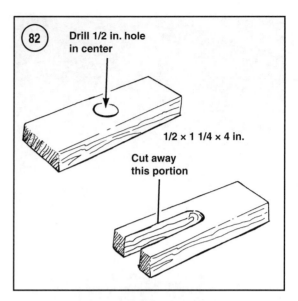

**82** Drill 1/2 in. hole in center

1/2 × 1 1/4 × 4 in.

Cut away this portion

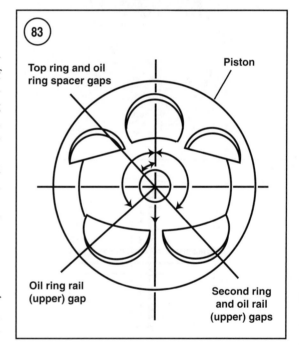

**83**

Top ring and oil ring spacer gaps

Piston

Oil ring rail (upper) gap

Second ring and oil rail (upper) gaps

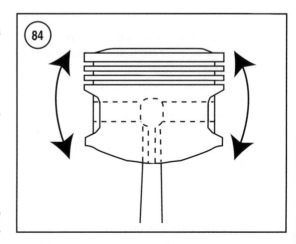

**84**

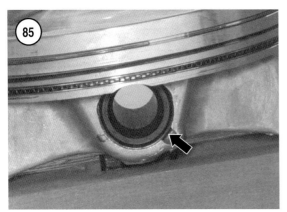

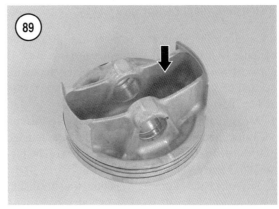

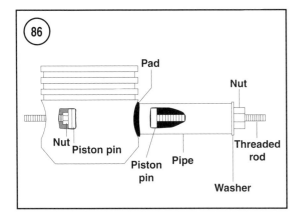

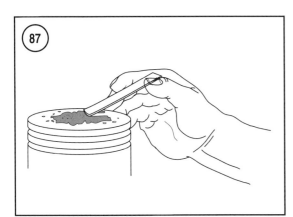

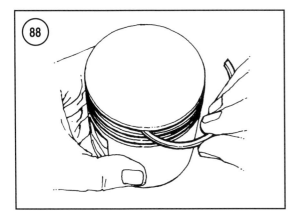

that can gouge or scratch the surface. This type of damage can cause hot spots on the piston when the engine is running.

3. Clean the piston pin bore, ring grooves and piston skirt. Clean the ring grooves with a soft brush (such as a toothbrush), or use a broken piston ring (**Figure 88**) to remove carbon and oil residue. Polish any mild galling or discoloration off the piston skirt with fine emery cloth and oil.

4. Inspect the piston crown for wear or damage. If the piston is pitted, overheating is likely occurring. This can be caused by a lean fuel mixture and/or pre-ignition. If damage is evident, perform troubleshooting procedures as described in Chapter Two.

5. Inspect the ring grooves for dents, nicks, cracks or other damage. The grooves should be square and uniform around the circumference of the piston. Particularly inspect the top compression ring groove. It is lubricated the least and is nearest the combustion temperatures. If the oil ring appears worn, or if the oil ring was difficult to remove, the piston has likely overheated and distorted. Replace the piston if any damage is detected.

6. Inspect the piston skirt. If the skirt shows signs of severe galling or partial seizure (bits of metal imbedded in the skirt), replace the piston.

7. Inspect the interior of the piston (**Figure 89**). Check the crown, skirt, piston pin bores and bosses for cracks or other damage. Check the circlip grooves for cleanliness and damage. Replace the piston if damaged.

8. Measure the piston pin bores with a small hole gauge and micrometer (**Figure 90**). Measure each bore horizontally and vertically. Record the measurements. Compare the largest measurement to the specifications in **Table 4**. Record this measurement to determining the piston pin-to-piston bore clearance, as described in this section.

9. Inspect the piston ring-to-ring groove clearance as described in this section.

## Piston-to-Cylinder Clearance Check

Calculate the clearance between the piston and cylinder to determine if the parts can be reused. If parts are not within specification, replace the cylinder and/or piston assembly. Clean and dry the piston and cylinder before measuring.

1. Measure the outside diameter of the piston. Measure 10 mm (0.39 in.) up from the bottom edge of the piston skirt and 90° to the direction of the piston pin (**Figure 91**). Record the measurement.

2. Determine the clearance by subtracting the piston measurement from the largest cylinder bore measurement. Determine the cylinder measurements as described in *Inspection* in *Cylinder* in this chapter. If the clearance exceeds the specification in **Table 4**, replace the piston.

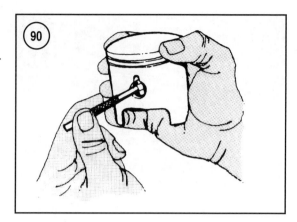

## Piston Pin and Connecting Rod Inspection

1. Clean the piston pin in solvent, then dry.

2. Inspect the pin for wear or discoloration from overheating.

3. Inspect the piston pin bore in the connecting rod (**Figure 92**). Check for scoring, uneven wear, and discoloration from overheating.

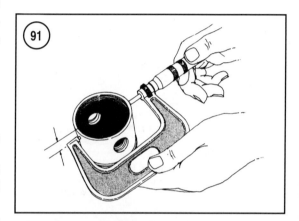

4. Lubricate the piston pin and slide it into the connecting rod. Slowly rotate the pin and check for radial play (**Figure 93**). If play is detectable, one or both of the parts are worn. Specifications for the connecting rod are not available. Therefore, measure the piston pin where it contacts the rod. If it is within specification, replace the rod. If the pin is not within specification, replace the pin and recheck for play in the connecting rod. If play still exists, replace the rod.

5. Determine the piston pin clearance as follows:

   a. Measure the piston pin outside diameter at both ends (**Figure 94**), using a micrometer. Record the measurements. Replace the pin if any measurements exceed the service limit in **Table 4**.

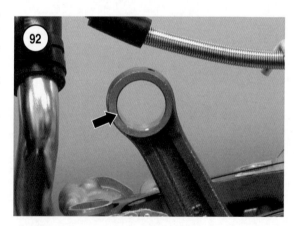

   b. Subtract the smallest piston pin measurement from the largest piston pin bore measurement. This measurement is described in *Piston Inspection* in this section. Replace the piston and pin if they exceed the service limit in **Table 4**.

## Piston Ring Removal and Inspection

> *WARNING*
> *The piston ring edges are sharp. Be careful when handling them.*

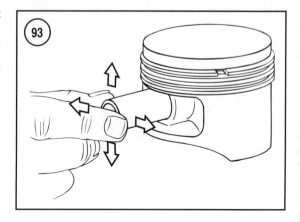

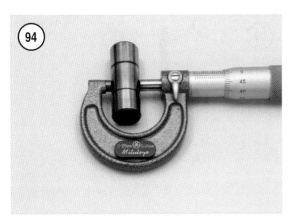

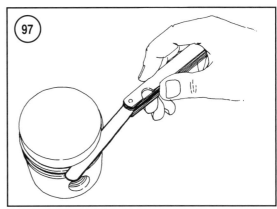

4

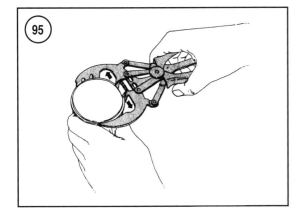

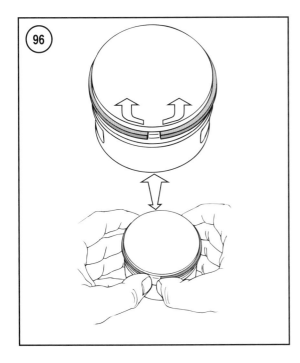

*NOTE*
*There are two ways to remove the rings:*
*with a ring expander tool (**Figure 95**)*
*or by hand (**Figure 96**). The ring ex-*
*pander tool is useful because it re-*

moves the rings without damaging
them or scratching the piston. If this
tool is not available, remove the rings
by carefully spreading their end gaps
with two thumbs and sliding them off
the top of the piston.

*NOTE*
*The top and second rings have iden-*
*tification marks near their end gaps.*
*These marks are not always visible*
*on used rings. If the rings are going*
*to be reused, mark them for location*
*and direction during disassembly. On*
*original equipment pistons and rings,*
*the top ring is wider than the second*
*ring.*

1. Remove the piston rings from the piston, starting
with the top ring and working down.
2. Remove the oil ring assembly by first removing
the top rail, followed by the bottom rail. Remove the
expander ring last.
3. Clean and inspect the piston as described in *Piston
Inspection* in this section.
4. Check the piston ring-to-ring groove clearance as
follows:
    a. Clean the rings and grooves so accurate
       measurements can be made with a flat feeler
       gauge.
    b. Install the top ring into the groove so the ring is
       fully seated in the groove.
    c. Insert a flat feeler gauge between the ring and
       groove (**Figure 97**). Record the measurement.
       Repeat this step at other points around the pis-
       ton. Replace the rings if any measurement ex-
       ceeds the service limit in **Table 4**. If excessive
       clearance remains after new rings are installed,
       replace the piston.
    d. Repeat Steps b and c for the second compres-
       sion ring. The oil control ring side clearance is
       not measured.

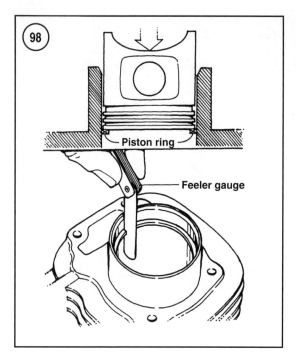

Piston ring

Feeler gauge

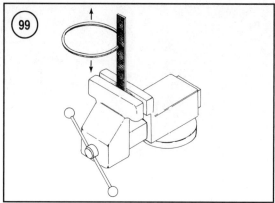

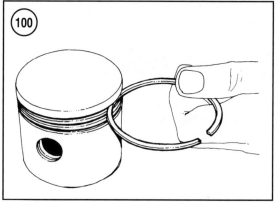

5. Inspect the end gap of each ring as follows:
   a. Insert a ring into the bottom of the cylinder. Use the piston to push the ring squarely into the cylinder (**Figure 98**) approximately 10 mm (0.039 in.).
   b. Measure the end gap with a feeler gauge (**Figure 98**). Replace the rings as a set if any gap measurement exceeds the service limit in **Table 4**. If new rings are installed, gap the new rings after the cylinder has been serviced. If the new ring gap is too small, carefully widen the gap using a fine-cut file as shown in **Figure 99**. Work slowly and measure often.

*NOTE*
*Measure only the ring rails of the oil control ring. It is not necessary to measure the expander spacer.*

6. Roll each ring around its piston groove and check for binding or snags (**Figure 100**). Repair minor damage with a fine-cut file.

**Piston Ring Installation**

If installing new piston rings, hone or deglaze the cylinder. This is necessary to roughen and crosshatch the cylinder surface. The newly honed surface is important in controlling wear and lubrication of the new rings, helping them seat and seal properly. A dealership can hone the cylinder for a minimal cost. Refer to *Inspection* in *Cylinder* in this chapter to determine if the cylinder should be honed.

1. Check that the piston and rings are clean and dry.
2. Install the oil control, middle and top rings into their respective grooves as follows:

*WARNING*
*Piston ring edges are sharp. Be careful when handling.*

*CAUTION*
*When installing the top and middle rings, check that the top mark, or manufacturer's numbers are facing up. The oil control ring is not marked.*

*CAUTION*
*Install rings using a ring expander (**Figure 95**) or by hand (**Figure 96**). Spread the rings only enough to clear the piston.*

   a. Install the oil ring expander into the bottom groove.
   b. Install the oil ring rails into the bottom groove; one above and one below the expander.
   c. Install the middle ring. Make sure the top mark, or manufacturer's numbers, is facing up.

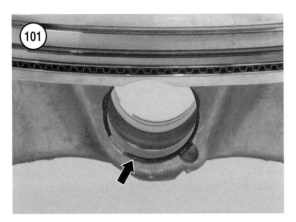

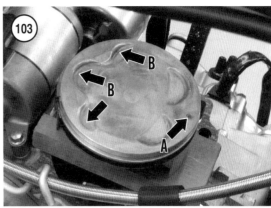

3. Install a new circlip (**Figure 101**) into the piston bore groove so the gap does not align with the notch on the piston.
4. Lubricate the piston pin, piston pin bores and connecting rod bore with engine oil.
5. Start the piston pin (**Figure 102**) into the open piston pin bore.

*CAUTION*
*The piston must he installed correctly to accommodate piston pin offset and prevent the valves from striking the piston. Failure to install the piston correctly can lead to severe engine damage.*

d. Install the top ring. Make sure the top mark, or manufacturer's numbers, is facing up.
3. Make sure all rings rotate freely in their grooves.

**Piston Installation**

1. Install the piston rings onto the piston as described in this section.

*CAUTION*
*Never install used circlips, as engine damage could occur. Circlips fatigue and distort during removal, even though they appear reusable.*

2. Make sure all parts are clean and ready to install. Install new piston pin clips.

6. Install the piston onto the connecting rod so the punch mark stamped on the piston crown is forward (A, **Figure 103**). Make sure the three intake valve indentions on the piston crown (B, **Figure 103**) face the intake (rear) side of the engine.
7. Align the piston with the rod, then slide the pin through the rod and into the opposite piston pin bore.
8. Install the remaining piston pin clip (**Figure 101**) into the piston bore groove so the gap does not align with the notch on the piston.
9. Position the ring end gaps as shown in **Figure 83**.
10. Install the cylinder as described in this chapter.
11. Refer to Chapter Five for break-in procedures.

**Table 1 GENERAL ENGINE SPECIFICATIONS**

| Item | Specification |
|---|---|
| Cylinder arrangement | Single-cylinder |
| Engine type | Four-stroke, DOHC, five-valve head |
| | (continued) |

**Table 1 GENERAL ENGINE SPECIFICATIONS (continued)**

| Item | Specification |
|---|---|
| Bore x stroke | |
| 2004-2005 models | 95 × 62 mm (3.74 × 2.44 in.) |
| 2006 models | 95 × 63.4 mm (3.74 × 2.50 in.) |
| Compression ratio | |
| 2004-2005 models | 11.9:1 |
| 2006-on models | 11.2:1 |
| Displacement | |
| 2004-2005 models | 439 cc (26.8 cu. in.) |
| 2006-on models | 449 cc (27.4 cu. in.) |
| Ignition type | Electronic |
| Ignition timing | 7.5° BTDC @ 1800 rpm |
| Ignition advancer type | Throttle position sensor and electronic |
| Cooling system | Liquid cooled |
| Lubrication system | |
| Type | Wet sump, forced pressure |
| Oil pump | Trochoid |

**Table 2 CAMSHAFT SPECIFICATIONS**

| Item | Standard mm (in.) | Service limit mm (in.) |
|---|---|---|
| Cam base circle diameter | | |
| Intake | 22.550-22.650 | 22.450 |
| | (0.8878-0.8917) | (0.8839) |
| Exhaust | 22.494-22.594 | 22.394 |
| | (0.8856-0.8895) | (0.8817) |
| Cam lobe height | | |
| Intake | 31.200-31.300 | 31.100 |
| | (1.2283-1.2323) | (1.2244) |
| Exhaust | 30.950-31.050 | 30.850 |
| | (1.2185-1.2224) | (1.2146) |
| Cam cap inside diameter | 22.000-22.021 | – |
| | (0.8661-0.8670) | |
| Cam journal outside diameter | | |
| 2004-2005 models | 21.967-21.980 | – |
| | (0.8648-0.8654) | – |
| 2006-on models | 21.959-21.972 | – |
| | (0.8645-0.8650) | – |
| Camshaft bearing oil clearance | | |
| 2004-2005 models | 0.020-0.054 | 0.080 |
| | (0.0008-0.0021) | (0.0032) |
| 2006-on models | 0.028-0.062 | 0.080 |
| | (0.0011-0.0024) | (0.0032 |
| Camshaft runout | – | 0.03 |
| | | (0.0012) |

**Table 3 CYLINDER HEAD SPECIFICATIONS**

| Item | Standard mm (in.) | Service limit mm (in.) |
|---|---|---|
| Cylinder head warp | – | 0.05 |
| | | (0.002) |
| Valve clearance (cold) | | |
| Intake | 0.10-0.15 | – |
| | (0.0039-0.0059) | |
| Exhaust | 0.20-0.25 | – |
| | (0.0079-0.0098) | |

(continued)

**Table 3 CYLINDER HEAD SPECIFICATIONS (continued)**

| Item | Standard mm (in.) | Service limit mm (in.) |
|---|---|---|
| Valve guide inside diameter | | |
| Intake | 4.500-4.512 | 4.550 |
| | (0.1772-0.1776) | (0.1791) |
| Exhaust | 5.000-5.012 | 5.050 |
| | (0.1969-0.1973) | (0.1988) |
| Valve stem outside diameter | | |
| Intake | 4.475-4.490 | 4.445 |
| | (0.1762-0.1768) | (0.1750) |
| Exhaust | 4.965-4.980 | 4.935 |
| | (0.1955-0.1961) | (0.1943) |
| Valve stem runout | – | 0.01 |
| | | (0.0004) |
| Valve stem-to-guide clearance | | |
| Intake | 0.010-0.037 | 0.08 |
| | (0.0004-0.0015) | (0.0031) |
| Exhaust | 0.020-0.047 | 0.10 |
| | (0.0008-0.0019) | (0.0039) |
| Valve face width | | |
| Intake and exhaust | 2.26 | – |
| | (0.089) | |
| Valve seat width | | |
| Intake and exhaust | 0.90-1.10 | – |
| | (0.035-0.043) | |
| Valve margin | 1.0 | 0.85 |
| | (0.039) | (0.033) |
| Valve spring free length | | |
| Intake | 37.03 | 35.17 |
| | (1.458) | (1.385) |
| Exhaust | 37.68 | 35.79 |
| | (1.483) | (1.409) |
| Valve spring pressure (installed) | | |
| Intake | 111.3-127.9 N | – |
| | (25.02-28.75 lb.) | |
| Exhaust | 127.4-146.4 N | – |
| | (28.64-32.91 lb.) | |
| Valve spring tilt | – | 1.6 mm |
| | | (0.06 in.) |

4

**Table 4 CYLINDER AND PISTON SPECIFICATIONS**

| Item | Standard mm (in.) | Service limit mm (in.) |
|---|---|---|
| Cylinder | | |
| Bore | 95.00-95.010 | – |
| | (3.7402-3.7406) | |
| Taper | – | 0.05 |
| | | (0.0020) |
| Out of round | – | 0.05 |
| | | (0.0020) |
| Piston | | |
| Outside diameter* | 94.945-94.960 | – |
| | (3.7380-3.7386) | |
| Piston to cylinder clearance | 0.040-0.065 | |
| | (0.0016-0.0026) | |
| Service limit | | |
| 2004-2005 models | 0.10 (0.004) | |
| 2006-on models | 0.15 (0.006) | |
| Piston-pin bore inside diameter | 20.004-20.015 | 20.045 |
| | (0.7876-0.7880) | (0.789) |
| Piston pin outside diameter | 19.991-20.000 | 19.971 |
| | (0.7870-0.7874) | (0.786) |
| | (continued) | |

**Table 4 CYLINDER AND PISTON SPECIFICATIONS (continued)**

| Item | Standard mm (in.) | Wear limit mm (in.) |
|---|---|---|
| Piston to cylinder clearance (continued) | | |
| Piston pin clearance | 0.004-0.024 | 0.074 |
| | (0.0002-0.0009) | (0.0029) |
| Piston rings | | |
| Ring-to-groove clearance | | |
| Top | 0.030-0.065 | 0.12 |
| | (0.0012-0.0026) | (0.005) |
| Second | 0.020-0.055 | 0.12 |
| | (0.0008-0.0022) | (0.005) |
| Ring end gap (installed) | | |
| Top | 0.20-0.30 | 0.55 |
| | (0.008-0.012) | (0.022) |
| Second | 0.35-0.50 | 0.85 |
| | (0.014-0.020) | (0.034) |
| Piston rings (continued) | | |
| Ring thickness | | |
| Top | 1.20 | – |
| | (0.047) | |
| Second | 1.00 | – |
| | (0.039) | |

*Measured at a point 10 mm (0.39 in.) from the bottom of the piston skirt. Refer to text.

**Table 5 ENGINE TOP END TORQUE SPECIFICATIONS**

| Item | N•m | in.-lb. | ft.-lb. |
|---|---|---|---|
| Camshaft cap bolts* | 10 | 88 | – |
| Camshaft chain bolt | 7 | 62 | – |
| Camshaft chain tensioner mounting bolts | 10 | 88 | – |
| Cylinder head bolts* | | Refer to procedure | |
| Cylinder head cover bolts | 10 | 88 | – |
| Cylinder head nuts | 10 | 88 | – |
| Cylinder mounting bolt | 10 | 88 | – |
| Engine mounting block bolts | 33 | – | 24 |
| Exhaust heat shield mounting bolts* | 7 | 62 | – |
| Exhaust pipe bolt (2004 and 2005 models)* | 24 | – | 18 |
| Exhaust pipe nut (2004 and 2005 models)* | 13 | 115 | – |
| Exhaust pipe nuts (2006-on models) | 14 | – | 10 |
| Muffler mounting bolts | 34 | – | 25 |
| Oil tube banjo bolts | | | |
| Front | 20 | – | 15 |
| Upper and rear | 18 | – | 13 |
| Upper engine bracket bolts | 26 | – | 19 |
| Upper engine mounting bolts | 40 | – | 29 |

*Refer to text.

NOTE: Refer to the Supplement at the back of the manual for information unique to 2009-on YFZ450R models.

# ENGINE LOWER END

Throughout the text there is frequent mention of the left and right sides of the engine. This refers to the engine as it sits in the frame, not how it may be placed on the workbench.

**Table 1** and **Table 2** are at the end of this chapter.

## ENGINE

### Service in the Frame

The following components can be serviced with the engine mounted in the frame:

1. Cylinder head cover.
2. Camshafts.
3. Cylinder head.
4. Cylinder and piston.
5. Water pump.
6. Clutch.
7. Oil pump.
8. Balancer.
9. Carburetor.
10. Alternator.
11. Starter.
12. Exhaust system.

### Removal/Installation

1. Park the vehicle on a level surface and set the parking brake.
2. Remove the fuel tank as described in Chapter Eight.
3. Remove the front fender as described in Chapter Fifteen.
4. Disconnect the electrical cable from the negative battery terminal (Chapter Nine).
5. Drain the engine oil as described in Chapter Three.
6. Drain the engine coolant as described in Chapter Three.
7. Remove the exhaust system as described in Chapter Four.
8. Remove the carburetor as described in Chapter Eight.
9. Remove the drive chain as described in Chapter Eleven.
10. Loosen the clamp and detach the radiator hose from the water pump inlet tube (**Figure 1**).
11. Loosen the clamp and detach the radiator hose from the cylinder head tube (**Figure 2**).

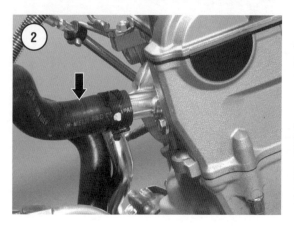

12. Remove the ignition coil/spark plug cap from the spark plug (A, **Figure 3**).

13. Detach the cylinder head breather hose (B, **Figure 3**) and oil tank breather hose (C) from the cylinder head cover.

14. Remove the bolt securing the clutch and parking brake cable bracket (**Figure 4**).

15. Remove the bolts securing the parking brake cable bracket (A, **Figure 5**) to the frame.

16. Push back the boot, then disconnect the wire connector (B, **Figure 5**) from the starter terminal.

17. Detach the crankcase breather hose (A, **Figure 6**) from the engine.

18. Remove the clamp bolt (B, **Figure 6**) that secures the negative battery terminal wire and clutch cable to the engine.

*NOTE*
*In Steps 19 and 21 the oil tube and O-ring may remain in the engine (**Figure 7**).*

19. Remove the retaining bolt (A, **Figure 8**) and separate the oil fitting from the left side of the engine. Remove the oil tube and O-ring.

20. Pull the neutral switch connector (B, **Figure 8**) off the switch terminal.

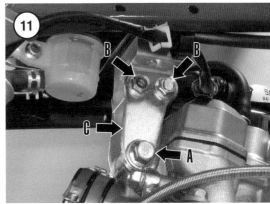

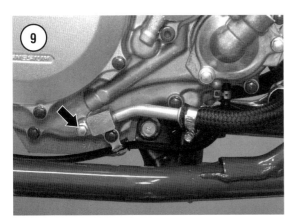

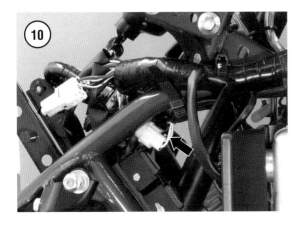

21. Remove the retaining bolt (**Figure 9**) and separate the oil fitting from the right side of the engine. Remove the oil tube and O-ring.

22. Disconnect the stator (white) and pickup coil (black) connectors (**Figure 10**).

23. Detach the plastic bands securing the stator and pickup coil wires to the frame. Note the wire routing for reinstallation.

24. Remove the right footrest (Chapter Fifteen) and rear brake pedal (Chapter Fourteen).

25. Verify that all engine wiring and hoses have been disconnected from the frame.

26. If the engine is going to be disassembled, consider removing the following parts for ease of service and weight reduction during engine removal.

    a. Alternator (Chapter Nine).

    b. Starter (Chapter Nine).

    c. Camshaft and cylinder head (Chapter Four).

    d. Cylinder and piston (Chapter Four).

    e. Clutch (Chapter Six).

    f. External shift mechanism (Chapter Six).

    g. Oil pump (this chapter).

27. Place tape or other material on the frame to protect it and the engine.

28. Remove the upper engine mounting bolt and washer (A, **Figure 11**).

29. Remove the bracket bolts (B, **Figure 11**), then remove the brackets (C).

30. Remove the retaining bolts (A, **Figure 12**), then remove the engine mounting block (B).

31. Place a jack underneath the engine and support the engine with just enough pressure to remove weight from the lower engine mounting bolts when removing them in the following steps. Place a block of wood between the jack and engine to protect the crankcase.

32. Remove the nut, then remove the front engine mounting bolt (A, **Figure 13**).

33. On each side, remove the mounting bracket bolts (B, **Figure 13**), then remove the brackets (C).

34. Remove the nut (**Figure 14**), then remove the lower mounting bolt.

> *NOTE*
> *The rear mounting bolt also serves as the swing arm pivot bolt. Pull the bolt out only enough to allow engine removal. Allow the bolt to remain in the left side of the swing arm so it will stay in place.*

35. Remove the nut and washer (**Figure 15**), then withdraw the rear mounting bolt enough to release the engine.

36. Remove the engine out through the right side of the frame.

37. Reverse the removal steps to install the engine while noting the following:

   a. Lubricate the rear engine mounting bolt before installation. The bolt also serves as the swing arm pivot bolt.

   b. Tighten all engine mounting bolts finger-tight, then tighten all bolts to the specified torque.

   c. Tighten the front engine mounting bracket bolts to 38 N•m (28 ft.-lb.).

   d. Tighten the front engine mounting bolt to 66 N•m (48 ft.-lb.).

   e. Tighten the rear engine mounting bolt to 100 N•m (74 ft.-lb.).

   f. Install the engine mounting block (B, **Figure 12**) so the cutout is toward the right side. Tighten the mounting block bolts (A, **Figure 12**) to 33 N•m (24 ft.-lb.).

   g. Tighten the upper engine bracket bolts to 26 N•m (19 ft.-lb.).

   h. Tighten the upper engine mounting bolt to 40 N•m (29 ft.-lb.).

   i. Install a new O-ring onto each oil tube (**Figure 7**). Lubricate the O-ring and insert the oil tube into the oil passage. Install the oil fitting on each side (A, **Figure 8** and **Figure 9**). Tighten the bolt to 8 N•m (71 in.-lb.).

   j. Install the right footrest and rear brake pedal.

   k. Tighten the parking brake cable bracket bolts to 10 N•m (88 in.-lb.).

   l. Tighten the bracket bolt that secures the clutch cable and negative battery terminal wire to 10 N•m (88 in.-lb.).

   m. Fill the engine with oil as described in Chapter Three.

   n. Fill the cooling system as described in Chapter Three.

   o. Adjust the throttle cable, clutch cable and drive chain as described in Chapter Three.

   p. Start the engine and check for leaks and proper operation.

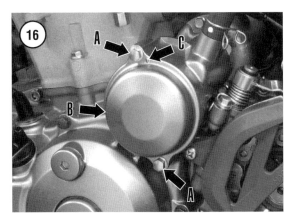

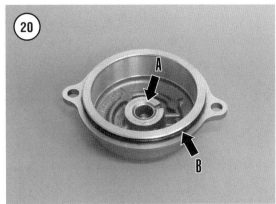

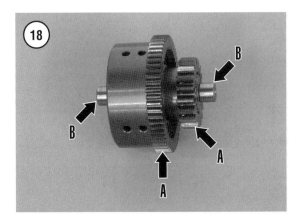

q. If the engine was overhauled, observe the *Engine Break-in* procedure in this chapter.

## TORQUE LIMITER

The torque limiter prevents damage to the starter and engine components should kickback occur.

### Removal/Inspection/Installation

1. Remove the cover bolts (A, **Figure 16**), then remove the cover (B).
2. Remove the torque limiter (**Figure 17**).
3. Inspect the torque limiter for damaged gear teeth (A, **Figure 18**) or other damage. Inspect the shaft (B, **Figure 18**) on the torque limiter.

> *NOTE*
> *If the gear teeth on the torque limiter are damaged, also inspect the gear teeth on the starter idle gear as described in this chapter.*

> *NOTE*
> *The torque limiter is available only as a unit assembly.*

4. Inspect the bearing bore in the crankcase (**Figure 19**). Also inspect the shaft on the torque limiter.
5. Inspect the bearing bore in the cover (A, **Figure 20**). Replace the cover if damaged. Also inspect the shaft on the torque limiter.
6. Install the torque limiter making sure the gear teeth engage properly.
7. If necessary, install a new O-ring onto the cover (B, **Figure 20**). Lubricate the O-ring.
8. Install the cover so the projection (C, **Figure 16**) is up. Tighten the cover bolts to 10 N•m (88 in.-lb.).

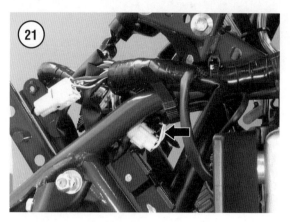

## LEFT CRANKCASE COVER

The left crankcase cover must be removed for access to the flywheel and stator assembly, and to remove the balancer shaft from the engine.

### Removal and Installation

1. Disconnect the electrical cable from the negative battery terminal (Chapter Nine).
2. Drain the engine oil as described in Chapter Three.
3. Remove the front fender as described in Chapter Fifteen.
4. Disconnect the stator (white) and pickup coil (black) connectors (**Figure 21**).
5. Detach the plastic bands securing the stator and pickup coil wires to the frame. Note the wire routing for reinstallation.
6. Remove the shift pedal (Chapter Six).
7. Remove the torque limiter as described in this chapter.
8. Detach the crankcase breather hose (**Figure 22**) from the engine.

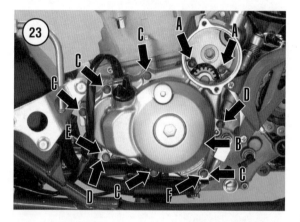

> *CAUTION*
> *Two of the crankcase cover bolts are located inside the torque limiter compartment (A, **Figure 23**). Note the length of each bolt as it is removed.*

9. Remove the nine bolts securing the crankcase cover (B, **Figure 23**). If necessary, lightly tap the cover to free it from the engine. Remove and discard the gasket.
10. Account for the two dowels that may remain in the crankcase (**Figure 24**) or cover.
11. Remove the two access plugs (**Figure 25**) from the cover and inspect the O-ring on each plug. Lubricate the O-rings.
12. If necessary, inspect the stator and pickup coil as described in *Alternator* in Chapter Nine.

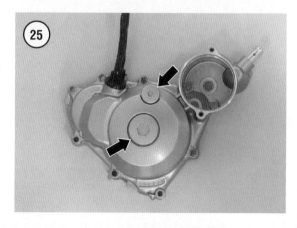

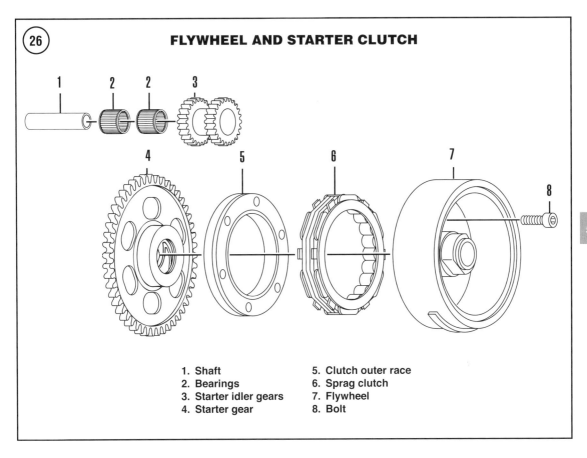

**26 FLYWHEEL AND STARTER CLUTCH**

1. Shaft
2. Bearings
3. Starter idler gears
4. Starter gear
5. Clutch outer race
6. Sprag clutch
7. Flywheel
8. Bolt

**5**

13. Reverse the removal steps to install the left crankcase cover while noting the following:
   a. Make sure both dowels (**Figure 24**) are in place.
   b. Install a new cover gasket.
   c. Note the length and location of the bolts: 20 mm (A, **Figure 23**), 30 mm (C), 40 mm (D).
   d. Install the loop-shaped wire retainer onto the lower, front bolt (E, **Figure 23**).
   e. Install the flat wire retainer onto the lower bolt (F, **Figure 23**).
   f. Tighten the crankcase cover bolts in a crossing pattern to 10 N•m (88 in.-lb.).

### STARTER IDLE GEAR

**Removal/Inspection/Installation**

Refer to **Figure 26**.
1. Remove the left crankcase cover as described in this chapter.
2. Remove the idle gear (**Figure 27**).
3. Remove the bearings (A, **Figure 28**) and shaft (B).
4. Inspect the idle gear for abnormal wear or tooth damage. Replace if necessary.
5. Inspect the bearings. Replace if necessary.

6. Inspect the shaft for abnormal wear or damage. Replace if necessary.

7. Make sure the shaft fits snugly in the bores in the crankcase and crankcase cover.

8. Installation is the reverse of removal. Lubricate all parts with engine oil.

## FLYWHEEL (ALTERNATOR ROTOR) AND STARTER CLUTCH

The alternator rotor mounted on the flywheel contains the magnets that energize the alternator stator coils. The alternator rotor and flywheel are available only as a unit assembly. The flywheel can be removed with the engine in the frame.

### Flywheel Puller

A flywheel puller is required to remove the flywheel from the crankshaft. Use one of the following pullers:

1. Yamaha flywheel puller (part No. 90890-04142).
2. Motion Pro flywheel puller (part No. 08-0390).

### Removal

Refer to **Figure 26**.

1. Remove the left crankcase cover as described in this chapter.

> *CAUTION*
> *Do not damage any projections on the flywheel rim when holding the flywheel. Doing so will affect pickup coil operation.*

2. Prevent flywheel rotation using a flywheel holding tool (A, **Figure 29**).

3. Loosen the flywheel retaining nut (B, **Figure 29**), then remove the nut and washer.

> *CAUTION*
> *Do not try to remove the flywheel without a puller. Any attempt to do so will damage the crankshaft and flywheel.*

> *CAUTION*
> *If the flywheel will not loosen, do not force the puller. Excessive force will strip the flywheel threads, causing damage. Take the engine to a dealership and have them remove the flywheel.*

4. Thread the flywheel puller (**Figure 30**) onto the flywheel. Make sure the puller fully engages the flywheel threads. Tighten the puller bolt against the crankshaft end.

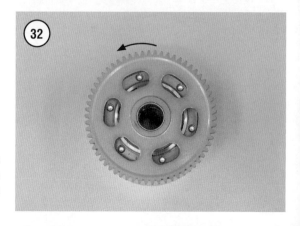

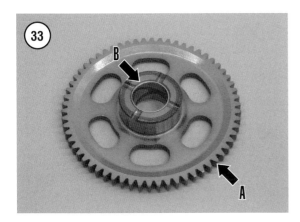

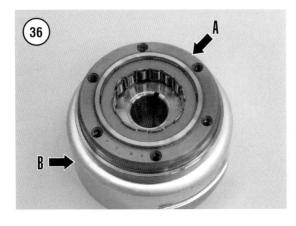

5. Hold the puller flats with a wrench and gradually tighten the flywheel puller bolt until the flywheel pops off the crankshaft taper.

6. Remove the puller from the flywheel.

7. Remove the flywheel and starter clutch assembly.

8. Remove the Woodruff key (A, **Figure 31**).

9. Remove the starter gear (B, **Figure 31**).

10. Inspect and lubricate the parts as described in this section.

11. Reverse the removal steps to install the flywheel and starter clutch while noting the following:

    a. Lubricate the starter gear and crankshaft with engine oil.

    b. Rotate the starter gear clockwise while installing the flywheel to engage the starter clutch.

    c. Tighten the flywheel nut to 65 N•m (48 ft.-lb.).

**Inspection**

1. Check starter clutch operation as follows:

    a. With the starter gear facing up, turn the gear counterclockwise (**Figure 32**). The gear should turn freely and smoothly in that direction.

    b. Attempt to turn the gear clockwise. The gear should not turn.

    c. If the gear turns in both directions or is always locked, disassemble and inspect the starter clutch assembly.

2. Remove the starter gear from the flywheel. Extract the gear from the clutch while turning the gear counterclockwise.

3. Clean and inspect the clutch assembly (**Figure 26**).

    a. Inspect the starter gear teeth (A, **Figure 33**) for wear or damage.

    b. Inspect the starter gear bushing (B, **Figure 33**) and crankshaft for damage. Install the gear onto the crankshaft. The gear should rotate smoothly with no play.

    c. Inspect the clutch rollers (**Figure 34**). The rollers should be undamaged and operate smoothly.

4. To replace the one-way clutch, perform the following:

    a. Secure the flywheel with a strap or band wrench.

    b. Using an impact driver, remove the one-way clutch mounting bolts (**Figure 35**).

    c. Separate the clutch assembly (A, **Figure 36**) from the flywheel (B).

    d. Install the one-way clutch into the outer race so the flange on the one-way fits into the recess in the outer race as shown in **Figure 37**.

    e. Apply a medium strength threadlocking compound to the threads of each mounting bolt (**Figure 35**).

f. Install the one-way clutch mounting bolts finger-tight, then tighten to 16 N•m (12 ft.-lb.).
5. Lubricate the clutch rollers with engine oil.
6. Install the clutch sprocket into the flywheel. Turn
the sprocket counterclockwise and twist it squarely into
the flywheel. When the sprocket is fully seated, check
that it turns only in the counterclockwise direction.
7. Clean and inspect the flywheel components.

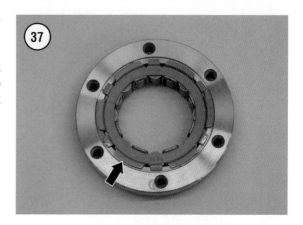

*WARNING*
*Replace the flywheel if damaged. The*
*flywheel can fly apart at high crank-*
*shaft speeds, causing personal injury*
*and damage to the motorcycle.*

a. Inspect the flywheel for cracks and damage.
b. Inspect the taper in the bore of the flywheel
and on the crankshaft for damage.

*NOTE*
*A bent or sheared Woodruff key will*
*cause flywheel misalignment, resulting*
*in incorrect ignition timing.*

c. Inspect the Woodruff key (A, **Figure 31**),
crankshaft keyway, flywheel nut and washer
for damage.

## CAMSHAFT CHAIN AND GUIDES

The camshaft chain and guides are located behind
the flywheel and starter clutch on the left side of the
crankcase (**Figure 38**). The front camshaft chain
guide can be removed after removal of the cylinder
head (Chapter Four).

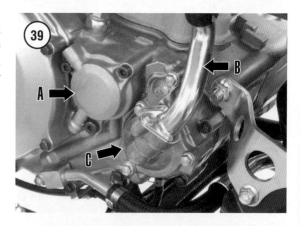

### Removal/Inspection/Installation

1. Remove the cylinder head (Chapter Four).
2. Remove the flywheel and starter clutch as described in this chapter.
3. If not previously removed, remove the front chain
guide (A, **Figure 38**).
4. Remove the rear chain guide retaining bolts (B,
**Figure 38**).
5. Remove the rear chain guide (C, **Figure 38**).
6. Lower the chain (D, **Figure 38**) through the crankcase and remove it from the crankshaft sprocket.
7. Inspect the camshaft chain for wear and damage.
Check for excessive play between the links, indicating worn rollers and pins. If chain replacement is
necessary, also inspect the crankshaft drive sprocket
and the camshaft sprockets.
8. Inspect the guides for excessive wear (grooves),
cuts or other damage. Replace if excessively worn
or damaged.

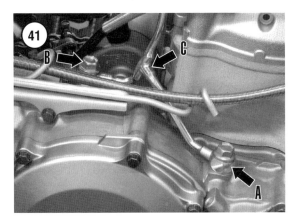

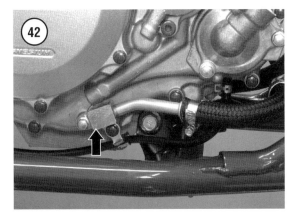

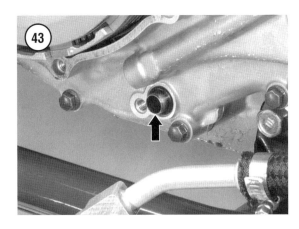

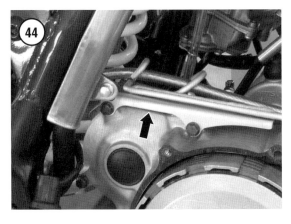

9. Reverse the removal steps to install the camshaft chain and guides. Tighten the rear cam chain guide retaining bolts to 10 N•m (88 in.-lb.).

## RIGHT CRANKCASE COVER

The right crankcase cover must be removed for access to the external shift mechanism, oil pump, water pump bearings, balancer gears and primary drive gears.

### Removal and Installation

1. Drain the engine oil as described in Chapter Three, then remove the oil filter cover (A, **Figure 39**) and filter.
2. Drain the engine coolant (Chapter Three), then remove the coolant pipe (B, **Figure 39**) and water pump housing (C) as described in Chapter Ten.
3. Remove the exhaust pipe as described in Chapter Four.
4. Remove the right footrest (Chapter Fifteen) and rear brake pedal (Chapter Fourteen).
5. Remove the upper oil tube banjo bolt at the cylinder head (**Figure 40**).
6. Remove the lower banjo bolt (A and B, **Figure 41**) at the crankcase. Remove the oil tube (C, **Figure 41**), fittings and sealing washers.
7. Remove the bolt securing the oil hose end (**Figure 42**). Do not lose the oil tube and O-ring which may remain in the fitting or in the cover (**Figure 43**).
8. Remove the clutch cover as described in Chapter Six. Two of the clutch cover bolts also retain the crankcase cover.

*NOTE*
*Two upper, rear crankcase cover bolts retain the parking brake cable bracket (**Figure 44**).*

9. Remove the bolts securing the crankcase cover to the engine. If necessary, lightly tap the cover to loosen it from the engine.
10. After the cover is removed, account for the dowels and two O-rings at the locations shown in **Figure 45**.
11. Remove and discard the cover gasket.
12. Refer to the appropriate sections in this chapter for servicing the balancer gears, primary drive gear and oil pump. Refer to Chapter Ten if servicing the water pump and seal assembly. Service the external shift mechanism as described in Chapter Six.
13. On 2007-on models, remove the oil nozzle (**Figure 46**). Clean the oil nozzle and oil passage in the cover.
14. Reverse the removal steps to install the right crankcase cover. Note the following:

5

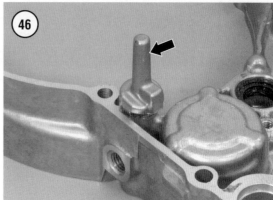

a. On 2007-on models, install a new O-ring (**Figure 47**) onto the oil nozzle. Install the oil nozzle so the flange (A, **Figure 48**) on the nozzle engages the slot (B) in the cover.

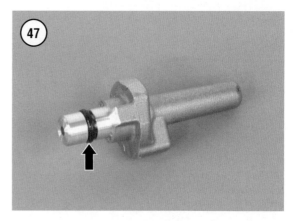

b. Install all the dowels. Place a new, lubricated O-ring onto the dowels at the water passage (A, **Figure 49**) and the oil passage (B).

c. Install a new cover gasket.

d. When installing the cover, make sure the flat side of the water pump impeller shaft (**Figure 50**) engages in the end slot of the balancer shaft (C, **Figure 49**).

e. Tighten the crankcase cover bolts in a crossing pattern and in several steps. Tighten the bolts to 12 N•m (106 in.-lb.).

f. Install new sealing washers on the oil banjo bolts.

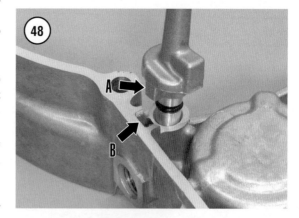

g. Attach the oil tube assembly to the engine. Tighten the front oil tube bolt (A, **Figure 41**) to 20 N•m (15 ft.-lb.). Tighten the upper bolt (**Figure 40**) and rear bolt (B, **Figure 41**) to 18 N•m (13 ft.-lb.).

h. Lubricate a new O-ring and insert the oil tube into the oil passage (**Figure 43**). Install the oil fitting end and tighten the oil fitting bolt to 8 N•m (71 in.-lb.).

i. Fill the engine with oil as described in Chapter Three.

j. Fill the cooling system as described in Chapter Three.

k. Check for leaks after running the engine.

## BALANCER AND PRIMARY DRIVE GEARS

**Removal**

1. Remove the right crankcase cover as described in this chapter.

2. If the balancer shaft must be removed, it must be removed from the left side of the engine. To access

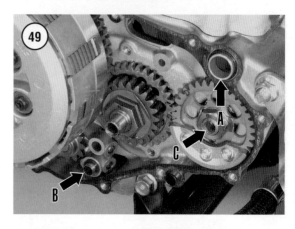

5

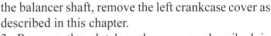

the balancer shaft, remove the left crankcase cover as described in this chapter.

3. Remove the clutch and cover as described in Chapter Six. After the clutch housing is loosened, leave it on the mainshaft until the nuts in the following step have been loosened. The housing is used to aid in the removal of the nuts.

4. Loosen the nuts securing the primary drive gear and balancer gear as follows:

    a. Bend the lockwashers (**Figure 51**) away from the nuts.

    b. If removed, temporarily reinstall the clutch housing on the mainshaft (A, **Figure 52**).

    c. Place a discarded gear or gear holding tool (B, **Figure 52**) at the mesh point of the primary drive gear and clutch housing gear. This jam gear will prevent the gears from turning so the primary drive gear nut can be loosened. Hold the gear at the lower mesh point when loosening the balancer shaft nut.

*CAUTION*
*Inserting a screwdriver or other tool into the gear teeth to prevent gear rotation may damage the gear teeth.*

    d. Loosen the nut on the primary drive gear (C, **Figure 52**) and/or on the balancer gear (D).

    e. Remove the gear holder and clutch housing.

5. Remove the nut and washer securing the primary drive gear, then remove the gear (A, **Figure 53**).

6. Remove the balancer drive gear (B, **Figure 53**) from the crankshaft.

7. Remove the nut and washer (A, **Figure 54**) from the balancer gear (B), then remove the gear.

8. The balancer shaft must be properly oriented so it will come out of the engine. Remove the balancer shaft as follows:

    a. Turn the shaft so the weight is positioned as shown in **Figure 55**.

    b. Pull the balancer shaft from the engine. If necessary, slightly turn the shaft back and forth during removal.

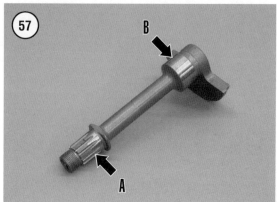

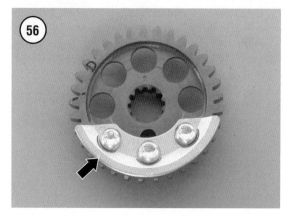

## Inspection

1. Wash and dry all parts.
2. Inspect the gear teeth and splines for wear and damage.
3. Inspect the balancer weight plate (**Figure 56**) bolts for looseness. Tighten the plate bolts securely.
4. Inspect the balancer shaft splines (A, **Figure 57**) and bearing surface (B) for damage.
5. Inspect the balancer shaft bearings (**Figure 58**) for roughness or play.
6. Replace any damaged parts.

## Installation

1. Insert the shaft into the engine so the flat spot on the shoulder of the shaft (**Figure 59**) will pass the crankshaft flywheels inside the engine.
2. Pass the balancer shaft through the engine.
3. Turn the balancer shaft and find the one spline that is different from the other splines (**Figure 60**). This master spline is used to index the balancer gear so it is in proper balance with the engine.
4. Find the index mark on the balancer gear which indicates the master spline (**Figure 61**). Install the balancer gear on the balancer shaft while aligning the master splines.

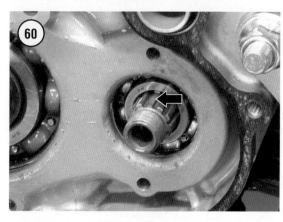

5. Place a new lockwasher on the balancer shaft, engaging the tab on the washer with the hole in the gear (A, **Figure 62**).

6. Finger-tighten the nut on the balancer shaft. The nut will be tightened later in this procedure.

7. Turn the balancer shaft so the index mark on the balancer gear is positioned as shown in B, **Figure 62**.

8. Find the master splines on the crankshaft and balancer drive gear. The balancer drive gear master spline is under the punch mark near the gear hub (A, **Figure 63**).

9. Locate the index mark (B, **Figure 63**) on the balancer gear. This mark must align with the index mark on the balancer drive gear (C, **Figure 63**) when it is installed.

10. Install the balancer drive gear onto the crankshaft while aligning the master splines. Make sure the index mark on the balancer drive gear (C, **Figure 63**) aligns with the mark (B) on the balancer gear.

11. If the index marks are not aligned, remove the balancer drive gear and reposition the balancer gear. The index marks must align or engine balance will not be correct.

12. Install the primary drive gear on the crankshaft (**Figure 64**) so the grooved side is out.

13. Place a new lockwasher on the crankshaft, then finger-tighten the nut (**Figure 65**).

14. Temporarily reinstall the clutch housing (A, **Figure 52**) on the mainshaft.

15. Using the same procedure during gear removal, place a gear holder tool (B, **Figure 52**) or discarded gear on the primary drive gear and clutch housing gear to prevent rotation.

16. Tighten the primary gear nut (C, **Figure 52**) to 75 N•m (55 ft.-lb.).

17. Tighten the balancer gear nut (D, **Figure 52**) to 50 N•m (37 ft.-lb.).

18. Remove the gear holder tool or discarded gear.

19. Bend the lockwashers against the flats on the nuts (**Figure 66**).

20. Install the clutch cover and clutch as described in Chapter Six.

21. If the balancer shaft was removed, install the left crankcase cover as described in this chapter.

22. Install the right crankcase cover as described in this chapter.

## OIL PUMP

### Removal/Installation

Refer to **Figure 67**.

1. Remove the clutch as described in Chapter Six, and remove the right crankcase cover (this Chapter).

2. Remove the snap ring (A, **Figure 68**) and washer (B) from the oil pump drive gear (C), then remove the gear.

3. Remove the tube and O-ring from the oil pump (**Figure 69**).

> *NOTE*
> *If the pump will be disassembled, loosen, but do not remove the screw (A, Figure 70) that holds the pump assembly together. Loosen the screw while the pump is still mounted.*

4. Remove the three mounting bolts from the oil pump (B and C, **Figure 70**), then remove the pump.

5. Remove the dowel from the engine case (**Figure 71**).

6. Disassemble and inspect the oil pump and drive gear as described in this section.

7. Reverse the preceding steps to install the oil pump while noting the following:

   a. Lubricate the oil pump rotors and crankcase surfaces with engine oil.

   b. Install the two short bolts in locations (B, **Figure 70**) and the long bolt in location (C). Tighten the bolts to 10 N•m (88 in.-lb.).

   c. Install a new, lubricated O-ring on the dowel (**Figure 71**).

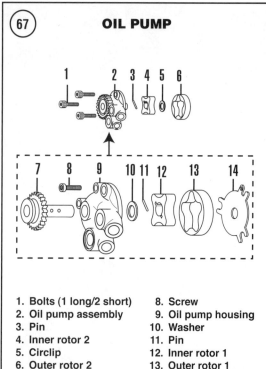

**OIL PUMP**

1. Bolts (1 long/2 short)
2. Oil pump assembly
3. Pin
4. Inner rotor 2
5. Circlip
6. Outer rotor 2
7. Drive gear and shaft
8. Screw
9. Oil pump housing
10. Washer
11. Pin
12. Inner rotor 1
13. Outer rotor 1
14. Cover

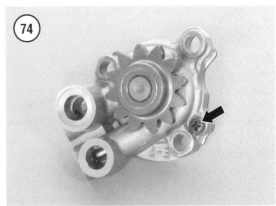

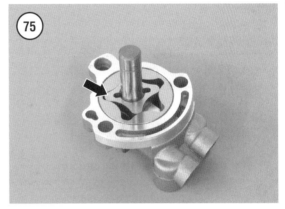

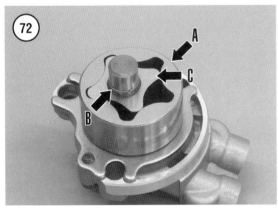

d. Install the oil pump drive gear and apply engine oil to all friction points on the drive gear.

e. Install right crankcase cover as described in this chapter, and then install the clutch (Chapter Six).

### Disassembly

Refer to **Figure 67**.

1. Remove the top outer rotor (A, **Figure 72**).
2. Remove the circlip (B, **Figure 72**), then remove the top inner rotor (C).
3. Remove the pin from the shaft (**Figure 73**).
4. Remove the oil pump cover screw (**Figure 74**), and remove the cover from the pump.
5. Remove the lower inner rotor and outer rotor (**Figure 75**).
6. Remove the pin (A, **Figure 76**) and washer (B) from the driveshaft
7. Remove the driveshaft from the housing.

### Cleaning and Inspection

*NOTE*
*Oil pump components (7 through 14, **Figure 67**) are available only as a unit assembly.*

An excessively worn or damaged oil pump will not maintain oil pressure and should be repaired or replaced before it causes engine damage. Inspect the oil pump carefully when troubleshooting a lubrication or oil pressure problem.

Refer to **Table 1** when measuring the oil pump components in this section. Replace parts that are out of specification or show damage as described in this section.

1. Clean and dry all parts. Place the parts on a clean, lint-free cloth.

2. Inspect the drive gear teeth (A, **Figure 77**) for wear or damage. Inspect the shaft (B, **Figure 77**) and bore (C) for scoring. Replace the gear if it is worn or damaged.

3. Inspect the oil pump driven gear and driveshaft. Inspect the teeth (A, **Figure 78**) for wear or damage. Inspect the shaft (B, **Figure 78**) for scoring. Replace the gear if it is worn or damaged.

4. Check the oil pump body for:
   a. Warped or cracked mating surfaces.
   b. Rotor bore damage.

5. Check the oil pump rotors for:
   a. Cracked or damaged outer surface.
   b. Worn or scored inner mating surfaces.

6. If the oil pump housing and rotors are in good condition, check the operating clearances as follows:
   a. Assemble the driveshaft and housing. Place the washer (B, **Figure 76**) on the shaft, then insert the pin (A) through the shaft.
   b. Install the inner set of rotors and the pump shaft into the pump housing.
   c. Using a flat feeler gauge, measure the clearance between the outer rotor and the oil pump housing (**Figure 79**) and refer to the body clearance specification in **Table 1**. If out of specification, replace the oil pump assembly.
   d. Using a flat feeler gauge, measure the clearance between the inner rotor tip and the outer rotor (**Figure 80**) and refer to the tip clearance specification in **Table 1**. If out of specification, replace the oil pump assembly.

## Assembly

Refer to **Figure 67**. During assembly of the oil pump, lubricate the parts with engine oil.

1. Assemble the pump shaft and housing. Place the washer (B, **Figure 76**) on the shaft, then insert the pin (A) through the shaft.

2. Install the inner set of rotors over the pump shaft and into the pump housing (**Figure 75**).

3. Install the cover onto the housing and tighten the oil pump cover screw (**Figure 74**) to 2 N•m (18 in.-lb.).

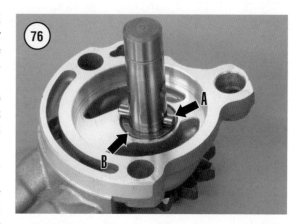

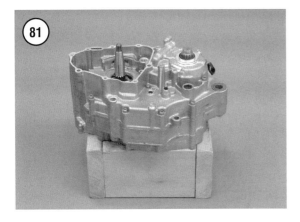

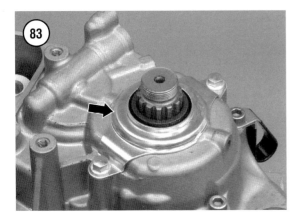

4. Insert the pin into the shaft (**Figure 73**).

5. Place the inner rotor (C, **Figure 72**) onto the pump shaft, then secure it to the shaft with a new circlip (B).

6. Turn the driven gear to assure that the pump turns freely.

7. Place the outer rotor onto the pump assembly (A, **Figure 72**).

8. Install the oil pump as described in this section.

## CRANKCASE

*NOTE*
*References to the right or left side of the engine refer to the engine as it sits in the frame, not how it may be placed on the workbench.*

The following procedures describe the disassembly and reassembly of the crankcase. The crankcase halves must be split for access to the crankshaft and transmission assemblies.

### Disassembly

1. Prior to disassembly of the crankcase, remove the following parts if not removed during engine removal:

    a. Starter (Chapter Nine).
    b. Piston (Chapter Four).
    c. Flywheel.
    d. Cam chain and guides.
    e. Clutch (Chapter Six).
    f. Oil pump.
    g. External shift mechanism (Chapter Six).
    h. Primary drive gear.
    i. Balancer.

2. As components are removed, keep each part or assembly separated from the other components. Keep seals and O-rings oriented with their respective parts.

3. Place the engine on wooden blocks with the left side facing up (**Figure 81**).

4. Remove the neutral switch (**Figure 82**).

5. Remove the sprocket shaft cover (**Figure 83**).

6. Remove the spacer from the countershaft (**Figure 84**).

7. Remove the O-ring from the groove in the countershaft (**Figure 85**).

*NOTE*
*For assembly, make a diagram during disassembly that identifies the location and size of each crankcase bolt.*

8. Working in a crossing pattern, loosen each crankcase bolt (**Figure 86**) 1/4 turn. Loosen the bolts until they can be removed by hand. Remove the bolts, along with the clutch cable holder and hose guide.

9. Grasp both halves of the crankcase and turn it over so the right case faces up.

10. Remove the snap ring (A, **Figure 87**) and spacer (B) from the countershaft.

11. Locate the tabbed pry points (**Figure 88**) around the mating surfaces of the crankcase.

12. Loosen the crankcase halves by tapping around the perimeter with a soft mallet.

13. Using a soft mallet, alternately tap on the reinforced bosses on the right crankcase half while carefully prying in small increments at the pry points. Work slowly and separate the case equally. Do not allow the case to bind. If binding occurs, reseat the case halves and start again.

> *CAUTION*
> *Do not hammer or pry on areas of the crankcase that are not reinforced. Do not pry on gasket surfaces.*

14. Slowly raise and remove the right crankcase half.

15. Remove the dowels between the case halves (**Figure 89**). The dowel at the bottom of the case half is also fitted with an O-ring (**Figure 90**).

> *NOTE*
> *The transmission shafts and forks are pinned together. These parts and the shift drum must be removed and installed as a unit.*

16. To remove the transmission, hold the crankcase upright (**Figure 91**), then alternately tap the ends of the countershaft and shift drum with a soft mallet.

17. Remove the transmission as an assembly (**Figure 92**).

18. Disassemble and inspect the transmission as described in Chapter Seven.

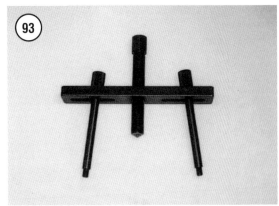

*CAUTION*
*Do not attempt to drive the crankshaft out of the crankcase. Doing so will damage the crankshaft and bearing.*

*NOTE*
*A crankshaft removal tool (**Figure 93**), Yamaha part No. 90890-01135, or equivalent tool, is required to remove the crankshaft.*

19. To remove the crankshaft, attach the crankshaft separating tool and bolts to the left crankcase half and crankshaft (**Figure 94**).

20. Tighten the center bolt to push the crankshaft out of the case half.

21. Inspect the crankcase and crankshaft assembly as described in this section.

22. Remove the oil pipe (**Figure 95**) from the right crankcase as follows:

    a. Remove the bolt from the outside of the case (**Figure 96**).

    b. Pull the pipe and O-rings from the case.

    c. Clean the holes (A, **Figure 97**) in the pipe and inspect for damage.

23. Remove the bolts (**Figure 98**) securing the strainer in the right case half.

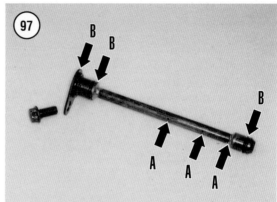

24. Remove the strainer from the case. Clean and inspect the fittings and screen (**Figure 99**).

## Assembly

The Yamaha crankshaft installation tool part No. YU-90050 is required to pull the crankshaft into the bearing. The tool consists of a pot (A, **Figure 100**), bolt (B), adapter (C) and spacer (D).

> *NOTE*
> *Prior to assembly, lubricate all O-rings and the lip of each seal with engine oil. Wrap splined shafts with tape to prevent damage to the seals. Lubricate all bearings and the transmission and crankshaft assemblies with engine oil.*

1. Install the oil strainer onto the right crankcase half. Tighten the bolts (**Figure 98**) to 10 N•m (88 in.-lb.).
2. Install new O-rings (B, **Figure 97**) onto the oil delivery pipe.
3. Install the oil pipe (**Figure 95**) into the right crankcase half. Tighten the bolt to 10 N•m (88 in.-lb.).
4. Insert the crankshaft into the bearing in the left case half. Hold the connecting rod at TDC using a rubber band (**Figure 101**).

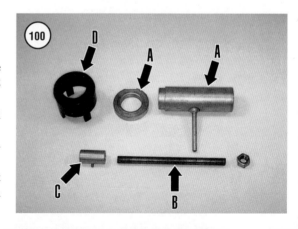

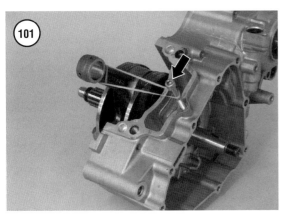

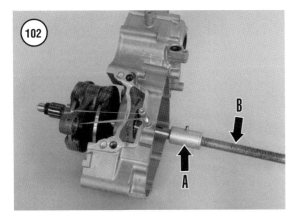

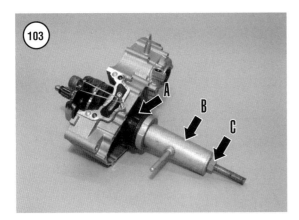

*CAUTION*
*Do not use a hammer to drive the crankshaft into the bearing.*

5. Thread the adapter (A, **Figure 102**) onto the crankshaft, then thread the bolt (B) into the adapter.

6. Place the spacer (A, **Figure 103**) and pot (B) over the bolt. The spacer must seat parallel to the case.

7. Thread the nut (C, **Figure 103**) onto the bolt and against the pot.

8. While holding the connecting rod at TDC, tighten the installation tool nut until the crankshaft seats against the bearing.

9. Remove the installation tool from the crankshaft. Install the flywheel nut on the end of the crankshaft to protect the threads during crankcase assembly.

10. Place the left case half on blocks as shown in **Figure 104**.

11. To ease installation, make sure the O-ring is not installed on the left end of the countershaft.

12. Mesh the two shafts together (**Figure 105**).

13. To ease installation, temporarily remove first gear from the countershaft (**Figure 106**).

14. Hold the assembly in one hand, with the countershaft positioned as shown in (**Figure 107**). With the transmission upside down in this position, assembly and installation will be easier.

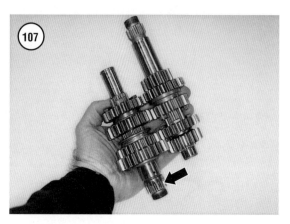

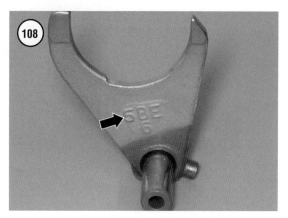

*NOTE*
*The shift forks are marked on both sides. One side is marked C, L or R according to location. The opposite side is marked with an identifying number (Figure 108).*

15. Install all shift forks so the identifying marks on the side of each fork (**Figure 108**) will face the right case half when installed (**Figure 109**).

16. Install the C shift fork into the mainshaft third gear groove (**Figure 110**).

17. Install the L shift fork into the countershaft fourth gear groove (**Figure 111**).

18. Install the R shift fork into the countershaft fifth gear groove (**Figure 112**).

19. Identify the threaded end of the shift drum (**Figure 113**). When installed, this end must face the right case.

20. Mesh the shift drum with the shifting forks. Make sure that the small end of the shift drum (A, **Figure 114**) faces the splines (B) on the countershaft.

21. While holding the transmission assembly together, turn it over and install it into the crankcase (**Figure 115**). When installed, make sure all shift drum pins engage with the shift drum. Spin the shafts and turn the shift drum by hand to check operation. It is normal for the shafts to move, as they are pinned to the forks.

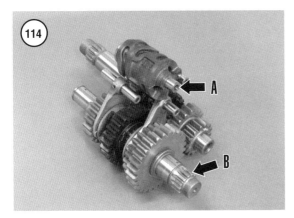

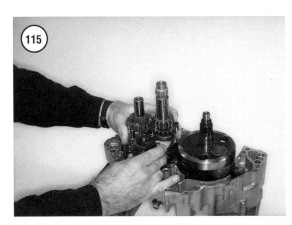

22. Install first gear onto the countershaft (**Figure 116**).

23. Insert the two dowels into the case (**Figure 117**). Install the O-ring onto the dowel at the bottom of the case half (**Figure 118**).

24. Make sure all mating surfaces are clean and dry.

25. Apply a nonhardening, liquid gasket sealant such as Yamabond 1215 or Yamabond 4 to all mating surfaces on the right case and around the threaded hole (**Figure 119**).

26. Make sure the connecting rod is at TDC.

27. Seat the right case half squarely onto the left case half. If necessary, use a soft mallet to seat the case. Do not raise the case once it is seated.

28. Insert the crankcase bolts (**Figure 120**) into the holes indicated below and finger-tighten. Note the position of the hose holder.

    a. 50 mm (A, **Figure 120**).
    b. 60 mm (B, **Figure 120**).
    c. 75 mm (C, **Figure 120**).
    d. Hose holder (D, **Figure 120**).

29. Tighten the bolts in a crossing pattern in three steps to 12 N•m (106 in.-lb.).

30. Install the O-ring into the countershaft groove (**Figure 121**).

31. Place the spacer onto the countershaft (**Figure 122**) with the notches inward.

32. Check the transmission for proper shifting as follows:

a. Install the shift drum stopper (A, **Figure 123**), stopper lever (B) and retaining bolts. The torsion spring for the lever is not required. Hold the stopper lever against the drum stopper during the shifting check.

b. Turn the shift drum stopper and align its raised ramp with the stopper lever (**Figure 124**). This is the neutral position. The mainshaft and countershaft should turn independently of one another.

c. Turn the mainshaft while turning the shift drum stopper clockwise. Stop when the stopper lever can seat between the ramps of the shift drum stopper (**Figure 125**). This is the first gear position. The mainshaft and countershaft should be meshed together.

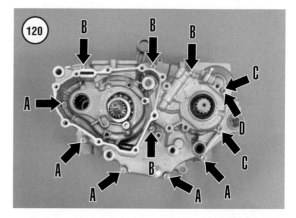

d. Turn the shift drum stopper counterclockwise. Turn the shift drum stopper past neutral, then place the stopper lever between the ramps to check the remaining gears for proper engagement. The mainshaft and countershaft should mesh whenever the transmission is in gear.

e. Remove the shift drum stopper and stopper lever when the check is completed. If the transmission did not engage properly, disassemble the crankcase and inspect the transmission for proper assembly or damaged parts.

33. Install the spacer (A, **Figure 126**) and snap ring (B) onto the countershaft. Install the snap ring so the flat side is toward the shaft end.

34. Install the neutral switch and tighten to 20 N•m (15 ft.-lb.).

35. Continue with engine assembly, as described in this chapter and Chapter Four.

## Inspection

1. Remove the oil seals as described in this chapter. Also refer to *Service Methods* in Chapter One.
2. Remove all sealer and residue from the gasket surfaces.
3. Clean the crankcase halves with solvent.
4. Using clean solvent, flush each bearing.
5. Dry the halves with compressed air.

> *WARNING*
> *When drying a bearing with compressed air, do not allow the inner bearing race to rotate. The air can spin the bearing at excessive speed, possibly causing bearing damage.*

6. Blow through each oil passage with compressed air.

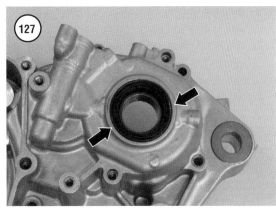

7. Lightly lubricate the bearings with engine oil before inspecting their condition.

8. Inspect the bearings for roughness, pitting, galling and play. Replace any bearing that is not in good condition. Always replace the opposite bearing at the same time. Refer to *Service Methods* in Chapter One and *Crankcase Seal and Bearing Replacement* in this chapter.

9. Inspect the clutch release lever bearing and, if necessary, replace as described in this chapter.

10. Inspect the cases for fractures around all mounting and bearing bosses, stiffening ribs and threaded holes. If repair is required, have the cases inspected by a dealership.

11. Check all threaded holes for damage or buildup. Clean threads with the correct size metric tap. Lubricate the tap with kerosene or aluminum tap fluid.

## CRANKCASE SEAL AND BEARING REPLACEMENT

Refer to *Service Methods* in Chapter One for general bearing and seal removal and installation techniques.

Refer to the appropriate chapter for specific removal and installation techniques that are unique to this engine.

### Countershaft Seal Replacement

When replacing the countershaft seal, located in the left case half, care must be taken when prying the seal from the case. Two oil passages are located in the bore at the locations shown in **Figure 127**. To prevent damage when prying the seal, keep the tool away from these two openings.

### Crankcase Bearings

1. When replacing crankcase bearings, note the following:

a. Remove bearing retainers (A, **Figure 128**) before attempting bearing removal.

b. If a hex bolt is used to secure the bearing retainer (B, **Figure 128**), apply threadlocking compound to the bolt threads and tighten to 10 N•m (88 in.-lb.).

c. If a Torx head bolt is used to secure the bearing retainer (C, **Figure 128**), tighten the bolt to 12 N•m (106 in.-lb.).

d. The main bearing retainers are secured by Torx head bolts (A, **Figure 129**). Tighten the bolts to 12 N•m (106 in.-lb.). Using a punch, depress the edge of the bolt head into the depression (B, **Figure 129**) in the bearing retainer. Do not disfigure the Torx hole in the bolt head.

e. Identify and record the size code of each bearing before it is removed from the case. This will eliminate confusion when installing the bearings in their correct bores.

f. Record the orientation of each bearing in its bore. Note if the size code faces toward the inside or outside of the case.

2. The following list identifies the left crankcase bearings. Refer to **Figure 130**:

a. Countershaft bearing (A, **Figure 130**).

b. Mainshaft bearing (B, **Figure 130**).

c. Crankshaft bearing (C, **Figure 130**).

d. Balancer shaft bearing (D, **Figure 130**).

3. The following list identifies the right crankcase bearings. Refer to **Figure 131**:

a. Countershaft bearing (A, **Figure 131**).

b. Mainshaft bearing (B, **Figure 131**).

c. Crankshaft bearing (C, **Figure 131**).

d. Balancer shaft bearing (D, **Figure 131**).

e. Shift drum bearing (E, **Figure 131**).

## Clutch Release Lever Bearing

The clutch release lever bearing (A, **Figure 132**) is located at the top of the left crankcase.

1. Insert the release lever shaft into the crankcase and check for excessive play or roughness in the bearing in the crankcase (**Figure 133**).

2. If bearing replacement is required, refer to *Service Methods* in Chapter One and remove the damaged bearing from the bore.

3. Clean the bore in the crankcase.

4. Install the new bearing so it sits just below the seal seat (B, **Figure 132**).

5. Install a new seal.

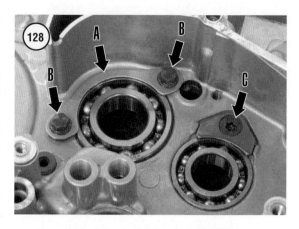

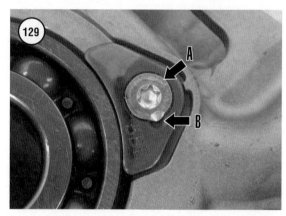

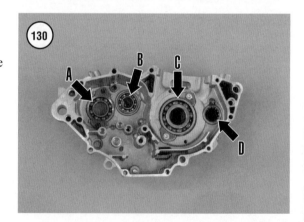

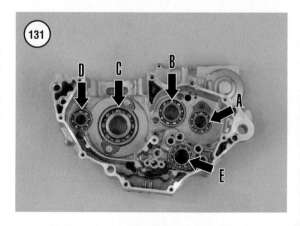

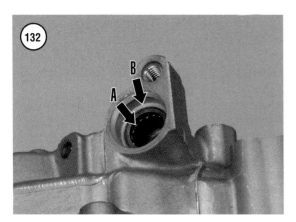

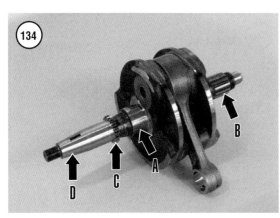

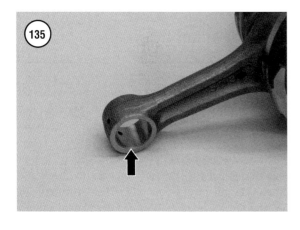

## CRANKSHAFT

### Inspection

Carefully handle the crankshaft assembly during inspection. Do not place the crankshaft where it could accidentally roll off the workbench. The crankshaft is an assembly-type, with its two halves joined by the crankpin. The crankpin is pressed into the flywheels and aligned, both vertically and horizontally, with calibrated equipment.

If the crankshaft assembly shows signs of wear, or is out of alignment, have a dealership inspect, overhaul or replace the crankshaft. Inspect the crankshaft assembly as follows:

1. Clean the crankshaft with solvent.
2. Dry the crankshaft with compressed air.
3. Blow through all passages with compressed air.
4. Inspect the crankshaft bearing surfaces (A, **Figure 134**) for scoring, heat discoloration or other damage.
5. Inspect the splines (B, **Figure 134**), sprocket (C) and shaft taper (D) for signs of wear or damage. The two halves of the crankshaft are available separately, if one side must be replaced.
6. Inspect the piston pin end of the connecting rod (**Figure 135**) as follows:
   a. Inspect the rod end for scoring, galling or heat damage.
   b. A specification for the bore diameter is not available. If the piston pin does not show signs of wear, and fits in the bore with no perceptible radial play, the rod end is considered in good condition.
7. Inspect the crankpin end of the connecting rod as follows:
   a. Slide the connecting rod to one side and check the connecting rod side clearance with a flat feeler gauge (**Figure 136**). Refer to **Table 1** for service limits.
   b. Inspect the connecting rod for radial clearance (**Figure 137**). Mount the crankshaft in a set of

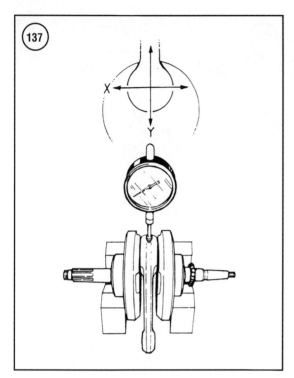

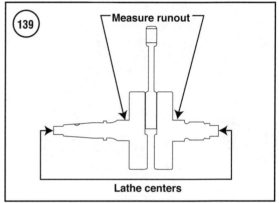

Measure runout

Lathe centers

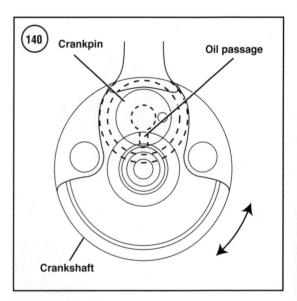

Crankpin

Oil passage

Crankshaft

V-blocks and accurately measure play. Refer to **Table 1** for specification. If tools are not available, grasp the rod and feel for radial play in all directions. There should be no perceptible play. If in doubt about the condition, check with a dealership.

8. Measure the width of the flywheels (**Figure 138**). Measure at the machined edge and at 90° intervals. Record the measurements. Have the crankshaft retrued if the measurements are not identical. Refer to **Table 1** for service limits.

9. Place the crankshaft between lathe centers (**Figure 139**) or equivalent and measure crankshaft runout with a dial indicator. Measure at both bearing surfaces. If the runout exceeds the service limit listed in **Table 1**, have the crankshaft trued by a dealership.

### Overhaul

Crankshaft overhaul requires a 20 ton capacity press, holding jigs, crankshaft alignment jig, dial indicators and a micrometer or vernier caliper. For this reason, refer crankshaft overhaul to a dealership. If having the crankshaft rebuilt, instruct the dealership or shop to align the crankshaft to the crankpin oil passages as shown in **Figure 140**.

### ENGINE BREAK-IN

If the rings are replaced, a new piston installed, the cylinder block rebored or honed or major lower end

work performed, the engine should be broken in just as though it were new. The performance and service life of the engine depends greatly on a careful and sensible break-in.

During break-in, oil consumption will be higher than normal. It is therefore important to check and correct the oil level frequently (Chapter Three). At no time during the break-in or later should the oil level be allowed to drop below the minimum level. If the oil level is low, the oil will overheat resulting in insufficient lubrication and increased wear.

For the first 0-10 hours, do not operate the engine above half throttle. Stop the engine and allow it to cool for approximately 5 to 10 minutes after each hour of operation. Avoid prolonged steady running at one speed, no matter how moderate, and hard acceleration.

Between 10-20 hours do not operate the engine above 3/4 throttle.

After break-in avoid extended periods of full throttle operation. Occasionally vary engine speed.

After one month, change the engine oil and filter as described in Chapter Three. It is essential to perform this service to ensure that all of the particles produced during break-in are removed from the lubrication system.

### Table 1 ENGINE LOWER END SPECIFICATIONS

|  | New mm (in.) | Service limit mm (in.) |
|---|---|---|
| Connecting rod |  |  |
|   Side clearance | 0.15-0.45 (0.006-0.018) | 0.50 (0.002) |
|   Big end radial play | 0.010-0.025 (0.0004-0.0010) | – |
| Crankshaft dimensions |  |  |
|   Width | 61.95-62.00 (2.439-2.441) | – |
|   Runout | 0.03 (0.0012) | 0.05 (0.002) |
| Oil pump |  |  |
|   Body clearance | 0.09-0.17 (0.0035-0.0067) | 0.24 (0.0094) |
|   Tip clearance | 0.07-0.12 (0.0028-0.0047) | 0.20 (0.008) |
|   Bypass valve pressure setting* | 40-80 kPa (5.8-11.6 psi) | – |

*No testing procedures supplied by the manufacturer.

### Table 2 ENGINE LOWER END TORQUE SPECIFICATIONS

| Item | N•m | in.-lb. | ft.-lb. |
|---|---|---|---|
| Balancer gear nut | 50 | – | 37 |
| Clutch cable/battery terminal bracket bolt | 10 | 88 | – |
| Crankcase bearing retainer bolts* |  |  |  |
|   Hex bolt | 10 | 88 | – |
|   Torx head bolt | 12 | 106 | – |
| Crankcase cover bolts | 12 | 106 | – |
| Engine mounting block bolts | 33 | – | 24 |
| Flywheel nut | 65 | – | 48 |
| Front engine mounting bolt | 66 | – | 48 |
| Front engine mounting bracket bolts | 38 | – | 28 |
| Left crankcase cover bolts | 10 | 88 | – |
| Neutral switch | 20 | – | 15 |
| Oil fitting bolt* | 8 | 71 | – |
| Oil pipe bolt | 10 | 88 | – |
| Oil pump bolts | 10 | 88 | – |
| Oil pump cover screw | 2 | 18 | – |
| Oil strainer bolts | 10 | 88 | – |
| Oil tube banjo bolts* |  |  |  |
|   Front | 20 | – | 15 |
|   Upper and rear | 18 | – | 13 |
| Parking brake cable bracket bolts | 10 | 88 | – |
| Primary gear nut | 75 | – | 55 |
| Rear cam chain guide bolts | 10 | 88 | – |
| Rear engine mounting bolt (swing arm pivot)* | 100 | – | 74 |
| Right crankcase cover bolts | 10 | 88 | – |
| Starter clutch mounting bolts* | 16 | – | 12 |
| Torque limiter cover bolts | 10 | 88 | – |
| Upper engine bracket bolts | 26 | – | 19 |
| Upper engine mounting bolt | 40 | – | 29 |

*Refer to text.

5

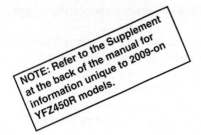

NOTE: Refer to the Supplement at the back of the manual for information unique to 2009-on YFZ450R models.

**CHAPTER SIX**

# CLUTCH AND EXTERNAL SHIFT MECHANISM

This chapter provides service procedures for the clutch, clutch release mechanism and external shift mechanism.

**Table 1** and **Table 2** are at the end of this chapter.

## CLUTCH COVER

### Removal/Installation

The clutch assembly is located behind the clutch cover on the right side of the engine. The clutch may be serviced with the engine mounted in the frame after removing the clutch cover.

1. Drain the engine oil as described in Chapter Three.

2. Remove the negative battery terminal bolt (A, **Figure 1**). The bolt also retains the clutch cable bracket.

3. Detach the clutch cable from the clutch release lever (B, **Figure 1**).

> *NOTE*
> *Loosen the clutch cover bolts 1/4 turn at a time in a crossing pattern.*

4. Remove the seven bolts from the perimeter of the clutch cover (A, B and C, **Figure 2**).

5. Remove the cover and account for the two dowels (**Figure 3**) which may remain in the cover or crankcase.

6. Remove the cover gasket.

7. Reverse the removal steps to install the clutch cover assembly while noting the following:

    a. Install a new cover gasket.

    b. Be sure the dowels are in place (**Figure 3**).

    c. Install the cover bolts in the locations identified in **Figure 2**: (A) 30 mm, (B) 40 mm, (C) 80 mm.

    d. Tighten the cover bolts in steps in a crossing pattern to 10 N•m (88 in.-lb.).

    e. Fill the engine with oil as described in Chapter Three.

    f. Tighten the negative battery terminal bolt to 10 N•m (88 in.-lb.).

    g. Adjust the clutch lever as described in Chapter Three.

## CLUTCH

### Operation

The clutch is a wet (operates in the engine oil) multi-plate design. The clutch assembly is located on the right side of the engine. The clutch hub is mounted on the splines on the transmission mainshaft. The

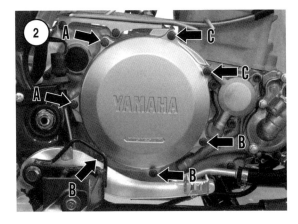

outer clutch housing is driven by the primary drive gear on the crankshaft.

Pulling in the clutch lever on the handlebar actuates the clutch release mechanism on the left crankcase cover. The clutch release shaft presses against a pushrod that passes through the transmission mainshaft. Forcing the pushrod assembly against the pressure plate disengages the clutch.

## Removal

Refer to **Figure 4**.

1. Remove the clutch cover as described in this chapter.
2. Remove the clutch spring bolts (A, **Figure 5**). Loosen the bolts evenly in several steps. Remove the bolts and springs from the clutch.
3. Remove the pressure plate (B, **Figure 5**).

> *NOTE*
> *Do not lose the ball which may fall out when removing the short pushrod.*

4. Remove the short pushrod assembly (A, **Figure 6**) from the mainshaft.

> *CAUTION*
> *Unless replacement is required, keep the clutch plates in the order removed.*

5. Remove the steel plates and friction plates (B, **Figure 6**) from the clutch hub.
6. Remove the damper spring and spring seat (**Figure 7**) from the clutch hub.
7. If necessary, remove the ball inside the mainshaft (**Figure 8**) using a magnet. Also remove the long pushrod (**Figure 9**) from the mainshaft.
8. Bend the tabs on the lockwasher (A, **Figure 10**) away from the nut.

> *CAUTION*
> *To prevent damage in Step 9, be sure to position the clutch holder tool squarely onto the clutch hub splines.*

9. Attach a clutch holding tool (B, **Figure 10**) to the clutch hub.
10. While grasping the holding tool, loosen the nut (C, **Figure 10**).
11. Remove the clutch nut and lockwasher.
12. Remove the holding tool from the clutch hub.
13. Remove the clutch hub (**Figure 11**) from the transmission mainshaft.
14. Remove the thrust washer (**Figure 12**) from the shaft.
15. Remove the clutch housing (**Figure 13**).
16. Inspect the clutch assembly as described in this section.

## Inspection

Refer to **Table 1** for clutch specifications.
1. Clean and dry all parts.
2. Inspect the friction plates (**Figure 14**) as follows:

> *NOTE*
> *If any friction plate is damaged or out of specification as described in the following steps, replace all of the friction plates as a set.*

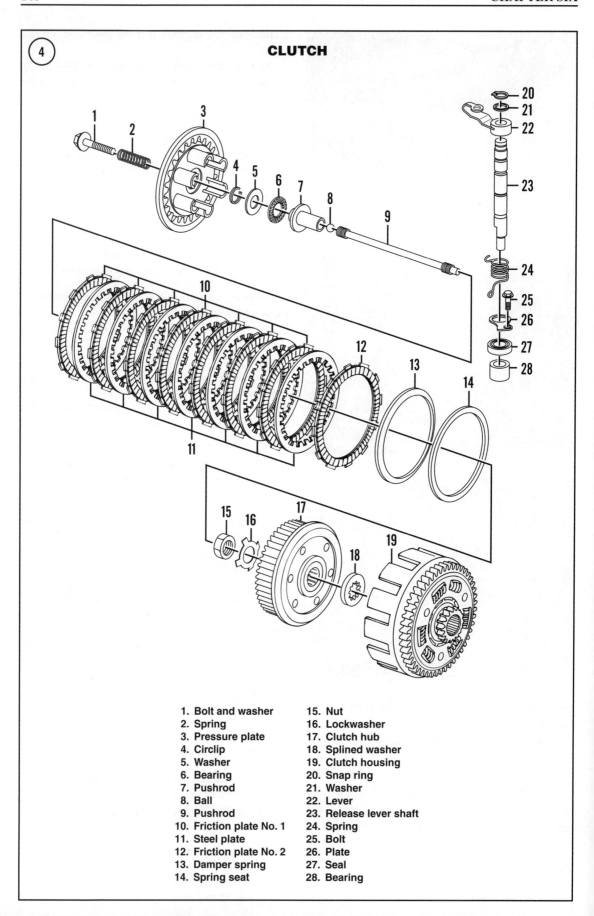

## CLUTCH

1. Bolt and washer
2. Spring
3. Pressure plate
4. Circlip
5. Washer
6. Bearing
7. Pushrod
8. Ball
9. Pushrod
10. Friction plate No. 1
11. Steel plate
12. Friction plate No. 2
13. Damper spring
14. Spring seat
15. Nut
16. Lockwasher
17. Clutch hub
18. Splined washer
19. Clutch housing
20. Snap ring
21. Washer
22. Lever
23. Release lever shaft
24. Spring
25. Bolt
26. Plate
27. Seal
28. Bearing

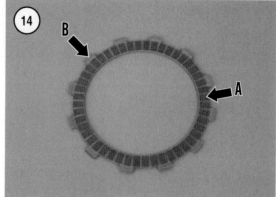

a. Inspect the friction material (A, **Figure 14**) for excessive or uneven wear, cracks and other damage. Inspect the plate tangs (B, **Figure 14**) for damage. The sides of the tangs must be smooth where they contact the clutch housing slots; otherwise, the plates cannot engage and disengage correctly. If the tangs are damaged, inspect the clutch housing slots carefully as described in this section.

b. Measure the thickness of each friction plate (**Figure 15**). Measure at several places around the plate and refer to **Table 1**.

3. Inspect the steel clutch plates (**Figure 16**) as follows:

a. Inspect the clutch plates for cracks, damage or color change. Overheated clutch plates will have a blue discoloration.

b. Check the clutch plates for an oil glaze buildup. Remove buildup by lightly sanding both sides of each plate with 400 grit sandpaper placed on a surface plate or piece of glass.

c. Place each clutch plate on a surface plate or piece of glass and check for warp (**Figure 17**). If the clutch plates are warped, compare the measurement to the service limit in **Table 1**. If any are warped beyond the specification, replace the entire set.

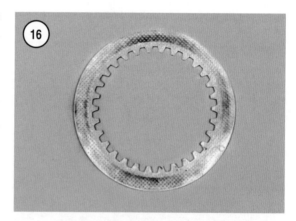

d. The clutch plate inner teeth mesh with the clutch hub splines. Check the clutch plate teeth for any roughness or damage. The teeth contact surfaces must be smooth; otherwise, the plates cannot engage and disengage correctly. If the clutch plate teeth are damaged, inspect the clutch hub splines carefully as described in this section.

4. Inspect the clutch hub for the following conditions:

a. Galled or otherwise damaged plate contact surface (A, **Figure 18**).

b. Inspect the splines (B, **Figure 18**) for rough spots, grooves or other damage. Repair minor

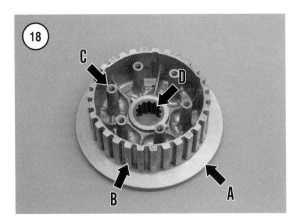

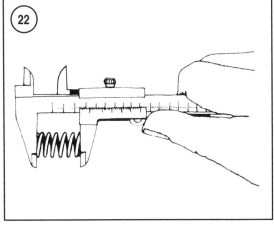

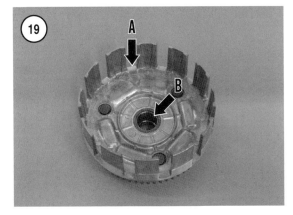

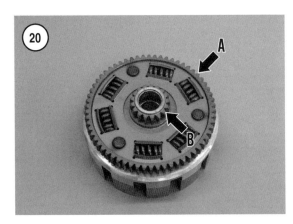

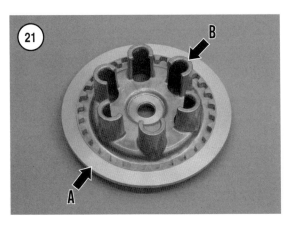

damage with a file or oil stone. If the damage is excessive, replace the clutch hub.

   c. Damaged bolt towers and threads (C, **Figure 18**).

   d. Inspect the inner splines (D, **Figure 18**) for damage.

5. Inspect the clutch housing for the following conditions:

   a. Inspect the slots (A, **Figure 19**) for cracks or galling. Repair minor damage with a file. If the damage is excessive, replace the clutch housing.

   b. Inspect the bushing (B, **Figure 19**). The bushing is not available separately.

   c. Inspect the clutch housing gear (A, **Figure 20**) for excessive wear, pitting, chipped gear teeth or other damage. If the clutch housing gear is excessively worn or damaged, check the primary drive gear assembly for the same wear conditions.

   d. Inspect the oil pump drive gear (B, **Figure 20**).

6. Inspect the pressure plate (**Figure 21**) for the following conditions:

   a. Galled or otherwise damaged plate contact surface (A, **Figure 21**).

   b. Cracks or other damage.

   c. Inspect the spring pockets (B, **Figure 21**) for damage.

7. Inspect the clutch springs for damage and length (**Figure 22**). Replace the springs if the free length is less than the limit specified in **Table 1**.

8. Inspect the ball and ends of the short pushrod and long pushrod. Replace the ball or pushrod if galled or otherwise damaged.

9. Inspect the short pushrod (**Figure 23**). Check that the bearing and washer operate smoothly. Replace the parts if roughness or wear is detected. Whenever the circlip on the rod is removed, always install a new circlip during reassembly.

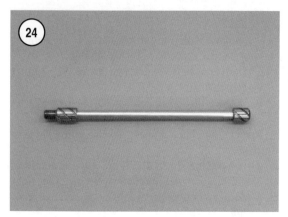

10. Inspect the long pushrod (**Figure 24**). Check the rod for wear and straightness. Replace the rod if it is worn or bent. If the left pushrod end is damaged, remove and inspect the clutch release lever assembly as described in this chapter.

## Installation

Refer to **Figure 4**. Where noted in the following procedure, lubricate components with engine oil.
1. If removed, install the clutch release lever and shaft assembly as described in this chapter.

*NOTE*
*Make sure the primary gear and oil pump gear mesh properly when installing the clutch housing in Step 2.*

2. Lubricate the transmission mainshaft and clutch housing bore, then slide the housing (**Figure 13**) onto the shaft.
3. Place the thrust washer (**Figure 12**) onto the shaft.
4. Install the clutch hub (**Figure 11**) onto the shaft.
5. Place a new lockwasher (**Figure 25**) onto the shaft, engaging the bent tabs with the clutch hub.
6. Finger-tighten the nut (C, **Figure 10**) onto the shaft.

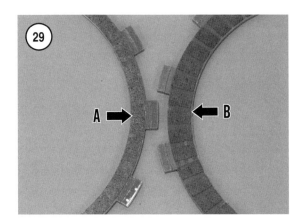

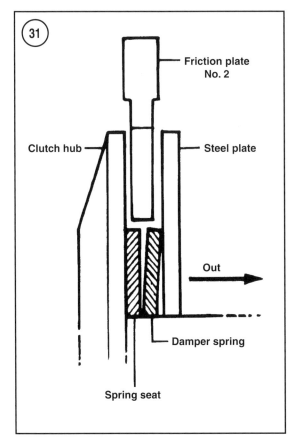

Friction plate No. 2

Clutch hub

Steel plate

Out

Damper spring

Spring seat

*CAUTION*
*To prevent damage in Step 7, be sure to position the clutch holder tool squarely onto the clutch hub splines.*

7. Attach a clutch holding tool (B, **Figure 10**) to the clutch hub.

8. While grasping the holding tool, tighten the nut to 75 N•m (55 ft.-lb.).

9. Remove the holding tool from the clutch hub.

10. Bend the tabs on the lockwasher over the sides of the nut.

11. Lubricate the long pushrod, then insert it into the mainshaft so the large end enters first (**Figure 26**).

12. Lubricate, then install the ball (**Figure 8**) into the mainshaft.

13. Install the damper spring seat (**Figure 27**) onto the clutch hub.

14. Install the damper spring (**Figure 28**) onto the clutch hub so the side marked outside (concave side) faces out.

15. Identify the single friction plate No. 2 in the clutch pack. Friction plate No. 2 has a larger inside diameter (A, **Figure 29**) than the remaining No. 1 friction plates (B).

16. Lubricate the friction plates and steel plates with engine oil.

17. Install friction plate No. 2 (**Figure 30**) around the damper spring seat and damper spring. Push it on until it is seated correctly.

18. Refer to **Figure 31** and note the assembly order of the spring seat, damper spring and friction plate No. 2.

19. Install a steel plate and push it on until it is completely seated against friction plate No. 2.

20. Beginning with a friction plate, alternately install friction plates and steel plates into the clutch housing and clutch hub.

21. Lubricate the short pushrod and bearing assembly (**Figure 32**), then insert it with the ball into the mainshaft.

22. Install the pressure plate (**Figure 33**).

23. Install the clutch springs on the clutch hub bosses (A, **Figure 34**).

24. Finger-tighten the bolts with washers (B, **Figure 34**).

25. Tighten the clutch spring bolts to 8 N•m (71 in.-lb.). Tighten the bolts evenly in several stages using a crossing pattern.

26. Install the clutch cover as described in this chapter.

## CLUTCH RELEASE LEVER ASSEMBLY

The clutch must be partially disassembled to remove the clutch release lever shaft. Refer to **Figure 4**.

### Removal/Inspection/Installation

1. Remove the long pushrod from the mainshaft by performing Steps 1-4 and Step 7 in *Removal* in *Clutch* in this chapter.
2. Remove the drive sprocket cover (**Figure 35**).
3. Remove the retaining bolt (A, **Figure 36**).
4. Remove the release lever assembly (B, **Figure 36**) from the left crankcase cover.
5. To disassemble the release lever assembly, detach the snap ring (A, **Figure 37**) and separate the lever (B) and shaft (C). Account for any washers.
6. Inspect the splines on the lever and shaft end for damage.
7. Inspect the shaft for damage and excessive wear, including the pushrod cavity (**Figure 38**). Excessive wear will prevent clutch disengagement. Also check wear on the pushrod end as described in the Clutch section.
8. Check the release lever spring (D, **Figure 37**) for damage and tension.
9. Inspect the shaft seal in the crankcase (**Figure 39**). Replace if worn or damaged.
10. Inspect and, if necessary, replace the release lever shaft bearing in the crankcase as described in Chapter Five.
11. When assembling the release lever assembly note following:

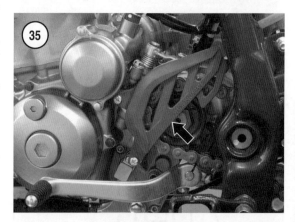

   a. Align the punch marks (**Figure 40**) on the lever and shaft end.
   b. Make sure the washer is installed before installing the snap ring (A, **Figure 37**).
   c. Note the proper position of the spring (D, **Figure 37**).

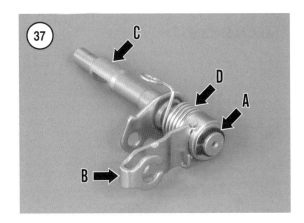

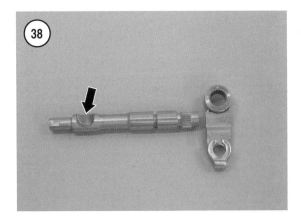

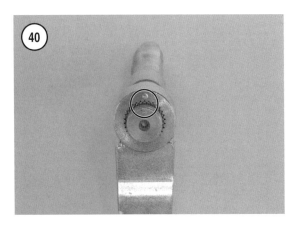

12. Reverse the removal steps to install the clutch release lever assembly while noting the following:

   a. Lubricate the shaft with engine oil.

   b. Tighten the clutch release shaft retainer bolt (A, **Figure 36**) to 10 N•m (88 in.-lb.).

## EXTERNAL SHIFT MECHANISM

The external shift mechanism includes the shift pedal, shaft and linkages that connect to the shift drum located inside the crankcase. Other than the shift pedal, all other components of the external shift mechanism are located in the right crankcase cover.

### Removal

Refer to **Figure 41**.

1. Remove the shift pedal clamp bolt (A, **Figure 42**), then remove the shift pedal (B).

2. Remove the oil pump drive gear as described in *Oil Pump* in Chapter Five.

3. Pull the shift shaft, spring and washer assembly (**Figure 43**) from the engine. Remove the washer (A, **Figure 44**) if it remains in the engine.

4. Remove the roller from the lever (B, **Figure 44**).

*NOTE*
*Be careful when handling the pawl holder assembly. It contains loose pairs of springs, pawl pins and pawls.*

5. Remove the bolts (A, **Figure 45**) securing the shift guide (B), then remove the guide and the pawl holder assembly (C).

6. Remove the shift drum stopper (A, **Figure 46**) and stopper lever (B) as follows:

   a. Loosen, but do not completely remove, the shift drum stopper bolt (C, **Figure 46**).

   b. Push the stopper lever to one side using a screwdriver.

   c. Remove the shift drum stopper and bolt.

   d. Remove the bolt securing the stopper lever, then remove the lever.

7. Inspect the parts as described in this section.

### Inspection

1. Inspect the shift shaft and spring assembly. Refer to **Figure 47** during the following checks:

   a. Inspect the splines (A, **Figure 47**) on the shaft for damage.

   b. Inspect the shaft for straightness.

   c. Inspect the engagement hole (B, **Figure 47**) for wear. The hole should be symmetrical and not worn.

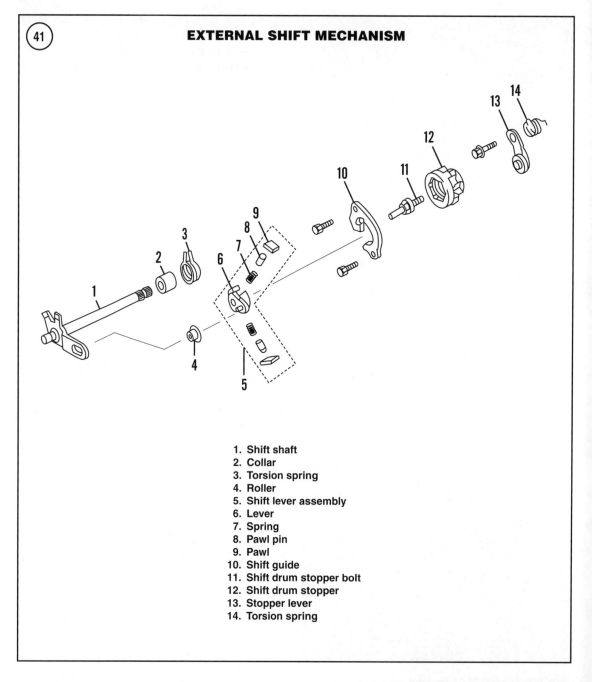

**41**

## EXTERNAL SHIFT MECHANISM

1. Shift shaft
2. Collar
3. Torsion spring
4. Roller
5. Shift lever assembly
6. Lever
7. Spring
8. Pawl pin
9. Pawl
10. Shift guide
11. Shift drum stopper bolt
12. Shift drum stopper
13. Stopper lever
14. Torsion spring

d. Inspect the spring (C, **Figure 47**) for wear and fatigue cracks.

e. Replace any parts that are worn or damaged.

2. Inspect the pawl holder assembly, roller and shift guide. Refer to **Figure 48** during the following checks:

a. Inspect the shift guide (A, **Figure 48**) for wear.

b. Inspect the roller (B, **Figure 48**) for wear. The roller should be symmetrical with no perceptible wear.

c. Inspect the springs and pawl pins (C, **Figure 48**) for wear.

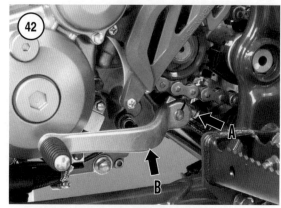

**42**

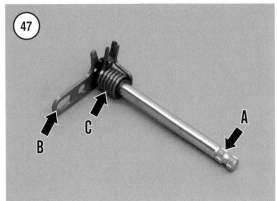

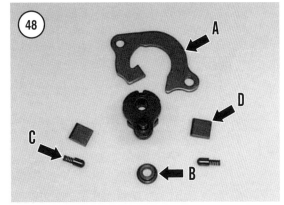

6

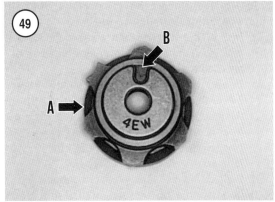

    d. Inspect the pawls (D, **Figure 48**) for wear at their square end. The ends must be square in order to stay engaged in the shift drum stopper.

    e. Replace any parts that are worn or damaged.

3. Inspect the shift drum stopper as follows:

    a. Inspect the detents (A, **Figure 49**) in the back of the stopper. The detents must not be worn, or faulty shifting will occur.

    b. Inspect the depressions in the front side of the stopper for wear or damage. If the depressions are rounded at their shoulders, the pawls in the shift lever assembly can slip. Replace the stopper if it is worn or damaged.

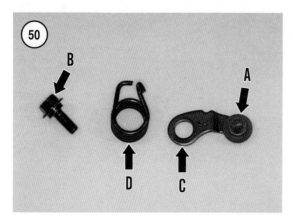

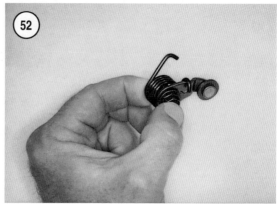

4. Inspect the stopper lever assembly. Refer to **Figure 50** during the following checks:

   a. Inspect the roller (A, **Figure 50**) on the lever. It must be symmetrical, turn freely, but be firmly attached to the lever.

   b. Inspect the fit of the shouldered bolt (B, **Figure 50**) in the lever hole (C). The bolt must fit in the hole firmly, but not bind or drag when the lever is pivoted.

   c. Inspect the spring (D, **Figure 50**) for wear or fatigue.

   d. Replace any parts that are worn or damaged.

5. Inspect the pin on the end of the shift drum (**Figure 51**) for wear or damage. The pin must be in good condition in order to properly engage with the notch in the back of the shift drum stopper (B, **Figure 49**).

**Installation**

Refer to **Figure 41**.

1. Assemble the stopper lever, bolt and spring as shown in **Figure 52**. Apply threadlocking compound to the bolt threads.

2. Install the stopper lever assembly (A, **Figure 53**), seating the spring (B) against the engine case. Finger-tighten the bolt.

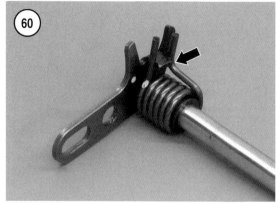

3. Pry and hold the stopper lever to one side so the shift drum stopper and bolt (**Figure 54**) can be installed. The notch on the back of the shift drum stopper (B, **Figure 49**) must engage with the pin on the shift drum (**Figure 51**). Note that a punch mark on the front of the shift drum stopper (**Figure 55**) corresponds with the notch on the back.

4. Release the stopper lever and let it rest against the shift drum stopper.

5. Tighten the stopper lever bolt to 10 N•m (88 in.-lb.). Push the lever with a screwdriver to verify the lever will pivot properly.

6. Tighten the shift drum stopper bolt to 30 N•m (22 ft.-lb.).

7. Insert the springs and pawl pins and pawls into the pawl holder, making sure that the rounded ends of the pawls are seated in the holder (**Figure 56**). The pawls must compress and retract smoothly in the lever. Lubricate the pawl assembly with engine oil.

8. Fit the holder assembly into the shift guide (**Figure 57**).

9. Lubricate the shift drum stopper bolt with engine oil. Slide the pawl holder and guide assembly onto the shaft of the shift drum stopper bolt (**Figure 58**). Apply medium-strength threadlocking compound to the threads of the guide bolts, then tighten the bolts to 10 N•m (88 in.-lb.).

10. Place the roller onto the pawl holder, installing the wide portion of the roller first (**Figure 59**). Lubricate the roller with engine oil.

11. If removed, slide the spring and washer onto the shift shaft. The spring ends (**Figure 60**) must press against the lever on opposite sides.

12. Lubricate the shaft and slowly slide it through the engine cases. As the lever and spring approach the engine, position the spring ends (A, **Figure 61**) on each side of the pin (B). Engage the roller (C, **Figure 61**) with the slot in the lever (D). Lubricate the contact areas of the spring and the lever.

13. Install the oil pump drive gear as described in Chapter Five.

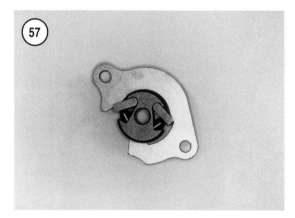

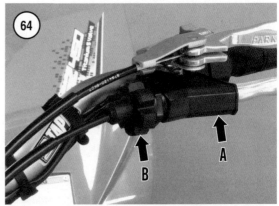

14. Install the shift pedal and clamp bolt.

## CLUTCH CABLE

### Removal/Installation

1. Remove the negative battery terminal bolt (A, **Figure 62**). The bolt also retains the clutch cable bracket.

2. Detach the clutch cable from the clutch release lever (B, **Figure 62**).

3. Disengage the clutch cable from the holder on the cylinder head (**Figure 63**).

4. Push back the boot (A, **Figure 64**) on the adjuster (B).

5. Turn the adjuster (**Figure 65**) all the way in.

6. Disengage the cable end from the lever assembly by passing the cable through the slots in the lever and adjuster.

7. Note the routing of the cable, then remove the cable.

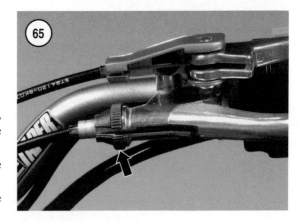

8. Reverse the removal steps to install the cable while noting the following:

    a. Lubricate the cable prior to installation (Chapter Three).

    b. Tighten the negative battery terminal bolt to 10 N•m (88 in.-lb.).

    c. Adjust clutch lever free play as described in Chapter Three.

## Table 1 CLUTCH SPECIFICATIONS

| Item | Standard mm (in.) | Service limit mm (in.) |
|------|-------------------|------------------------|
| Clutch spring free length | | |
| 2004-2006 models | 51.8 (2.04) | 50.0 (1.97) |
| 2007-on models | 47.8 (1.88) | 46.0 (1.81) |
| Friction plate thickness | 2.90-3.10 (0.114-0.122) | 2.80 (0.110) |
| Steel plate warp | – | 0.20 (0.008) |
| Shift pedal height (above footrest) | 25.0 (0.98 in.) | |

## Table 2 CLUTCH TORQUE SPECIFICATIONS

| Item | N•m | in.-lb. | ft.-lb. |
|------|-----|---------|---------|
| Clutch cover bolts | 10 | 88 | – |
| Clutch hub nut | 75 | – | 55 |
| Clutch release shaft retainer bolt | 10 | 88 | – |
| Clutch spring bolts | 8 | 71 | – |
| Negative battery terminal bolt | 10 | 88 | – |
| Shift drum stopper bolt | 30 | – | 22 |
| Shift guide bolts* | 10 | 88 | – |
| Shift pedal clamp bolt | 12 | 106 | – |
| Stopper lever bolt | 10 | 88 | – |
| *Refer to text. | | | |

6

# CHAPTER SEVEN

# TRANSMISSION AND INTERNAL GEARSHIFT MECHANISM

This chapter covers service for the transmission and internal shift mechanism. The external shift mechanism is covered in Chapter Six. Transmission and internal shift mechanism service requires crankcase disassembly as described in Chapter Five.

**Table 1** and **Table 2** are at the end of this chapter.

## TRANSMISSION SERVICE NOTES

1. Parts with two different sides, such as gears, circlips and shift forks, can be installed backward. To maintain the correct alignment and position of the parts during disassembly, store each part in order and in a divided container.

2. The circlips are a tight fit on the transmission shafts and will bend and twist during removal. Install new circlips during transmission assembly.

3. To avoid bending and twisting the new circlips during installation, use the following installation technique:

   a. Open the new circlip with a pair of circlip pliers while holding the back of the circlip with a pair of pliers (**Figure 1**).

   b. Slide the circlip down the shaft and seat it into the correct transmission groove. Check the circlip to make sure it seats in the groove completely.

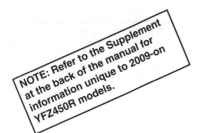

4. When installing circlips, align the circlip opening with the shaft groove as shown in **Figure 2**.

5. Circlips and flat washers have one sharp edge and one rounded edge (**Figure 3**). Install the circlips with the sharp edge facing away from the gear producing the thrust.

## MAINSHAFT

*NOTE*
*A hydraulic press is required to disassemble and assemble the mainshaft*

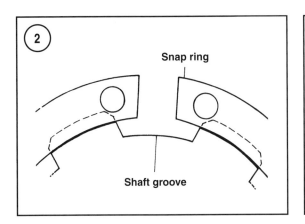

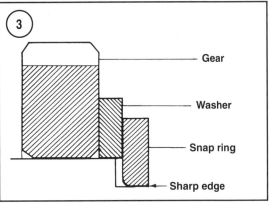

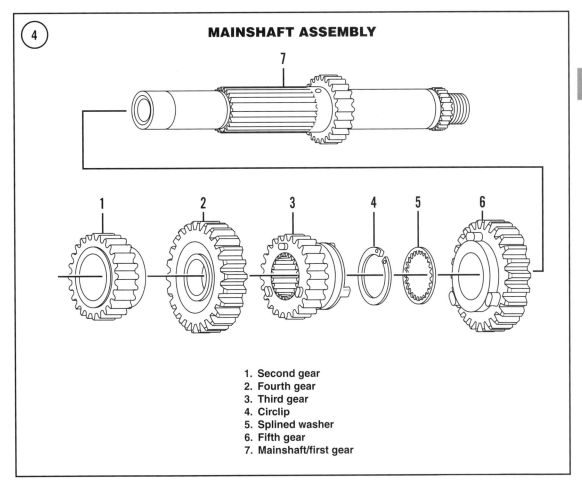

## MAINSHAFT ASSEMBLY

1. Second gear
2. Fourth gear
3. Third gear
4. Circlip
5. Splined washer
6. Fifth gear
7. Mainshaft/first gear

components. *If a press is not available, refer service to a dealership.*

### Disassembly

Refer to **Figure 4**.

1. Clean the assembled mainshaft (**Figure 5**) in solvent and dry with compressed air.

2. Install a bearing splitter onto the second gear (**Figure 6**).

*CAUTION*
*Before pressing the gear off the mainshaft, make sure no mainshaft parts will be damaged. Be prepared to catch the mainshaft.*

3. Using a hydraulic press, force the second gear off the mainshaft.

4. Remove fourth gear (**Figure 7**).

5. Remove third gear (A, **Figure 8**).

6. Remove the circlip (**Figure 9**).

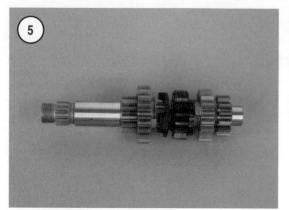

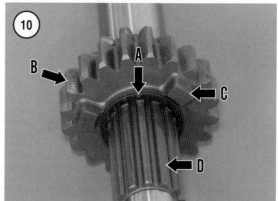

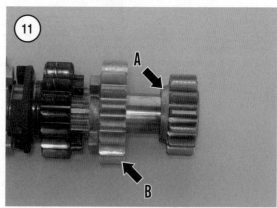

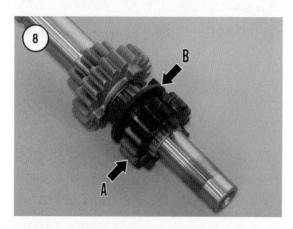

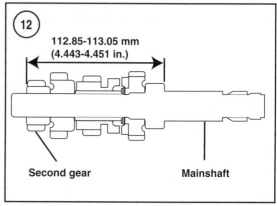

112.85-113.05 mm
(4.443-4.451 in.)

Second gear

Mainshaft

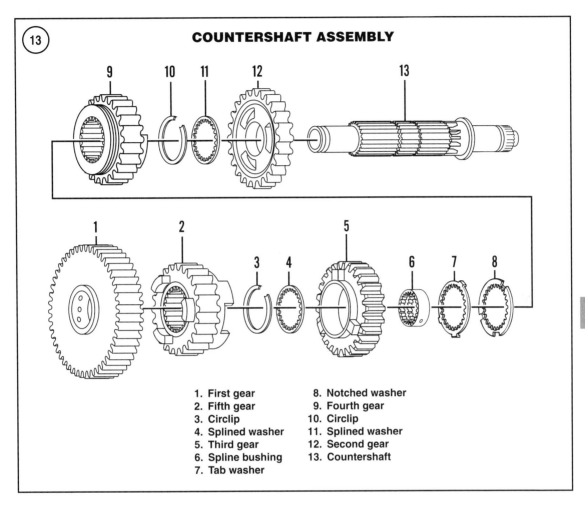

**COUNTERSHAFT ASSEMBLY**

1. First gear
2. Fifth gear
3. Circlip
4. Splined washer
5. Third gear
6. Spline bushing
7. Tab washer
8. Notched washer
9. Fourth gear
10. Circlip
11. Splined washer
12. Second gear
13. Countershaft

7. Remove the washer (A, **Figure 10**) and fifth gear (B).

**Inspection**

Refer to *Transmission Inspection* in this chapter.

**Assembly**

Refer to **Figure 4**.

1. Lubricate all parts with molybdenum disulfide oil.

2. Install fifth gear (B, **Figure 10**) onto the mainshaft. The gear dogs (C, **Figure 10**) must face toward the shaft splines (D).

3. Install the washer (A, **Figure 10**) and a new circlip (**Figure 9**) onto the shaft. The flat side of both parts must face away from fifth gear. Make sure the circlip seats fully in the shaft groove.

4. Install third gear (A, **Figure 8**) so the shift groove (B) faces toward fifth gear.

5. Install fourth gear (**Figure 7**) on the shaft. The gear dogs must face toward third gear.

6. Place second gear onto the mainshaft so the shoulder (A, **Figure 11**) is toward fourth gear (B).

7. Using a hydraulic press, install second gear onto the shaft so the distance between second gear and first gear is 112.85-113.05 mm (4.443-4.451 in.). Refer to **Figure 12**.

> *CAUTION*
> *After pressing second gear onto mainshaft, verify that fourth gear rotates freely. Otherwise, recheck gear location.*

8. Wrap and store the assembly (**Figure 5**) until it is ready for installation into the crankcase. Install the complete transmission assembly as described in *Crankcase* in Chapter Five.

**COUNTERSHAFT**

**Disassembly**

Refer to **Figure 13**.

1. Clean the assembled countershaft (**Figure 14**) in solvent and dry with compressed air.

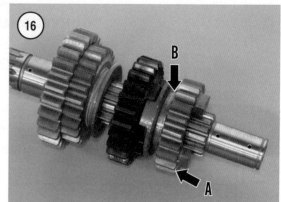

2. Remove first gear (**Figure 15**).

3. Remove fifth gear (A, **Figure 16**).

4. Remove the circlip (**Figure 17**).

5. Remove the spline washer (A, **Figure 18**) and third gear (B).

6. Remove the spline bushing (**Figure 19**).

7. Remove the tab lockwasher (A, **Figure 20**). Rotate the notched spline washer (B, **Figure 20**) to clear the spline groove and remove it.

8. Remove fourth gear (A, **Figure 21**).

9. Remove the circlip (A, **Figure 22**) and spline washer (B).

10. Remove second gear (A, **Figure 23**).

## Inspection

Refer to *Transmission Inspection* in this chapter.

## Assembly

Refer to **Figure 13**.

1. Lubricate all parts with molybdenum disulfide oil.

2. Install second gear (A, **Figure 23**) onto the countershaft. The dog slots (B, **Figure 23**) must face toward the shaft splines (C).

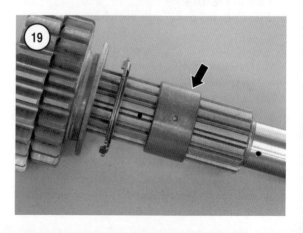

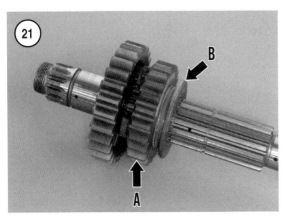

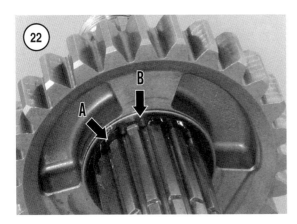

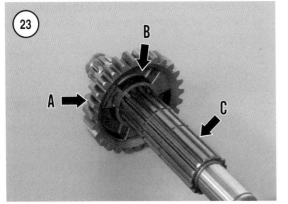

3. Install the spline washer (B, **Figure 22**) and a new circlip (A) onto the shaft. The flat side of both parts must face out. Make sure the circlip seats fully in the shaft groove.

4. Install fourth gear (A, **Figure 21**) so the shift groove (B) faces out.

5. Slide on the notched spline washer (A, **Figure 24**). This washer is symmetrical (both sides are flat). Slightly rotate the spline washer so it is locked in the countershaft groove and held in place by the splines.

6. Position the tab lockwasher (B, **Figure 24**) with the locking arms facing toward the notched spline washer (A).

7. Slide on the tab lockwasher and insert the locking arms into the notches in the spline washer as shown in **Figure 25**.

8. Align the oil hole in the third gear bushing (A, **Figure 26**) with the countershaft oil hole (B) and slide on the third gear bushing.

*CAUTION*
*The oil holes may not align. Position the bushing so its oil hole is over the spline next to the countershaft oil hole.*

9. Install third gear (B, **Figure 18**) onto the bushing so the gear dogs (C) face out.

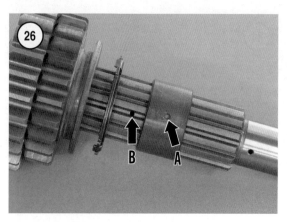

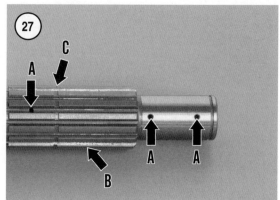

10. Install the splined washer (A, **Figure 18**) and a new circlip (**Figure 17**) onto the shaft. The flat side of both parts must face out. Make sure the circlip seats fully in the shaft groove.

11. Install fifth gear (A, **Figure 16**) so the shift groove (B) faces toward third gear.

12. Install first gear (**Figure 15**) so the shift dogs face in toward fifth gear.

13. Wrap and store the assembly (**Figure 14**) until it is ready for installation into the crankcase. Install the complete transmission assembly as described in *Crankcase* in Chapter Five.

### TRANSMISSION INSPECTION

#### Shaft Inspection

1. Inspect each shaft for the following:
    a. Clean oil holes (A, **Figure 27**).
    b. Worn or-damaged splines (B, **Figure 27**).
    c. Rounded or damaged circlip grooves (C, **Figure 27**).
    d. Damaged threads (A, **Figure 28**). Mildly damaged threads can be trued with a thread die.
    e. Damaged O-ring groove (B, **Figure 28**).
    f. Wear, galling or other damage on the bearing/bushing surfaces (C, **Figure 28**). A blue discoloration on any surface indicates excessive heat.
    g. Broken or damaged gear teeth on the mainshaft.
    h. Shaft runout. With the shaft mounted between lathe centers or a centering jig, use a dial indicator to measure runout. Measure on a smooth surface near the center of the shaft. Refer to **Table 2** for the specification.
2. Assemble the shafts as described in this chapter.

#### Gear, Bushing and Washer Inspection

1. Inspect the gears for the following:

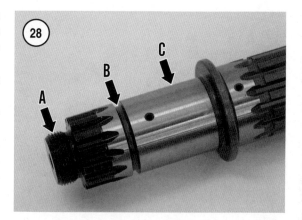

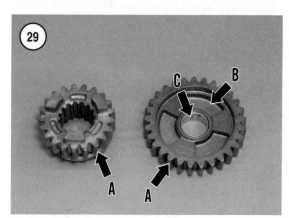

    a. Broken or damaged teeth (A, **Figure 29**).
    b. Worn, damaged or rounded dog slots (B, **Figure 29**).
    c. Scored, galled or fractured bore (C, **Figure 29**). The oil pockets should not be worn away A blue discoloration indicates excessive heat.
    d. Worn or damaged shift fork groove (A, **Figure 30**).
    e. Worn or damaged splines (B, **Figure 30**).
    f. Worn, damaged or rounded gear dogs (C, **Figure 30**). Any wear on the dogs and mating recesses should be uniform. If the dogs are not worn evenly, the remaining dogs will be over

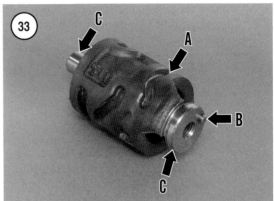

*Rounded dogs will cause the transmission to jump out of gear.*

g. Smooth gear operation on the shafts. Bored gears should fit firmly on the shaft, yet spin smoothly and freely. Splined gears should fit snugly at their position on the shaft, yet slide smoothly and freely from side to side. If a gear is worn or damaged, also replace the gear it mates to on the other shaft.

2. Inspect the bushing and gear bore (**Figure 31**). There should be no signs of wear or damage.

3. Install the parts onto their shafts as described in this chapter.

## SHIFT DRUM AND FORKS

When the transmission is shifted, the shift drum and fork assembly engages and disengages pairs of gears on the transmission shafts (**Figure 32**). Cam grooves in the shift drum move the shift forks, which slide the gears along the mainshaft and countershaft.

It is important that the shift drum grooves, shift forks and mating gear grooves be in good condition. Too much wear between the parts will cause unreliable and poor engagement of the gears. This can lead to premature wear of the gear dogs and other parts.

stressed and possibly fail. Check the engagement of the dogs by placing the gears at their appropriate positions on the countershaft, then twisting the gears together. Check for positive engagement in both directions. If damage is evident, also check the condition of the shift forks as described in this chapter.

*NOTE*
*The side of the gear dogs that carries the engine load will wear and eventually become rounded. The unloaded side of the dogs will remain unworn.*

### Inspection

1. Clean all parts in solvent and dry with compressed air.

2. Inspect the shift drum. Check for:

    a. Worn or damaged grooves (A, **Figure 33**). The grooves should be a uniform width.

    b. Worn shift drum stopper pin (B, **Figure 33**).

    c. Worn or damaged bearing surfaces (C, **Figure 33**).

3. Inspect each shift fork for:

    a. Worn or damaged fingers (A, **Figure 34**).

b. Worn or damaged guide pin (B, **Figure 34**). The pin should be symmetrical and not flat on the sides.

c. Bends, cracks or scoring.

d. Worn or damaged pivot shafts (C, **Figure 34**).

4. Inspect the fit of each fork guide pin with the appropriate groove in the shift drum. The pin should fit with slight lateral play.

5. Inspect the fit of each fork in the matching gear groove. The forks should fit with slight lateral play.

6. Inspect the fit of each fork in the corresponding bore in the right and left crankcase halves. The fork shaft should slide smoothly in the bore.

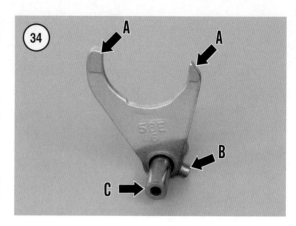

### Table 1 TRANSMISSION SPECIFICATIONS

| Transmission | Constant mesh, 5-speed |
|---|---|
| Shift pattern | 1-N-2-3-4-5 |
| Primary reduction ratio | 2.818 (62/22) |
| Final reduction ratio | 2.714 (38/14) |
| Transmission gear ratios | |
|   First gear | 2.416 (29/12) |
|   Second gear | 1.928 (27/14) |
|   Third gear | 1.562 (25/16) |
|   Fourth gear | 1.277 (23/18) |
|   Fifth gear | 1.050 (21/20) |

### Table 2 TRANSMISSION SERVICE SPECIFICATIONS

| Item | Standard mm (in.) | Service limit mm (in.) |
|---|---|---|
| Countershaft runout | – | 0.08 (0.003) |
| Mainshaft runout | – | 0.08 (0.003) |
| Mainshaft second gear position* | 112.85-113.05 (4.443-4.451) | – |
| *Refer to text. | | |

**CHAPTER EIGHT**

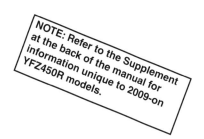

NOTE: Refer to the Supplement at the back of the manual for information unique to 2009-on YFZ450R models.

# FUEL SYSTEM AND EMISSION CONTROL

8

The fuel system consists of the carburetor, fuel tank, and fuel shutoff valve and air filter.

Routine air filter service is covered in Chapter Three.

The handlebar throttle housing and carburetor are equipped with switches that operate as part of the Throttle Override System (TORS). Refer to *Switches* in Chapter Nine.

**Table 1** and **Table 2** are at the end of this chapter.

## CARBURETOR

### Operation

The carburetor is a float type, slide valve, constant velocity carburetor.

The carburetor is equipped with an air cutoff valve. The air cutoff valve operates during high vacuum conditions that cause a lean fuel mixture, such as engine braking. The diaphragm-actuated valve shuts the air passage to the slow jet thereby enriching the fuel mixture to prevent afterburn in the exhaust system.

A diaphragm type accelerator pump enriches the fuel mixture when the throttle is opened rapidly.

A starter (choke) system supplies the rich mixture needed to start a cold engine. A hot start valve pre-vents an excessively rich mixture when starting a hot engine.

Refer to *Carburetor Adjustment and Rejetting* in this chapter.

### Removal/Installation

1. Remove the seat, fuel tank cover and side covers as described in Chapter Fifteen.
2. Remove the air box as described in this chapter.
3. Disconnect the throttle position sensor connector (A, **Figure 1**).
4. Disconnect the TORS connector (B, **Figure 1**).
5. Loosen the clamp, then detach the fuel hose (**Figure 2**) from the carburetor.
6. Remove the bolt securing the rear brake fluid reservoir (**Figure 3**), then move the reservoir to gain access to the throttle cable cover screws.
7. Remove the screws (A, **Figure 4**), then remove the throttle cable cover (B).
8. Loosen the throttle cable nuts (A, **Figure 5**), then disconnect the throttle cable from the carburetor pulley (B).
9. Loosen the hose clamp screw (**Figure 6**).
10. Remove the carburetor.
11. Reverse the removal steps to install the carburetor while noting the following:

a. Position the clamp on the intake tube so the slot in the clamp band (A, **Figure 7**) fits over the hose rib (B).

b. If damaged, install a new gasket onto the throttle cable cover.

c. Tighten the throttle cable cover screws to 4 N•m (35 in.-lb.).

d. Adjust the throttle cable and idle speed as described in Chapter Three.

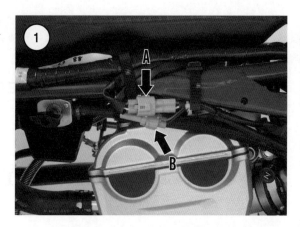

### Disassembly

Refer to **Figure 8**.

1. Disconnect and label the carburetor vent and drain hoses (**Figure 9**).

> *NOTE*
> *Do not loosen or remove the throttle position sensor (TPS) from the carburetor unless it is necessary to adjust or replace the sensor (A, **Figure 10**). Refer to Chapter Nine for inspection, replacement and adjustment of the sensor.*

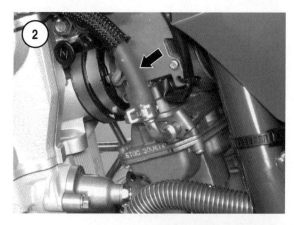

2. Remove the TORS switch cover screws (B, **Figure 10**), then remove the cover (C).

3. Remove the nut (A, **Figure 11**), lockwasher and switch arm (B).

4. Back out the idle speed screw (A, **Figure 12**) for access to the center switch housing screw.

> *CAUTION*
> *The TORS switch housing screws use threadlocking compound. Adequately support the carburetor to prevent damage and use an impact driver to loosen the screws.*

5. Remove the TORS switch housing screws (B, **Figure 12**). Remove the switch housing assembly (C, **Figure 12**).

6. Remove the O-ring on the switch housing (**Figure 13**).

7. Unscrew the hot start valve cap (A, **Figure 14**), then remove the hot start valve assembly (**Figure 15**).

8. Unscrew the starter (choke) body (B, **Figure 14**).

9. Remove the spring (A, **Figure 16**) and plunger (B).

10. Remove the screws from the top cover (**Figure 17**), and then remove the cover and gasket.

11. Remove the jet needle holder (**Figure 18**) and jet needle (**Figure 19**).

12. Remove the throttle shaft screw (**Figure 20**).

13. Turn the throttle shaft so the throttle valve assembly (A, **Figure 21**) can be disengaged from the valve lever rollers (B).

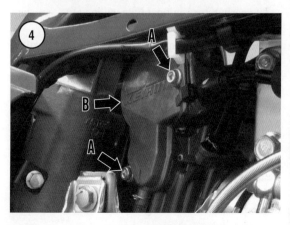

14. Remove the throttle valve from the carburetor (**Figure 22**).

15. Remove the accelerator pump cover (**Figure 23**). Remove the O-ring (A, **Figure 24**), spring (B) and diaphragm (C).

16. Remove the air cutoff valve cover (**Figure 25**), spring, diaphragm and O-ring.

17. Remove the float bowl screws, then remove the float bowl (**Figure 26**).

18. Push up the accelerator pump link lever (A, **Figure 27**), then remove the pump rod (B) by pulling it out of the actuator arm (C).

19. Remove the pilot screw as follows:

a. Count and record the number of turns required to lightly seat the pilot screw (**Figure 28**) into the carburetor.

b. Remove the pilot screw, spring, washer and O-ring (**Figure 29**).

*NOTE*
*If the O-ring is stuck in the bottom of the pilot screw bore, carefully extract it with a piece of wire.*

20. Remove the float pin (A, **Figure 30**), float (B, **Figure 30**) and fuel valve (**Figure 31**).

21. Remove the main jet (**Figure 32**).

22. Remove the needle jet (A, **Figure 33**).

23. Remove the fuel baffle (B, **Figure 33**).

24. Remove the starter jet (A, **Figure 34**).

25. Remove the pilot jet (B, **Figure 34**).

26. Remove the pilot air jet (**Figure 35**).

*NOTE*
*Do not remove the throttle shaft. It is available only as part of the carburetor body assembly.*

27. Clean and inspect the parts as described in this section.

**Cleaning and Inspection**

*CAUTION*
*Do not attempt to clean the jet orifices or seats with wire or drill bits. These items can scratch the surfaces and alter flow rates or cause leaking.*

1. Clean all the parts. Remove all sediment from inside the float bowl, and clean all carburetor passages and hoses with compressed air.

*CAUTION*
*Do not submerge the throttle position sensor or wiring harness in solvent. Only wipe the outside of the unit and wiring harness with a dry cloth.*

2. Inspect all of the jets. Check that all holes, in the ends and sides, are clean and undamaged.

3. Inspect the pilot screw assembly (**Figure 29**). Inspect the tip for damage or bends.

4. Inspect the accelerator pump (**Figure 36**) and air cutoff valve (**Figure 8**) assemblies for wear and damage. Inspect the diaphragm for cracks, tears or brittleness. Check the spring for weakness or damage. Check the passages in each cover for clogging.

5. Inspect the float and fuel valve assembly:

8

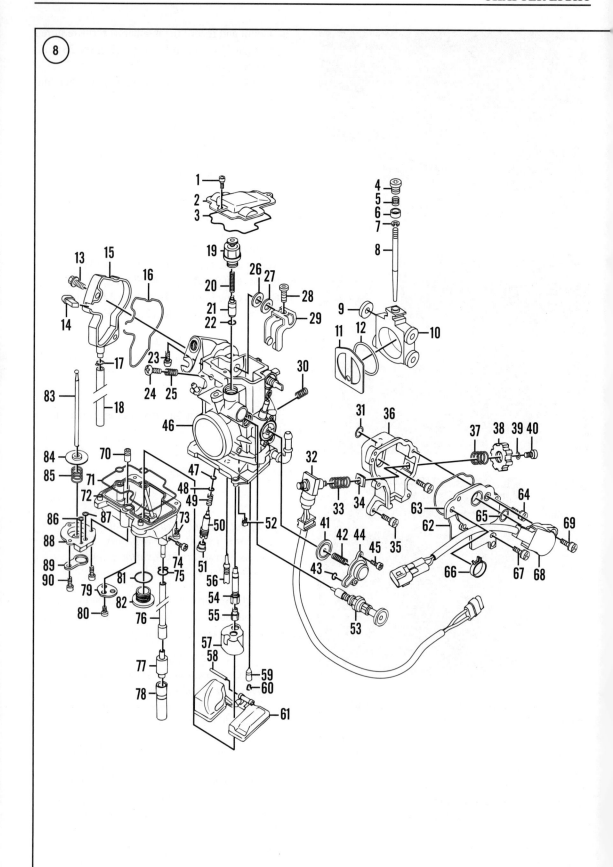

## CARBURETOR

1. Bolt
2. Top cover
3. O-ring
4. Jet needle holder
5. Spring
6. Collar
7. Clip
8. Jet needle
9. Roller
10. Throttle valve
11. Throttle valve plate
12. O-ring
13. Bolt
14. Grommet
15. Throttle pulley cover
16. O-ring
17. Clip
18. Hose
19. Hot start valve cap
20. Spring
21. Hot start valve
22. O-ring
23. Bolt
24. Accelerator pump adjusting screw
25. Spring
26. Metal washer
27. Plastic washer
28. Throttle shaft screw
29. Valve lever
30. Pilot air jet
31. O-ring
32. TORS switch
33. Spring
34. Plate
35. Screw
36. Switch housing
37. Spring
38. Idle speed knob
39. O-ring
40. Screw
41. Air cutoff diaphragm
42. Spring
43. O-ring
44. Air cutoff valve cover
45. Screw
46. Carburetor body
47. O-ring
48. Washer
49. Spring
50. Pilot screw
51. Plug
52. Starter jet
53. Starter (choke) body
54. Needle jet
55. Main jet
56. Pilot jet
57. Baffle
58. Float pin
59. Fuel valve
60. Clip
61. Float
62. O-ring
63. Cover
64. Screw
65. O-ring
66. Wire guide
67. Screw
68. Throttle position sensor (TPS)
69. Bolt
70. Accelerator pump jet
71. O-ring
72. Float bowl
73. Screw
74. Drain screw
75. Clip
76. Hose
77. Tube
78. Hose
79. Hose guide
80. Screw
81. O-ring
82. Drain bolt
83. Accelerator pump rod
84. Accelerator pump diaphragm
85. Spring
86. O-ring
87. O-ring
88. Accelerator pump cover
89. Hose guide
90. Screw

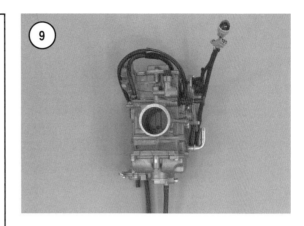

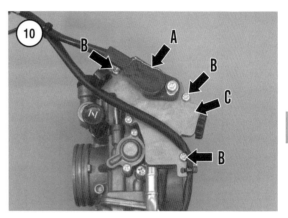

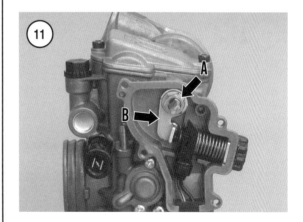

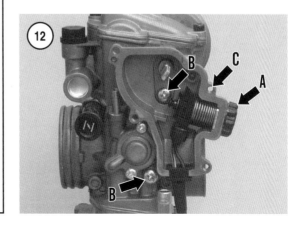

8

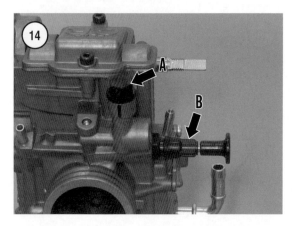

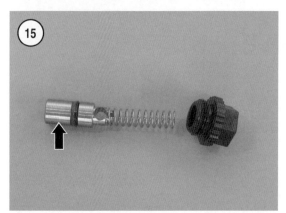

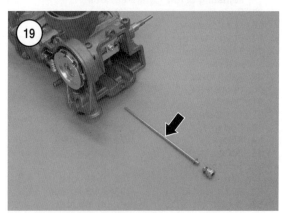

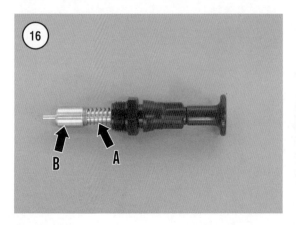

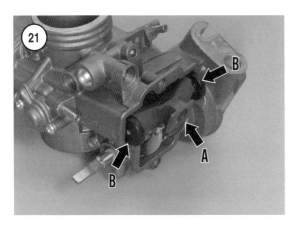

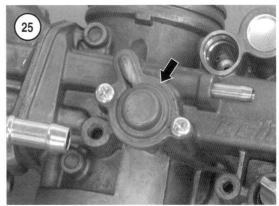

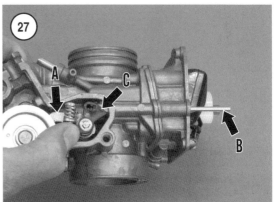

8

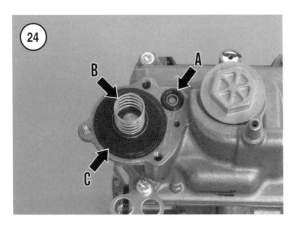

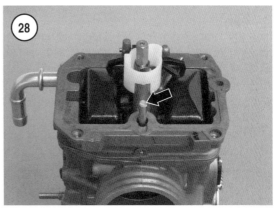

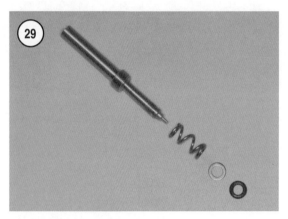

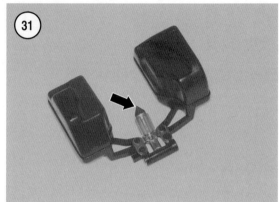

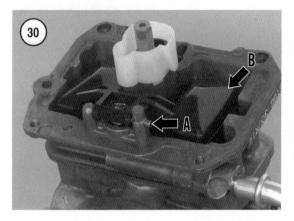

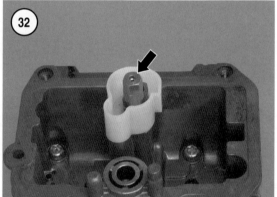

a. Inspect the tip of the fuel valve (**Figure 37**). If it is stepped or damaged, replace the fuel valve and seat.

b. Lightly press on the spring-loaded pin in the fuel valve. The pin should easily move in and out of the valve. If it is varnished with fuel residue, replace the fuel valve and seat.

c. Inspect the fuel valve seat (**Figure 38**). The seat should be clean and scratch-free; otherwise, the fuel valve will not seat properly and the carburetor will overflow. The carburetor body must be replaced if the seat is damaged.

d. Submerge the float in water and check for leaks. Replace the float if liquid is detected inside the float.

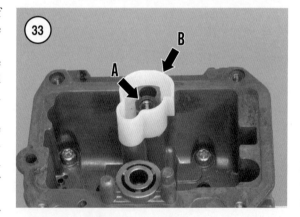

6. Inspect the starter (choke) plunger (**Figure 39**) for wear or damage. Hold the housing and operate the knob by hand. If there is any sticking or binding, check for a bent shaft. Check the spring for damage.

7. Inspect the throttle valve assembly (**Figure 40**) as follows:

a. Remove the needle holder, spring, collar and jet needle.

b. The jet needle must be smooth and evenly tapered. Replace if stepped, dented, worn or bent.

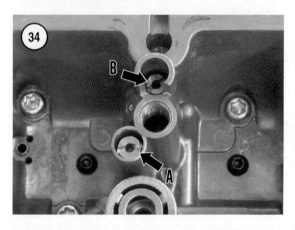

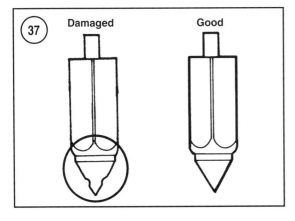

c. Check the throttle valve plate for cracks or other damage.

d. Check that the rollers on the throttle valve turn freely.

e. Inspect the fit of the throttle valve assembly in the carburetor body. The assembly should fit snugly, but easily slide through the bore. If drag or binding is felt, inspect the bore and throttle valve for excessive wear, roughness and other damage.

f. Install the jet needle, collar, spring and needle holder.

8. Replace the float bowl O-ring (A, **Figure 41**) if leaking or damaged.

9. Inspect and, if necessary, clean the accelerator pump jet (B, **Figure 41**).

10. Check the fit of the throttle shaft in the carburetor. The shaft must rotate without binding or wobbling. If the throttle shaft or shaft bores in the carburetor body are worn, replace the carburetor.

11. Refer to *Switches* in Chapter Nine and check operation of the TORS carburetor switch.

**Assembly**

Refer to **Figure 8**.

*NOTE*
*Perform Steps 1-4 if the throttle shaft, pushrod link lever and accelerator pump rod were removed.*

1. Install the pilot air jet (**Figure 35**).
2. Install the pilot jet (B, **Figure 34**).
3. Install the starter jet (A, **Figure 34**).
4. Hook the fuel valve (**Figure 42**) onto the float tab.
5. Place the float and valve assembly into the carburetor while inserting the valve into the seat.
6. Install the float pin (A, **Figure 30**).
7. Check the float height as described in this chapter.
8. Install the fuel baffle (B, **Figure 33**).
9. Install the needle jet (A, **Figure 33**).

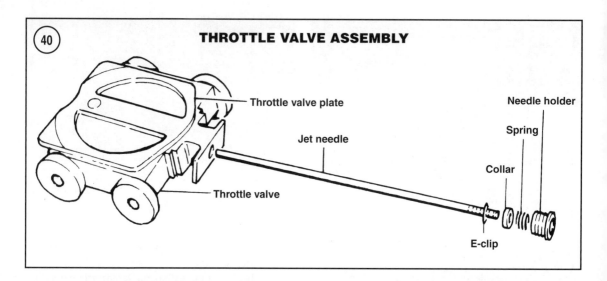

THROTTLE VALVE ASSEMBLY

Throttle valve plate

Needle holder

Spring

Jet needle

Collar

Throttle valve

E-clip

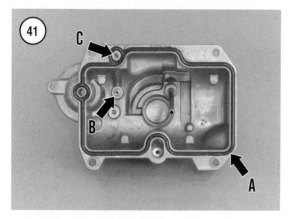

10. Install the main jet (**Figure 32**).

11. Install the pilot screw assembly (**Figure 29**). Lightly seat the screw, then turn it out the number of turns recorded during disassembly. If the number of turns is not known, refer to **Table 1** for the standard setting.

12. Install the accelerator pump rod (B, **Figure 27**) into the carburetor. The ball end must be toward the arm (A, **Figure 27**). Push the ball end into the arm until properly engaged.

13. Install the O-ring (A, **Figure 41**) into the float bowl groove.

14. Align the passage in the float bowl (C, **Figure 41**) with the accelerator pump rod and install the float bowl (**Figure 43**). Install the hose guides and the float bowl mounting screws. Tighten the screws securely.

15. Install the air cutoff valve O-ring (A, **Figure 44**), diaphragm (B) and spring (C). Install the cover (**Figure 45**) and tighten the screws securely.

16. Install the accelerator pump as follows:
   a. Install the accelerator pump diaphragm (A, **Figure 46**) so the spring seat on the diaphragm faces out.

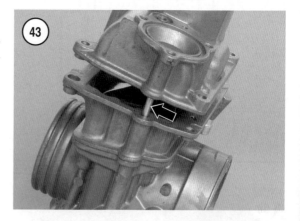

   b. Install the spring (B, **Figure 46**), the small O-ring (C) and the large O-ring (D).
   c. Install the cover.
   d. Tighten the cover screws securely.

17. Install the throttle valve assembly as follows:
   a. Turn the throttle shaft so the valve lever rollers (A, **Figure 47**) are at the top of the carburetor.
   b. Insert the throttle valve into the carburetor so the throttle valve plate (B, **Figure 47**) faces the engine side of the carburetor.

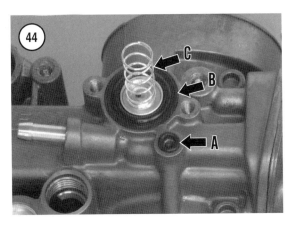

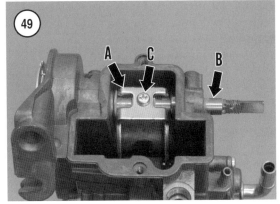

8

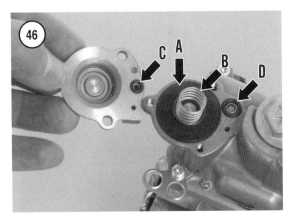

c. Engage the throttle valve with the valve lever rollers (**Figure 48**).

d. Align the valve lever (A, **Figure 49**) with the throttle shaft (B). Apply threadlocking compound onto the throttle shaft screw. Install the screw (C, **Figure 49**) through the valve lever and thread into the throttle shaft. Tighten the screw securely.

e. Operate the throttle to check the throttle valve for proper operation.

18. Install the O-ring into the top cover.

19. Install the top cover (**Figure 17**). Tighten the screws securely.

20. Install a new O-ring (**Figure 50**) onto the hot start valve plunger. Install the plunger and spring into the carburetor. Tighten the cap securely.

21. Install a new O-ring onto the starter (choke) valve plunger (**Figure 51**). Install the starter (choke) plunger and tighten the nut securely.

*NOTE*
*Pull the plunger knob on the starter valve to make sure it operates correctly.*

22. Install a new O-ring onto the switch housing (**Figure 13**).

23. Install the TORS switch housing (C, **Figure 12**). Apply threadlocking compound to the screws (B, **Figure 12**) and tighten securely.

24. Install the switch arm (B, **Figure 11**), lockwasher and nut (A). Tighten the nut securely.

25. Install a new gasket (**Figure 52**) onto the TORS switch cover. Install the cover (C, **Figure 10**). Apply threadlocking compound to the cover screws and tighten the screws securely.

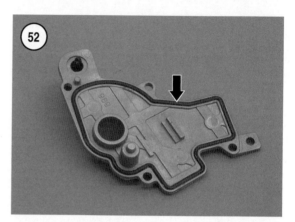

26. Check and adjust the accelerator pump timing as follows:

   a. Pull up the throttle valve, then insert a 3.40 mm (0.134 in.) rod into the throttle bore (**Figure 53**). Carefully allow the throttle valve to rest on the rod.

   b. Turn the accelerator pump adjusting screw (A, **Figure 54**) until free play can be felt at the link lever (B).

   c. Place a finger against the link lever (B, **Figure 54**) and slowly turn the adjusting screw (A) until free play has just been removed from the link lever.

   d. Remove the rod.

27. Connect the carburetor hoses.

28. Install the carburetor as described in this section.

29. Adjust the carburetor as described in Chapter Three.

## FLOAT ADJUSTMENT

### Float Height

The float and fuel valve maintain a constant fuel level in the float chamber. As fuel is used, the float lowers and allows more fuel past the valve. As the fuel level rises, the float closes the valve when the required fuel level is reached. If the float is out of adjustment, the fuel level will be too high or low. An incorrect float level can cause poor engine performance.

1. Remove the carburetor as described in this chapter.

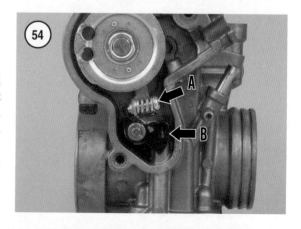

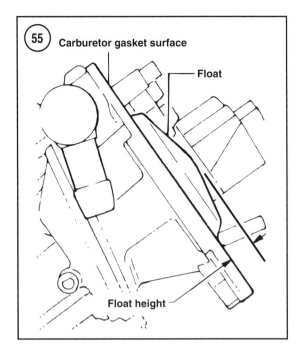

**55** Carburetor gasket surface

Float

Float height

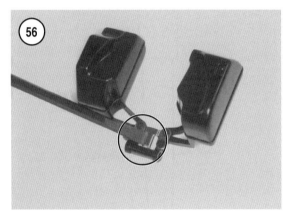

**56**

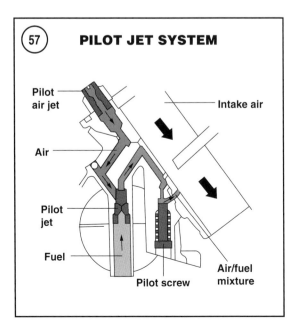

**57** **PILOT JET SYSTEM**

Pilot air jet

Intake air

Air

Pilot jet

Fuel

Pilot screw

Air/fuel mixture

2. Remove the float bowl.

3. Lightly touch the float to ensure the fuel valve is seated.

4. Hold the carburetor so the fuel valve remains seated, but the spring-loaded pin in the valve is not compressed by the float tab (**Figure 55**). The tab should only touch the pin.

5. Measure the distance from the carburetor gasket surface to the highest point on the float (**Figure 55**). Refer to **Table 1** at the end of this chapter for float height specifications.

6. If the float height is incorrect, remove the float from the carburetor and bend the float tab (**Figure 56**) in the appropriate direction to raise or lower the float. Recheck the height after adjusting the float.

7. Install the float bowl. Tighten the screws securely.

8. Install the carburetor as described in this chapter.

**Fuel Level**

Fuel level measurement procedures or specifications are not available from the manufacturer.

## CARBURETOR ADJUSTMENT AND REJETTING

The performance of the carburetor is affected by altitude, temperature, humidity and riding conditions. If the machine is not running or performing up to expectations, check the following before adjusting or changing the components in the carburetor:

1. Throttle cables. Make sure the throttle cables are not dragging and are correctly adjusted.

2. Make sure the air filter is clean.

3. Make sure there is fuel flow from the fuel tank to the carburetor.

4. Make sure the timing is correct and the throttle position sensor is operating correctly.

5. Make sure the muffler is not restricted.

6. Make sure the brakes are not dragging.

### Carburetor Circuits

Before disassembling the carburetor, understand the function of the pilot, needle and main jet systems. When evaluating or troubleshooting these systems, keep in mind that their operating ranges overlap one another during the transition from closed to fully open throttle.

*Pilot jet system*

The pilot system consists of the pilot air jet, pilot jet and pilot screw (**Figure 57**). The pilot system controls the air/fuel ratio from closed throttle to 1/8 throttle. The pilot jet draws fuel from the float chamber and mixes it with air from the pilot air jet. The air/fuel mixture then passes to the pilot screw, where it is regulated and discharged into the airstream in the carburetor bore. Turning the pilot screw in will decrease the mixture flow to the engine, while turning the screw out will increase the flow.

The pilot jet is interchangeable with jets that will provide a leaner or richer air/fuel mixture. Replacing the standard pilot jet with a larger numbered jet will enrich the mixture. Pilot jets with a smaller number will lean the mixture.

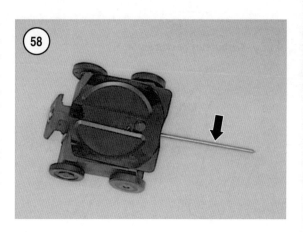

### Jet needle

The jet needle (**Figure 58**) is connected to the throttle valve and controls the mixture from approximately 1/4 to 3/4 throttle. The jet needle passes through the needle jet, and regulates the air/fuel mixture emitted from the jet into the carburetor throat. The jet needle taper, diameter and clip position determine fuel flow through the needle jet (**Figure 59**). In the closed throttle position, the tapered needle shuts off flow from the needle jet. As the throttle is opened, the needle allows fuel to pass by the taper, and between the straight portion of the needle and jet wall.

The position of the needle in the jet can be adjusted by removing the needle clip and positioning it on a higher or lower groove in the needle. Raising the clip will lower the needle into the jet, creating a lean condition. Lowering the clip will raise the needle, creating a rich condition.

Adjust the needle if it is determined the engine will perform better for the loads or climate in which it is operated. Do not adjust the needle in an attempt to correct other problems that may exist with the carburetor. Engine damage can occur if riding conditions do not warrant an overly rich or lean fuel mixture.

The jet needle is interchangeable with needles that will provide a leaner or richer air/fuel mixture.

Replacement needles all have the same starting point for the tapers. The difference in the needles is the taper angle and their diameter at the straight portion.

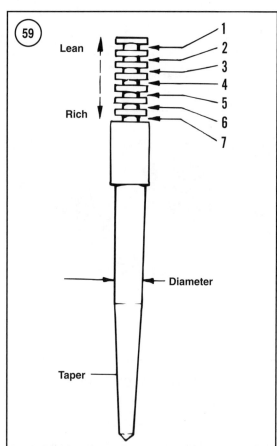

### Main jet

The main jet at the bottom of the needle jet controls the mixture from approximately 3/4 to full throttle. The main jet is numbered and is interchangeable with jets that will provide a leaner or richer air/fuel mixture. Replacing the standard jet with a larger numbered jet will make the mixture richer. Jets with a smaller number will make the mixture leaner.

The main jet can be accessed by removing the cap on the bottom of the float chamber. Carburetor removal is not necessary.

### Accelerator pump jet

Rapid throttle opening produces a lean mixture that can cause engine stalling. To richen the mixture, the accelerator pump ejects fuel into the throttle bore. The accelerator pump jet in the float bowl (B, **Figure 41**) determines the amount of fuel discharged during accelerator pump operation.

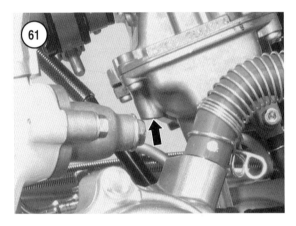

limited accessibility, a pilot screw adjustment tool is helpful (*motionpro.com*).

1. The engine must be in good mechanical running condition.

2. Remove the pilot screw plug (**Figure 60**) as follows:

   a. Remove the carburetor as described in this chapter.

   b. Remove the float bowl, then remove the plug in the float bowl.

   c. Install the float bowl, then install the carburetor.

*CAUTION*
*Seat the pilot screw lightly in Step 3 or the screw tip can break off into the pilot screw bore.*

3. Lightly seat the pilot screw (**Figure 61**), then back it out two turns.

4. Start and allow the engine to reach operating temperature. Ride the ATV for ten minutes and turn off the engine.

5. Attach a shop tachometer to the engine following the manufacturer's directions.

6. Adjust the idle speed as described in *Carburetor* in Chapter Three.

7. Turn the pilot screw (**Figure 61**) in or out slowly to obtain the highest engine idle speed possible.

8. Operate the throttle slowly two or three times, then turn the idle speed screw (A, **Figure 62**) and reset the idle speed to 1750-1850 rpm.

9. While reading the tachometer, turn the pilot screw in (clockwise) until the idle speed drops 50 rpm. Then turn the pilot screw 1/2 turn out (counterclockwise).

10. If necessary, readjust the idle speed.

11. Turn off the engine and disconnect the shop tachometer.

12. Test ride the ATV. Open the throttle slowly, but evenly. The engine should pull smoothly. Do not open the throttle quickly. Doing so will involve the accelerator pump system, which will mask pilot screw operation.

## Changing the Needle or Jets

When changing the needle or jets, observe the following practices:

1. Record all settings or clip position of the part being removed.

2. Check that the pilot system is adjusted correctly before changing the needle or main jet.

3. To check a main jet, run the ATV at full throttle in an open area. Shut off the engine while it is running at full throttle, then pull in the clutch and coast to a stop. Remove the spark plug and check it for a lean or rich condition. Refer to *Spark Plug* in Chapter Three for possible spark plug conditions.

## Pilot Screw Adjustment

The pilot screw is sealed. A plug (**Figure 60**) is installed at the bottom of the pilot screw bore in the float bowl to prevent routine adjustment. The pilot screw is preset and routine adjustment should not be necessary unless the pilot screw is replaced. There is no specification for the starting position of the pilot screw or an adjustment procedure. The following describes adjustment of the pilot screw using engine rpm to find the optimum pilot screw position.

A tachometer that can indicate a change of 50 rpm or less is required to adjust the pilot screw. Due to

8

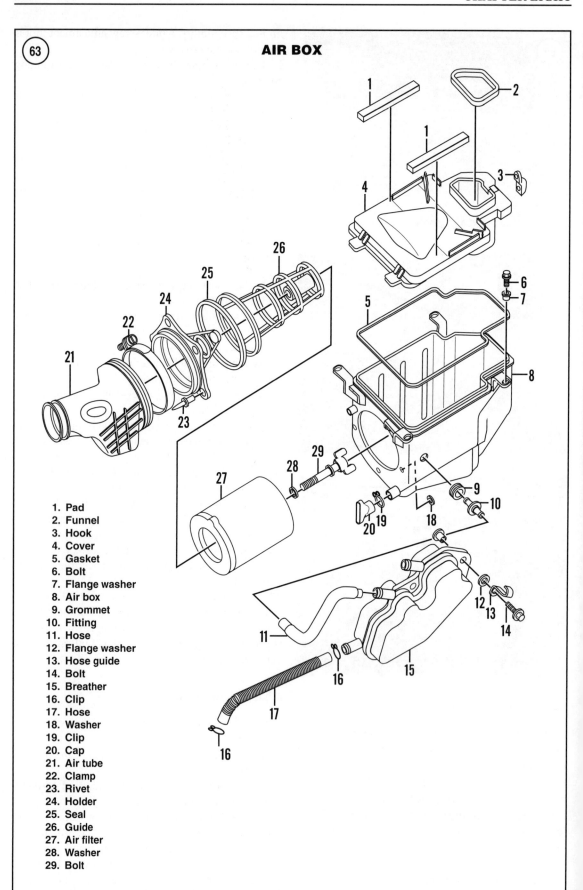

**AIR BOX**

63

1. Pad
2. Funnel
3. Hook
4. Cover
5. Gasket
6. Bolt
7. Flange washer
8. Air box
9. Grommet
10. Fitting
11. Hose
12. Flange washer
13. Hose guide
14. Bolt
15. Breather
16. Clip
17. Hose
18. Washer
19. Clip
20. Cap
21. Air tube
22. Clamp
23. Rivet
24. Holder
25. Seal
26. Guide
27. Air filter
28. Washer
29. Bolt

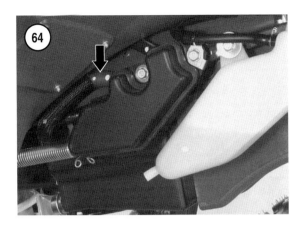

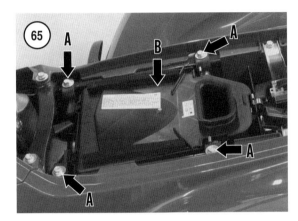

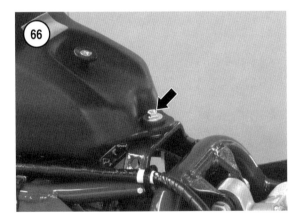

## AIR BOX

### Removal/Installation

Refer to **Figure 63**.
1. Remove the seat as described in Chapter Fifteen.
2. Disconnect the breather hose from the air box (**Figure 64**).
3. Loosen the air tube clamp (B, **Figure 62**).
4. Remove the air box retaining bolts (A, **Figure 65**).
5. Remove the air box (B, **Figure 65**).
6. Inspect the air box for cracks and other damage.
7. Reverse the removal steps to install the air box.

## FUEL TANK

### Fuel Tank Raising/Lowering

The fuel tank may be raised for access to components below, such as the spark plug and ignition coil.
1. Remove the seat, fuel tank cover and side covers as described in Chapter Fifteen.
2. Remove the fuel tank retaining bolt (**Figure 66**).
3. Pull back and raise the rear of the fuel tank, then install a long bolt or other support under the fuel tank (**Figure 67**).
4. Reverse the procedure to lower the fuel tank back into place. Tighten the fuel tank retaining bolt to 7 N•m (62 in.-lb.).

### Removal/Installation

1. Remove the seat, fuel tank cover and side covers as described in Chapter Fifteen.
2. Loosen the clamp and detach the fuel hose (**Figure 68**) from the fuel valve.
3. Remove the fuel tank retaining bolt (**Figure 66**).

*NOTE*
*Each front fuel tank mounting leg is slotted with a large hole at the end that allows disengagement from the mounting posts (Figure 69).*

4. Pull back the fuel tank and disengage the front mounting legs from the mounting posts. Remove the fuel tank.
5. If necessary, remove the retaining screws and remove the fuel tank shield (**Figure 70**).
6. Reverse the removal steps to install the fuel tank while noting the following:
   a. Install the flanged spacers in the fuel tank mounting holes so the flange is on the underside.
   b. Tighten the fuel tank retaining bolt to 7 N•m (62 in.-lb.).

8

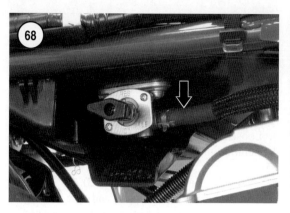

## FUEL VALVE

### Removal/Inspection/Installation

1. Remove the fuel tank as described in this chapter.
2. Drain the fuel from the tank. Refer to *Safety* in Chapter One.
3. Remove the two screws (**Figure 71**) securing the fuel valve to the tank, then pull the valve straight out of the tank.
4. Remove the two screws (**Figure 72**) securing the valve cover, then pull the lever and cover assembly out of the fuel valve.
5. Disassemble, clean and inspect the parts (**Figure 73**).
   a. Inspect for buildup in the screen filters. If buildup is evident, lightly scrub the screens with a nylon brush and solvent. Carefully blow compressed air through the screen, from the inside to the outside.
   b. Inspect and clean buildup from the valve passages.
   c. Replace all O-rings.
   d. The wave washer must be capable of applying pressure to the outside of the lever. If resistance is not felt when tightening the valve cover screws, the washer is fatigued.
   e. Inspect the remaining parts for damage.
6. When assembling the valve note the following:
   a. Lightly lubricate the O-rings.
   b. When filling the tank, start with a small amount of fuel and check for leaks. Operate the lever and check that all positions are leak-free.

## THROTTLE CABLE

### Removal/Installation

1. Remove the seat, fuel tank cover and side covers as described in Chapter Fifteen.
2. Push back the boot (A, **Figure 74**) on the handlebar throttle housing, then loosen the cable nut (B) and turn the adjuster (C) in to create slack in the cable.

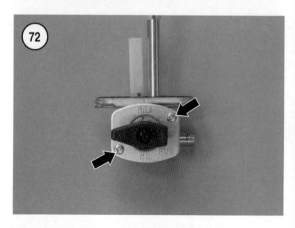

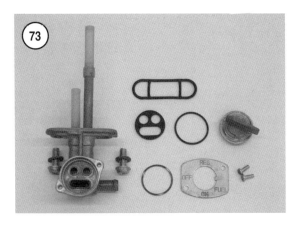

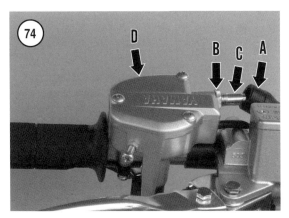

3. Remove the bolt securing the rear brake fluid reservoir (**Figure 75**), then move the reservoir to gain access to the throttle cable cover screws.

4. Remove the screws (A, **Figure 76**), then remove the throttle cable cover (B).

5. Loosen the throttle cable nuts (A, **Figure 77**), then disconnect the throttle cable from the carburetor pulley (B).

6. Remove the cover (D, **Figure 74**) on the handlebar throttle housing. Detach the cable end from the throttle lever (**Figure 78**) and remove the cable from the throttle housing.

7. Note how the cable is routed, then remove the cable from the frame.

8. Reverse the removal steps to install the new cable. Note the following:

    a. Clean the housings and levers before assembly.

    b. Lubricate the cable and cable ends.

    c. Adjust the throttle cable as described in Chapter Three.

    d. Tighten the throttle cable cover screws to 4 N•m (35 in.-lb.).

## CRANKCASE BREATHER SYSTEM

All models are equipped with a closed crankcase breather system. This system routes crankcase vapors into the crankcase breather (A, **Figure 79**). Crankcase

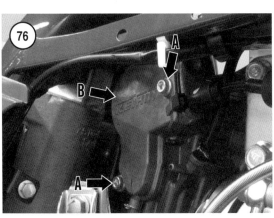

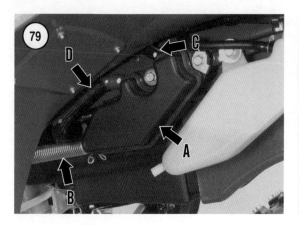

vapor passes through the lower hose (B, **Figure 79**) to the rear of the crankcase (**Figure 80**). The upper crankcase hose (C, **Figure 79**) connects the crankcase breather to the cylinder head (**Figure 81**). After passing through the crankcase breather, vapor flows through a hose (D, **Figure 79**) to the air box where it is drawn through the intake system and burned.

## Inspection/Cleaning

Inspect the breather hoses. Replace any cracked or deteriorated hoses. Make sure the hose clamps are in place and tight.

### Table 1 CARBURETOR SPECIFICATIONS

| Carburetor type | Keihin FCR |
| --- | --- |
| Accelerator jet | |
| 2004-2005 models | 50 |
| 2006-on models | 40 |
| Cutaway | 1.5 |
| Jet needle | |
| 2004-2005 models | NDSR |
| 2006-on models | NGNR |
| Jet needle clip position | 4th groove |
| Main jet No. | |
| 2004-2005 models | 158 |
| 2006-on models | 155 |
| Pilot air jet No. | |
| 2004-2005 models | 100 |
| 2006-on models | 70 |
| Pilot jet No. | 42 |
| Pilot screw initial setting | 1 7/8 turns out |
| Starter jet No. | 90 |
| Float height | 8 mm (0.32 in.) |
| Idle speed | 1750-1850 rpm |

### Table 2 CARBURETOR TORQUE SPECIFICATIONS

| Item | N•m | in.-lb. | ft.-lb. |
| --- | --- | --- | --- |
| Throttle cable cover screws | 4 | 35 | – |
| Fuel tank retaining bolt | 7 | 62 | – |

# CHAPTER NINE

# ELECTRICAL SYSTEM

9

This chapter contains service and test procedures for electrical systems and components. Refer to Chapter One for electrical system fundamentals and Chapter Two for troubleshooting.

Refer to the back of the manual for wiring diagrams.

**Tables 1-9** are at the end of this chapter.

## ELECTRICAL COMPONENT REPLACEMENT

Most dealerships and parts suppliers will not accept the return of any electrical part. If the exact cause of an electrical system malfunction cannot be determined, have a dealership retest that specific system to verify the test results. This may help avert the possibility of purchasing an expensive part that does not fix the problem.

Consider any test results carefully before replacing a component that tests only slightly out of specification, especially resistance. A number of variables can affect test results dramatically. These include the testing meter's internal circuitry, ambient temperature and conditions under which the machine has been operated. All instructions and specifications have been checked for accuracy; however, successful test results depend to a great extent upon individual accuracy.

## CONTINUITY TESTING

Circuits, switches, light bulbs and fuses can be checked for continuity (a completed circuit) using an ohmmeter connected to the appropriate color-coded wires in the circuit. Tests can be made at the connector or at the part. Use the following procedure as a guide to performing general continuity tests.

*CAUTION*
*When performing continuity checks, do not turn on the ignition switch. Damage to parts and test equipment could occur. Also, verify that power from the battery is not routed directly into the test circuit, regardless of ignition switch position.*

1. Refer to the wiring diagram at the back of this manual and find the part to be checked.
2. Identify the wire colors leading to the part and determine which pairs of wires should be checked. For any check, the circuit should begin at the connector, pass through the part, then return to the connector.
3. Determine when continuity should exist.
   a. Typically, whenever a switch or button is turned on, it closes the circuit, and the meter should indicate continuity.

b. When the switch or button is turned off, it opens the circuit, and the meter should not indicate continuity.

4. Trace the wires from the part to the nearest connector. Separate the connector.

5. Connect an ohmmeter to the connector half that leads to the part being checked. If the test is being made at the terminals on the part, remove all other wires connected to the terminals so they do not influence the meter reading.

6. Operate the switch/button and check for continuity.

## ELECTRICAL CONNECTORS

Electrical connectors are easily susceptible to corrosion-causing moisture which can cause poor electrical connections, leading to component failure. Troubleshooting an electrical circuit with one or more corroded electrical connectors can be time-consuming and frustrating.

When reconnecting electrical connectors, pack them with a dielectric grease compound. Dielectric grease is specially formulated for sealing and waterproofing electrical connections without interfering with current flow. Use only this compound or an equivalent designed for this specific purpose. Do not use a substitute that may interfere with the current flow within the electrical connector. Do not use silicone sealant.

After cleaning both the male and female connectors, make sure they are thoroughly dry. Apply dielectric grease to the interior of one of the connectors prior to connecting the connector halves. For best results, the compound should fill the entire inner area of the connector. On multi-pin connectors, also pack the backside of both the male and female side with the compound to prevent moisture from entering the connector. After the connector is fully packed, wipe all excessive compound from the exterior.

## NEGATIVE BATTERY TERMINAL

Some service procedures require disconnection of the battery cable from the negative battery terminal.

1. Remove the seat as described in Chapter Fifteen.

2. Remove the bolt and disconnect the cable from the negative battery terminal (A, **Figure 1**).

3. Move the cable out of the way and secure it so it cannot accidentally touch the battery terminal.

4. Reconnect the cable to the negative battery terminal and tighten the bolt securely.

5. Install the seat.

## BATTERY

*WARNING*
*Even though the battery is a sealed type, protect eyes, skin and clothing; electrolyte is corrosive and can cause severe burns and permanent injury. The battery case may be cracked and leaking electrolyte. If electrolyte gets into the eyes, flush both eyes thoroughly with clean, running water and get immediate medical attention. Always wear safety goggles when servicing the battery.*

*WARNING*
*While batteries are being charged, highly explosive hydrogen gas forms in each cell. Some of this gas escapes through filler cap openings and may form an explosive atmosphere in and around the battery. This condition can persist for several hours. Sparks, an open flame or a lighted cigarette can ignite the gas, causing an internal battery explosion and possible serious personal injury.*

*NOTE*
*Recycle the old battery. When replacing the old battery, be sure to turn in the old battery at that time. The lead plates and the plastic case can be recycled. Most dealerships accept old batteries in trade when purchasing a new one. Never place an old battery in household trash; it is illegal, in most states, to place any acid or lead (heavy metal) contents in landfills.*

### Safety Precautions

Take the following precautions to prevent an explosion.

1. Do not smoke or permit any open flame near any battery being charged or which has been recently charged.

2. Do not disconnect live circuits at the battery. A spark usually occurs when a live circuit is broken.

3. To prevent accidental shorts that could blow a fuse when working on the electrical system, always disconnect the negative battery cable from the battery as described in this chapter.

4. Be sure the battery cables are connected to their proper terminals. Connecting the battery backward

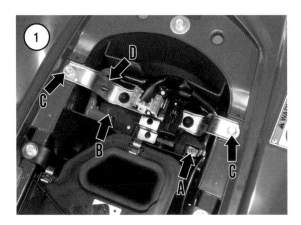

reverses the polarity and damages the rectifier and ignition system.

5. Take care when connecting or disconnecting a battery charger. Turn the power switch off before making or breaking connections. Poor connections are a common cause of electrical arcs, which cause explosions.

6. Do not remove the sealing caps from the top of the battery. The electrolyte level cannot be serviced.

7. Keep children and pets away from the charging equipment and the battery.

## Type

A sealed, maintenance-free battery is installed on all models. The battery electrolyte level cannot be serviced. When replacing the battery, use a sealed type; do not install a non-sealed battery. Never attempt to remove the sealing caps from the top of the battery. The battery does not require periodic electrolyte inspection or refilling. Refer to **Table 1** for battery specifications.

## Removal/Installation

The battery is installed in the compartment located underneath the seat.

1. Read *Safety Precautions* in this section.
2. Turn the ignition switch off.
3. Remove the seat as described in Chapter Fifteen.
4. Disconnect the negative battery cable (A, **Figure 1**) from the negative battery terminal.
5. Disconnect the positive battery cable (B, **Figure 1**) from the positive battery terminal.
6. Remove the battery bracket bolts (C, **Figure 1**), then remove the bracket (D).
7. Lift the battery out of the battery compartment.
8. After the battery has been serviced or replaced, install it by reversing the preceding removal steps while noting the following:

a. Install the battery into the frame with the negative terminal on the left side of the frame.
b. Tighten the bracket bolts to 7 N•m (62 in.-lb.).
c. Always connect the positive battery cable first (B, **Figure 1**), then the negative cable (A).
d. Coat the battery leads with dielectric grease or petroleum jelly.

## Cleaning/Inspection

1. Read *Safety Precautions* in this section.
2. Remove the battery from the ATV as described in this section. Do not clean the battery while it is mounted in the ATV.
3. Clean the battery exterior with a solution of warm water and baking soda. Rinse thoroughly with clean water.
4. Inspect the battery. Look for bulges or cracks in the case, leaking electrolyte or corrosion buildup.
5. Check the battery terminal bolts and nuts for corrosion and damage. Clean parts with a solution of baking soda and water, and rinse thoroughly. Replace if damaged.
6. Check the battery cable clamps for corrosion and damage. If corrosion is minor, clean the battery cable clamps with a stiff brush. Replace excessively worn or damaged cables.

## Testing

The maintenance-free battery can be tested while mounted in the ATV. A digital voltmeter is required for this procedure. Refer to **Table 1** for battery voltage readings for the maintenance free battery.

1. Read *Safety Precautions* in this section.

*NOTE*
*To prevent false test readings, do not test the battery if the battery terminals are corroded. Remove and clean the battery and terminals as described in this section, then reinstall it.*

2. Connect a digital voltmeter between the battery negative and positive leads. Note the following:

a. If the battery voltage is 13.0-13.2 volts (at 20° C [68° F]), the battery is fully charged. Refer to **Table 3**.
b. If the battery voltage is below 12.8 volts (at 20° C [68° F]), the battery is undercharged and requires charging. See **Table 3**.

3. If the battery is undercharged, recharge it as described in this section. Then test the charging system as described in this chapter.

9

## Charging

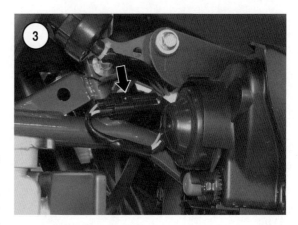

Refer to *Battery Initialization* in this section if the battery is *new*.

To recharge a maintenance-free battery, a digital voltmeter and a charger (**Figure 2**) with an adjustable or automatically variable amperage output are required. If this equipment is not available, have the battery charged by a shop with the proper equipment. Excessive voltage and amperage from an unregulated charger can damage the battery and shorten service life.

The battery should only self-discharge approximately one percent of its given capacity each day. If a battery not in use, without any loads connected, loses its charge within a week after charging, the battery is defective.

If the ATV is not used for long periods of time, an automatic battery charger with variable voltage and amperage outputs is recommended for optimum battery service life.

1. Remove the battery as described in this section.
2. Connect the positive charger lead to the positive battery terminal and the negative charger lead to the negative battery terminal.
3. Set the charger at 12 volts and switch it on. Normally, a battery should be charged at a slow charge rate of 1/10 its given capacity. **Table 1** lists the battery capacity and charge rate for all models.
4. After the battery has been charged, turn the charger OFF, disconnect the leads and check the battery with a digital voltmeter. It should be within the limits specified in **Table 1**. If it is, and remains stable for one hour, the battery is charged.

### Battery Initialization

A new battery must be fully charged before installation. Failure to do so reduces the life of the battery. Using a new battery without an initial charge causes permanent battery damage. That is, the battery will never be able to hold more than an 80% charge. Charging a new battery after it has been used will not bring its charge to 100%. When purchasing a new battery from a dealership or parts store, verify its charge status. If necessary, have them perform the initial or booster charge before accepting the battery.

## CHARGING SYSTEM

The charging system consists of the battery, alternator and a voltage regulator/rectifier. A 15-amp main fuse protects the circuit. Refer to the main wiring diagram at the end of this manual.

The stator coil assembly contains charging coils and lighting coils. The alternating current generated by the charging coils is rectified to direct current. The voltage regulator maintains constant voltage to the battery and additional electrical loads (such as lights or ignition) despite variations in engine speed and load.

### Charging Voltage Test

This procedure tests charging system operation. It does not measure maximum charging system output. To obtain accurate test results, the battery must be fully charged (13.0 volts or higher).

1. Start and run the engine until it reaches normal operating temperature, then turn the engine OFF.
2. Connect a digital voltmeter to the battery terminals.

*NOTE*
*Do not disconnect either battery cable when making this test.*

3. Start the engine and allow it to idle.
4. Gradually increase engine speed to 5000 rpm and read the voltage indicated on the voltmeter. Compare this with the regulated voltage reading in **Table 2**.

*NOTE*
*If the battery is often discharged, but charging voltage tested normal during Step 4, the battery may be damaged.*

5. If the regulated voltage is too low, check for an open or short circuit in the charging system wiring harness, an open or short in the alternator or a damaged regulator/rectifier.
6. If the regulated voltage is too high, check for a poor regulator/rectifier ground, a damaged regulator/rectifier or a damaged battery.

### Regulated (Lighting) Voltage Test

Current generated by the alternator rotor and lighting coils in the stator coil assembly illuminates the headlights and taillight/brake light. The regulator/rectifier regulates the voltage (the current remains alternating current).

The following test applies to the lighting circuit portion of the regulator/rectifier. Refer to the appropriate sections in this chapter for service on the alternator, stator coils and lights.

1. Disconnect the headlight connector (**Figure 3**).
2. Connect an AC voltmeter to the harness end of the connector as follows:
   a. Negative lead to black wire terminal.
   b. Positive lead to yellow or green wire terminal. Note that yellow wire feeds the low headlight beam, and the green wire feeds the high headlight beam.
3. Start the engine and allow it to idle.
4. Set the headlight switch to the low or high position and read the voltmeter.
5. If the voltage is too low, check for an open or short circuit in the wiring harness, an open or short in the alternator or a damaged regulator/rectifier.

### Regulator/Rectifier Removal/Installation

1. Disconnect the cable from the negative battery terminal as described in this chapter.
2. Remove the front fender as described in Chapter Fifteen.
3. Disconnect the regulator/rectifier electrical connector (A, **Figure 4**).
4. Remove the bolts (B, **Figure 4**) securing the regulator/rectifier (C) to the frame bracket and remove it.
5. Install by reversing the preceding removal steps. Make sure the electrical connector is secure and corrosion-free.

### ALTERNATOR

The alternator consists of the flywheel rotor and stator coil assembly. The rotor is a part of the flywheel. The stator coil assembly is located inside the left crankcase cover. The stator coil consists of separate coils that generate voltage for the charging system and lighting system.

Refer to Chapter Five for removal and installation of the flywheel and left crankcase cover.

### Rotor Testing

The rotor is permanently magnetized and cannot be tested except by replacing it with a known good one. The rotor can lose magnetism from old age or a sharp hit, such as dropping it onto a concrete floor. Replace the flywheel if the rotor is defective or damaged.

### Stator Coil

#### *Resistance test*

The stator coil can be tested while mounted on the engine.

1. Disconnect the cable from the negative battery terminal as described in this chapter.

2. Remove the front fender as described in Chapter Fifteen.

3. Disconnect the regulator/rectifier electrical connector (**Figure 5**).

4. To check the charging coil, connect the positive probe of an ohmmeter to the white wire terminal in the stator coil end of the connector and the negative probe to engine ground. Measure the resistance and refer to **Table 2**.

5. To check the lighting coil, connect the positive probe of an ohmmeter to the yellow wire terminal in the stator coil end of the connector and the negative probe to engine ground. Measure the resistance and refer to **Table 2**.

6. Replace the stator if the resistance is not as specified.

*NOTE*
*Before replacing the stator assembly, check the electrical wires to and within the electrical connector, including the stator connector, for any opens or poor connections.*

7. If the stator coil fails the test, replace it as described in this section.

8. Make sure the electrical connector is secure and corrosion-free.

9. Connect the negative battery cable.

10. Install the front fender.

### Removal/installation

*NOTE*
*The stator coil and pickup coil are wired together and must be serviced as a unit assembly.*

1. Remove the left crankcase cover as described in Chapter Five.

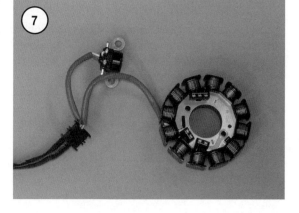

2. Remove the bolts securing the wire retainer (A, **Figure 6**) and remove the retainer.

3. Remove the stator coil mounting bolts (B, **Figure 6**).

4. Remove the pickup coil mounting bolts (C, **Figure 6**).

5. Pull the wire harness grommet out of the crankcase cover notch.

6. Remove the stator coil and pickup coil assembly (**Figure 7**).

7. Do not clean the stator coils with solvent. Wipe off with a clean rag.

8. Install the stator coil by reversing the preceding steps, while noting the following:

    a. Apply sealant to the grooves in the wiring harness grommet before inserting it into the crankcase cover notch.

    b. Insert the tab on the backside of the stator into the notch in the cover (**Figure 8**).

    c. Tighten the stator coil mounting bolts to 7 N•m (62 in.-lb.).

    d. Tighten the pickup coil mounting bolts to 10 N•m (88 in.-lb.).

    e. Tighten the stator wire retainer bolts to 7 N•m (62 in.-lb.).

**IGNITION SYSTEM**

The YFZ450 is equipped with an electronic ignition system. Refer to the wiring diagrams at the end of this manual.

### Ignition System Precautions

Note the following to protect ignition system components.

1. Never disconnect any of the electrical connections while the engine is running.

2. Keep all connections between the various units clean and tight. Apply dielectric grease to all electri-

cal connectors before reconnecting them. This will help seal out moisture.

3. When operating the starter with the spark plug removed, make sure the spark plug or a spark plug checker is installed in the plug cap, and the plug or checker is grounded. If not, excessive resistance may damage the CDI module. Refer to *Spark Test* in Chapter Two.

4. Make sure the CDI module is mounted correctly as described in this chapter.

### Throttle Override System (TORS)

The TORS disables the ignition system if the throttle sticks in the open position.

### *TORS switches*

The throttle override system includes two switches, a throttle switch contained in the throttle housing on the handlebar, and the carburetor switch.

Refer to *Switches* in this chapter for testing and replacement procedures.

### Direct Ignition Coil

The ignition coil is an integral part of the spark plug cap, eliminating the spark plug secondary wire.

### *Removal/installation*

1. Disconnect the cable from the negative battery terminal as described in this chapter.

2. Raise the fuel tank as described in Chapter Eight.

3. Disconnect the ignition coil primary connector (A, **Figure 9**) from the direct ignition coil (B).

4. Pull straight up on the ignition coil (**Figure 10**) and disengage it from the top of the spark plug. Remove it from the cylinder head cover.

5. Install by reversing the removal steps while noting the following.

    a. Push straight down on the ignition coil so it securely engages the spark plug and the cylinder head cover.

    b. Make sure the electrical connector is free of corrosion.

### *Testing*

The ignition coil must be at a minimum temperature of 20° C (68° F) during this test. If necessary, start the engine and let it warm to normal operating temperature. Otherwise, remove and warm the coil prior to testing.

1. Remove the direct ignition coil as described in this section.

2. Measure the primary coil resistance between the positive and the negative terminals on the ignition coil (**Figure 11**). Record the measured resistance.

3. Measure the secondary coil resistance between the ignition coil terminal and the spark plug terminal (**Figure 12**). Record the measured resistance.

4. Replace the ignition coil if either measurement is outside the range specified in **Table 4** or if the coil is damaged.

## Pickup Coil

The pickup coil is located inside the left crankcase cover.

### *Resistance test*

The pickup coil can be tested while mounted on the engine.

1. Disconnect the cable from the negative battery terminal as described in this chapter.

2. Remove the front fender as described in Chapter Fifteen.

3. Disconnect the pickup coil electrical connector (**Figure 13**).

4. Connect the negative probe of an ohmmeter to the red wire terminal and the positive probe to the white wire terminal in the pickup coil end of the connector. Measure the resistance and refer to **Table 4**.

5. Replace the pickup coil if the resistance is not as specified.

### *Removal/installation*

The stator coil and pickup coil are wired together and must be serviced as a unit assembly. Refer to *Stator Coil* in *Alternator* in this chapter for removal and installation procedures.

## CDI Module

The YFZ450 is equipped with a capacitor discharge ignition (CDI) control module. The CDI module controls ignition timing using an electrical signal from the pickup coil as the timing source.

### *Testing*

Test specifications for the CDI module are not available from the manufacturer. Determining

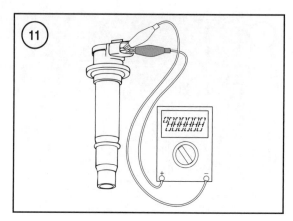

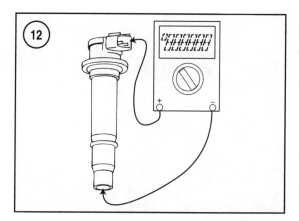

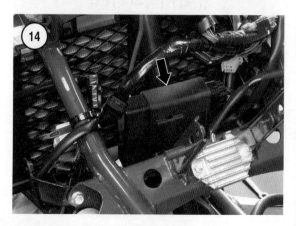

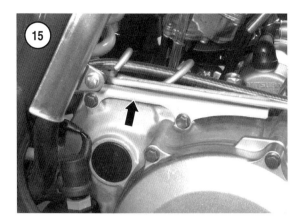

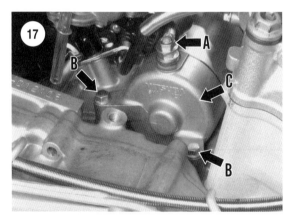

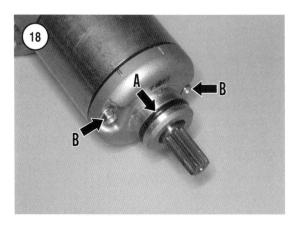

whether the module is faulty requires eliminating other possible causes through troubleshooting.

### Removal/installation

The CDI module (**Figure 14**) is mounted on a bracket under the front fender.
1. Disconnect the cable from the negative battery terminal as described in this chapter.
2. Remove the front fender as described in Chapter Fifteen.
3. Disconnect the electrical connectors from the CDI module.
4. Remove the module from the rubber mount.
5. Reverse the removal steps to install the CDI module.

## STARTER

The starting system consists of the starter, starter gears, starting circuit cutoff relay, starter relay, neutral switch, clutch switch and starter button. Refer to the wiring diagram at the end of this manual.

Refer to **Table 5** for starter specifications.

> *CAUTION*
> *Do not operate the starter for more than 5 seconds at a time. Wait approximately 10 seconds between starting attempts.*

### Troubleshooting

Refer to Chapter Two.

### Removal/Installation

1. Disconnect the cable from the negative battery terminal as described in this chapter.
2. Remove the exhaust system as described in Chapter Four.
3. Remove the parking brake cable holder (**Figure 15**).
4. Remove the bolts (**Figure 16**) securing the banjo fittings to the engine. Remove the oil tubes, fittings and sealing washers.
5. Push back the rubber cap, then remove the nut and starter cable terminal (A, **Figure 17**) from the starter.
6. Remove the starter mounting bolts (B, **Figure 17**).
7. Remove the starter (C, **Figure 17**).
8. If necessary, service the starter as described in this section.
9. Install the starter by reversing the removal steps while noting the following:
   a. Lubricate the starter O-ring (A, **Figure 18**) with grease.

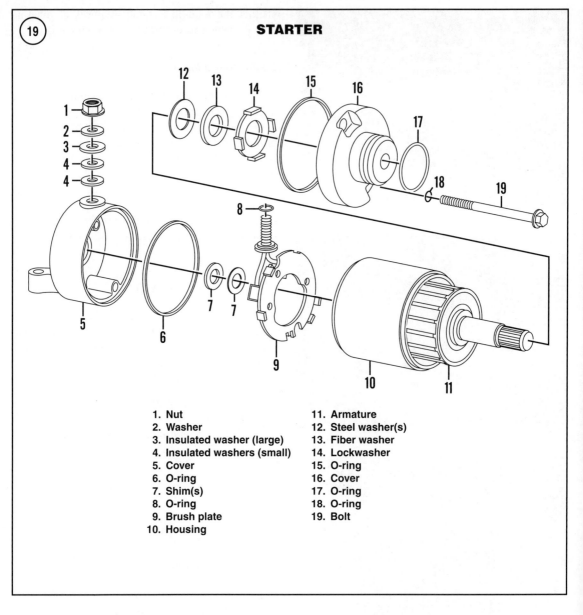

**STARTER**

1. Nut
2. Washer
3. Insulated washer (large)
4. Insulated washers (small)
5. Cover
6. O-ring
7. Shim(s)
8. O-ring
9. Brush plate
10. Housing
11. Armature
12. Steel washer(s)
13. Fiber washer
14. Lockwasher
15. O-ring
16. Cover
17. O-ring
18. O-ring
19. Bolt

b. Clean any rust or corrosion from the starter cable eyelet.

c. Tighten the starter mounting bolts (B, **Figure 17**) to 10 N•m (88 in.-lb.).

**Disassembly**

Refer to **Figure 19**.

1. Find the alignment marks on the case and both end covers. If necessary, scribe new marks.

2. Remove the case bolts (B, **Figure 18**) and O-rings.

*NOTE*
*Record the thickness and alignment of each shim and washer removed during disassembly.*

*NOTE*
*The number of shims used in each starter varies. The starter may be equipped with a different number of shims from that shown in the following photographs.*

3. Remove the front cover (A, **Figure 20**) and lock-washer (B).

4. Remove the fiber washer (C, **Figure 20**) and steel washer(s) (D) from the armature shaft.

5. Remove the end cover (A, **Figure 21**).

6. Remove the rear shim set (B, **Figure 21**).

7. Withdraw the armature from the housing (C, **Figure 21**).

*CAUTION*
*Do not immerse the wire windings in the case or the armature coil in sol-*

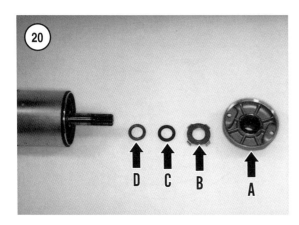

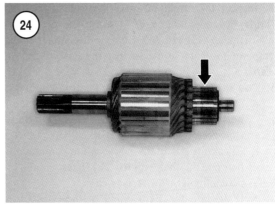

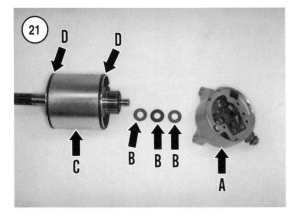

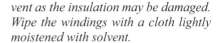

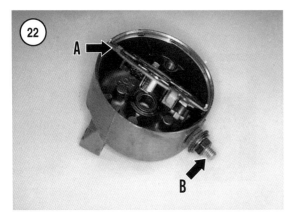

*vent as the insulation may be damaged. Wipe the windings with a cloth lightly moistened with solvent.*

8. Clean all grease, dirt and carbon from the armature, housing and end covers.

**Inspection**

*NOTE*
*The O-rings and brush holder assembly are the only replaceable parts. If other parts are defective, replace the starter.*

1. Pull the brush holder assembly (A, **Figure 22**) out of the end cover.
2. Pull the spring away from each brush and pull the brushes out of their guides.
3. Measure the length of each brush. If the length is less than the service limit in **Table 5**, replace both brushes as a set. When replacing the brushes, note the following:
   a. Soldering is not necessary when replacing the starter brushes.
   b. The brushes are not available separately.
4. Remove the terminal bolt and brush holder (B, **Figure 22**) as an assembly (**Figure 23**). Be sure to install the washer set in the order shown in **Figure 19**.
5. Inspect the brush springs and replace them if weak or damaged.
6. Inspect the commutator (**Figure 24**). The mica must be below the surface of the copper bars. Measure the mica undercut, the distance between the top of the mica and the top of the adjacent copper bars (**Figure 25**). If the mica undercut is less than the specification in **Table 5**, have the commutator serviced by a dealership.
7. Inspect the commutator copper bars for discoloration. A discolored pair of bars indicates grounded armature coils.

8. Inspect the armature shaft for excessive wear, scoring or other damage. Measure the commutator diameter (**Figure 26**). Replace the starter if the commutator diameter is less than the service limit in **Table 5**.

9. Use an ohmmeter and perform the following:

    a. Check for continuity between the commutator bars (**Figure 27**). There should be continuity (low resistance) between pairs of bars.

    b. Check for continuity between the commutator bars and the shaft (**Figure 28**). There should be no continuity (low resistance).

    c. If the armature fails either of these tests, replace the starter.

10. Inspect the front cover seal and bearing. Replace the front cover if either part is excessively worn or damaged.

11. Inspect the end cap bushing. Replace the starter if the bushing is damaged.

12. Inspect the housing (C, **Figure 21**) for cracks or other damage. Inspect for loose, chipped or damaged magnets.

13. Inspect the O-rings (D, **Figure 21**) and replace them if worn or damaged.

## Assembly

1. If removed, install the brushes into their holders, and secure the brushes with the springs.

2. Install the brush holder assembly in the rear cover. Align the holder locating tab with the notch in the end cap (**Figure 29**).

3. Lubricate two new O-rings with lithium grease, and install an O-ring (D, **Figure 21**) onto each end of the housing.

4. Slide the armature into the housing.

5. Install the correct number of shims (B, **Figure 21**) as noted during disassembly onto the armature shaft next to the commutator.

6. Install the end cap onto the armature. Hold the end cap over the armature, and turn the armature during installation so the brushes engage the commutator properly. Do not damage the brushes during this step. Also, make sure the armature is not turned upside down so the shims cannot slide off the end of the shaft. Once the end cap is installed, align the marks (A, **Figure 30**) on the housing case and end cover.

7. Install the correct number of shims (A, **Figure 31**) onto the armature shaft.

8. Install the lockwasher (B, **Figure 31**) into the front cover so the lockwasher tabs engage the slots in the cover.

9. Install the front cover over the armature shaft. Align the marks on the front cover with those on the housing (B, **Figure 30**).

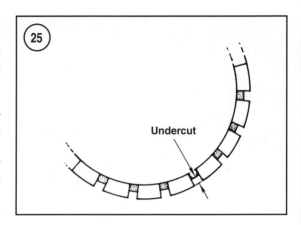

Undercut

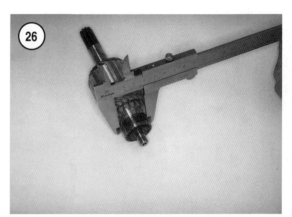

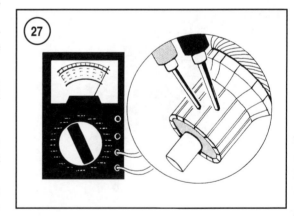

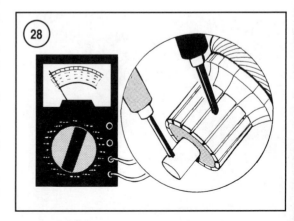

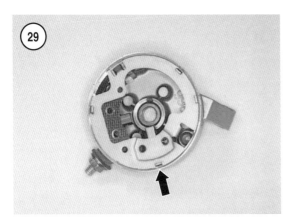

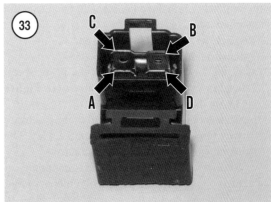

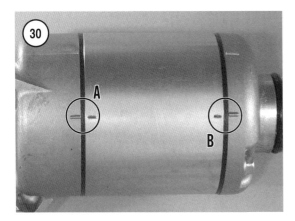

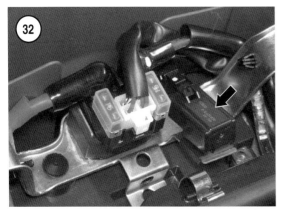

10. Apply blue Loctite (No. 242) to the case bolt threads, and install the bolts, washers and lockwashers. Tighten the bolts securely.

11. Lubricate a new front-cover O-ring with lithium grease, and install it onto the front cover (A, **Figure 18**).

12. Clean the cover mounting lugs of all dirt and other contaminants. The lugs provide the ground for the starter so there must be good contact between them and the crankcase.

### STARTING CIRCUIT CUTOFF SYSTEM

The starting circuit cutoff system uses a cutoff relay that does not allow current to the starter relay unless the transmission is in neutral or unless the clutch lever is pulled in. Included in the relay unit is a diode that prevents current flow from the neutral switch back through the clutch switch.

### Removal/Installation

1. Disconnect the negative battery cable as described in this chapter.

2. Unhook the starting circuit cutoff relay (**Figure 32**) from the mounting bracket.

3. Disconnect the connector from the starting circuit cutoff relay.

4. Install by reversing the preceding removal steps.

### Relay Testing

1. Remove the relay as described in this section.

2. Disconnect the electrical connector from the relay.

3. Connect a fully charged 12 volt battery to the relay. Connect the positive battery terminal to the red/black wire terminal (A, **Figure 33**) and the negative battery terminal to the black/yellow wire terminal (B).

4. Connect the ohmmeter positive test lead to the red/black wire terminal (A, **Figure 33**) on the relay and connect the negative lead to the yellow/black

wire terminal (C) on the relay. The ohmmeter should show continuity.

5. Replace the relay if it fails this test.

6. Proceed as follows to test the diode:

   a. Using an ohmmeter, connect the positive test lead to the sky blue wire terminal (D, **Figure 33**) on the relay.

   b. Connect the negative test lead to the red/black wire terminal (A, **Figure 33**) on the relay. The ohmmeter should indicate continuity.

   c. Reverse the test leads and check continuity in the opposite direction. The ohmmeter should indicate no continuity.

   d. Replace the cutoff relay if it fails these tests.

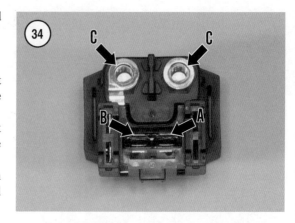

## STARTER RELAY

### Testing

1. Remove the starter relay as described in this section.

2. Check the continuity of the starter relay by performing the following:

   a. Connect the positive terminal of a fully charged 12-volt battery to the starter relay blue/black wire terminal (A, **Figure 34**).

   b. Connect the negative battery terminal to the yellow/black relay terminal (B, **Figure 34**).

   c. Check for continuity between the starter relay terminals (C, **Figure 34**).

3. Replace the starter relay if it fails this test.

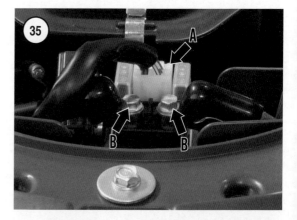

### Removal/Installation

1. Disconnect the negative battery cable as described in this chapter.

2. Disconnect the starter relay electrical connector (A, **Figure 35**).

3. Slide the rubber boots off the two large cable leads.

4. Disconnect the two large cable leads (B, **Figure 35**) from the starter relay switch.

5. Remove the starter relay switch from the mounting bracket.

6. Transfer the 15-amp main fuse and spare fuse to the new starter relay switch.

7. Install by reversing the preceding removal steps.

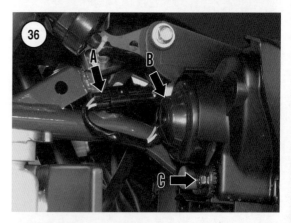

## LIGHTING SYSTEM

The lighting system includes the headlights, headlight relays (2006-on models), taillight/brake light and indicator lights and resistor (2006-on models). Refer to **Table 6** for bulb specifications. Always use the correct bulb. Using the wrong size bulb gives a dim light or causes the bulb to burn out prematurely.

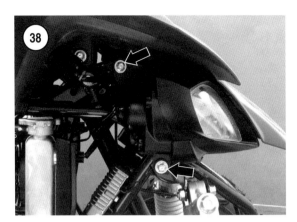

2. Remove the headlight mounting bolts, washers and spacers (**Figure 38**) and remove the headlight.

3. Reverse the removal steps to install the headlight housing. Push the inner housing grommet onto the mounting stud on the frame (**Figure 39**).

### Headlight Adjustment

The headlight beam may be adjusted vertically by turning the adjustment bolt (C, **Figure 36**) on each headlight. Turn the bolt clockwise to lower the beam.

### Headlight Relays 2006-on Models

The headlight relays are mounted on the front, left frame downtube (**Figure 40**). The headlight relays are identical. Refer to the wiring diagram in this manual to determine which relay connects to the high or low beam in the headlight.

#### *Removal/installation*

1. Disconnect the negative battery cable as described in this chapter.

2. Disengage the headlight relay (**Figure 40**) from the rubber mount.

*NOTE*
*Pry up the tabs on the relay nearest the connector.*

3. Disconnect the electrical connector from the headlight relay (**Figure 41**).

4. Reverse the removal steps to install the relay.

#### *Continuity test*

The following test procedure applies to either headlight relay.

1. Remove the headlight relay as described in this section.

### Headlight Bulb Removal/Installation

*WARNING*
*If the headlight just burned out or it was just turned off, it will be hot! Do not touch the bulb until it cools.*

*CAUTION*
*The headlights are equipped with quartz-halogen bulbs. Traces of oil on this type of bulb reduces the life of the bulb. Do not touch the bulb glass. Clean any oil or other chemicals from the bulb with an alcohol-moistened cloth.*

1. Disconnect the headlight connector (A, **Figure 36**).

2. Pull back the rubber cover (B, **Figure 36**).

3. Push in the bulb holder, then turn it counterclockwise and remove the bulb and holder.

4. Remove the bulb (**Figure 37**) from the holder.

5. Reverse the removal steps to install the bulb and headlight. Start the engine and check the headlight operation. If necessary, perform *Headlight Adjustment* as described in this section.

### Headlight Housing Removal/Installation

1. Disconnect the headlight connector (A, **Figure 36**).

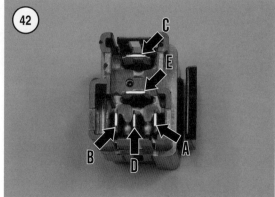

2. Use jumpers to connect the positive terminal of a 12-volt battery to relay terminal (A, **Figure 42**); connect the battery negative terminal to terminal (B).

3. Connect the ohmmeter positive test probe to relay terminal (C, **Figure 42**); connect the negative test probe to relay terminal (D). The relay should have continuity.

4. Disconnect the battery from the relay.

5. Connect the ohmmeter positive test probe to relay terminal (C, **Figure 42**); connect the negative test probe to relay terminal (E). The relay should have continuity.

6. Replace the relay if it fails any portion of this test.

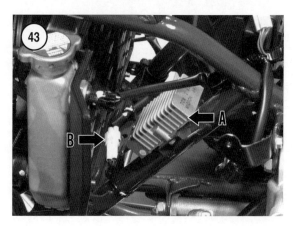

### Resistor 2006-on Models

A resistor is wired into the lighting circuit between the high beam headlight relay and ground. Refer to the wiring diagram at the back of this manual. The resistor is mounted on a right, front downtube (A, **Figure 43**).

### *Testing*

1. Remove the front fender as described in Chapter Fifteen.

2. Disconnect the connector (B, **Figure 43**).

3. Using an ohmmeter measure the resistance between the resistor connector terminals.

4. Replace the resistor if the measured resistance is not as specified in **Table 7**.

### *Removal/installation*

1. Remove the front fender as described in Chapter Fifteen.

2. Disconnect the resistor connector (B, **Figure 43**).

3. Remove the mounting bolts, then remove the resistor (A, **Figure 43**).

4. Reverse the removal steps to install the resistor. Tighten the mounting bolts securely.

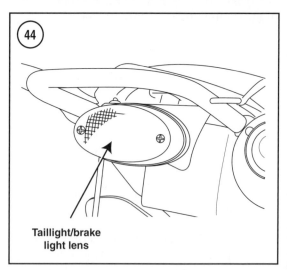

Taillight/brake
light lens

### Taillight/Brake Light Bulb Replacement 2004-2005 Models

1. Remove the lens mounting screws, then remove the lens (**Figure 44**).

2. Turn the bulb counterclockwise and remove it.

3. Install the bulb into the taillight socket and turn it clockwise until it locks into place.

4. Install the lens.

5. Check taillight and brake light operation.

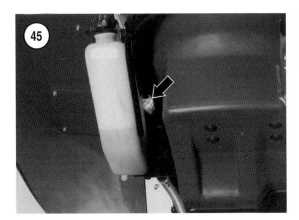

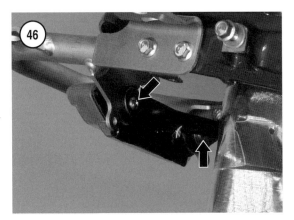

## Taillight/Brake Light Bulb Replacement
## 2006-on Models

2006-on models are equipped with a LED-lighted taillight/brake light assembly. The entire assembly must be replaced if it is faulty.

1. Disconnect the connector (**Figure 45**).
2. Remove the taillight housing mounting screws and washers (**Figure 46**).
3. Remove the taillight/brake light assembly.
4. Reverse the removal steps to install the taillight/brake light assembly.

## Indicator Lights

Indicator lights for coolant temperature and neutral are mounted on a panel forward of the handlebar.

### Coolant light testing

1. Make sure the engine stop switch is in the RUN position.
2. Turn the ignition switch to ON.
3. Shift the transmission into neutral, or pull in the clutch lever.
4. Push the start switch. The coolant temperature light should come on. If not, check for a faulty indicator light bulb, faulty diode or circuit problem.

*NOTE*
*Refer to the wiring diagram in this manual to identify the coolant indicator light circuit diode using wire color.*

5. Use the following procedure to check the diode.
   a. Disconnect the diode (**Figure 47**) from the wiring.
   b. Using an ohmmeter, connect the positive test lead to the blue/black wire terminal on the diode.
   c. Connect the negative test lead to the white/blue wire terminal on the diode. The ohmmeter should indicate continuity.
   d. Reverse the test leads and check continuity in the opposite direction. The ohmmeter should indicate no continuity.
   e. Replace the diode if it fails these tests.

### Neutral light testing

1. Turn the ignition switch on.
2. Shift the transmission into neutral.
3. The neutral light should come on. If not, check for a faulty indicator light bulb or circuit problem.

### Bulb removal/installation

1. Remove the front fender as described in Chapter Fifteen.
2. Pull out the indicator lens (**Figure 48**).
3. Push the grommet (**Figure 49**) out of the panel, then remove the bulb.

## COOLING SYSTEM

## Radiator Fan Testing

1. Remove the front fender as described in Chapter Fifteen.
2. Disconnect the electrical connector (**Figure 50**).

3. Connect a fully charged 12 volt battery to the connector as follows:

   a. Positive battery lead to the blue terminal.

   b. Negative battery lead to the black terminal.

4. The fan should operate. If it is faulty, replace it as described in Chapter Ten.

5. Reconnect the electrical connector to the main harness.

6. Install the front fender.

## Radiator Fan Circuit Breaker Testing

A circuit breaker contained in a small vinyl pack protects the fan circuit.

1. Remove the front fender as described in Chapter Fifteen.

2. Disconnect the circuit breaker leads (A, **Figure 51**).

3. Using an ohmmeter measure the resistance between the circuit breaker leads.

4. If the resistance is greater than 0, replace the circuit breaker (B, **Figure 51**).

## Coolant Temperature Switch (Thermoswitch) Testing

There are two thermoswitches. One switch controls the coolant indicator light. Another switch controls operation of the radiator fan. Both switches are located on the radiator. The switches are designed to open and close at different temperatures; they are not identical. Although the specifications vary, the testing procedure is the same for both switches.

1. Drain the cooling system as described in Chapter Three.

2. Disconnect the electrical connector from the indicator light thermoswitch (A, **Figure 52**) or the radiator fan thermoswitch (B).

3. Unscrew and remove the thermoswitch from the radiator.

*NOTE*
*Make sure the switch terminals do not get wet.*

4. Place the switch in a pan filled with a 50:50 mixture of coolant (water/antifreeze) (A, **Figure 53**). Support the switch so the threads are covered with the coolant and so that the sensor is away from the bottom of the pan.

5. Place a shop thermometer (B, **Figure 53**) in the pan. Use a thermometer that is rated higher than the test temperature.

6. Connect an ohmmeter or continuity tester to the two terminals on top of the switch.

7. Heat the coolant to the specified temperatures in **Table 7** and check for continuity between the termi-

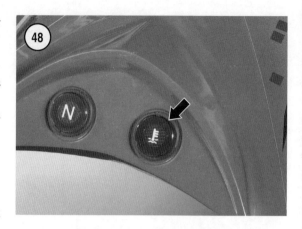

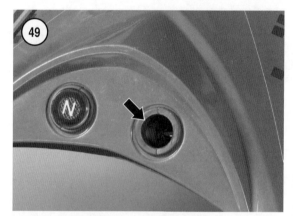

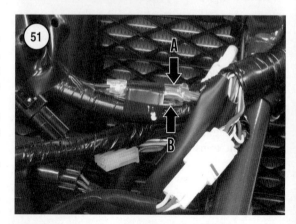

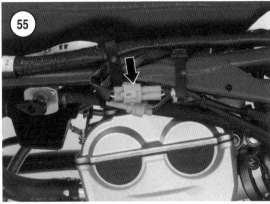

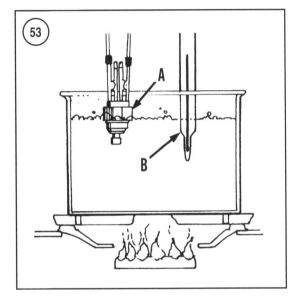

11. Install the thermoswitch and tighten to 28 N•m (21 ft.-lb.).

12. Connect the electrical connector to the thermo unit.

13. Refill the cooling system as described in Chapter Three.

## THROTTLE POSITION SENSOR

*CAUTION*
*Do not loosen the throttle position sensor (TPS) screw, except to adjust or replace the sensor. If the screw is loosened, adjust the TPS as described in this section. Failing to adjust the TPS unit will reduce engine performance.*

The throttle position sensor (TPS) installed on the carburetor (**Figure 54**) provides the CDI module with an electronic signal that coincides with the throttle valve position. The CDI module then adjusts ignition timing for the immediate engine load. The TPS unit must be accurately adjusted so the signal represents the actual throttle position.

Carburetor removal is not necessary to perform the following checks and adjustment.

### Testing

The manufacturer does not provide test specifications for the TPS. If the TPS will not perform as described in the adjustment procedure, replace the TPS.

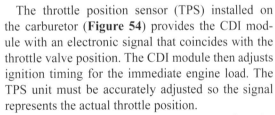

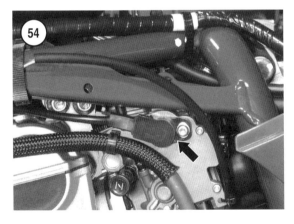

nals on the switch. Maintain the coolant at the specified temperature in **Table 7** for three minutes before testing.

8. Allow the coolant to cool while checking for continuity between the terminals on the switch.

9. If the continuity test does not match those listed in **Table 7**, replace the switch.

10. Install a new O-ring onto the thermoswitch.

### CDI Input Voltage Check

The input voltage from the CDI unit to the TPS must be correct in order for the TPS to function properly. Check the CDI unit as follows:

1. Disconnect the TPS connector (**Figure 55**).

2. Connect the positive lead of a voltmeter to the blue wire connector terminal in the connector end

that leads to the CDI. Connect the negative tester lead to the black wire connector terminal.
3. Start the engine and run at idle speed.
4. Compare the reading to the TPS input voltage specification in **Table 7**. If the reading is not within specifications, replace the CDI unit as described in this chapter.
5. Reattach the connector.

### TPS Removal/Installation/Adjustment

The TPS unit can be replaced and adjusted with the carburetor installed on the motorcycle.
1. Disconnect the TPS connector (**Figure 55**).

> *NOTE*
> *A tamper resistant T-25 bit will be required to loosen and tighten the TPS Torx screw.*

2. Remove the Torx screw securing the TPS (**Figure 54**) to the carburetor. Remove the unit.
3. Install a new O-ring onto the TPS.
4. Install the new TPS, checking that the slot in the unit couples with the throttle shaft tang. Temporarily tighten the screw.
5. Start the engine and check the idle speed as described in *Carburetor* in Chapter Three. Shut off the engine.
6. Adjust the TPS sensor output voltage as follows:
   a. Reattach the TPS connector (**Figure 55**).

> *CAUTION*
> *In substep b, do not insert the electrical conductors too far into the TPS connector. Doing so may damage the waterproof material in the connector. Also make sure the conductors do not touch as a short-circuit between the terminals may damage the TPS and CDI units.*

   b. Insert thin electrical conductors into the TPS connector yellow wire and black wire terminal positions (**Figure 56**).
   c. Switch a digital voltmeter to the DCV scale.

> *NOTE*
> *A digital voltmeter is required to accurately read the small amount of voltage measured in this procedure.*

   d. Connect the positive voltmeter lead to the yellow wire terminal and the negative voltmeter lead to the black wire terminal (**Figure 56**).
   e. Start and run the engine.
   f. Loosen the screw and turn the TPS until the required TPS output voltage listed in **Table 7**

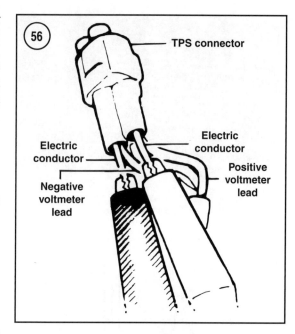

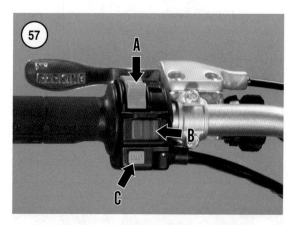

is achieved. Tighten the screw and recheck the measurement.
   g. Reattach the TPS connector (**Figure 55**).

### SWITCHES

#### Left Handlebar Switch Assembly

The left handlebar switch assembly houses the headlight switch (A, **Figure 57**), engine stop switch (B) and starter switch (C). The switches can be checked for continuity using an ohmmeter connected to the appropriate color-coded wires in the connector plug. Refer to *Continuity Testing* in this chapter for the test procedure.

> *NOTE*
> *The switches mounted in the left handlebar switch housing are not available separately. If one switch is damaged, replace the housing as an assembly.*

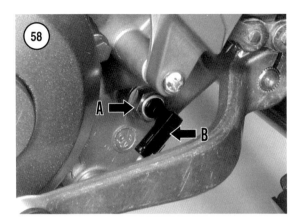

a. The ohmmeter must read continuity with the transmission in neutral.
b. The ohmmeter must read infinity with the transmission in gear.
c. If either reading is incorrect, check the wiring harness for damage or dirty or loose-fitting terminals. If the wiring harness is good, replace the neutral switch.
5. Reconnect the switch connector.
6. Start the engine and check the operation of the neutral switch indicator light with the transmission in neutral and in gear.

*Removal/installation*

1. Shift the transmission into neutral.
2. Remove the external shift mechanism as described in Chapter Six.
3. Disconnect the electrical connector (B, **Figure 58**) from the neutral switch.
4. Unscrew the neutral switch and washer (A, **Figure 58**) from the crankcase.
5. Make sure the sealing washer (**Figure 59**) is installed on the neutral switch. Install the neutral switch into the lower crankcase and tighten to 20 N•m (15 ft.-lb.).
6. Connect the electrical connector to the neutral switch. Push it on and make sure it is seated correctly.
7. Install the external shift mechanism.

**Front Brake Light Switch**

The front brake light switch is mounted on the front master cylinder assembly.

*Testing*

The switch can be checked for continuity using an ohmmeter connected to the appropriate color-coded wires in the connector plug. Refer to *Continuity Testing* in this chapter for the test procedure.

*Removal/installation 2004-2006 models*

1. Insert a small tool to depress the barb that retains the switch housing in the master cylinder (**Figure 60**).
2. Pull out the switch from the master cylinder.
3. Disconnect the switch connector and remove the switch.
4. Reverse the preceding steps to install the switch.
5. Check brake light operation.

*Removal/installation*

1. Remove the front fender as described in Chapter Fifteen.
2. Remove or cut any clamps securing the switch wiring harness to the handlebar.
3. Pull back the large rubber boot and disconnect the switch assembly electrical connectors.
4. Remove the screws securing the switch to the handlebar and remove the switch assembly.
5. Install by reversing the preceding steps.

**Neutral Switch**

The neutral switch is mounted on the left crankcase (A, **Figure 58**).

*Testing*

1. Shift the transmission into neutral.
2. Disconnect the connector (B, **Figure 58**).
3. Connect one lead of an ohmmeter to the neutral switch terminal and the other ohmmeter lead to a good engine ground.
4. Read the ohmmeter scale with the transmission in neutral, and then in gear. Note the following:

9

### Removal/installation 2007-on models

1. Disconnect the two electrical connectors (A, **Figure 61**) from the front brake light switch.
2. Remove the mounting screw (B, **Figure 61**) and brake switch.
3. Reverse the preceding steps to install the switch.
4. Check brake light operation.

## Rear Brake Light Switch

### Testing

1. Remove the right side cover as described in Chapter Fifteen.
2. Disconnect the brake light switch wires at the electrical connector beneath the fuel tank.
3. Connect the leads of an ohmmeter or continuity tester between the connector terminals. The tester should indicate continuity when the rear brake pedal is depressed and infinity when the pedal is released.
4. If necessary, replace the rear brake light switch if it fails to operate as described.

### Removal/installation

1. Remove the right side cover as described in Chapter Fifteen.
2. Disconnect the brake light switch wires at the electrical connector beneath the fuel tank.
3. Remove the cover (**Figure 62**) around the brake reservoir hose and switch wires.
4. Detach the spring (A, **Figure 63**) from the brake light switch.
5. Unscrew the brake light switch from the mounting nut (B, **Figure 63**).
6. Reverse the removal steps to install the brake light switch.
7. Refer to Chapter Three and adjust the rear brake light switch.

## Ignition Switch Removal/Installation

1. Remove the front fender as described in Chapter Fifteen.
2. Unscrew the switch retaining nut (A, **Figure 64**), then remove the ignition switch (B).
3. Reverse the removal steps to install the ignition switch.
4. Turn the ignition switch on and check operation.

## TORS Switches

The throttle override system (TORS) consists of two switches in parallel that connect the ignition

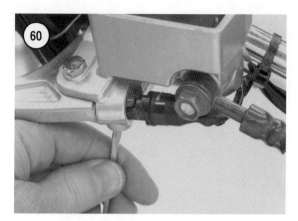

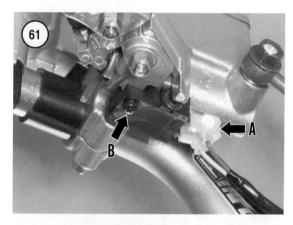

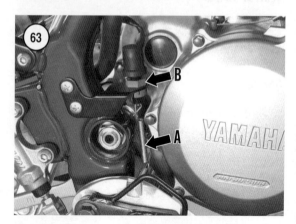

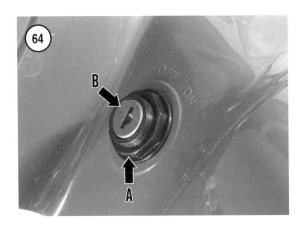

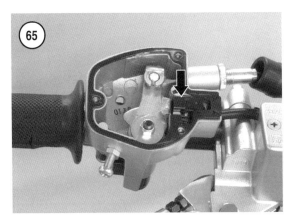

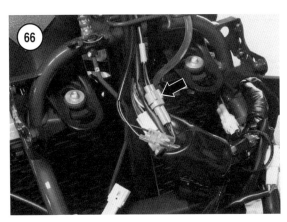

module to ground. The circuitry stops current flow from the ignition module to the ignition coil, which stops the engine, if the carburetor sticks open when the throttle is closed.

The TORS switches are located in the handlebar throttle housing and on the carburetor. Note the following:

1. The handlebar TORS switch is closed (continuity) when the throttle lever is pushed.
2. The carburetor TORS switch is closed (continuity) when the throttle is closed.

### Throttle lever switch testing/removal/installation

The throttle lever switch (**Figure 65**) is mounted in the throttle housing.

1. Check the throttle cable adjustment as described in Chapter Three. Adjust if necessary.
2. Remove the front fender as described in Chapter Fifteen.
3. Push back the rubber cover, then disconnect the gray throttle lever switch electrical connector (**Figure 66**). The connector has two wires, black and black/yellow.
4. Check for continuity between the black/yellow wire and the black wire.
5. Push the throttle lever to full throttle position. If the switch is good, the tester will indicate continuity.
6. Release the throttle lever. If the switch is good, the tester will indicate no continuity.
7. If the switch fails this test, replace the switch.
8. To replace the throttle lever switch (**Figure 65**):
   a. Remove the throttle lever housing cover and gasket.
   b. Remove the screw securing the switch to the throttle lever housing.
   c. Lift the switch out of the housing and remove it.
   d. Reverse the preceding steps to install the new switch. Push the grommet on the switch wiring harness into the throttle lever housing.
9. Reconnect the wiring harness connectors.

### Carburetor switch testing

The carburetor switch (**Figure 67**) is installed in the TORS housing on the carburetor. Do not attempt to remove the switch from the housing. If the switch is faulty, the TORS switch housing assembly must be replaced as described in Chapter Eight.

1. Check the throttle cable adjustment as described in Chapter Three. Adjust if necessary.
2. Remove the left side cover as described in Chapter Fifteen.
3. Disconnect the gray carburetor switch electrical connector (**Figure 68**).

4. Check for continuity between the black/yellow wire and the black wire.

5. Push the handlebar throttle lever to full throttle position. If the switch is good, the tester will indicate no continuity.

6. Release the throttle lever. If the switch is good, the tester will indicate continuity.

7. If the switch fails this test, replace the switch. To replace the carburetor switch, refer to *Carburetor* in Chapter Eight and remove and install the TORS switch housing as described in the disassembly and reassembly procedures.

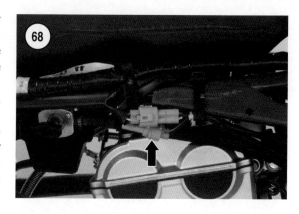

### Table 1 BATTERY SPECIFICATIONS

| | |
|---|---|
| Type | GT7B-4, maintenance-free (sealed)* |
| Capacity | 12 volt 6.5 amp hour |
| Voltage (@ 68° F/20° C) | |
|   Fully charged | 13.0-13.2 volts |
|   Need charging | Below 12.8 volts |

*A maintenance free battery is installed on all models described in this manual. Because this type of battery requires a high-voltage charging system, do not install a standard type battery.

### Table 2 ALTERNATOR AND CHARGING SYSTEM SPECIFICATIONS

| | |
|---|---|
| Alternator | |
|   Type | AC magneto |
|   Model number | F5TG (Moric) |
|   Normal output | 14 volts/120 watts @ 5000 rpm |
|   Charging coil resistance | 0.288-0.432 ohm* |
|   Lighting coil resistance | 0.224-0.336 ohm* |
| Voltage regulator/rectifier | |
|   Model number | SH712AB (Shindengen) |
|   Regulator no-load regulated voltage | |
|     DC | 14.1-14.9 volts |
|     AC | 13.0-14.0 volts |
|   Rectifier capacity | |
|     DC | 8.0 amps |
|     AC | 12.0 amps |

*Test must be made at an ambient temperature of 68° F (20° C). Do not test when the engine or component is hot.

### Table 3 MAINTENANCE-FREE BATTERY VOLTAGE READINGS

| State of charge | Voltage reading |
|---|---|
| 100% | 13.0-13.2 |
| 75% | 12.8 |
| 50% | 12.5 |
| 25% | 12.2 |
| 0% | 12.0 volts or less |

## Table 4 IGNITION SYSTEM SPECIFICATIONS

| Type | Capacitor discharge ignition |
|---|---|
| Model number | 5TG (Moric) |
| Ignition timing | 7.5 degrees BTDC @ 1800 rpm |
| Advancer type | Electronic |
| Pickup coil resistance | 248-372 ohms* |
| Ignition coil | |
| Model number | J0474 (Denso) |
| Primary resistance | 0.08-0.10 ohms* |
| Secondary resistance | 4560-6840 ohms* |

*Test must be made at an ambient temperature of 68° F (20° C). Do not test when the engine or component is hot.

## Table 5 STARTER SPECIFICATIONS

| Item | New mm (in.) | Service limit mm (in.) |
|---|---|---|
| Starter motor model number | SM-14 (Mitsuba) | – |
| Brush length | 10 (0.39) | 3.5 (0.14) |
| Commutator outer diameter | 28 (1.10) | 27 (1.06) |
| Mica undercut | 0.7 (0.03) | – |

## Table 6 BULB SPECIFICATIONS

| Item | Wattage |
|---|---|
| Headlight (high/low beam) | 30/30W (2) |
| Tail/brake light | 5/21 W |
| Instrument illumination light | 2 W (3) |
| Indicator lights | 1.7 W (2) |

## Table 7 SENSOR, SWITCH AND RESISTOR TEST READINGS

| Item | Test readings |
|---|---|
| Coolant temperature thermoswitch | |
| Indicator light | |
| Heating phase | |
| Less than 243-253° F (117-123°C) | No continuity |
| More than 243-253° F (117-123° C) | Continuity |
| Cooling phase | |
| More than 234-244° F (112-118° C) | Continuity |
| Less than 234-244° F (112-118° C) | No continuity |
| Radiator fan thermoswitch (2004-2005 models) | |
| Heating phase | |
| Less than 203-214° F (95-101° C) | No continuity |
| More than 203-214° F (95-101° C) | Continuity |
| Cooling phase | |
| More than 192-203° F (89-95° C) | Continuity |
| Less than 192-203° F (89-95° C) | No continuity |
| Radiator fan thermoswitch (2006-2009 models) | |
| Heating phase | |
| Less than 216-226° F (102-108° C) | No continuity |
| More than 216-226° F (102-108° C) | Continuity |
| Cooling phase | |
| More than 207-217° F (97-103° C) | Continuity |
| Less than 207-217° F (97-103° C) | No continuity |

(continued)

**Table 7 SENSOR, SWITCH AND RESISTOR TEST READINGS (continued)**

| Item | Test readings |
|------|---------------|
| Lighting resistor resistance (2006-2009 models) | 2.755-3.045 ohms @ 77° F (25° C) |
| Throttle position sensor | |
|   Input voltage | 5 volts |
|   Output voltage | 0.58-0.78 volt |

**Table 8 FUSE SPECIFICATION**

| Main fuse | 15 amp |
|-----------|--------|

**Table 9 ELECTRICAL SYSTEM TORQUE SPECIFICATIONS**

| Item | N•m | in.-lb. | ft.-lb. |
|------|-----|---------|---------|
| Battery bracket bolts | 7 | 62 | – |
| Neutral switch | 20 | – | 15 |
| Pickup coil mounting bolts | 10 | 88 | – |
| Starter mounting bolts | 10 | 88 | – |
| Stator coil mounting bolts | 7 | 62 | – |
| Stator wire retainer bolts | 7 | 62 | – |
| Thermoswitch | 28 | – | 21 |

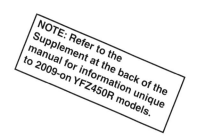

NOTE: Refer to the Supplement at the back of the manual for information unique to 2009-on YFZ450R models.

# COOLING SYSTEM

**10**

This chapter covers radiator, coolant reservoir, radiator fan and water pump. For routine cooling system maintenance, refer to Chapter Three. For electrical test procedures, refer to Chapter Nine.

**Table 1** and **Table 2** are at the end of this chapter.

## COOLING SYSTEM SERVICE NOTES

*WARNING*
*Do not remove the radiator cap (**Figure 1**), remove the coolant drain plug or disconnect coolant hoses when the engine and radiator are hot. The coolant is very hot and under pressure. Scalding fluid and steam may be emitted which could cause personal injury.*

*WARNING*
*Antifreeze is toxic. Do not discharge coolant containing antifreeze into storm sewers, septic systems, or onto the ground. Place used antifreeze in the original container and dispose of it according to local regulations. Do not store coolant where it is accessible to children or pets.*

### Inspection

The pressurized cooling system consists of the radiator, water pump, radiator cap, electric cooling fan and coolant reservoir.

*CAUTION*
*Drain and flush the cooling system as described in Chapter Three. Refill the system with the specified type, mixture and quantity of coolant (**Table 1**). Do not reuse the old coolant, as it deteriorates with use. Do not operate the cooling system with only distilled water, even in climates where antifreeze protection is not required; doing so will promote internal engine corrosion.*

It is important to keep the coolant level to the FULL mark on the coolant reserve tank (**Figure 2**).

1. Check the level with the engine at normal operating temperature and the ATV on a level surface (Chapter Three).

2. If the level is low, remove the reservoir tank cap and add coolant to the reserve tank, not to the radiator.

3. Check the coolant hoses and clamps for looseness or damage.

4. Start the engine and allow it to idle. If steam is observed at the muffler, a head gasket might be damaged. If enough coolant leaks into the cylinder, the cylinder could hydrolock, thus preventing the engine from being cranked. Coolant may also be present in the engine oil. If the oil on the dipstick is foamy or milky-looking, there is coolant in the oil. If so, correct the problem before returning the ATV to service.

*CAUTION*
*If the engine oil is contaminated with coolant, change the oil and filter after performing the repair.*

5. Check the radiator for clogged or damaged fins. Refer radiator repair to a dealership.

6. Check all coolant hoses for cracks or damage. Replace all questionable parts. Make sure the hose clamps are tight, but not so tight that they cut the hoses. Refer to *Hoses and Hose Clamps* in this chapter section.

7. When troubleshooting the cooling system for loss of coolant, pressure test the system as described in this chapter.

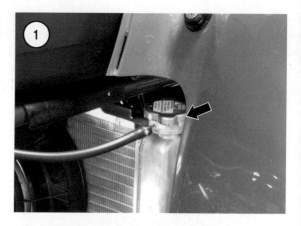

### PRESSURE TEST

A cooling system tester is required for the following tests.

1. Park the ATV on level ground.

2. Remove the radiator cap (**Figure 1**).

3. Pressure test the radiator cap (**Figure 3**) using a cooling system tester. Refer to the manufacturer's instructions when making the tests. The specified radiator cap pressure is 108-137 kPa (15.6-19.8 psi). Replace the radiator cap if it does not hold pressure or if the relief pressure is too high or too low.

4. Pressure test the radiator and cooling system (**Figure 4**). Apply a pressure of 137 kPa (19.8 psi). If the cooling system will not hold the specified pressure, determine the source of leakage and repair as needed.

5. Reinstall the radiator cap (**Figure 1**).

### HOSES AND CLAMPS

Hoses deteriorate with age. Inspect them periodically and replace them whenever they show signs of

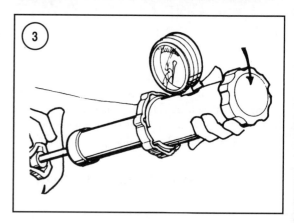

cracks or leaks. To be safe, replace the hoses every two years. Whenever any component of the cooling system is removed, inspect the hoses and clamps to determine if replacement is necessary.

### Inspection

1. With the engine cool, check the cooling hoses for brittleness, hardness or cracks. Replace hoses in this condition.

2. With the engine hot, examine the hoses for swelling along the entire hose length. Replace hoses that show signs of swelling.

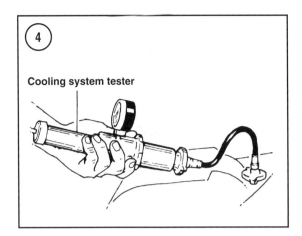

Cooling system tester

3. Twist the hose end to break the seal and remove it from the connecting joint. If the hose has been on for some time, it may have become fused to the joint. If so, insert a small screwdriver or pick tool between the hose and joint. While working the tool around the joint, carefully pry the hose loose.

*CAUTION*
*Do not apply excessive force to a hose when attempting to remove it. Many of the hose connectors are fragile and can be easily damaged.*

4. Examine the connecting joint for cracks or other damage. Repair or replace parts as required. Remove rust and corrosion with a wire brush.
5. Inspect the hose clamps and replace if necessary.
6. Slide the hose clamp over the outside of the hose and then install the hose over its connecting joint. Make sure the hose clears all obstructions and is routed properly.

*NOTE*
*If it is difficult to install a hose on a joint, apply some antifreeze into the end of the hose where it seats onto its connecting joint.*

7. With the hose positioned correctly on the joint, position the clamp back away from the end of the hose slightly. Tighten the clamp securely, but not so much that the hose is damaged.

*NOTE*
*If installing coolant hoses onto the engine while it is removed from the frame, check the position of the hose clamp(s) to make sure it can be loosened when installed in the frame.*

8. Refill the cooling system as described in *Cooling System* in Chapter Three. Start the engine and check for leaks.

**RADIATOR**

**Removal/Installation**

1. Remove the front fender as described in Chapter Fifteen.
2. Drain the coolant as described in Chapter Three.
3. Remove the radiator fan as described in this chapter.
4. Disconnect the electrical connectors (**Figure 5**) from the thermoswitches on the radiator.
5. Disengage the electrical wires from the hooks on the left side of the grille. Note wire routing.
6. Detach the coolant reservoir hose from the radiator (A, **Figure 6**).

3. Check the area around each hose clamp. Signs of rust around clamps indicate possible leaks from a damaged or over-tightened clamp.

**Removal/Installation**

Remove/install hoses when the engine is cool.
1. Drain the cooling system as described in *Cooling System* in Chapter Three.
2. Loosen the hose clamps from the hose to be replaced. Slide the clamps along the hose and out of the way.

7. Detach the lower (outlet) radiator hose (B, **Figure 6**).

8. Detach the upper (inlet) radiator hose (**Figure 7**).

*NOTE*
*The lower radiator retaining bolts also secure the fender brace.*

9. Remove the lower radiator retaining bolts (C, **Figure 6**), then remove the fender brace (D).

10. Remove the upper radiator retaining bolts (**Figure 8**) and remove the radiator.

11. If necessary, remove the grill retaining screw (A, **Figure 9**) and separate the grill (B) from the radiator.

12. Reverse the removal steps to install the radiator. Note the following:

   a. Make sure the mounting grommets (A, **Figure 10**) are in good condition. Replace otherwise.

   b. Make sure the radiator fan retaining nut plates (B, **Figure 10**) are installed before installing the radiator.

   c. Install a cup washer onto each upper radiator retaining bolt. Tighten the radiator retaining bolts to 7 N•m (62 in.-lb.).

   d. Refill the coolant system as described in Chapter Three.

   e. Check for leaks.

**Inspection**

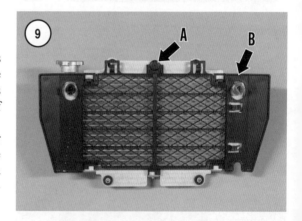

1. Inspect the radiator cap top and bottom seals (**Figure 11**) for deterioration or damage. Check the spring for damage. Pressure test the radiator cap as described in this chapter. Replace the radiator cap if necessary.

2. Clean off the exterior of the radiator with a water hose on low pressure. Spray both the front and the back to remove all dirt and debris. Carefully use a whiskbroom or stiff paintbrush to remove any stubborn debris.

*CAUTION*
*Do not press too hard on the cooling fins and tubes, as they may be damaged and cause a leak.*

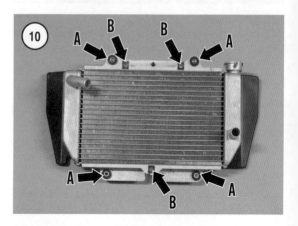

3. Straighten any bent cooling fins with a broad-tipped screwdriver.

4. Check for cracks or coolant leaks (usually a moss-green colored residue). If leaks, blockage or damage are evident, take the radiator to a dealership.

5. Check the mounting brackets for cracks or damage.

6. To prevent oxidation to the radiator, touch up any area where the black paint is worn off.

## COOLANT RESERVOIR

### Removal/Installation

1. Mark the coolant hoses for proper installation.
2. Detach the reservoir vent hose (A, **Figure 12**).
3. Detach the coolant hose (B, **Figure 12**).
4. While holding the reservoir, remove the reservoir retaining bolts (C, **Figure 12**) and remove the reservoir.
5. Remove the reservoir cap, then pour the coolant into a container.
6. Reverse the removal steps to install the reservoir. Fill with coolant as described in Chapter Three.

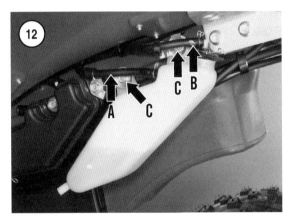

## RADIATOR FAN

The radiator fan is mounted on the backside of the radiator.

### Testing

To test the fan motor and switch, refer to Chapter Nine.

### Removal/Installation

1. Remove the front fender as described in Chapter Fifteen.
2. Disconnect the fan connector (**Figure 13**).
3. Detach the fan vent hose (A, **Figure 14**).
4. Remove the lower fan retaining bolt (B, **Figure 14**).
5. Hold the fan, remove the upper retaining bolt (C, **Figure 14**) on each side and remove the radiator fan.
6. Reverse the removal steps to install the radiator fan while noting the following:
   a. Make sure the nut plates (B, **Figure 10**) are properly positioned on the radiator frame.
   b. Tighten the retaining bolts to 9 N•m (80 in.-lb.).
   c. If removed, install the fan vent hose as shown in **Figure 15**.

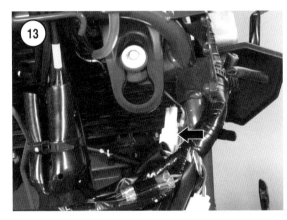

## WATER PUMP HOUSING

The water pump (A, **Figure 16**) is located in the right crankcase cover. To inspect the condition of the impeller or water passages, the outer housing can be removed without removing the crankcase cover. However, to service the seals or bearing, the right crankcase cover must be removed.

**10**

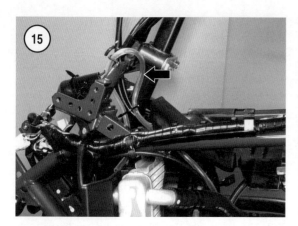

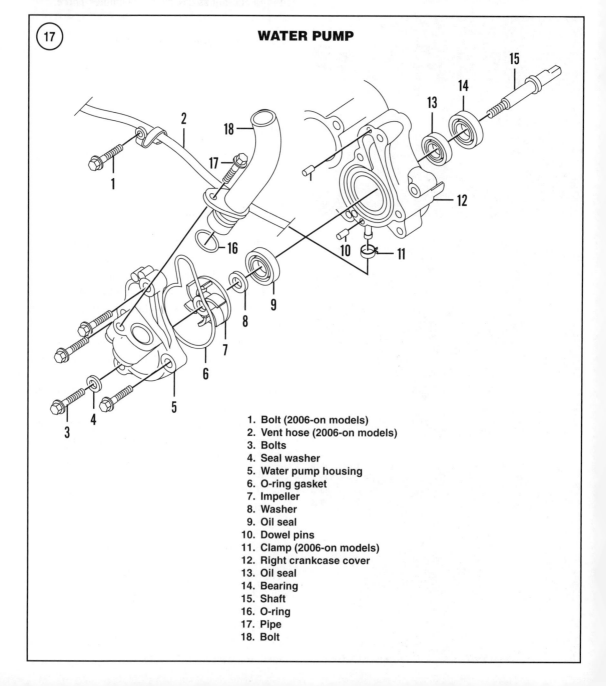

**WATER PUMP**

1. Bolt (2006-on models)
2. Vent hose (2006-on models)
3. Bolts
4. Seal washer
5. Water pump housing
6. O-ring gasket
7. Impeller
8. Washer
9. Oil seal
10. Dowel pins
11. Clamp (2006-on models)
12. Right crankcase cover
13. Oil seal
14. Bearing
15. Shaft
16. O-ring
17. Pipe
18. Bolt

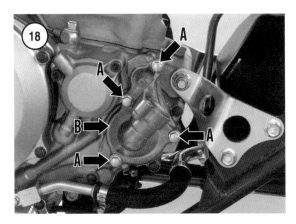

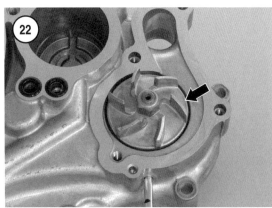

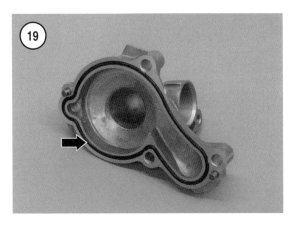

## Removal/Installation

Refer to **Figure 17**.

1. Drain the cooling system as described in Chapter Three.

2. Remove the outer housing as follows:

   a. Remove the bolt (B, **Figure 16**) securing the coolant pipe (C).

   b. Pull the coolant pipe from the water pump housing.

   c. Remove the four bolts (A, **Figure 18**) securing the water pump housing, then remove the housing (B).

   d. Account for the dowel between the cover and housing.

3. Disassemble and inspect the pump as described in *Bearing and Seal Remova/Installation* in *Water Pump* in this chapter.

4. Reverse the preceding steps to install the housing while noting the following:

   a. Install a new O-ring onto the housing (**Figure 19**).

   b. Install a new seal washer onto the bottom housing bolt.

   c. Tighten the water pump housing bolts to 10 N•m (88 in.-lb.).

   d. Install a new, lubricated O-ring onto the coolant pipe (**Figure 20**).

   e. Tighten the coolant pipe retaining bolt to 10 N•m (88 in.-lb.).

## WATER PUMP

### Bearing and Seal Removal/Installation

Refer to **Figure 17**.

1. Remove the right crankcase cover as described in Chapter Five.

2. Hold the impeller shaft with a wrench (**Figure 21**) so the impeller (**Figure 22**) can be removed.

*CAUTION*
*Place the wrench on the large impeller flats. The small flats must remain un-damaged as they must properly engage with the balancer shaft.*

3. Remove the washer from the shaft (**Figure 23**).
4. Remove the impeller shaft from the housing (**Figure 24**).
5. Remove the outer seal as follows:
   a. Place a folded shop cloth over the housing so it will not get damaged.
   b. Pry the seal out of the housing (**Figure 25**).
6. Remove the inner seal and bearing together as follows:
   a. Place a bearing driver onto the seal.
   b. Carefully drive the bearing and seal from the housing.

*CAUTION*
*Do not apply pressure to the inner bearing race or the bearing will be damaged. Apply pressure to the outer race only.*

7. Inspect the bearing for roughness and play. Check for radial and axial play (**Figure 26**). Replace the bearing if necessary.
8. Inspect the impeller and shaft.
   a. Inspect the impeller (A, **Figure 27**) for damage and deposits.
   b. Inspect the impeller shaft (B, **Figure 27**) for deposits and wear at the bearing and seal surfaces. Also check that the shaft is straight.
9. Inspect the bore in the housing for damage (**Figure 28**).
10. Install the bearing and inner seal (**Figure 29**) as follows:
   a. Pack lithium-base grease in the lip of a new seal. The inner seal is smaller than the outer seal.
   b. Drive the seal into the housing, with the closed side of the seal facing out (away from the engine). To seat the seal, use a driver that is slightly smaller than the outside diameter of the seal.

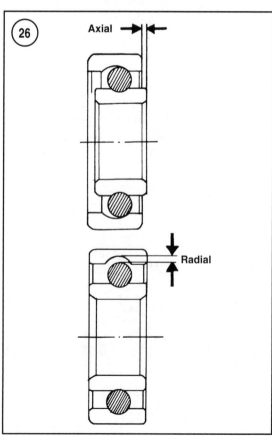

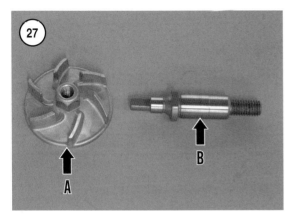

*CAUTION*
*Do not apply pressure to the inner bear-*
*ing race or the bearing will be damaged.*
*Apply pressure to the outer race only.*

11. Install the outer seal as follows:
   a. Pack lithium-base grease in the lip of a new seal.
   b. Position the seal with its closed side facing in (toward the engine).
   c. Drive the seal (**Figure 25**) into the housing, using a driver that is slightly smaller than the outside diameter of the seal.
12. Install the impeller and impeller shaft as follows:
   a. Lubricate the shaft with engine oil.
   b. Working from the back side of the housing, carefully twist the threaded end of the shaft through the bearing and seals. Seat the shaft (**Figure 30**) against the bearing.
   c. Place a new washer (**Figure 23**) on the impeller shaft, then thread the impeller (**Figure 22**) onto the shaft.

*CAUTION*
*Place the wrench on the large impeller*
*flats. Do not damage the small impeller*
*flats, as they must properly engage with*
*the balancer shaft.*

   d. Hold the impeller shaft with a wrench and tighten the impeller to 14 N•m (124 in.-lb.).
13. Install the right crankcase cover as described in Chapter Five.
14. Install the water pump housing as described in this chapter.

c. Position the bearing over the housing. The manufacturer's marks on the bearing should face in (toward engine). Drive the bearing into the housing until its outer race is even with the edge of the bore.

**Table 1 COOLING SYSTEM SPECIFICATIONS**

| Coolant type | Ethylene glycol containing corrosion inhibitors for aluminum engines |
|---|---|
| Coolant mixture | 50:50 (antifreeze/soft or distilled water) |

(continued)

**Table 1 COOLING SYSTEM SPECIFICATIONS (continued)**

| | |
|---|---|
| Coolant capacity | |
| Radiator and engine | 1.3 L (1.37 qt.) |
| Reservoir | 0.29 L (0.31 qt.) |
| Radiator cap pressure relief | 108-137 kPa (15.6-19.8 psi) |

**Table 2 COOLING SYSTEM TORQUE SPECIFICATIONS**

| Item | N•m | in.-lb. | ft.-lb. |
|---|---|---|---|
| Coolant pipe retaining bolt | 10 | 88 | – |
| Radiator retaining bolts | 7 | 62 | – |
| Radiator fan retaining bolts | 9 | 80 | – |
| Water pump housing bolts | 10 | 88 | – |
| Water pump impeller | 14 | 124 | – |

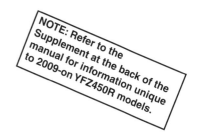

NOTE: Refer to the Supplement at the back of the manual for information unique to 2009-on YFZ450R models.

# WHEELS, TIRES AND DRIVE CHAIN

This chapter covers the wheels, tires, drive chain and sprockets. Routine maintenance procedures for these components are in Chapter Three.

**Tables 1-4** are at the end of this chapter.

## WHEEL

### Removal/Installation

1. Park the ATV on level ground and set the parking brake.
2. Loosen the lug nuts (**Figure 1**).
3. Raise and support the ATV so the wheel is off the ground.
4. Remove the lug nuts and washers from the studs, then remove the wheel from the hub. If more than one wheel will be removed, mark each wheel so it can be installed in its original location.
5. On the front wheel, if damaged or dirty, remove the outer brake disc guard (**Figure 2**).
6. Clean the lug nuts, washers and studs. If studs are broken or damaged, replace them.
7. On the front wheel, if removed, install the outer brake disc guard onto the hub. Install the burred side against the hub.
8. Install the wheel onto the studs with the valve stem facing out.

> *WARNING*
> *If more than one wheel has been removed, check that the tire direction arrow (on the tire sidewall, if applicable) row is pointing forward, when the wheel is mounted.*

9. Install the washers and finger-tighten the lug nuts.
10. Lower the ATV to the ground. Tighten the lug nuts in several steps in a crossing pattern. Tighten the nuts to 45 N•m (33 ft.-lb.).
11. Raise the ATV and spin the wheel, checking that the wheel runs true.
12. Lower the ATV to the ground.

### Inspection

1. Inspect the wheel for damage which may affect true wheel rotation, tire seating or wheel strength. Replace a damaged wheel.

> *CAUTION*
> *Do not remove the wheel bearings for inspection purposes as they can be damaged during the removal process. Remove the wheel bearings only if replacement is required. Refer to Chapter Twelve or Chapter Thirteen for wheel bearing replacement procedures.*

2. Mount the wheel on its hub and tighten the nuts to 45 N•m (33 ft.-lb.).
3. Support the ATV securely so the wheel can rotate.
4. Mount a dial indicator against the rim as shown in **Figure 3** to measure radial and lateral runout. Turn

11

the tire slowly by hand and read movement indicated on dial indicator. Refer to **Table 1** for runout limits. Note the following:

    a. If runout limit is excessive, first check condition of wheel assembly. If the wheel is bent or otherwise damaged, it may require replacement.

    b. If wheel condition is okay but runout is excessive, remove the wheel and inspect the hub as described in Chapter Twelve or Chapter Thirteen.

5. Remove dial indicator and lower vehicle to ground.

## TIRES

The YFZ450 is equipped with tubeless, low pressure tires designed specifically for off-road use. Rapid tire wear will occur if the ATV is ridden on paved surfaces.

### Tire Changing

> *CAUTION*
> *If the tire is difficult to remove or install using the proper tools, do not take a chance on damaging the tire or rim sealing surface. Take the tire and rim to a dealership and have them service the tire.*

> *NOTE*
> *The operating conditions in which an ATV may operate can create a seal that makes tire bead and wheel separation extremely difficult. K&L Supply Co. offers a heavy-duty tire breakdown tool (**Figure 4**) that is available through the dealership or parts supplier.*

1. Remove the valve stem cap and core and deflate the tire. Do not reinstall the core at this time.

2. Lubricate the tire bead and rim flanges with a rubber tire lubricant. Press the tire sidewall/bead down to allow the lubricant to run into and around the bead area. Also apply lubricant to the area where the bead breaker arm will contact the tire sidewall.

3. Position the wheel into the bead breaker tool (**Figure 5**).

4. Slowly work the bead breaker tool, making sure the tool arm seats against the inside of the rim, and break the tire bead away from the rim.

5. Apply hand pressure against the tire on either side of the tool to break the rest of the bead free from the rim.

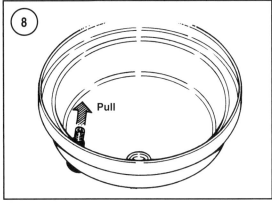

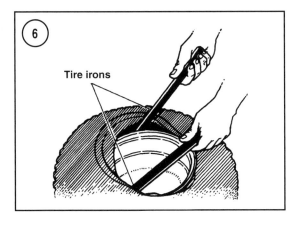

*Damage to these areas may cause an air leak and require replacement of the tire or rim.*

8. Lubricate the tire beads and rim flanges as described in Step 2. Pry the bead over the rim with two tire irons (**Figure 6**). Take small bites with the tire irons. Place rim protectors between the tire irons and the rim.

9. When the upper tire bead is free, lift the second bead up into the center rim well and remove it as described in Step 8.

10. Clean and dry the rim.

11. Inspect the sealing surface on both sides of the rim (**Figure 7**). If the rim is bent, it may leak air.

12. To replace the air valve, perform the following:

a. Support the rim and pull the valve stem out of the rim. Discard the valve stem.

b. Lubricate the new valve stem with a tire lubricant.

c. Pull a new valve stem into the rim, from the inside out, until it snaps into place (**Figure 8**).

13. Inspect the tire for cuts, tears, abrasions or any other defects.

14. Clean the tire and rim of any lubricant used during removal.

*WARNING*
*When mounting the tire, use only clean water as a tire lubricant. Other lubricants may leave a slippery residue on the tire that would allow the tire to slip on the rim, causing a loss of air pressure.*

*WARNING*
*The tire tread pattern is directional. Position the tire onto the rim so the rotation arrow on the tire sidewall faces in the correct direction of wheel rotation.*

6. If the rest of the tire bead cannot be broken loose, raise the tool, rotate the tire/rim assembly and repeat Step 4 and Step 5 until the entire bead is broken loose from the rim.

7. Turn the wheel over and repeat Steps 2-6 to break the opposite side loose.

*CAUTION*
*When using tire irons in the following steps, work carefully so that the tire or rim sealing surfaces are not damaged.*

*NOTE*
*If the tire is difficult to install, place the tire outside in the sun or in an enclosed car. The higher temperatures will soften the tire and help with installation.*

15. Install the tire onto the rim starting with the side opposite the valve stem. Push the first bead over the rim flange. Force the bead into the center of the rim to help installation (**Figure 9**).
16. Install the rest of the bead with tire irons (**Figure 10**).
17. Repeat the preceding steps to install the second bead onto the rim.
18. Install the valve stem core, if necessary.

*WARNING*
*Never exceed the maximum inflation pressure specified on the tire sidewall.*

19. Apply water to the tire bead and inflate the tire to seat the tire onto the rim. Check that the rim lines on both sides of the tire are parallel with the rim flanges as shown in **Figure 11**. If the rim flanges are not parallel, deflate the tire and break the bead. Then lubricate the tire with water again and reinflate the tire.
20. When the tire is properly seated, remove the air valve to deflate the tire and wait one hour before putting the tire into service. After one hour, inflate the tire to the pressure in **Table 2**.
21. Check for air leaks and install the valve cap.

### Cold Patch Repair

Use the manufacturer's instructions for the tire repair kit. If there are no instructions, use the following procedure.
1. Remove the tire as described in this section.
2. Prior to removing the object that punctured the tire, mark the puncture location with chalk or crayon. Remove the object.
3. Working on the inside of the tire, roughen the area around the hole larger than the patch (**Figure 12**). Use the cap from the tire repair kit or a pocket knife. Do not scrape too vigorously or additional damage may occur.
4. Clean the area with a non-flammable solvent. Do not use an oil base solvent as it will leave a residue rendering the patch useless.
5. Apply a small amount of patch cement to the puncture and spread it evenly.
6. Allow the cement to dry until tacky–usually 30 seconds or so is sufficient.
7. Remove the backing from the patch.

*CAUTION*
*Do not touch the newly exposed rubber or the patch will not stick firmly.*

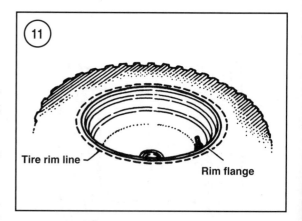

Tire rim line

Rim flange

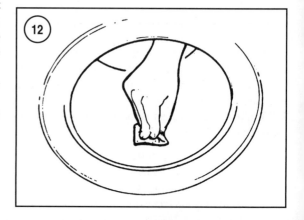

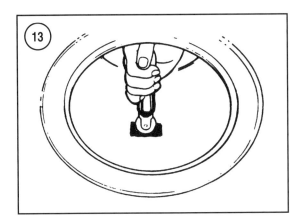

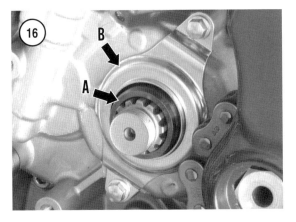

8. Center the patch over the hole. Hold the patch firmly in place for about 30 seconds to allow the cement to dry. If available, use a roller to press the patch into place (**Figure 13**).

9. Dust the area with talcum powder.

## SPROCKETS

Check the condition of both sprockets and the drive chain, as described in Chapter Three. If either the chain or sprockets are worn, replace all drive components. Using new sprockets with a worn chain, or a new chain on worn sprockets will shorten the life of the new part.

### Drive Sprocket and Guard Removal/Installation

1. Shift the transmission into gear and set the parking brake.

2. Remove the sprocket cover (**Figure 14**).

*NOTE*
*The chain can now be removed from the drive sprocket without removing the sprocket. If the drive sprocket must be removed, leave the chain on the sprocket until the sprocket nut is loosened.*

3. Bend the lockwasher tabs away from the sprocket nut (**Figure 15**), then remove the nut, lockwasher and sprocket from the shaft. Discard the lockwasher. A new one must be used during installation. Mark the outside face of the sprocket. If reused, install the sprocket in its original direction.

4. Clean and inspect the sprocket and chain (Chapter Three).

*NOTE*
*If oil is leaking past the countershaft spacer, remove the spacer to determine the cause.*

5. If necessary, twist and remove the countershaft spacer (A, **Figure 16**) and shaft O-ring (A, **Figure 17**).

   a. Clean and inspect the output shaft spacer (**Figure 18**). Inspect the inner and outer surfaces that contact the O-ring and crankcase seal. The surfaces should be smooth and free of corrosion or damage.

   b. If a leak is evident at the crankcase seal (**Figure 18**), remove the seal cover (B, **Figure 16**) and replace the seal as described in Chapter Five. Tighten the seal retainer bolts to 10 N•m (88 in.-lb.).

6. Reverse the preceding steps to install the drive sprocket. Note the following:

11

a. Install a new, lubricated O-ring (A, **Figure 17**) onto the countershaft. The O-ring must seat in the shaft groove.

b. Install the countershaft spacer so the notched end faces in.

c. If reusing the sprocket, check that the sprocket is installed in its original direction.

d. Install a new lockwasher.

e. Tighten the sprocket nut to 75 N•m (55 ft.-lb.).

f. Tighten the sprocket cover bolts securely.

g. Adjust the chain (Chapter Three).

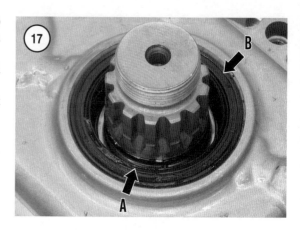

### Driven Sprocket
### Removal/Installation

If the drive sprocket will be replaced, loosen the drive sprocket shaft nut before raising the swing arm to remove the driven sprocket. The resistance of the machine sitting on the ground will aid in loosening the nut.

1. Shift the transmission into gear and set the parking brake.

2. Loosen the sprocket mounting bolts (**Figure 19**).

3. Remove the left rear wheel as described in this chapter.

4. Remove the sprocket from the hub.

5. Clean and inspect the sprocket and bolts. Inspect the sprocket and chain (Chapter Three).

6. Reverse the preceding steps to install the driven sprocket. Note the following:

> *NOTE*
> *On 2006-on models install the left rear wheel if necessary to move the axle forward.*

a. If necessary, refer to Chapter Three and move the axle forward as described in *Drive Chain* to mount the chain.

b. Mount the sprocket with *38* mark facing out.

c. Tighten the sprocket bolts to the torque specified in **Table 4**.

d. Adjust the chain (Chapter Three).

### DRIVE CHAIN

Refer to Chapter Three for O-ring type chain cleaning, lubrication, adjustment and measurement. Refer to **Table 3** in this chapter for chain specifications.

When checking the condition of the chain, also check the condition of the sprockets (Chapter Three). If either the chain or sprockets are worn, replace all drive components. Using new sprockets with a worn chain, or a new chain on worn sprockets will shorten the life of the new part.

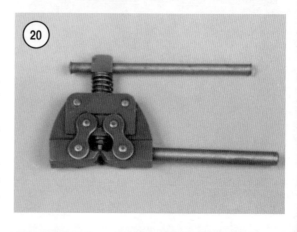

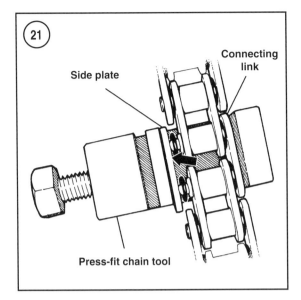

21

Side plate

Connecting link

Press-fit chain tool

22

Replacing the endless O-ring drive chain with a chain that uses a clip-type master link is not recommended. However, a chain that can be assembled using a permanent, press-fit master link is acceptable. If a chain breaker tool (**Figure 20**) and link riveting tool (**Figure 21**) are available, this can be a more convenient way to replace the chain, rather than disassembling the swing arm.

## Chain With No Master Link
## Removal/Installation

1. Increase drive chain slack as described in Chapter Three.

2. Remove the rear wheels as described in this chapter.

3. Remove the drive sprocket guard as described in this chapter.

4. Remove the shock absorber as described in Chapter Thirteen.

5. Lift the chain off the sprockets.

> *WARNING*
> *If necessary, get assistance in handling the swing arm.*

> *NOTE*
> *With the swing arm disconnected from the shock absorber and linkage, it is recommended to check the condition of the swing arm bearings as described in Chapter Thirteen.*

6. Remove the swing arm bolt (**Figure 22**) and pull back the swing arm.

7. Lower the swing arm and remove the chain.

8. Reverse this procedure to install the chain. Note the following:
   a. Clean and inspect the bores in the swing arm, engine case and frame.
   b. Apply waterproof grease to the parts and bores.
   c. Tighten the swing arm pivot bolt to 100 N•m (74 ft.-lb.).
   d. Adjust the chain (Chapter Three).

## Chain With Press-Fit Master Link
## Removal/Installation

1. Increase drive chain slack as described in *Drive Chain* in Chapter Three.

2. Support the machine so the rear wheels are off the ground.

3. Choose a convenient location along the drive chain for attaching a chain breaker tool (**Figure 20**).

4. Attach the tool to the drive chain and drive a link pin from the chain. Remove the chain.

5. Install the new chain and route it over the sprockets.
   a. Shift the transmission into neutral.
   b. If necessary, attach a wire to the end of the chain to route it behind the sprocket guard and over the drive sprocket.
   c. After the chain is routed over the sprockets, remove the chain slack and position the ends together. Shift the transmission into gear to prevent the drive sprocket from rotating.

6. Secure the chain ends with the master link. Check that the O-rings are on the master link pins. Insert the link from the back side of the chain.

7. Place the chain link sideplate on the master link. The identification marks must face out.

8. Stake the link pins using a chain riveting tool (**Figure 21**).

9. Adjust the chain (Chapter Three).

11

### Table 1 TIRE AND WHEEL SPECIFICATIONS

| | |
|---|---|
| Tires | |
| Type | |
| Front | |
| 2004-2005 models | Dunlop KT331A |
| 2006-on models | Dunlop KT341 |
| Rear | |
| 2004-2005 models | Dunlop KT335 |
| 2006-on models | Dunlop KT355A |
| Size | |
| Front | |
| 2004-2005 models | AT21 × 7-10 |
| 2006-on models | AT21 × 7R-10 |
| Rear | AT20 × 10-9 |
| Wheels | |
| Front rim size | 10 × 5.5 AT |
| Rear rim size | 9 × 8.5 AT |
| Rim runout limit – radial or lateral | 2.0 mm (0.08 in.) |

### Table 2 TIRE INFLATION PRESSURE*

| | psi (kPa) |
|---|---|
| 2004-2005 models | |
| Front | 4.4 (30) |
| Rear | 5.1 (35) |
| 2006-on models | |
| Front | 4.0 (27.5) |
| Rear | 4.4 (30) |

*Tire inflation pressure is for original equipment tires. Aftermarket tires may require different inflation pressure.

### Table 3 DRIVE CHAIN SPECIFICATIONS

| | |
|---|---|
| Drive chain | |
| Manufacturer | Daido |
| Type | 520MX |
| Number of links | 96 |
| Drive chain slack | 25-35 mm (0.98-1.38 in.) |
| Sprocket sizes | |
| Drive (front) | 14 teeth |
| Driven (rear) | 38 teeth |

### Table 4 WHEEL AND DRIVE CHAIN TORQUE SPECIFICATIONS

| Item | N•m | in.-lb. | ft.-lb. |
|---|---|---|---|
| Drive sprocket nut* | 75 | – | 55 |
| Drive sprocket seal retainer bolts | 10 | 88 | – |
| Driven sprocket nuts | | | |
| 2004-2005 models | 55 | – | 40 |
| 2006-on models | 72 | – | 53 |
| Swing arm pivot bolt | 100 | – | 74 |
| Wheel lug nuts* | 45 | – | 33 |

*Refer to text.

NOTE: Refer to the Supplement at the back of the manual for information unique to 2009-on YFZ450R models.

# FRONT SUSPENSION AND STEERING

This chapter provides service information for the front suspension and steering including toe-in adjustment. Refer to Chapter Three for shock adjustment procedures. Refer to Chapter Eleven for wheel and tire service information.

**Table 1** and **Table 2** are at the end of this chapter.

## HANDLEBAR

### Adjustment

1. Withdraw the fuel tank vent hose (A, **Figure 1**) from the handlebar cover (B).
2. Push up and remove the handlebar cover (B, **Figure 1**).
3. Loosen the rear handlebar holder bolts (A, **Figure 2**), then the front holder bolts (B).
4. Tilt the handlebar to the desired position.
5. Tighten the front holder bolts (B, **Figure 2**), then tighten the rear holder bolts (A). Tighten the bolts to 23 N•m (17 ft.-lb.).

### Removal/Installation

1. Withdraw the fuel tank vent hose (A, **Figure 1**) from the handlebar cover (B).
2. Push up and remove the handlebar cover (B, **Figure 1**).
3. Remove cable and hose bands.
4. Remove the front master cylinder as described in Chapter Fourteen.

5. Remove the throttle housing screws, clamp and throttle housing (**Figure 3**). Place the throttle housing out of the way.
6. Remove the screws and the clutch lever clamp (**Figure 4**), then remove the clutch lever assembly and place out of the way.
7. Remove the switch housing as described in the *Left Handlebar Switch Assembly* in *Switches* in Chapter Nine.
8. Remove the handlebar holder bolts (A and B, **Figure 2**), then remove the handlebar.
9. If removal of the grips is necessary, use solvent or a spray lubricant under the grip to soften the adhesive. Compressed air can also be used to lift and free the grips. Remove the collar from the handlebar and install it on the new handlebar.
10. Inspect the handlebar as described in this section.
11. Reverse the removal steps to install the handlebar while noting the following:
   a. The punch marks on the handlebar holders must face forward (**Figure 5**). Tighten the front holder bolts (B, **Figure 2**), followed by the rear holder bolts (A). Tighten all bolts to 23 N•m (17 ft.-lb.). There should be a gap between the top and bottom holders at the rear of the holders.
   b. Make sure the notch on the collar engages the throttle housing (**Figure 6**).
   c. If new grips will be installed, clean the handlebar grip surface with solvent, such as electrical contact cleaner. Apply a hand grip cement following the manufacturer's instructions.

12

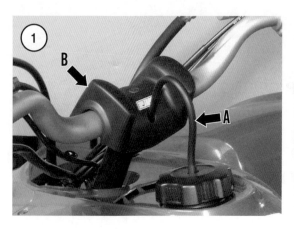

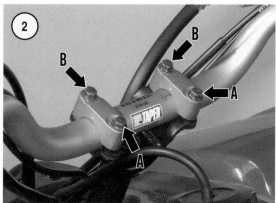

d. Check the riding position and adjust the handlebar as described in this section. Turn the handlebar side to side and check for cable binding.

**Inspection**

1. Inspect the handlebar for cracks, bends or other
damage. If the handlebar is made of aluminum, check
closely where the handlebar is clamped to the holders, and at the clutch lever. If cracks, scores or other
damage is found, replace the handlebar. Damage in
these areas can cause handlebar failure.

> *WARNING*
> *Never attempt to straighten, weld or*
> *heat a damaged handlebar. The metal*
> *can weaken and possibly break when*
> *subjected to the shocks and stresses*
> *that occur when riding the ATV.*

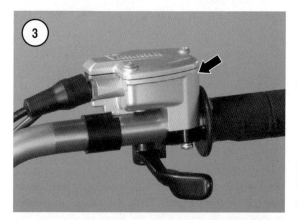

2. Inspect the threads on the mounting bolts and
in the holders. Clean all residue from the threads.
Replace damaged bolts.
3. Clean the handlebar holders and handlebar with
solvent or electrical contact cleaner.

### SHOCK ABSORBERS

Shock absorber adjustment procedures are in
Chapter Three.

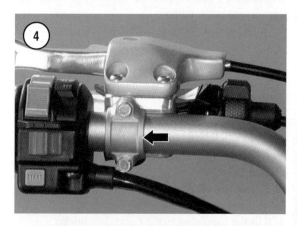

**Removal/Installation**

1. Support the vehicle with the front wheels off the
ground.
2. Remove the lower shock absorber nut, washer
and bolt (**Figure 7**).
3. Remove the upper shock absorber nut and bolt
(**Figure 8**), then remove the shock absorber.
4. Inspect the shock absorber as described in this
section.

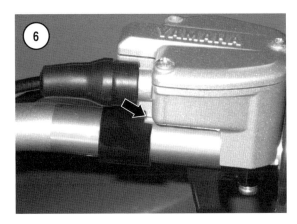

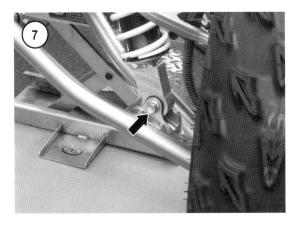

5. Install the shock absorber by reversing the preceding removal steps, while noting the following:

    a. Install a washer inside the nut on the lower shock retaining bolt.

*CAUTION*
*A self-locking nut is used on each shock absorber retaining bolt. Replace any nut that does not resist turning during installation.*

    b. Tighten the shock absorber retaining bolts to 45 N•m (33 ft.-lb.).

## Inspection

1. Inspect the shock absorber for gas or oil leaks. If found, refer service to a dealership.
2. Check the damper rod for bending, rust or other damage.
3. Inspect the spring (A, **Figure 9**) for damage.
4. Inspect the reservoir (B, **Figure 9**) for damage.

## FRONT WHEEL HUB

### Removal/Installation

1. Remove the front wheel and outer brake disc guard as described in Chapter Eleven.
2. Remove the brake caliper as described in Chapter Fourteen.
3. Remove the hub cap.
4. Remove the cotter pin, hub nut and washer (**Figure 10**).
5. Remove the wheel hub assembly (**Figure 11**).

*CAUTION*
*If the hub is corroded to the axle, place a drift against the back of the hub and tap it free. Do not strike the outer edge of the brake disc.*

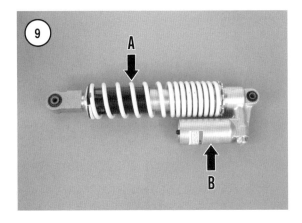

12

6. Remove the inner washer from the axle (**Figure 12**).

7. Inspect the front hub assembly (**Figure 13**) as described in this section.

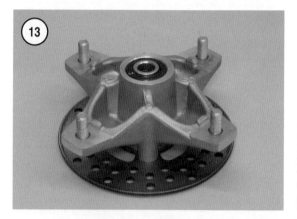

8. If additional suspension or steering components will be serviced, remove the inner brake disc guard (**Figure 14**).

9. If necessary, remove the brake disc from the hub as described in Chapter Fourteen.

10. Reverse this procedure to install the front hub. Note the following:

    a. Inspect the steering knuckle before installing the hub. Check for cracks and damage on bearing surfaces (A, **Figure 15**) and threads (B).

    b. Tighten the hub nut to 70 N•m (52 ft.-lb.).

    c. Install a new cotter pin.

    d. Install the caliper as described in Chapter Fourteen.

    e. Install the front wheel and brake guard as described in Chapter Eleven.

## Inspection

1. Remove the spacers (**Figure 16**) from both sides of the hub.

2. Inspect the seals (A, **Figure 17**) for damage.

3. Turn each bearing inner race (B, **Figure 17**) by hand. The bearing should roll smoothly and quietly. If binding or roughness is detected, replace both bearings as described in this section.

4. Check each bearing for axial and radial play (**Figure 18**). If obvious play is detected, replace the bearing as described in this section. Replace both bearings if either bearing is worn or damaged.

5. Check the tightness of the bearings in the hub. Replace the bearings and/or hub if they are loose.

6. Install the spacers if the bearings and seals are in good condition.

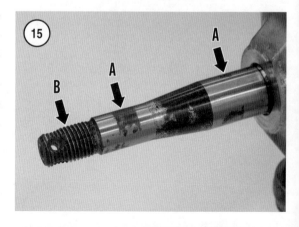

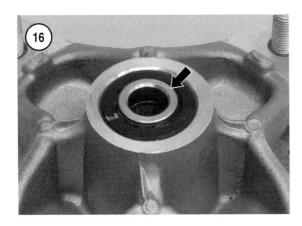

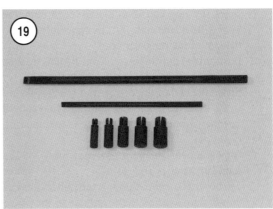

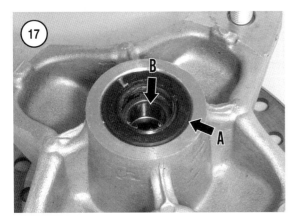

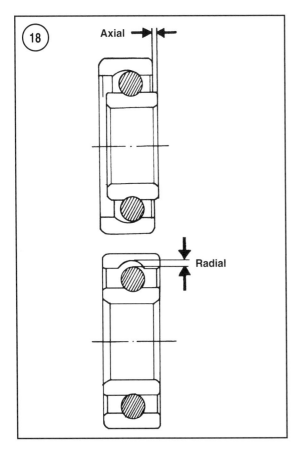

## Bearing and Seal Removal/Installation

Two methods for removing bearings from the wheel hub are provided in the following procedure. The first method (Step 3A) uses a wheel bearing removal set and the second method (Step 3B) uses common shop tools.

> *CAUTION*
> *In the following procedure, do not allow the wheel to rest on the brake disc. Support the wheel to prevent pressure against the disc.*

1. Pry the seals (A, **Figure 17**) from both sides of the hub. Protect the hub to prevent damage.
2. Examine the bearings. Note the following:
   a. The bearings are open on the outer face and shielded on the inner face. The new bearings must be installed with the open side facing out.
   b. If bearing damage is severe, determine which bearing is damaged the least. This bearing will be removed first.

3A. Remove the bearings using the wheel bearing removal set as follows:

> *NOTE*
> *The tools used in this procedure are part of the Kowa Seiki Wheel Bearing Remover set (**Figure 19**). The set is distributed by K & L Supply Co. through motorcycle dealerships. The set is designed so a proper-size remover head can be wedged against the inner bearing race. The bearing can then be driven from the hub (**Figure 20**).*

   a. Select the appropriate-size remover head. The small, split end of the remover must fit inside the bearing race.
   b. Insert the split end of the remover head into the bearing. Seat the remover head against the bearing.

c. Insert the tapered end of the driver through the back side of the hub. Fit the tapered end into the slot of the remover head.

d. Position the hub so the remover head is against a solid surface, such as a concrete floor.

e. Strike the end of the driver so it wedges firmly in the remover head. The remover head should now be jammed tight against the inner bearing race.

f. Reposition and support the assembly so the remover head is free to move and the driver can be struck again. Support the hub so there is no pressure applied to the outside of the brake disc.

g. Strike the driver, forcing the bearing and hub spacer from the hub.

h. Remove the driver from the remover head.

i. Repeat the procedure to remove the remaining bearing.

3B. Remove the bearings using a hammer, drift and heat gun, or propane torch. The purpose for using heat is to slightly expand the hub bores so the bearings can be removed with minimal resistance. Remove the bearings as follows:

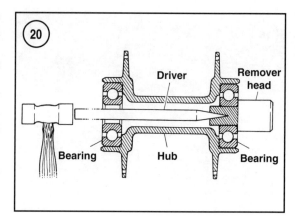

*WARNING*
*When using a heat gun or propane torch to heat the hub, care must be taken to prevent burning finished or combustible surfaces. Work in a well-ventilated area and away from combustible materials. Wear protective clothing, including eye protection and insulated gloves.*

a. Clean all lubricants from the wheel.

b. Insert a long drift into the hub. Move the hub spacer as needed for access to the bearing to be removed.

c. Heat the hub around the bearing to be removed. Keep the heat source moving at a steady rate and avoid heating the bearing. A large washer placed over the bearing will help insulate the bearing from the heat.

d. Turn the wheel over and use the drift to tap around the inner bearing race (**Figure 21**). To prevent bearing cocking, tap in several locations around the bearing. Drive the bearing out of the hub.

e. Remove the hub spacer (**Figure 22**).

f. Heat the hub around the remaining bearing and drive out the remaining bearing.

4. Clean and inspect all parts.

5. Inspect the hub bore (**Figure 23**) for:

a. Cracks, corrosion or other damage.

b. Fit of the new bearings. If a bearing easily enters the hub bore, replace the hub. The bearings must be a driven-fit.

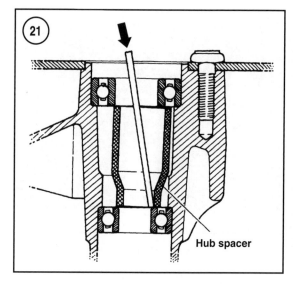

6. Inspect the hub spacer for:

a. Cracks, corrosion or other damage.

b. Fit. Check the fit of the spacer against the back side of the bearings. It should fit flat against the bearings. Repair minor nicks and flaring with a file. Do not grind or shorten the spacer. The spacer must remain its full length, in order to prevent binding of the bearings when the axle is tightened.

7. Before installing the new bearings, apply waterproof grease to bearings that are not lubricated by the manufacturer. Work the grease into the cavities between the balls and races.

8. Refer to *Service Methods* in Chapter One and install the bearings as described. Note the following:

a. Install each bearing so the open side is out.

b. After installing one of the bearings, install the spacer (**Figure 22**) so the tapered end is toward the wheel side of the hub.

9. Install the seals as described in *Service Methods* in Chapter One. Note the following:

a. Pack grease into the lips of the new seals.

b. Lubricate the seal bores.

c. Install the seal so the manufacturer's marks face out.

10. Install the spacers (**Figure 16**) on both sides of the hub.

## TIE RODS

### Removal/Installation

Refer to **Figure 24**.

1. Before removing the tie rods, make the following check for obvious play and wear.

a. Park the ATV on level ground with the wheels pointing straight ahead.

b. Lightly turn the handlebar toward the left, then right while observing the tie rod ends. It is not necessary to actually turn the wheels. If the tie rod ends move vertically (removing play) as pressure is applied, they are worn or damaged.

c. Repeat the check with the wheels fully locked to the left, then the right. If vertical play is observed in this position, this also indicates worn tie rod ends.

2. To improve access, remove the front wheel as described in Chapter Eleven.

3. Remove the cotter pin, nut and washer (**Figure 25**) from the tie rod end attached to the steering knuckle.

4. Install a hex nut onto the tie rod stud threads so it is flush with the end of the stud (**Figure 26**). The nut protects the stud threads.

5. Using as little force as needed, tap the stud free of the steering knuckle. Unscrew the nut and separate the tie rod from the steering knuckle.

6. If the tie rod end is seized in the bore consider the following:

a. Apply heat to the area around the joint using a heat gun or propane torch.

b. Use a ball joint remover (**Figure 27**) to separate the parts. If the tie rod end will be reused, there is a risk of tearing the rubber boot when using this tool.

7. Repeat the removal steps to remove the tie rod (**Figure 28**) from the steering shaft. If the tie rod end is seized in the bore, and must be driven out, it may be necessary to remove the upper control arm as described in this chapter to gain the necessary clearance.

8. Reverse the preceding steps to install the tie rods. Note the following:

a. Install the tie rods so the tie rod wrench flats (**Figure 29**) are nearer the steering knuckle.

b. Tighten both tie rod nuts to 25 N•m (18 ft.-lb.).

c. Install new cotter pins.

9. Check wheel toe-in as described in this section.

### Inspection

*CAUTION*
*The tie rod ends are packed with grease and sealed. Do not immerse the tie rod ends in solvent or any other liquid that could penetrate the boots. Wipe the ends with a shop cloth prior to inspection.*

1. Inspect the tie rod for straightness. Replace the rod if it is bent.

2. Inspect the ball joint boot for tears and the entry of moisture or dirt into the joint.

3. Grasp the ball joint (**Figure 30**) and swivel it in all directions, as well as vertically. Check for roughness, dryness and play. Replace the tie rod end if wear is detected.

### Tie Rod Ends Disassembly/Assembly

*NOTE*
*The outer tie rod end and locknut have left-hand threads. The inner tie rod end and locknut have right-hand threads. Note which direction each set of parts must be turned when loosening and tightening the parts.*

**12**

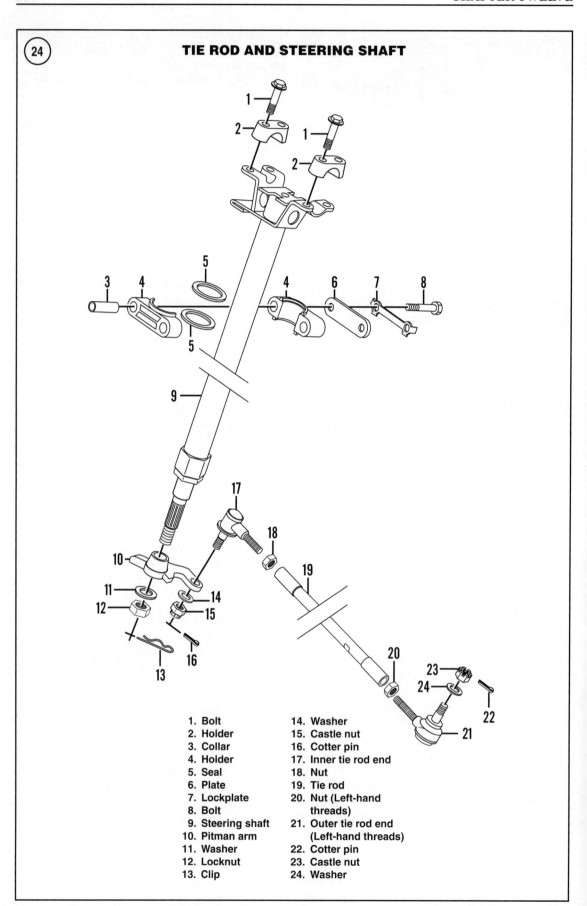

TIE ROD AND STEERING SHAFT

1. Bolt
2. Holder
3. Collar
4. Holder
5. Seal
6. Plate
7. Lockplate
8. Bolt
9. Steering shaft
10. Pitman arm
11. Washer
12. Locknut
13. Clip
14. Washer
15. Castle nut
16. Cotter pin
17. Inner tie rod end
18. Nut
19. Tie rod
20. Nut (Left-hand threads)
21. Outer tie rod end (Left-hand threads)
22. Cotter pin
23. Castle nut
24. Washer

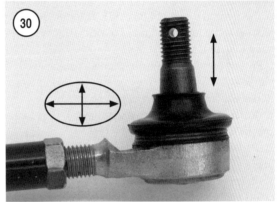

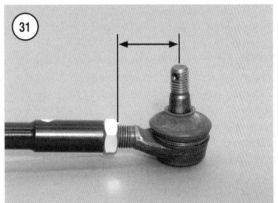

1. Measure the distance from the tie rod end center to the locknut (**Figure 31**). This will provide a starting point for installation of the tie rod end.

2. Hold the tie rod with a wrench placed on the tie rod flats (A, **Figure 32**).

3. Loosen the locknut (B, **Figure 32**) and remove the tie rod end (C).

4. Clean the tie rod threads.

5. Thread the correct tie rod end onto the tie rod.

6. Repeat the procedure for the remaining tie rod end.

7. Adjust the tie rod ends as follows:

   a. Turn the tie rod end until it is the distance from the locknut as measured in Step 1. The distance should be same at both ends.

b. Finger-tighten the locknuts to hold the positions. Tighten the locknuts after the tie rods have been installed and the toe-in adjustment has been made.

c. Check toe-in adjustment as described in this section.

### Toe-in Adjustment

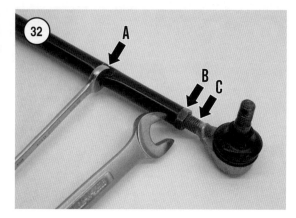

In order to maintain stable steering and minimize tire wear, the front wheels must be set for toe-in. When correctly set, the front of the tires will point in slightly, while the rear of the tires will point out. To check toe-in, measure the distance between the tires at the front and rear (**Figure 33**). If toe-in is incorrect, tie rod length is adjusted to bring the measurement to within specifications.

Proper toe-in adjustment cannot be achieved if the tie rods, wheel bearings or ball joints are worn. Replace worn parts before adjusting toe-in.

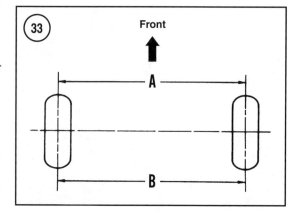

1. Refer to Chapter Eleven and inflate all tires to the specified pressure.

2. Park the ATV on level ground and set the parking brake.

3. Raise and support the ATV. The front wheels must be off the ground.

4. Point the handlebar straight ahead.

5. On both front tires, make a chalk mark at the center of the tread. The mark should be level with the centerline of the axle.

6. Measure distance A between the tires as shown in **Figure 33**. Record the measurement.

7. Rotate both wheels until the marks are at the back, and level with the axle.

8. Measure distance B between the tires as shown in **Figure 33**. Record the measurement.

9. Subtract measurement A from measurement B.

   a. If the difference is 2-12 mm (0.08-0.47 in.), toe-in is correct.

   b. If toe-in is not correct, perform Step 10.

10. Adjust both tie rods equally as follows:

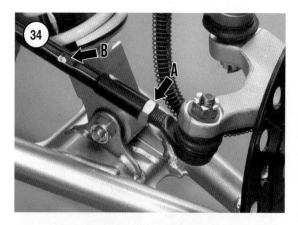

*NOTE*
*The outer tie rod end and locknut is a left-hand thread. The inner tie rod end and locknut is a right-hand thread. Note which direction each set of parts must be turned when loosening and tightening the parts.*

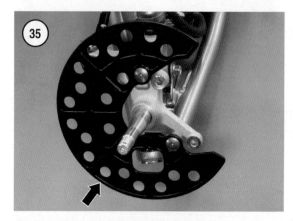

a. Loosen both tie rod end locknuts (A, **Figure 34**) on both tie rods.

b. Equally turn each tie rod with a wrench fitted to the flats on the rod (B, **Figure 34**).

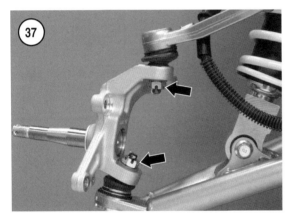

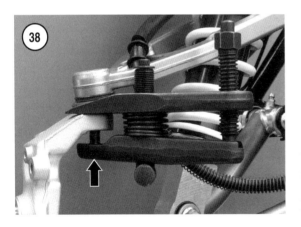

*NOTE*
*If the tie rods are not adjusted identically, handlebar alignment will not be centered with the wheels.*

c. Recheck the measurements.

d. Tighten the locknuts when toe-in is correct.

e. Turn the handlebar from side to side and check that all ball joints pivot properly.

f. Test ride the ATV slowly to ensure that all adjustments are correct.

## STEERING KNUCKLE

### Removal/Installation

1. Remove the front hub as described in this chapter.

2. Remove the inner brake disc guard (**Figure 35**).

3. Remove the brake hose guard (**Figure 36**).

4. Remove the outer tie rod end (**Figure 25**) as described in this chapter.

5. Remove the cotter pins and nuts (**Figure 37**) from the ball joint studs.

6. Remove the ball joints from the steering knuckle. Two methods of removal are as follows:

   a. If a ball joint remover (**Figure 38**) is available, it can be used to separate the parts. If the ball joint will be reused, there is a risk of tearing the rubber boot when using this tool.

   b. If a ball joint remover is not available, support the steering knuckle and thread a hex nut onto the stud. Use a heat gun or propane torch to heat the area around the joint, then drive the ball joint from the steering knuckle. If the ball joint will be reused, avoid damaging the threads.

7. Inspect the steering knuckle as described in this section.

8. Reverse the preceding steps to install the steering knuckle while noting the following:

   a. Tighten both ball joint nuts to 25 N•m (18 ft-lb.).

   b. Install new cotter pins.

### Inspection

1. Clean and dry the steering knuckle.

2. Inspect the following areas for cracks and other damage (**Figure 39**). If damage is detected, replace the steering knuckle.

   a. Cotter pin hole (A).

   b. Axle threads (B).

   c. Bearing surfaces (C).

   d. Bores (D).

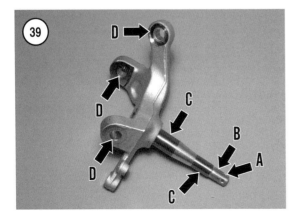

**12**

## CONTROL ARMS AND STEERING KNUCKLE

40

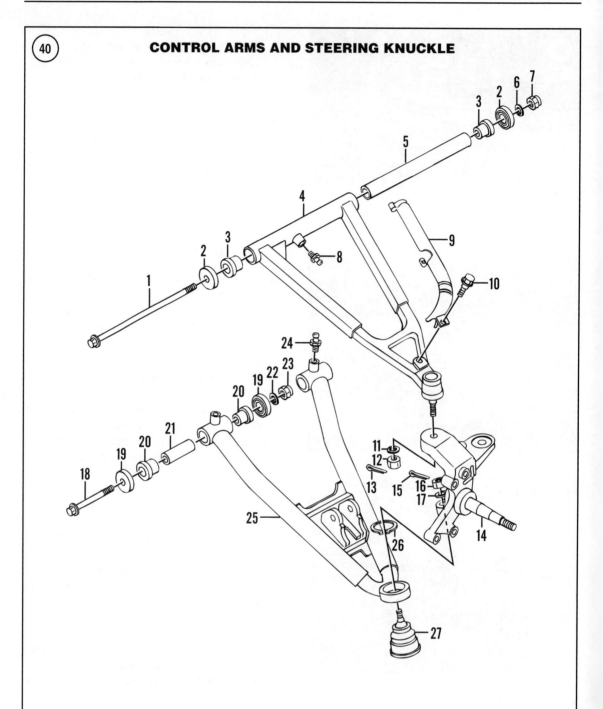

| | | |
|---|---|---|
| 1. Pivot bolt | 10. Bolt | 19. Cap |
| 2. Cap | 11. Washer | 20. Flange bushing |
| 3. Flange bushing | 12. Castle nut | 21. Spacer |
| 4. Upper control arm | 13. Cotter pin | 22. Washer |
| 5. Spacer | 14. Steering knuckle | 23. Locknut |
| 6. Washer | 15. Cotter pin | 24. Grease fitting |
| 7. Locknut | 16. Castle nut | 25. Lower control arm |
| 8. Grease fitting | 17. Washer | 26. Snap ring |
| 9. Brake hose guard | 18. Pivot bolt | 27. Ball joint |

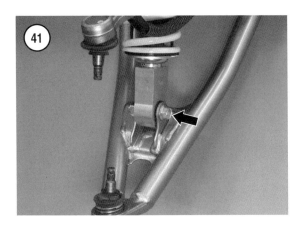

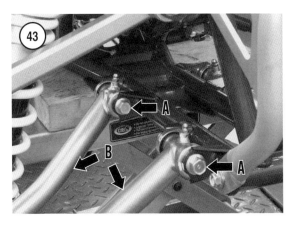

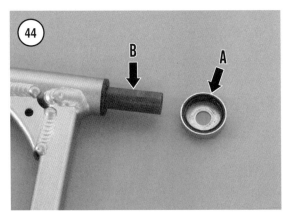

## CONTROL ARMS

Refer to **Figure 40**.

**Removal and Installation**

1. Remove the front bumper as described in Chapter Fifteen to allow control arm bolt removal.
2. Remove the steering knuckle as described in this chapter.
3. Remove the lower mounting bolt from the shock absorber (**Figure 41**). If increased work space is desired, remove the entire shock absorber as described in this chapter.
4. Remove the brake hose guard and detach the control arm ball joints as described in *Steering Knuckle* in this chapter.
5. Before removing the control arms, grasp each arm and move it side to side. If play is noticeable, check the bushings for wear as described in this section.
6. Remove the bolt (A, **Figure 42**) from the upper control arm, then remove the control arm assembly (B). If both upper control arms are removed, identify the arms so they can be installed in their original positions.
7. Remove the bolts (A, **Figure 43**) from the lower control arm, then remove the control arm assembly (B). If both lower control arms are removed, identify the arms so they can be installed in their original positions.
8. Inspect the control arms as described in this section.
9. Reverse the preceding steps to install the control arms. Note the following:
   a. If control arms on both sides have been removed, verify that they are being installed on the correct side of the ATV.
   b. Install the control arm pivot bolts so the heads face toward the front.
   c. Tighten the lower control arm bolts to 55 N•m (40 ft.-lb.).
   d. Tighten the upper control arm bolt to 38 N•m (28 ft.-lb.).
   e. Tighten the ball joint nuts to 25 N•m (18 ft.-lb.).
   f. Tighten the shock absorber retaining bolts to 45 N•m (33 ft.-lb.).

**12**

**Inspection**

1. Remove the caps (A, **Figure 44**) and pivot spacer (B) from the control arm. Keep all parts with their respective control arm.

*CAUTION*
*Unless the bushings are obviously damaged, do not remove them from the control arms. The bushings are made of synthetic material that is easily damage during removal.*

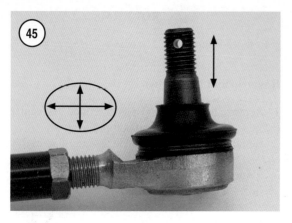

2. Clean the control arm parts.

> *NOTE*
> *The ball joints are packed with grease and sealed. Do not immerse the ball joints in solvent or any other liquid that could penetrate the boots. Wipe the ball joints clean with a shop cloth prior to inspection.*

3. Inspect all welded joints on the control arm. Check for fractures, bending or other damage. If damage is detected, replace the control arm.

4. Inspect the ball joint boots for tears and the entry of moisture or dirt into the joint.

5. Grasp each ball joint (**Figure 45**) and swivel it in all directions, as well as vertically. Check for roughness, dryness and play. The upper ball joint is not replaceable. If necessary, replace the lower ball joint as described in this section.

6. Inspect the control arm pivot assemblies.

   a. Insert each pivot spacer (B, **Figure 44**) into its bushing and check for play. If necessary, remove a damaged bushing by carefully prying at the edge of the bushing. When the bushing is unseated, twist it from the bore. Install a new bushing by lightly tapping it into place with a soft mallet.

   b. Check the fit of the bolt in the spacer. If play is evident, replace the worn parts.

   c. Check the fit of each cap (A, **Figure 44**) on the control arm. The cap should fit snugly to prevent the entry of moisture and dirt.

## Lower Control Arm Ball Joint
## Removal/Installation

Removal of the ball joint requires the removal/installation set (Yamaha part No. YM-01474, 90890-01474 and part No. YM-01480, 90890-01480 [**Figure 46**], or an equivalent).

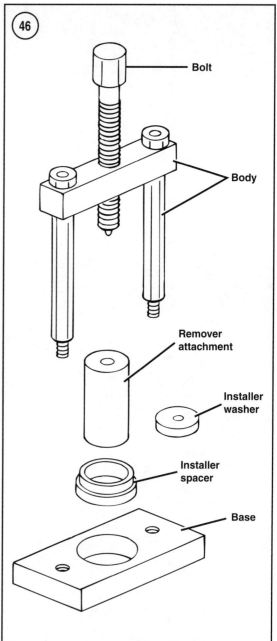

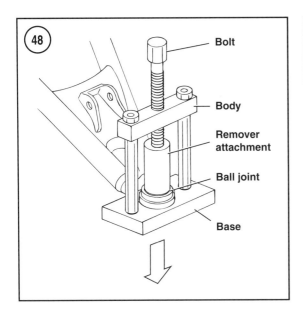

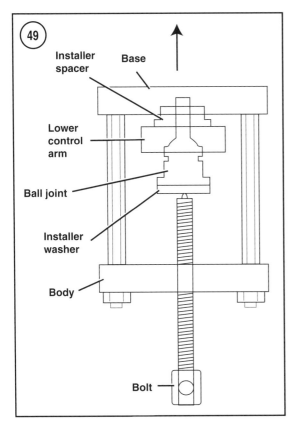

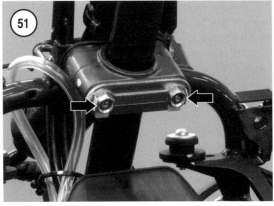

6. Force in the new ball joint by installing the tool as shown in (**Figure 49**).

7. Check that all parts are aligned and the ball joint can pass into the control arm.

8. Turn the bolt and apply pressure to the ball joint, driving it into the control arm.

9. Lubricate the ball joint and boot interior with waterproof grease, then install the snap ring, boot and clip.

## STEERING SHAFT

Refer to **Figure 24**.

### Removal/Installation

1. Remove the front fender (Chapter Fifteen).

2. Remove the fuel tank (Chapter Eight).

3. Remove the handlebar as described in this chapter. Reposition and secure the handlebar out of the way. Avoid kinking the cables and brake hose. Keep the brake fluid reservoir upright.

4. Remove the clip, nut and washer (**Figure 50**) from the end of the steering shaft. If the pitman arm must also be removed, remove the tie rod ends as described in this chapter.

1. Remove the clip, boot and snap ring from the ball joint (**Figure 47**).

2. Drive out the ball joint by installing the tool as shown in (**Figure 48**).

3. Center the bolt on the ball joint stud.

4. Center the base so the ball joint can pass through the hole in the base.

5. Turn the bolt and apply pressure to the ball joint, driving it from the control arm.

12

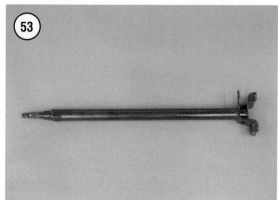

5. Bend the lockplate tabs away from the bolt heads, then remove the two bolts (**Figure 51**) from the steering shaft holders.

6. Lift and remove the steering shaft from the lower bearing (**Figure 52**).

7. Inspect the steering shaft assembly as described in this section.

8. Reverse the preceding steps to install the steering shaft while noting the following:

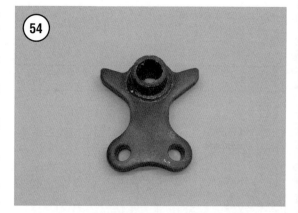

 a. Apply waterproof grease to the shaft splines, seals, bearing and steering shaft holder.

 b. When installing the steering shaft splines into the pitman arm splines, check that the wheels and handlebar mounts are centered with one another. Finger-tighten all bolts and verify correct alignment of the parts before tightening any bolts.

 c. Tighten the steering shaft nut to 180 N•m (132 ft.-lb.).

 d. Install a new lockplate onto the steering shaft holder.

 e. Tighten the steering shaft holder bolts to 23 N•m (17 ft.-lb.). Bend the lockplate tabs against the bolt heads.

 f. Check toe-in as described in *Tie Rods* in this chapter.

### Inspection

1. Wipe the steering shaft clean.

2. Inspect the steering shaft (**Figure 53**) for the following:

 a. Distortion or damage.

 b. Enlarged tie rod holes in the pitman arm, if removed.

 c. Cracked clip hole.

 d. Damaged threads.

3. Inspect the steering shaft holders and seals for wear or damage.

4. Inspect the pitman arm (**Figure 54**) for wear or damage.

5. Inspect the bearing by turning the inner race. The bearing should turn smoothly and have minimal, if any play.

6. If necessary, replace the bearing and seals as described in this section.

### Steering Shaft Bearing and Seals
### Removal/Installation

Refer to **Figure 24**.

1. Pry the upper and lower seals out of the bearing holder.

2. Remove the bearing retainer (**Figure 55**) from the bearing holder in the frame. Removal of the retainer requires a 30 mm hex tool (K&L Tool Part No. 35-8576, or an equivalent).

3. Drive the bearing out the top of the holder.

4. Clean the retainer and the bearing holder bore.

5. Apply waterproof grease to the new bearing and seals.

6. Insert the bearing into the bearing holder. Install the bearing so the manufacturer's marks face up.

7. Install and tighten the bearing retainer to 65 N•m (48 ft.-lb.).

8. Place the seals squarely over the bores in the bearing holder, then seat the seals into the bore. When driving the seals, use a driver or socket that fits against the outer edge of the seals.

**Table 1 STEERING AND FRONT SUSPENSION SPECIFICATIONS**

| | |
|---|---|
| Front suspension type | Double wishbone |
| Front shock absorber | |
|   Type | Gas/oil |
|   Travel | 110 mm (4.33 in.) |
|   Spring installed length | 255 mm (10.04 in.) |
|   Spring free length | 265 mm (10.43 in.) |
| Steering | |
|   Camber angle | −1.5° |
|   Caster angle | 5° |
|   Front wheel travel | 230 mm (9.06 in.) |
|   Kingpin angle | 15.4° |
|   Kingpin offset | 1.0 mm (0.04 in.) |
|   Toe-in | 2-12 mm (0.08-0.47 in.) |
|   Trail length | 21 mm (0.83 in.) |

**Table 2 FRONT SUSPENSION TORQUE SPECIFICATIONS**

| Item | N•m | in.-lb. | ft.-lb. |
|---|---|---|---|
| Ball joint nuts* | 25 | – | 18 |
| Handlebar holder bolts* | 23 | – | 17 |
| Hub nut* | 70 | – | 52 |
| Lower control arm bolts | 55 | – | 40 |
| Shock absorber retaining bolts | 45 | – | 33 |
| Steering shaft bearing retainer | 65 | – | 48 |
| Steering shaft holder bolts* | 23 | – | 17 |
| Steering shaft nut | 180 | – | 132 |
| Tie rod nuts* | 25 | – | 18 |
| Upper control arm bolt | 38 | – | 28 |
| *Refer to text. | | | |

12

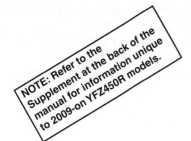
NOTE: Refer to the Supplement at the back of the manual for information unique to 2009-on YFZ450R models.

# CHAPTER THIRTEEN

# REAR AXLE AND SUSPENSION

This chapter covers the rear axle and suspension assemblies. Refer to Chapter Three for shock adjustment procedures. Refer to Chapter Eleven for wheel, tire and drive chain service information.

**Table 1** and **Table 2** are at the end of this chapter.

> *WARNING*
> *Self-locking nuts are used to retain some suspension components. Replace any nut that does not resist turning during installation.*

## WHEEL HUB

### Removal/Installation

1. Remove the rear wheels as described in Chapter Eleven.
2. Remove the cotter pin (**Figure 1**) and nut from the axle.
3. Pull the wheel hub (**Figure 2**) from the axle splines. If the other hub will be removed, mark the hubs so they can be reinstalled in the same position on the axle.

> *NOTE*
> *If the hub is stuck to the splines, use penetrating oil and a hub puller to slide the hub off the axle (**Figure 3**). Do not strike the hub.*

4. Inspect the hub for cracks, damaged splines and other damage. Replace broken studs.
5. Reverse this procedure to install the hub while noting the following:
   a. Apply grease to the hub splines and to the threads and seating surface before tightening the nut.
   b. Tighten the wheel hub nut to the specification in **Table 2**. After tightening the nut, continue turning it until the cotter pin hole is aligned. Do not loosen the nut to align the cotter pin hole.
   c. Install a new cotter pin.

## REAR AXLE

Refer to **Figure 4**.

### Removal

The rear brake caliper and driven sprocket can be removed with the axle installed. Before beginning removal, read the removal and installation procedures and have the required special tools on hand.

1. Park the ATV on level ground and block the front wheels.
2. Loosen the chain as described in Chapter Three.
3. Remove both setscrews in the axle nut (A, **Figure 5**).

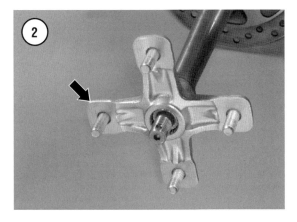

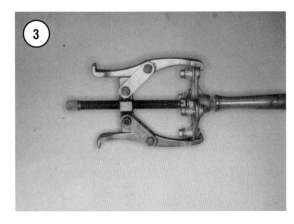

4. Push down the brake pedal to lock the rear brake.
5. Using Yamaha axle nut wrench 90890-06588, or equivalent, loosen the axle nut (B, **Figure 5**) as shown in **Figure 6**.

*NOTE*
*A suitable tool may be fabricated by grinding the opening of a 1 3/4-inch crows-foot wrench to fit the 46 mm axle nut (**Figure 6**).*

6. If sprocket or brake disc replacement is necessary, loosen the nuts or bolts while holding down the brake pedal.

7. Remove the rear axle hubs as described in this chapter.
8. Remove the rear brake caliper as described in Chapter Fourteen.
9. Remove the axle nut (A, **Figure 7**) and conical washer (B).

*NOTE*
*It is not necessary to remove the brake disc prior to removing the brake disc hub as shown in **Figure 7**.*

10. Remove the brake disc hub (C, **Figure 7**).
11. Before removing the axle, check the condition of the axle bearings. Grasp the end of the axle and move it in all directions. If excessive play is detected, replace the axle bearings as described in *Rear Axle Hub* in this chapter.
12. Reinstall the right side wheel hub (A, **Figure 8**).

*WARNING*
*Wear safety glasses when driving out the axle.*

*CAUTION*
*Excessive force may damage the axle, hub or swing arm. If the axle is frozen in the bearings or collar due to rust, remove the swing arm and refer disassembly to a dealership.*

13. Place a piece of pipe (B, **Figure 8**) against the wheel hub. Do not allow the pipe to contact the axle threads. Tap against the pipe to force the axle out the left side of the swing arm.
14. If necessary, remove the circlip (A, **Figure 9**), then remove the sprocket hub (B) from the rear axle.
15. Inspect the rear axle as described in this section.
16. Inspect the seals and bearings as described in *Rear Axle Hub* in this chapter.

**Inspection**

1. Clean the axle. All splines must be clean for inspection. Prevent any damage to the axle bearing surfaces during the inspection procedure.
2. At each end of the axle, inspect the following:
    a. Cotter pin holes (A, **Figure 10**). Check for cracks or fractures around the holes. Replace the axle if damaged.
    b. Wheel hub nut threads (B, **Figure 10**). Check for uniform and symmetrical threads. Screw the wheel hub nut onto the threads and check for roughness and play. If damage is detected, try restoring the threads with a thread die.
    c. Wheel hub splines (C, **Figure 10**). Check for worn, distorted and broken splines. Inspect the

**13**

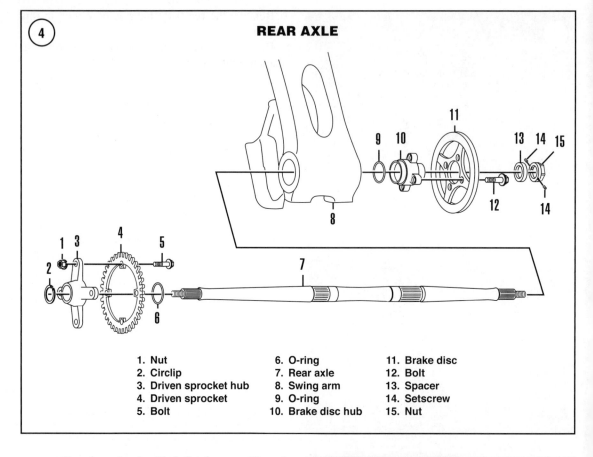

**REAR AXLE**

1. Nut
2. Circlip
3. Driven sprocket hub
4. Driven sprocket
5. Bolt
6. O-ring
7. Rear axle
8. Swing arm
9. O-ring
10. Brake disc hub
11. Brake disc
12. Bolt
13. Spacer
14. Setscrew
15. Nut

splines in each wheel hub for damage. Fit each hub onto its respective end of the axle and feel for play. If play or wear is detected, replace the parts.

d. Brake disc hub splines (A, **Figure 11**). Check for worn, distorted and broken splines. Inspect the fit of the brake hub on the splines. Check for looseness between the parts.

e. Driven sprocket hub splines (B, **Figure 11**). Check for worn, distorted and broken splines. Inspect the fit of the sprocket hub on the splines. Check for looseness between the parts.

3. Inspect the axle where it contacts the bearings in the rear axle hub (C, **Figure 11**). Check for scoring, galling and other damage. If damage is evident, inspect the bearings in the rear axle hub, as described in *Rear Axle Hub* in this chapter. Replace damaged parts.

4. Inspect the driven sprocket hub and brake disc hub for the following:

a. Remove the O-rings from the axle.

b. Cracks or fractures.

c. Inspect the condition of the hub splines.

5. Check the axle for straightness. Support the axle with V-blocks at locations shown at A, **Figure 12**. Measure runout using a dial indicator at locations B, **Figure 12**. Replace the axle if runout exceeds the

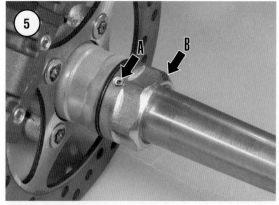

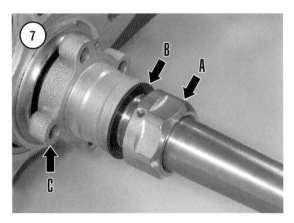

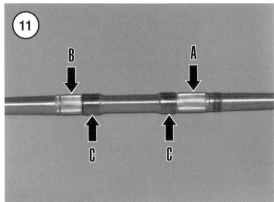

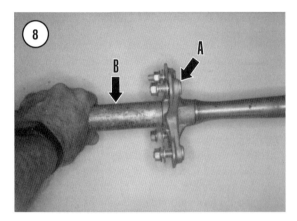

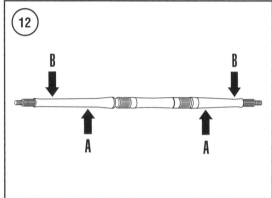

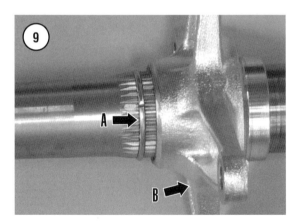

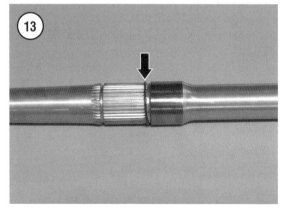

13

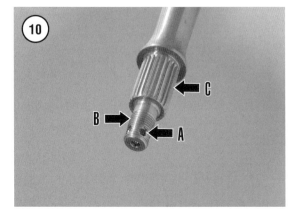

service limit in **Table 1**. When measuring runout, the runout is one-half the reading on the dial indicator.

**Installation**

Refer to **Figure 4**.
1. Apply grease to the lips of the seals in both sides of the rear axle hub.
2. Apply grease to the axle splines and axle bearing surfaces.
3. If removed, install a new, lubricated O-ring onto the axle (**Figure 13**), then install the drive sprocket hub (B, **Figure 9**) and the circlip (A, **Figure 9**).

*NOTE*
*Insert the axle through the drive chain*
*in Step 4 while installing the axle.*

4. Install the axle into the rear hub.
5. Install a new, lubricated O-ring onto the axle
(**Figure 14**).
6. Install the rear brake hub and disc, if not removed
from the hub.
7. Install the conical washer so the concave side is
toward the brake disc hub.
8. Apply threadlocking compound to the axle nut
threads, then install the nut using the axle nut wrench
(**Figure 6**).

*NOTE*
*Temporarily install a wheel hub. Hold*
*the wheel hub to prevent axle rotation*
*during Step 9.*

9A. On 2004-2005 models, tighten the axle nut to
100 N•m (74 ft.-lb.).
9B. On 2006-on models, tighten the axle nut to 240
N•m (176 ft.-lb.).
10. Apply threadlocking compound to the setscrew
threads. Tighten the setscrews in the axle nut to 7
N•m (62 in.-lb.).
11. Install the rear brake caliper as described in
Chapter Fourteen.
12. Install the drive chain as described in Chapter
Eleven.
13. Install the rear wheel hubs as described in this
chapter.
14. Install the rear wheels as described in Chapter
Eleven.

## REAR AXLE HUB (2004-2005 MODELS)

Refer to **Figure 15**.

### Removal/Installation

The swing arm contains the rear axle hub. The hub
contains the axle bearings and seals.
1. Remove the rear axle as described in this chapter.
2. Remove the nuts and washers (**Figure 16**) retaining
the brake caliper bracket. Apply penetrating oil and use
a wood block to evenly tap the bracket off the hub.
3. Inspect the axle hub assembly (**Figure 17**, typical) as described in this section.
4. Reverse the preceding procedure to install the hub
assembly while noting the following:
   a. Lubricate all splines and seals with waterproof
    grease.
   b. Tighten the axle hub retaining nuts to 85 N•m
    (62 ft.-lb.).

### Disassembly/Inspection/Assembly

1. Wipe the axle hub assembly clean. Do not immerse the hub assembly in solvent unless the bearings and seals require replacement.
2. Inspect the dust seals for tears, distortion or other
damage. If rust, dirt or moisture is evident behind
the seals, the seals are leaking. Replace the seals as
described in this section.
3. Inspect the bearings as follows:
   a. Turn each bearing inner race (**Figure 18**). Feel
    for roughness, noise or binding. The bearings
    should turn smoothly and quietly.
   b. Check for axial and radial (**Figure 19**) play.
    Replace the bearings if worn or damaged.
    Remove and install the bearings as described
    in this section.

*NOTE*
*Always replace bearings as a pair.*

4. After the bearings and seals have been inspected/
replaced, coat the surface of the spacer that fits inside
the swing arm with a film of waterproof grease.
5. Inspect the brake caliper bracket and bore. If the
bracket was seized to the axle hub, polish the interior of
the bore with emery cloth to remove corrosion. Apply
a film of waterproof grease to the cleaned bore.
6. Inspect the bolts, washers and nuts for corrosion
and damage.

### Seal Removal/Installation

Seals are used to prevent the entry of moisture and
dirt into the hub and bearings. Always install new
seals whenever the axle hub is being reconditioned.
Refer to *Seal Removal/Installation* in *Service
Methods* in Chapter One.

### Bearing Removal/Installation

1. Remove the seals.

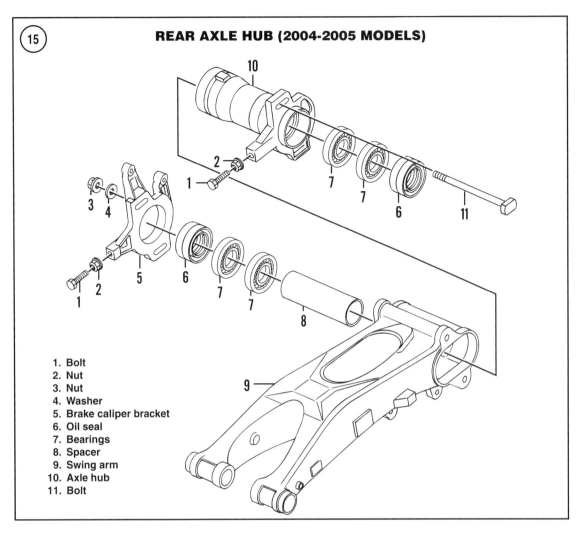

**REAR AXLE HUB (2004-2005 MODELS)**

1. Bolt
2. Nut
3. Nut
4. Washer
5. Brake caliper bracket
6. Oil seal
7. Bearings
8. Spacer
9. Swing arm
10. Axle hub
11. Bolt

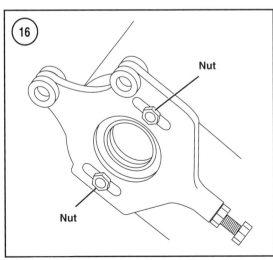

Nut

Nut

**REAR AXLE HUB (2006-ON MODELS)**

Refer to **Figure 21**.

2. Insert a drift into one side of the axle hub and push the spacer (**Figure 20**) between the bearings to one side.

3. Refer to *Bearings* in *Service Methods* in Chapter One and remove and install the bearings.

**Removal/Installation**

The swing arm contains the rear axle hub. The hub contains the axle bearings and seals.

13

1. Remove the rear axle as described in this chapter.
2. Remove the snap ring (A, **Figure 22**).
3. Remove the caliper mounting bracket (B, **Figure 22**).
4. Remove the axle hub pinch bolts at the back end of the swing arm (A, **Figure 23**). Then remove the gasket (B, **Figure 23**).
5. Remove the brake caliper bracket locating collar (A, **Figure 24**).
6. Remove the O-rings on the hub (B, **Figure 24**).
7. Lightly tap the axle hub (C, **Figure 24**) out the left side of the swing arm using a soft mallet.
8. Inspect the axle hub as described in this section.

### Disassembly/Inspection

1. Wipe the axle hub and swing arm clean. Do not immerse the axle hub in solvent unless the bearings and seals require replacement.
2. Inspect the caliper mounting bracket for damage.
3. Inspect the seals (A, **Figure 25**) for tears, distortion or other damage. If rust or moisture is evident on the inner bearing races or bearing spacer, the seals are leaking. Replace the bearings and seals as described in this section.
4. Inspect the bearings as follows:
    a. Turn each bearing inner race (B, **Figure 25**). Feel for roughness, noise or binding. The bearings should turn smoothly and quietly.
    b. Check for axial and radial (**Figure 19**) play. Replace the bearings if worn or damaged. Remove and install the bearings as described in this section.

*NOTE*
*Always replace bearings as a pair.*

5. After the bearings and seals have been inspected/replaced, prepare the axle hub for installation as follows:
    a. Install new, lubricated O-rings (**Figure 26**) onto the axle hub.
    b. Coat the exterior surface of the axle hub that fits inside the swing arm with waterproof grease.

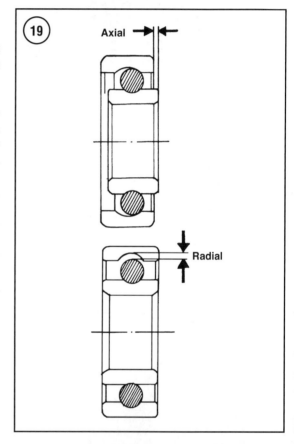

### Seal Removal/Installation

Seals are used to prevent the entry of moisture and dirt into the hub and bearings. Always install new seals whenever the axle hub is being reconditioned.

Refer to *Seal Removal/Installation* in *Service Methods* in Chapter One.

### Bearing Removal/Installation

1. Remove the seals as described in this section.

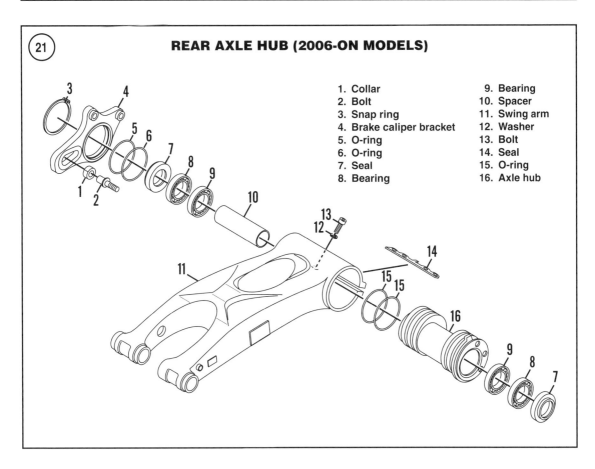

**REAR AXLE HUB (2006-ON MODELS)**

21

1. Collar
2. Bolt
3. Snap ring
4. Brake caliper bracket
5. O-ring
6. O-ring
7. Seal
8. Bearing

9. Bearing
10. Spacer
11. Swing arm
12. Washer
13. Bolt
14. Seal
15. O-ring
16. Axle hub

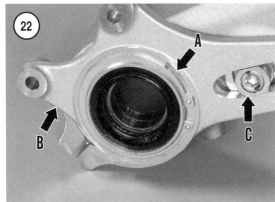

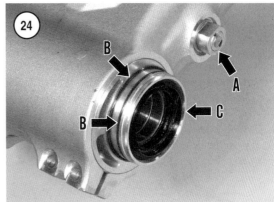

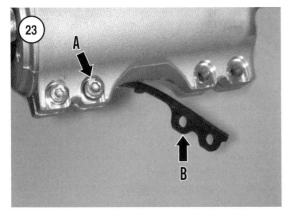

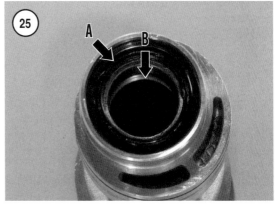

13

2. Insert a drift into one side of the axle hub and push the spacer (**Figure 20**) between the bearings to one side.

3. Refer to *Bearings* in *Service Methods* in Chapter One and remove and install the bearings.

## Installation

1. Install and seat the axle hub (**Figure 27**) into the swing arm from the left side. Work slowly to prevent damaging the O-rings on the hub.

> *NOTE*
> *The inner O-ring has a larger circumference than the outer O-ring.*

2. Install new, lubricated O-rings (B, **Figure 24**). The inner O-ring sits in the crevice between the face of the hub and the hub outer diameter. The outer O-ring sits in the inner groove. The outer groove accepts the snap ring.

3. Install the caliper bracket locating collar (C, **Figure 22**).

4. Apply grease to the inner contact surface of the caliper bracket.

> *NOTE*
> *Rotate the axle hub as needed to prevent contact between the swing arm and caliper bracket during bracket installation.*

5. Fit the caliper bracket onto the axle hub and engage it with the stopper collar.

6. Install a new snap ring (A, **Figure 22**).

7. Install the gasket (B, **Figure 23**) and pinch bolts (A). Tighten the axle hub pinch bolts to 21 N•m (15 ft.-lb.).

8. Install the rear axle as described in this chapter.

9. Adjust the chain as described in Chapter Three.

### SHOCK ABSORBER

The single shock absorber is a spring-loaded, hydraulically-damped unit with an integral oil/nitrogen reservoir. To adjust the shock absorber, refer to Chapter Three.

### Removal/Installation

1. Remove the seat as described in Chapter Fifteen.

2. Remove the left foot protector as described in Chapter Fifteen.

3. Remove the exhaust system as described in Chapter Four.

4. Support the ATV so the rear wheels are off the ground.

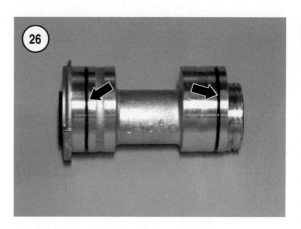

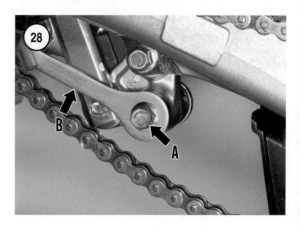

5. Place a jack or other support under the swing arm so it cannot fall.

6. Remove the connecting arm bolts (A, **Figure 28**), then remove the connecting arm (B) from the relay arm.

7. Remove the cotter pin (**Figure 29**) and lower shock absorber mounting bolt (**Figure 30**).

8. Remove the upper mounting bolt from the shock absorber and frame (**Figure 31**).

9. Remove the shock absorber. Inspect the unit as described in this section.

10. Reverse the preceding procedure to install the shock absorber while noting the following:

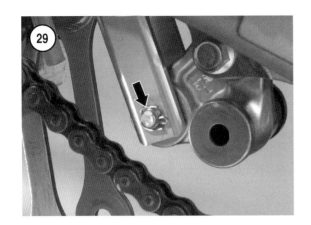

a. Lubricate all bearings, seals and pivot bolts with lithium grease.
b. Install the washers on the upper and lower shock absorber bolts so the flat side of the washer contacts the bolt head or the nut.
c. Tighten the upper shock absorber bolt to 80 N•m (59 ft.-lb.).
d. Tighten the lower shock absorber bolt to 43 N•m (32 ft.-lb.). Install a new cotter pin.
e. Insert the connecting arm bolt (A, **Figure 28**) from the left side. Tighten the bolts to 55 N•m (40 ft.-lb.).

**Inspection**

Individual parts are not available for the rear shock absorber.

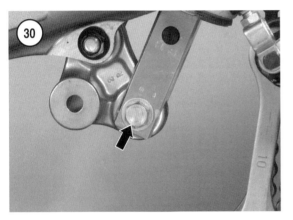

1. Inspect the shock absorber for gas or oil leaks.
2. Check the damper rod (A, **Figure 32**) for bending, rust or other damage.
3. Inspect the spring (B, **Figure 32**) for damage. The spring is not available seperately.
4. Inspect the reservoir (C, **Figure 32**) for damage.
5. Inspect the bearing, collar and seals in the upper end of the shock absorber (D, **Figure 32**) as follows:
    a. Check the seals for cracks, wear or other damage.
    b. Check the collar for cracks, scoring, wear or other damage.
    c. Check the needle bearing for wear, play, flat spots, rust or blue discoloration (overheating).
    d. Lubricate the collar with grease and insert it into the bearing. The collar should turn freely and smoothly with no play.
6. Inspect the lower mounting hole for damage and excessive wear.
7. If the shock is leaking, or if it is time to replace the shock oil, refer all service to a dealership.

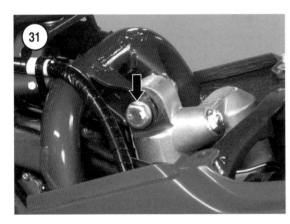

**13**

**SHOCK LINKAGE**

The shock linkage consists of the relay arm, connecting arm, pivot bolts, seals, collars, bushings and needle bearings. The linkage operates in a harsh environment, follow the service interval recommendations in Chapter Three.

*NOTE*
*Motion Pro tool No. 08-0213 may be used to remove and install the bearings in the shock linkage.*

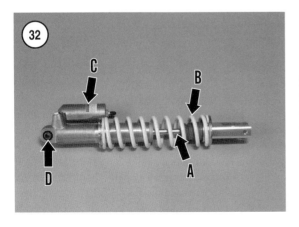

## Removal/Installation

The connecting arm and relay arm may be removed for service without removing the swing arm. This procedure details the removal and separation of the connecting arm and relay arm assemblies. Refer to **Figure 33**.

1. Clean the shock linkage components to prevent dirt from contaminating bearings during removal.
2. Remove the shock absorber as described in this chapter.
3. Remove the pivot bolt (A, **Figure 34**) from the connecting arm, then remove the connecting arm.
4. Remove the pivot bolt (B, **Figure 34**) from the relay arm, then remove the relay arm.
5. Disassemble/inspect/reassemble the connecting arm and relay arm as described in this section.
6. Reverse these steps to install the parts. Note the following:

   a. Lubricate all bearings, seals and collars with lithium grease.

   b. Note the L and R cast into the sides of the relay arm (A, **Figure 35**). Install the relay arm so the side marked L faces the left side of the swing arm.

   c. Tighten the swing arm to relay arm pivot bolt from the left side of the ATV. Tighten the bolt to 55 N•m (40 ft.-lb.).

   d. Tighten the connecting arm pivot bolt from the left side of the ATV. Tighten the bolt to 55 N•m (40 ft.-lb.).

## Disassembly/Inspection/Reassembly

1. On models so equipped, remove the dust covers from the relay arm (B, **Figure 35**).
2. Remove the spacer from the connecting arm (**Figure 36**).
3. Remove the spacers from the relay arm.
4. Pry the seals from the bearing bores (A, **Figure 37**).
5. Clean and dry the relay arm, connecting arm, seals, collars and bearings.
6. Inspect the following:

   a. Inspect the relay arm and connecting arm for cracks or bends. Check the pivot bolt holes for scoring, wear and elongation.

   b. Lay the connecting arm on a flat surface and check that both arms are parallel and the pivot bolt passes straight from one bore to the other.

   c. Check the pivot bolts for scoring, wear and other damage.

   d. Check the seals for cracks, wear or other damage.

   e. Check the collars for cracks, scoring, wear or other damage.

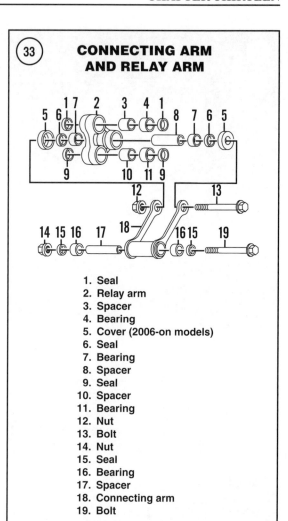

**33  CONNECTING ARM AND RELAY ARM**

1. Seal
2. Relay arm
3. Spacer
4. Bearing
5. Cover (2006-on models)
6. Seal
7. Bearing
8. Spacer
9. Seal
10. Spacer
11. Bearing
12. Nut
13. Bolt
14. Nut
15. Seal
16. Bearing
17. Spacer
18. Connecting arm
19. Bolt

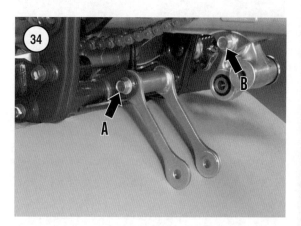

   f. Check the needle bearings (B, **Figure 37**) for wear, play, flat spots, rust or blue discoloration (overheating). Inspect the bearing cages for cracks, rust or other damage. Lubricate the collars with lithium grease and insert them into their respective bearings. The parts should turn freely and smoothly with no play. If play or roughness exists, replace the bearing as described in Step 7.

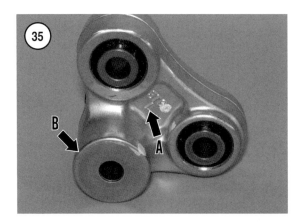

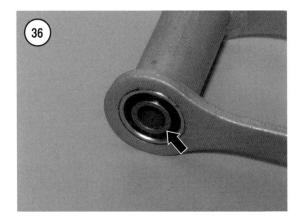

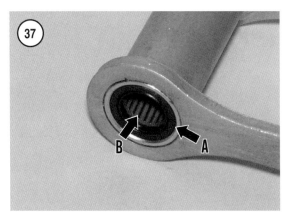

Replace bearings and collars as a set. If the bearing is in good condition, continue with Step 8.

7. Refer to *Bearings* in *Service Methods* in Chapter One and replace the needle bearings in the relay arm or connecting arm as follows:
   a. Support the part in a press.
   b. Place a driver on the outer race of the bearing and force the bearing out of the part.
   c. Clean and inspect the mounting bore.
   d. Lubricate the new bearing with lithium grease.
   e. Refer to **Table 1** for the required depth to insert the bearing(s). The depth is required so the seals can be seated in both sides of the bore.

   f. Place the new bearing squarely into the bore and force it into place.
   g. Measure the bearing depth and force in the bearing(s) as required.
8. Lubricate the bearings, seals and collars with lithium grease.
9. Install the seals and collars. Install the seals with the manufacturer's marks facing out.
10. Install the relay arm and connecting arm as described in this section.

## SWING ARM

### Bearing Inspection

The general condition of the swing arm bearings can be determined with the swing arm mounted on the ATV. Periodically check the bearings for play, roughness or damage. If the swing arm will be removed from the frame, make the check prior to removing the swing arm pivot bolt. If the swing arm will not be removed from the frame, perform the following steps before making the inspection.
1. Remove the rear wheels as described in Chapter Eleven.
2. Remove the shock absorber as described in this chapter.
3. Loosen the drive chain adjusters, then push the axle forward and lift the chain off the driven sprocket.
4. Check the bearings as follows:
   a. Grasp the ends of the swing arm and move it from side to side horizontally. There should be no detectable play in the bearings.
   b. Pivot the swing arm up and down. The bearings must pivot smoothly.
   c. If there is play or roughness in the bearings, remove the swing arm and inspect the bearing and pivot assembly for wear as described in this section.
5. Install the shock absorber as described in this chapter.
6. Install the wheels as described in Chapter Eleven.
6. Adjust the chain (Chapter Three).

### Removal/Installation

This procedure assumes the swing arm is being removed for service or replacement. Therefore, major assemblies attached to the swing arm are completely removed.

Refer to **Figure 38**.
1. Remove the hubs, axle, axle hub and shock absorber as described in this chapter.
2. Remove the parking brake cable and brake hose guides (**Figure 39**) from the swing arm.

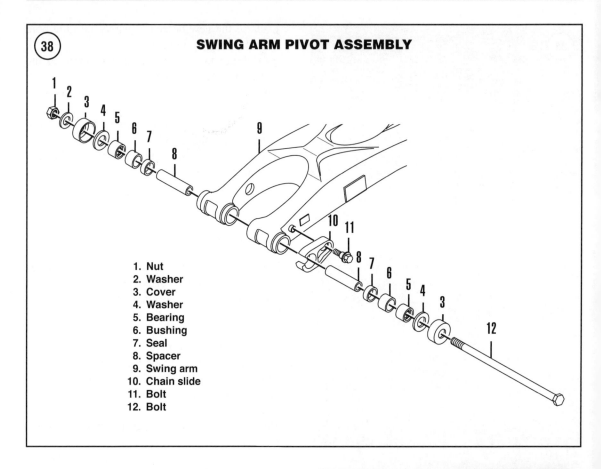

**(38)** **SWING ARM PIVOT ASSEMBLY**

1. Nut
2. Washer
3. Cover
4. Washer
5. Bearing
6. Bushing
7. Seal
8. Spacer
9. Swing arm
10. Chain slide
11. Bolt
12. Bolt

3. Remove the nut and washer (**Figure 40**).

4. Remove the swing arm pivot bolt (**Figure 41**).

5. Inspect and service the swing arm as described in this section.

6. Reverse the preceding steps to install the swing arm assembly while noting the following:

   a. Check that the chain is routed above and below the swing arm before inserting and tightening the swing arm pivot bolt.

   b. Tighten the swing arm bolt to 100 N•m (74 ft.-lb.).

   c. Adjust the chain (Chapter Three).

**Disassembly/Inspection/Assembly**

During disassembly, identify the parts so they may be inspected and reinstalled in their original locations. Refer to **Figure 38**.

1. On the left side, remove the cover (A, **Figure 42**) and chain slider (B).

2. If necessary, remove the washer inside the cover (**Figure 43**).

3. Remove the spacer (**Figure 44**) from the bearing.

4. If necessary, remove the inner seal (A, **Figure 45**).

5. Repeat for remaining swing arm leg.

6. Clean the parts. Inspect the swing arm casting. Check for fractures and other damage. If damaged,

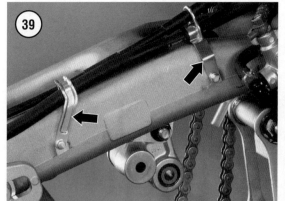

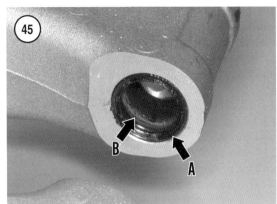

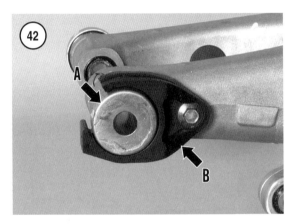

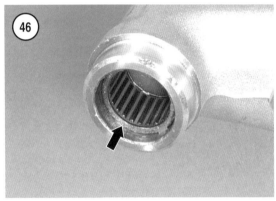

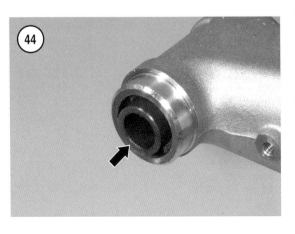

replace the swing arm, or have a dealership determine if it can be repaired.

7. Inspect the needle bearings (**Figure 46**) for wear, play, flat spots, rust or discoloration.

    a. If the rollers are blue, overheating has occurred.

    b. Inspect the bearing cages for cracks, rust or other damage.

    c. Lubricate the bearing and spacer, then insert the spacer (**Figure 44**) into the bearing. The spacer should turn freely and smoothly with no play. If play or roughness exists, replace the bearing as described in this section.

8. Inspect the bushings (B, **Figure 45**) for wear, play and deterioration. The bushings are a synthetic material and may not show obvious wear.

    a. Lubricate the spacer and insert it into the bushing. The spacer should turn freely and smoothly with no play.

    b. If play or roughness exists, replace the bushing as described in this section.

9. Inspect the cover assembly, seals, spacer and pivot bolt assembly.

    a. Inspect the seals for cracks, wear or deterioration.

    b. The cover should seal firmly over the bearing bore.

    c. Inspect the pivot bolt for straightness. Replace the bolt if bent.

**13**

10. Inspect the chain slider. Replace the slider if it is worn. Severe damage can occur to the swing arm if the chain wears through the slider.

11. Clean and inspect the chain rollers (**Figure 47**), attached to the frame. Replace the rollers if worn or seized.

12. Clean and inspect the pivot boss (**Figure 48**) at the rear of the engine. Lubricate the pivot with lithium grease.

13. Reverse the disassembly steps to assemble the swing arm. Note the following:

    a. If necessary, replace the bearings and bushings as described in this section.

    b. Apply lithium grease to the parts as they are assembled.

    c. Install the inner seals so the manufacturer's marks face out.

### Bearing and Bushing Removal/Installation

> *CAUTION*
> *The swing arm casting is brittle and must be supported properly. Failure to provide adequate support around the bearing bore can result in cracking of the casting. If in doubt, have a dealership remove and replace the parts. If the parts are severely seized in the bore, apply penetrating oil and work slowly.*

> *NOTE*
> *Motion Pro tool No. 08-0213 may be used to remove and install the bearings in the swing arm.*

Replace the bearings and bushings after disassembling, cleaning and inspecting the parts as described in this section. Replace bearings and bushings as a set. Refer to *Service Methods* in Chapter One for bearing removal and installation techniques while noting the following:

1. Install the bushings first, then install the bearings.

2. Install bearings to a depth of 5 mm (0.20 in.) from the bore opening.

3. Install bushings to a depth of 8 mm (0.31 in.) from the bore opening.

4. After bushing and bearing installation, insert the collars and check for fit and smooth operation.

### Table 1 REAR SUSPENSION SPECIFICATIONS

| | |
|---|---|
| Rear axle runout limit | 1.5 mm (0.06 in.) |
| Rear shock absorber | |
| 2004-2005 models | |
|   Type | Coil spring/gas-oil damper |
|   Travel | 116 mm (4.57 in.) |
|   Spring free length | 259 mm (10.20 in.) |
|   Spring rate | 46 N/mm (263 lb./in.) |
|   Stroke | 0-116 mm (0-4.57 in.) |
| 2006-on models | |
|   Type | Coil spring/gas-oil damper |
|   Travel | 126 mm (4.96 in.) |
|   Spring free length | 272 mm (10.71 in.) |
|   Spring rate | 36 N/mm (206 lb./in.) |
|   Stroke | 0-126 mm (0-4.96 in.) |
| | (continued) |

## Table 1 REAR SUSPENSION SPECIFICATIONS (continued)

| | |
|---|---|
| Connecting arm bearing depth | 4 mm (0.16 in.) |
| Relay arm bearing depth | |
|   2004-2005 models | |
|     Connecting arm bearings | 5 mm (0.20 in.) |
|     Shock arm bearing | 6.5 mm (0.26 in.) |
|     Swing arm bearing | 6 mm (0.24 in.) |
|   2006-on models | |
|     Connecting arm bearings | 5 mm (0.20 in.) |
|     Shock arm bearing | 5 mm (0.20 in.) |
|     Swing arm bearing | 4.6 mm (0.18 in.) |
| Swing arm pivot | |
|   End play service limit | 1.0 mm (0.04 in.) |
|   Side clearance service limit | 1.0 mm (0.04 in.) |
| Rear wheel travel | |
|   2004-2005 models | 256 mm (10.08 in.) |
|   2006-on models | 270 mm (10.63 in.) |
| Swing arm bushing depth | 8 mm (0.31 in.) |
| Swing arm bearing depth | 5 mm (0.20 in.) |

## Table 2 REAR SUSPENSION TORQUE SPECIFICATIONS

| Item | N•m | in.-lb. | ft-lb. |
|---|---|---|---|
| Axle hub retaining nuts (2004-2005 models) | 85 | – | 62 |
| Axle hub pinch bolts (2006-on models) | 21 | – | 15 |
| Axle nut* | | | |
|   2004-2005 models | 100 | – | 74 |
|   2006-on models | 240 | – | 176 |
| Axle nut setscrews* | 7 | 62 | – |
| Connecting arm bolts | 55 | – | 40 |
| Rear shock absorber | | | |
|   Upper bolt | 80 | – | 59 |
|   Lower bolt* | 43 | – | 32 |
| Swing arm pivot bolt | 100 | – | 74 |
| Swing arm to relay arm pivot bolt | 55 | – | 40 |
| Wheel hub nut* | | | |
|   2004-2005 models | 120 | – | 88 |
|   2006-on models | 200 | – | 147 |

*Refer to text.

13

NOTE: Refer to the Supplement at the back of the manual for information unique to 2009-on YFZ450R models.

# BRAKES

**Table 1** and **Table 2** are at the end of this chapter.

## BRAKE FLUID SELECTION

*WARNING*
*Do not intermix silicone based (DOT 5) brake fluid with glycol-based (DOT 4) brake fluid as it can cause brake system failure.*

When adding brake fluid, use DOT 4 brake fluid from a sealed container. DOT 4 brake fluid is glycol-based and draws moisture, which greatly reduces its ability to perform correctly. Purchase brake fluid in small containers and discard small leftover quantities. Do not store a container of brake fluid with less than 1/4 of the fluid remaining.

Do not reuse drained fluid. Discard old fluid properly.

## BRAKE SERVICE NOTES

*WARNING*
*Do not add to or replace the brake fluid with Silicone (DOT 5) brake fluid. It is not compatible with the system and may cause brake failure.*

*WARNING*
*Whenever working on the brake system, do not inhale brake dust. It may contain asbestos, which can cause lung injury and cancer. Wear a facemask that meets OSHA requirements for trapping asbestos particles, and wash hands and forearms thoroughly after completing the work.*

*WARNING*
*Do not use compressed air to remove brake dust. Brake pad residue is harmful. Use an aerosol brake cleaner to clean parts when servicing any component still installed on the ATV.*

The brake system transmits hydraulic pressure from the master cylinder to the brake caliper. This pressure is transmitted from the caliper to the brake pads, which grip both sides of the brake disc and slow the ATV. As the pads wear, the caliper piston moves out of the caliper bore to automatically compensate for pad wear. As this occurs the fluid level in the reservoir goes down, which must be raised with additional fluid. Refer to Chapter Three to check the brake system fluid level.

Proper service includes carefully performed procedures in a clean work environment. Debris that enters the system can damage the components and cause poor brake performance. Do not use sharp tools while servicing the master cylinder, caliper or piston. Any damage to these components could cause a loss of hydraulic pressure in the system. If there is any doubt about having the ability to correctly and safely service the brake system, have a professional technician perform the task.

Consider the following when servicing the brake system:

1. When properly maintained, hydraulic components rarely require disassembly. Make sure it is necessary.

2. Keep the reservoir covers in place to prevent the entry of moisture and debris.

3. Clean parts with DOT 4 brake fluid, an aerosol brake parts cleaner or isopropyl alcohol. Never use petroleum-based solvents on internal brake system components. They cause seals to swell and distort.

4. Do not allow brake fluid to contact plastic, painted or plated parts. It will damage the surface.

5. Dispose of brake fluid properly.

6. If the hydraulic system has been opened (not including the reservoir cover), the system must be bled to remove air from the system. Refer to *Brake Bleeding* in this chapter.

## FRONT BRAKE PADS

Brake pad life depends on riding habits and the brake pad compound. Replace the pads when they are worn to within 1 mm (0.040 in.) of the backing plate, or have been contaminated with oil or other chemicals.

### Removal/Installation

The brake pads can only be replaced by removing the caliper from the steering knuckle. Brake hose disconnection is not necessary. Keep the caliper supported and do not allow it to hang from the brake hose. Replace both pads as a set.

If the caliper will be rebuilt, or, if other damage is detected during this procedure, the pads can be removed when the caliper is at the workbench. Refer to *Front Brake Caliper* in this chapter for complete removal, repair and installation. Refer to **Figure 1**.

1. Remove the front wheel as described in Chapter Eleven.

2. Loosen the pad pins (**Figure 2**).

3. Remove the caliper mounting bolts (**Figure 3**), then remove the caliper from the disc. Avoid kinking the brake hose.

4. Remove the pad pins, then remove the pads (**Figure 4**).

*CAUTION*
*In the following step, monitor the level of fluid in the master cylinder reservoir. Brake fluid will back flow to the reservoir when the caliper piston is pressed into the bore. Do not allow brake fluid to spill from the reservoir, or damage can occur to painted and plastic surfaces. Immediately clean up any spills, flooding the area with water.*

*NOTE*
*Do not operate the brake lever with the pads removed. Doing so may force the caliper piston out of the bore.*

5. Push in the caliper pistons to create room for the new pads.

6. Remove the pad spring (**Figure 5**).

7. Clean the interior of the caliper and inspect for the following:
   a. Leaks or damage around the piston, bleeder valve and hose connection.
   b. Damaged or missing boots.
   c. Excessive drag of the caliper bracket when it is moved in and out of the caliper. If corrosion or water is detected around the rubber boots, clean the parts and lubricate with lithium-base grease.

8. Inspect the pad pins (A, **Figure 6**), pad spring (B) and mounting bolts (C). The pins and spring must be in good condition to allow the inner pad to slightly move when installed. Check that both small tabs on the spring are not corroded or missing.

9. Inspect the pads (**Figure 7**) for wear and damage.
   a. Replace the pads when they are worn to within 1 mm (0.040 in.) of the backing plate, as shown by the wear indicator (**Figure 8**). Always replace pads contaminated with oil or other chemicals.
   b. If the pads are worn unevenly, the caliper is probably not sliding correctly on the caliper bracket. The caliper must be free to float on the slide pin and retainer bolt. Buildup or corrosion on the parts can hold the caliper in one position, causing brake drag and excessive pad wear.

10. If so equipped, install the shim onto the back of the brake pad (**Figure 9**).

11. Install the pad spring with the small tabs pointing out.

12. Install the inner pad, seating the pad under the caliper bracket and against the piston.

13. Install the outer pad.

14. Align and install the pad pins. Tighten the pins after the caliper is installed.

**14**

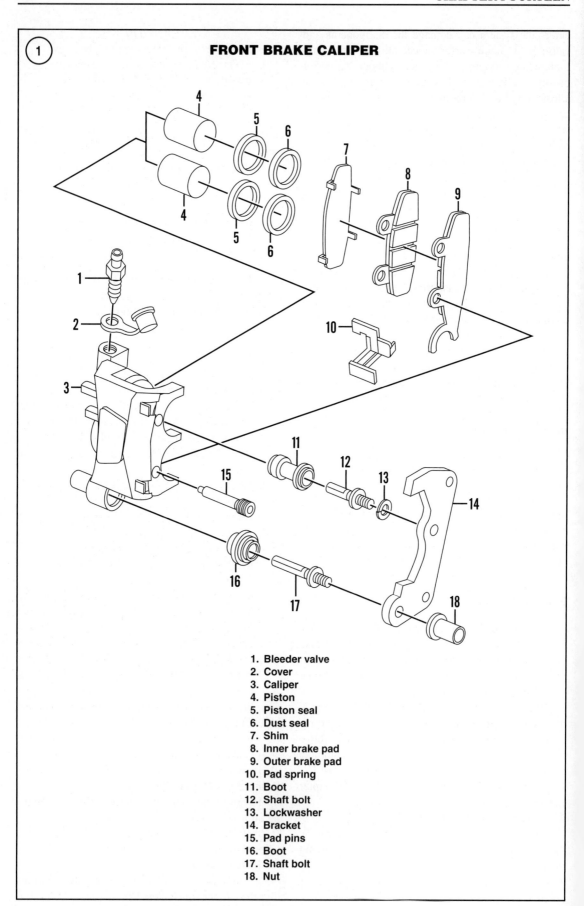

FRONT BRAKE CALIPER

1. Bleeder valve
2. Cover
3. Caliper
4. Piston
5. Piston seal
6. Dust seal
7. Shim
8. Inner brake pad
9. Outer brake pad
10. Pad spring
11. Boot
12. Shaft bolt
13. Lockwasher
14. Bracket
15. Pad pins
16. Boot
17. Shaft bolt
18. Nut

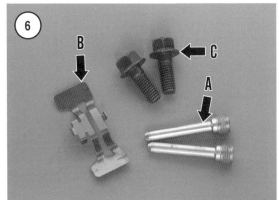

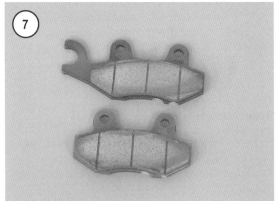

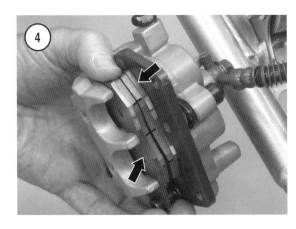

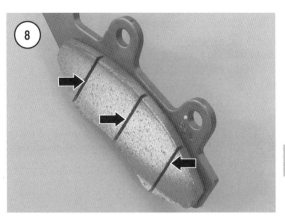

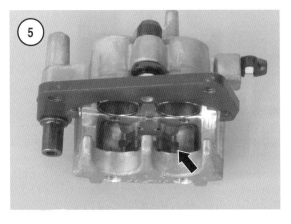

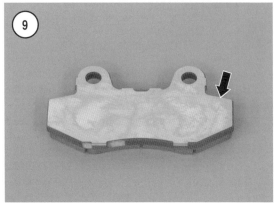

14

15. Spread the pads so there is clearance to fit the caliper over the brake disc.

16. Position the caliper over the brake disc and hub assembly, then slide the caliper down around the brake disc.

17. Install and tighten the front caliper mounting bolts to 28 N•m (21 ft.-lb.).

18. Apply threadlocking compound to the pad pins and tighten to 18 N•m (13 ft.-lb.).

19. Operate the brake lever several times to seat the pads.

20. Check the brake fluid reservoir and replenish or remove fluid as necessary as described in Chapter Three.

21. With the front hub raised, check that the hub spins freely and the brake operates properly.

22. Install the front wheel as described in Chapter Eleven.

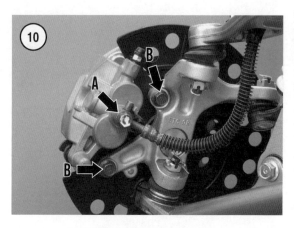

## FRONT BRAKE CALIPER

### Removal/Installation

Use the following procedure to remove the caliper from the steering knuckle:

1. Remove the front wheel as described in Chapter Eleven.

2. If the caliper will be disconnected from the brake hose, drain the system as described in this chapter. After draining, remove the brake hose union bolt and both washers (A, **Figure 10**). Tie a plastic bag around the end of the hose.

3A. If the caliper will be removed from the ATV, remove the caliper mounting bolts (B, **Figure 10**).

3B. If the caliper will be left attached to the brake hose:

    a. Remove the caliper mounting bolts (B, **Figure 10**) and secure the caliper with a length of wire. Do not allow the caliper to hang by the brake hose.

    b. Insert a spacer block between the brake pads.

*NOTE*
*The spacer block will prevent the pistons from being forced out of the caliper if the front brake lever is applied with the brake caliper removed.*

4. Service the caliper as described in this section.

5. Reverse the preceding procedure to install the caliper while noting the following:

    a. Install and tighten the caliper mounting bolts to 28 N•m (21 ft.-lb.).

    b. Install new seal washers on the union bolt. Position the pin on the brake hose end against the boss on the caliper, then tighten the union bolt to 27 N•m (20 ft.-lb.).

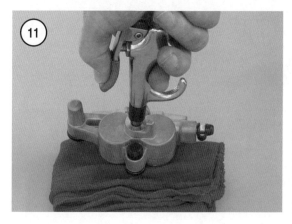

    c. If the caliper was rebuilt, or the brake hose disconnected from the caliper, fill and bleed the brake system as described in this chapter.

    d. Operate the brake lever several times to seat the pads.

    e. Check the brake fluid reservoir and replenish or remove fluid, as described in Chapter Three.

    f. With the front hub raised, check that the hub spins freely and the brake operates properly.

    g. Install the front wheel as described in Chapter Eleven.

### Disassembly

Refer to **Figure 1**.

*CAUTION*
*Do not try to pry out the piston. This will damage the piston and caliper bore.*

### *Removing the pistons hydraulically*

If the piston and dust seals are in good condition and there are no signs of brake fluid leaking from the bores, it may be possible to remove the pistons hydraulically. However, note that brake fluid will spill from the caliper once the pistons are free.

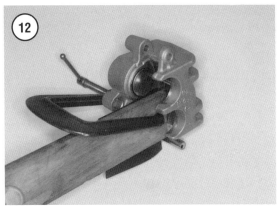

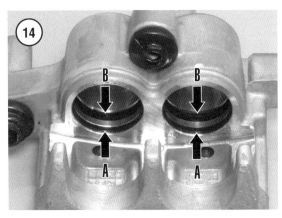

fluid leaking from the hose and reservoir. Temporarily reinstall the caliper bracket and mount the caliper onto the slider with its mounting bolts to hold it in place, then remove the union bolt and both washers.

7. Remove the dust seals (6, **Figure 1**) and piston seals (5) from the caliper bore grooves. Discard the seals.

8. Remove the bleeder valve and cover from the caliper.

9. Clean and inspect the caliper assembly as described in this section.

### *Removing the pistons with compressed air*

1. Remove the brake caliper as described in this section.

2. Remove the pads and the caliper bracket from the caliper.

3. Remove the pad spring from the caliper.

4. Make sure the bleeder valve is closed so air cannot escape.

> *WARNING*
> *Wear eye protection when using compressed air to remove the pistons, and keep your fingers away from the piston.*

5. Cushion the caliper pistons with a shop rag and position the caliper with the piston bores facing down. Apply compressed air through the brake hose port (**Figure 11**) to pop the pistons out. If only one piston came out, block its bore opening with a piece of thick rubber (old inner tube), wooden block and clamp as shown in **Figure 12**. Apply compressed air again and remove the remaining piston. Refer to **Figure 13**.

6. Use a small wooden or plastic tool and remove the dust seals (A, **Figure 14**) and piston seals (B) from the caliper bore grooves and discard them.

7. Remove the bleeder valve and its cover from the caliper.

8. Clean and inspect the brake caliper assembly as described in this section.

1. Remove the front brake caliper as described in this section. Do not loosen or remove the brake hose.

2. Remove the pads and caliper bracket from the caliper as described in this chapter.

3. Remove the pad spring from the caliper.

4. Hold the caliper with the pistons facing down in a pan and slowly operate the brake lever to push the pistons out of their bores. If both pistons move evenly, continue until they extend far enough to be removed by hand.

5. If the pistons do not move evenly, stop and push the extended piston back into its bore by hand, so that both pistons are even, then repeat. If the results are the same, reposition the extended piston again, then operate the brake lever while preventing the moving piston from extending. Install a strip of wood across the caliper to block the piston. If the other piston now starts to move, continue with this technique until both pistons move evenly and can be gripped and removed by hand. After removing the pistons, hold the caliper over the drain pan to catch the brake fluid draining through the caliper.

6. Remove the union bolt with an impact gun, if available. Otherwise, hold the caliper in a secure manner and remove the union bolt with hand tools. If the caliper cannot be held securely to remove the bolt, stuff paper towels into the caliper bores to absorb brake

**14**

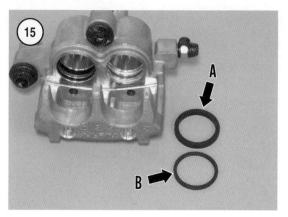

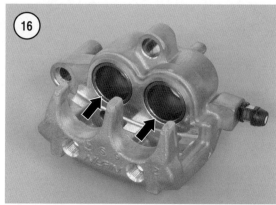

## Assembly

> *NOTE*
> *Use new DOT 4 brake fluid when lu-*
> *bricating the piston seals, pistons and*
> *caliper bores in the following steps.*

1. Install the bleeder valve and its cover into the caliper.
2. Soak the new piston and dust seals in brake fluid.
3. Lubricate the cylinder bores with brake fluid.

> *NOTE*
> *The piston seals (A, Figure 15) are*
> *thicker than the dust seals (B).*

4. Install a new piston seal into each rear bore groove (B, **Figure 14**).
5. Install a new dust seal into each front bore groove (A, **Figure 14**).
6. Lubricate the pistons with brake fluid.

> *CAUTION*
> *The tight piston-to-seal fit can make*
> *piston installation difficult. Make sure*
> *each seal fits squarely inside its bore*
> *groove. Do not install the pistons by*
> *pushing them straight in as they may*
> *bind in their bores and tear the seals.*

7. With the open side facing out, align a piston with the caliper bore. Rock the piston slightly to center it in the bore while at the same time pushing the lower end past the seals. When the lower end of the piston passes through both seals, push and bottom the piston (**Figure 16**) in the bore. After installing the other piston, clean spilled brake fluid from the area in front of the pistons to prevent brake pad contamination.

> *CAUTION*
> *In the following steps, use only lithium-*
> *based grease specified for brake use.*
> *Do not use brake fluid to lubricate the*
> *rubber boots or fixed shafts.*

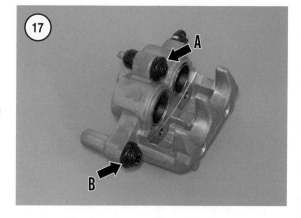

8. Pinch the open end of the large rubber boot and push this end through the mounting hole in the caliper until its outer shoulder bottoms (A, **Figure 17**). Make sure the boot opening faces toward the inside of the caliper. Partially fill the boot with lithium-based grease.
9. Install the small boot into the groove in the caliper (B, **Figure 17**). Partially fill the boot with lithium-based grease.
10. If removed, install the shafts into the caliper bracket. Note the location of the short shaft and lockwasher (**Figure 18**). Tighten the shafts securely.
11. Lubricate the caliper bracket shafts with lithium-base grease.
12. Align and slide the mounting bracket (**Figure 19**) onto the caliper body. Hold the caliper and slide the caliper bracket in and out by hand. Make sure there is no roughness or binding.
13. Install the brake caliper assembly as described in this section.
14. Install the brake pads as described in this section.

## Inspection

All models use a floating caliper design, in which the caliper slides, or floats, on threaded shafts mount-

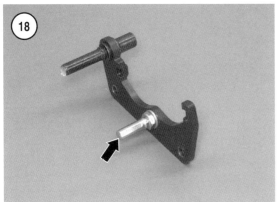

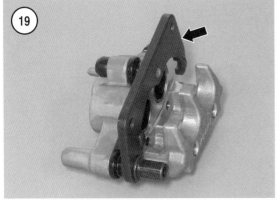

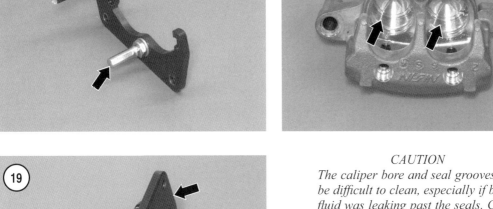

*CAUTION*
*The caliper bore and seal grooves can be difficult to clean, especially if brake fluid was leaking past the seals. Clean the grooves carefully to avoid damaging the grooves and bore surfaces.*

2. Inspect the caliper bracket, shafts and rubber boots as follows:
   a. Inspect the rubber boots for cracks, tearing, weakness or other damage.
   b. Inspect the shafts on the caliper bracket (**Figure 18**) for excessive or uneven wear. If the shaft is damaged, replace the shaft.
3. Check each cylinder bore for corrosion, pitting, deep scratches or other wear.
4. Measure the inside diameter of the caliper bores (**Figure 20**).
5. Check the pistons for wear marks, scoring, cracks or other damage.
6. Check the bleeder valve and cap for wear or damage. Make sure air can pass through the bleeder valve.
7. Check the union bolt for wear or damage. Discard the washers. Use new washers during assembly.
8. Inspect the brake pads and pad spring as described in *Front Brake Pads* in this chapter.

ed parallel with each other on the caliper and caliper bracket. Rubber boots around each shaft prevent dirt from damaging the shafts. If the shafts are worn or damaged the caliper can move out of alignment on the caliper bracket. This will cause brake drag, uneven pad wear and overheating. Inspect the rubber boots and shafts during caliper inspection as they play a vital role in brake performance.

Refer to **Figure 1** when servicing the front brake caliper assembly. Replace parts that are out of specification (**Table 1**) or damaged as described in this section.

*WARNING*
*Do not allow oil or grease on the brake components. Do not clean the parts with kerosene or other petroleum products. These chemicals cause the rubber brake system components to swell, which may cause brake failure.*

1. Clean and dry the caliper and the other metal parts. Clean the seal grooves carefully. If the contamination is difficult to remove, soak the caliper in a suitable solvent and then reclean. If any of the rubber parts are to be reused, clean them with isopropyl alcohol or new DOT 4 brake fluid. Do not use a petroleum-based solvent.

## FRONT MASTER CYLINDER

### Removal/Installation

1. Cover and protect the bodywork and area surrounding the master cylinder.

*CAUTION*
*Do not allow brake fluid to splash from the reservoir or hose. Brake fluid can damage painted and plastic surfaces. Immediately clean up any spills, with plenty of soapy water. Rinse thoroughly with clean water.*

14

2. Drain the brake system as described in this chapter.

3. Remove the cap and diaphragm and verify that the master cylinder is empty (**Figure 21**). Wipe the interior of the reservoir to absorb all remaining fluid.

4A. On 2004-2006 models, remove the brake light switch. Use a small tool to press on the barb that locks the switch to the master cylinder (**Figure 22**).

4B. On 2007-on models, disconnect the two electrical connectors (**Figure 23**) from the front brake light switch.

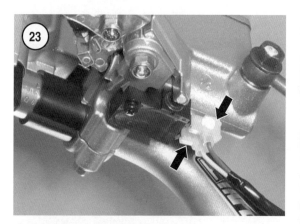

5. If the master cylinder will be rebuilt, remove the brake lever pivot bolt (A, **Figure 24**) while the master cylinder remains stable.

6. Remove the brake hose union bolt (B, **Figure 24**) from the master cylinder as follows:

   a. Remove the union bolt and seal washers from the brake hose. Have a shop cloth ready to absorb excess brake fluid that drips from the hose.

   b. Tie a plastic bag around the end of the hose.

7. Remove the bolts (**Figure 25**) securing the master cylinder to the handlebar, then remove the master cylinder.

8. Repair the master cylinder as described in this section.

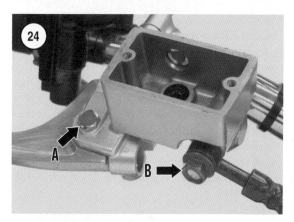

9. Reverse this procedure to install the master cylinder. Note the following:

   a. Check that the indentations on the handlebar collar are engaged with the throttle assembly and master cylinder.

   b. The mounting bracket must be installed so UP and the arrow are facing up. Tighten the upper bolt first, then the bottom bolt. Tighten the bolts to 7 N•m (62 in.-lb.).

   c. Position the brake hose fitting so it is slightly angled downward, keeping the hose straight.

   d. Install new seal washers on the union bolt. Tighten the bolt to 27 N•m (20 ft.-lb.).

   e. Check that the brake light operates when the lever is operated.

10. Fill the brake fluid reservoir and bleed the brake system as described in this chapter.

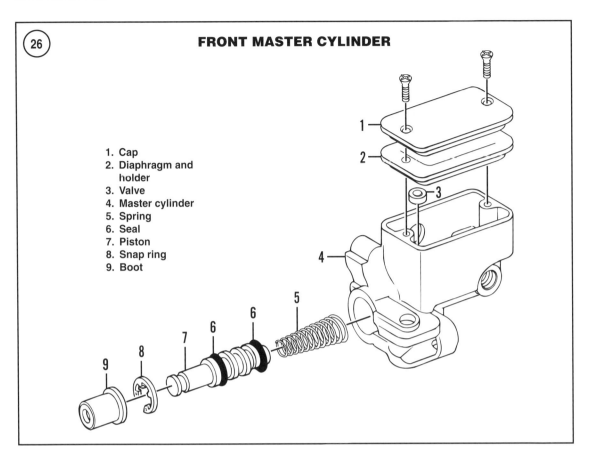

**FRONT MASTER CYLINDER**

26

1. Cap
2. Diaphragm and holder
3. Valve
4. Master cylinder
5. Spring
6. Seal
7. Piston
8. Snap ring
9. Boot

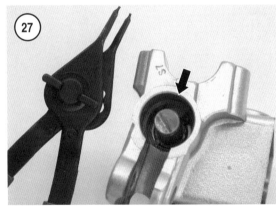

27

28

### Disassembly/Inspection/Reassembly

Refer to **Figure 26**. The piston, seals and spring are only available as a complete assembly.

1. Remove the master cylinder as described in this section.

2. On 2007-on models, remove the mounting screw and brake switch.

3. Remove the boot from the piston. The boot is a friction fit. To avoid damaging the boot on removal, apply penetrating lubricant around the perimeter of the boot. Carefully pull the bottom edge back so the lubricant can loosen the boot.

4. Remove the snap ring from the master cylinder (**Figure 27**) as follows:

    a. Press down on the piston to relieve pressure on the snap ring, then remove the snap ring.

    b. Slowly relieve the pressure on the piston.

5. Remove the piston assembly from the bore (**Figure 28**).

6. Clean all parts that will be reused with brake fluid or isopropyl alcohol.

7. Inspect the cylinder bore for wear, pitting or corrosion.

8. Measure the inside diameter of the cylinder bore (**Figure 29**). Refer to **Table 1** for specifications.

9. Inspect and clean the threads and orifices in the reservoir. Clean with compressed air.

14

10. Inspect the brake lever bore and pivot bolt for wear.

11. Inspect the diaphragm and reservoir cap for damage.

12. Inspect the mounting hardware and union bolt for corrosion and damage. Install new seal washers on the union bolt.

13. Assemble the piston, seals and spring (**Figure 30**) as follows:

    a. Soak the seals in DOT 4 brake fluid for 15 minutes. This will soften and lubricate the seals.

    b. Apply brake fluid to the piston so the seals can slide over the ends.

    c. Mount the seals on the piston. Identify the wide (open) side of both seals. When installed, the wide side of the seals must face in the direction of the arrow (**Figure 30**). Mount the seal with the small hole nearer the spring.

    d. Install and seat the spring onto the piston.

14. Install the piston and snap ring into the master cylinder as follows:

    a. Place the cylinder in a vise with soft jaws. Do not overtighten the vise or cylinder damage could occur.

    b. Lubricate the cylinder bore and piston assembly with brake fluid.

> *CAUTION*
> *In the following step, after the piston cups have entered the cylinder, hold the piston in place until the snap ring is installed. Anytime the cups come out of the cylinder there is a chance of damaging the cup lips during the reinsertion process.*

    c. Insert the piston assembly in the cylinder.

    d. While holding the piston in the cylinder, install the snap ring (**Figure 27**) so the flat side faces out.

15. Apply lithium-based grease to the inside of the boot. Seat the boot into the cylinder.

16. Install the lever and pivot bolt. Apply waterproof grease to the pivot bolt and lever contact point.

17. Loosely attach the diaphragm and cap to the reservoir.

18. On 2007-on models, install the brake switch and mounting screw.

19. Install the master cylinder as described in this section.

## REAR BRAKE PADS

Brake pad life depends on riding habits and brake pad compound. Replace the pads when they are worn to within 1 mm (0.040 in.) of the backing plate, or have been contaminated with oil or other chemicals.

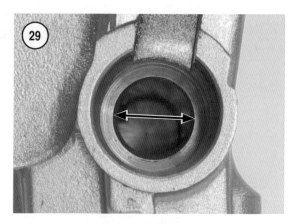

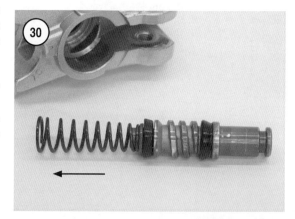

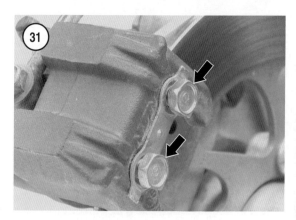

Brake pad removal/installation requires caliper removal from the swing arm. Brake hose disconnection from the caliper is not necessary. Keep the caliper supported and do not allow it to hang from the brake hose.

If the caliper will be rebuilt, or, if other damage is detected during this procedure, the pads can be removed when the caliper is on the workbench. Refer to *Rear Brake Caliper* in this chapter.

### Removal/Installation (2004-2005 Models)

1. Bend the tabs on the lockplate away from the pad pins, then loosen the pad pins (**Figure 31**).

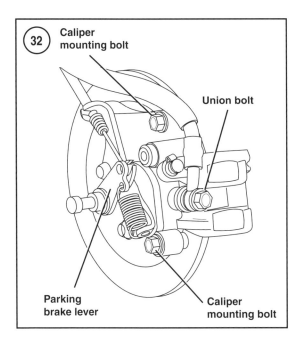

Figure 32

- Caliper mounting bolt
- Union bolt
- Parking brake lever
- Caliper mounting bolt

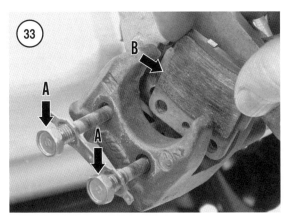

Figure 33

A, A, B

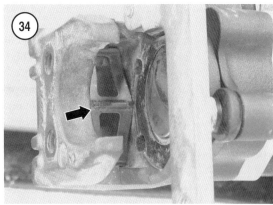

Figure 34

Figure 35

2. Remove the caliper mounting bolts (**Figure 32**). Avoid kinking the brake hose.

3. Press down on the pads to relieve the pressure on the pad pins, then remove the pins (A, **Figure 33**).

4. Remove the pads (B, **Figure 33**).

*CAUTION*
*In the following step, monitor the level of fluid in the master cylinder reservoir. Brake fluid will back flow to the reservoir when the caliper piston is pressed into the bore. Do not allow brake fluid to spill from the reservoir, or damage can occur to painted and plastic surfaces. Immediately clean up any spills with plenty of soapy water. Rinse thoroughly with clean water.*

*NOTE*
*Do not operate the brake pedal with the pads removed. Doing so may force*

*the caliper piston out of the bore. Refer to **Rear Brake Caliper** in this chapter for reassembly procedures.*

5. Push the caliper piston into the bore to create room for the new pads.

6. Remove the pad spring (**Figure 34**).

7. Clean the interior of the caliper and inspect for the following:

a. Leaks or damage around the piston, bleeder valve and hose connection.

b. Damaged or missing boots.

c. Excessive drag of the caliper bracket when it is moved in and out of the caliper. If corrosion or water is detected around the rubber boots, clean the parts and lubricate with lithium-based grease.

8. Inspect the pad pins, pad spring and mounting bolts. The pins and spring must be in good condition to allow the inner pad to slightly move when installed. Check that both small tabs on the spring are not corroded or missing.

9. Inspect the pads and shim on back of inner pad for wear and damage (**Figure 35**).

a. Replace the pads when they are worn to within 1 mm (0.040 in.) of the backing plate, as shown by the wear indicator (**Figure 36**). Always re-

14

place pads that have been contaminated with oil or other chemicals.

   b. If the pads are worn unevenly, the caliper is probably not sliding correctly on the caliper bracket. The caliper must be free to float on the slide pin and retainer bolt. Buildup or corrosion on the parts can hold the caliper in one position, causing brake drag and excessive pad wear.

10. Install the pad spring with the small tabs pointing out.

11. Install the shim onto the inner pad so the triangle (**Figure 35**) points in the direction of brake disc rotation.

12. Install the inner pad and shim, seating the pad under the caliper bracket and against the piston (**Figure 37**).

13. Install the outer pad.

14. Press down on the pads, then align and install the pad pins and a new lockwasher. Tighten the pins after the caliper is installed.

15. Spread the pads so there is clearance to fit the caliper over the brake disc.

16. Position the caliper onto the brake disc, then install and tighten the caliper mounting bolts to 31 N•m (23 ft.-lb.).

17. Tighten the pad pins to 18 N•m (13 ft.-lb.).

18. Bend the lockplate tabs against the mounting bolts.

19. Operate the brake lever several times to seat the pads.

20. Check the brake fluid reservoir and replenish or remove fluid, as described in Chapter Three.

21. With the rear axle raised, check that the axle spins freely and the brake operates properly.

**Removal/Installation (2006-on Models)**

1. Loosen but do not remove the pad pins (**Figure 38**).

2. Remove the caliper mounting bolts (**Figure 39**). Avoid kinking the brake hose.

3. Press down on the pads to relieve the pressure on the pad pins, then remove the pins (**Figure 40**).

4. Remove the pads.

> *CAUTION*
> *In the following step, monitor the level of fluid in the master cylinder reservoir. Brake fluid will back flow to the reservoir when the caliper piston is pressed into the bore. Do not allow brake fluid to spill from the reservoir, or damage can occur to painted and plastic surfaces. Immediately clean up any spills*

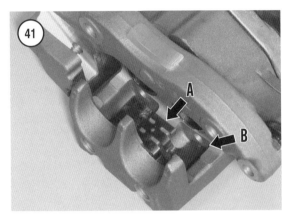

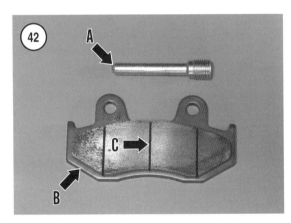

*with plenty of soapy water. Rinse thoroughly with clean water.*

*NOTE*
*Do not operate the brake pedal with the pads removed. Doing so may force the caliper piston out of the bore. Refer to **Rear Brake Caliper** in this chapter for reassembly procedures.*

5. Push the caliper pistons into the bore to create room for the new pads.
6. Remove the inner pad spring (A, **Figure 41**).

7. Clean the interior of the caliper and inspect for the following:
   a. Leaks or damage around the pistons, bleeder valve and hose connection.
   b. Damaged or missing boots.
   c. Excessive drag of the caliper bracket when it is moved in and out of the caliper. If corrosion or water is detected around the rubber boots, clean the parts and lubricate with lithium-base grease.
8. Inspect the pad pins (A, **Figure 42**), pad spring and mounting bolts. The pins and spring must be in good condition to allow the inner pad to slightly move when installed.
9. Inspect the pads (B, **Figure 42**) for wear and damage.
   a. Replace the pads when they are worn to within 1 mm (0.040 in.) of the backing plate, as shown by the wear indicator grooves (C, **Figure 42**). Always replace pads that have been contaminated with oil or other chemicals.
   b. If the pads are worn unevenly, the caliper is probably not sliding correctly on the caliper bracket. The caliper must be free to float on the slide shafts. Buildup or corrosion on the shafts can hold the caliper in one position, causing brake drag and excessive pad wear.
10. Install the pad spring with the small tabs pointing out and the clip (B, **Figure 41**) near the pistons.
11. Install the pads.
12. Press down on the pads, then align and install the pad pins. Tighten the pins after the caliper is installed.
13. Spread the pads so there is clearance to fit the caliper around the brake disc.
14. Position the caliper onto the brake disc, then install and tighten the caliper mounting bolts to 43 N•m (32 ft.-lb.).
15. Tighten the pad pins to 17 N•m (12 ft.-lb.).
16. Operate the brake lever several times to seat the pads.
17. Check the brake fluid reservoir and replenish or remove fluid, as described in Chapter Three.
18. With the rear axle raised, check that the axle spins freely and the brake operates properly.

**REAR BRAKE CALIPER
(2004-2005 MODELS)**

**Removal/Installation**

1. If the caliper will be disassembled, do the following:
   a. Drain the system as described in this chapter. After draining, loosen the brake hose union bolt (**Figure 43**) while the caliper is mounted.

14

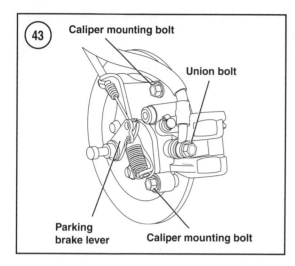

Caliper mounting bolt

Union bolt

Parking brake lever

Caliper mounting bolt

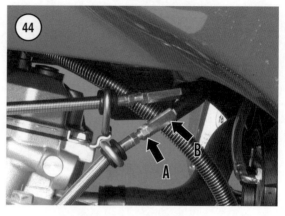

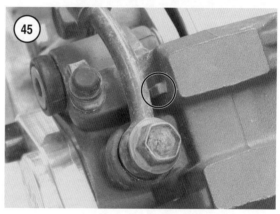

Leave the bolt finger-tight. It will be removed in a later step.

b. On the parking brake cable, loosen the locknut (A, **Figure 44**) and turn the cable adjuster (B) until there is enough slack in the cable to remove it from the parking brake lever (**Figure 43**).

*NOTE*
*If necessary, disengage the upper end of the parking brake cable from the handlebar lever to obtain sufficient cable slack.*

2. Remove the caliper mounting bolts (**Figure 43**). Remove the caliper from the disc. Avoid kinking the brake hose.

3A. If the caliper will be left attached to the brake hose, but not disassembled and serviced, do the following:

a. Suspend the caliper with a length of wire. Do not let the caliper hang from the brake hose.

b. Insert a wood block between the brake pads. This will prevent the caliper piston from extending out of the caliper if the brake lever is operated.

3B. If the caliper will be disassembled, do the following:

a. Remove the union bolt and seal washers from the brake hose. Have a shop cloth ready to absorb excess brake fluid that drips from the hose.

b. Tie a plastic bag around the end of the hose to prevent brake fluid from damaging other surfaces.

c. Drain excess brake fluid from the caliper.

d. Repair the caliper as described in this section.

4. Reverse this procedure to install the caliper while noting the following:

a. Install and tighten the caliper mounting bolts to 31 N•m (23 ft.-lb.).

b. If removed, install new seal washers on the union bolt. Seat the brake hose against the boss on the caliper (**Figure 45**), then tighten the union bolt to 30 N•m (22 ft.-lb.).

c. If the caliper was rebuilt, or the brake hose disconnected from the caliper, fill and bleed the brake system as described in this chapter.

5. Operate the brake lever several times to seat the pads.

6. Check the brake fluid reservoir and replenish or remove fluid as described in Chapter Three.

7. If necessary, adjust the parking brake cable (Chapter Three).

8. With the rear wheels raised, check that the disc spins freely and the brake operates properly.

**Disassembly**

Refer to **Figure 46**.

*CAUTION*
*Do not try to pry out the piston. This will damage the piston and caliper bore.*

*Removing the piston hydraulically*

If the piston and dust seals are in good condition and there are no signs of brake fluid leaking from the

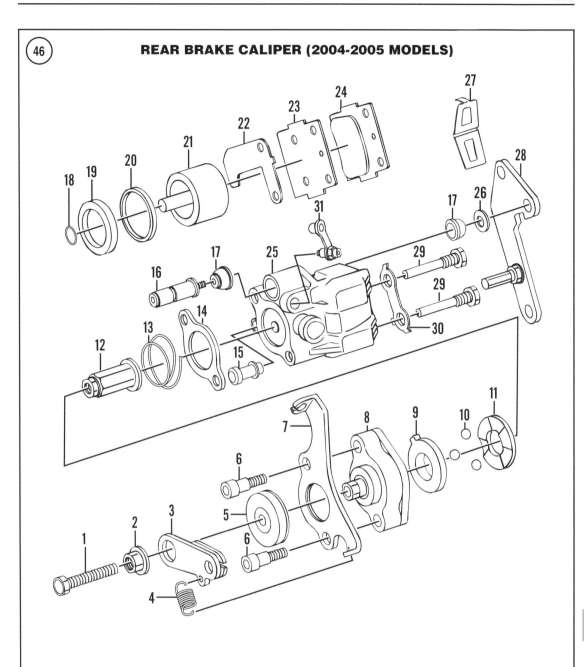

**REAR BRAKE CALIPER (2004-2005 MODELS)**

1. Adjust bolt
2. Locknut
3. Parking brake lever
4. Return spring
5. Boot
6. Bolt
7. Bracket
8. Parking brake housing
9. Inner race
10. Ball
11. Outer race
12. Nut
13. Spring
14. Gasket
15. Boot
16. Shaft bolt
17. Boot
18. O-ring
19. Piston seal
20. Dust seal
21. Piston
22. Shim
23. Inner brake pad
24. Outer brake pad
25. Brake caliper
26. Lockwasher
27. Pad spring
28. Bracket
29. Pad pins
30. Lockplate
31. Bleeder valve

14

bore, it may be possible to remove the piston hydraulically. However, note that brake fluid will spill from the caliper once the piston becomes free.

1. Remove the rear brake caliper as described in this section. Do not loosen or remove the brake hose.

2. Remove the rear brake pads as described in this chapter.

3. Remove the caliper bracket from the caliper. Have a supply of paper towels and a pan available to catch and wipe up spilled brake fluid.

4. Hold the caliper with the piston facing out and operate the brake pedal to push the piston out of the caliper bore.

5. Remove the union bolt with an impact gun (air or electric), if available. Otherwise, hold the caliper and caliper bracket against the swing arm with an adjustable wrench and remove the union bolt with hand tools.

6. Perform Steps 5-11 in *Removing the Piston With Compressed Air* in this secion.

### Removing the piston with compressed air

1. Remove the rear brake caliper as described in this section.

2. Remove the rear brake pads as described in this chapter.

3. Slide the caliper bracket out of the caliper.

> *WARNING*
> *Wear eye protection when using compressed air to remove the piston. Keep your fingers away from the piston.*

4. Cushion the piston with a shop rag and position the caliper with the piston bore facing down. Apply compressed air through the brake hose port (**Figure 47**) to force out the piston.

5. Remove the dust and piston seals (**Figure 48**) from the caliper bore grooves and discard them.

6. Remove the small O-ring (**Figure 49**) from the inside of the parking brake housing.

7. To remove the rear parking brake assembly, perform the following:

    a. Remove the return spring (4, **Figure 46**).

    b. Loosen the locknut (2, **Figure 46**) and remove the adjust bolt (1).

    c. Remove the parking brake lever (3, **Figure 46**).

    d. Remove the two bolts that hold the parking brake housing to the rear brake caliper. Then remove the parking brake housing.

    e. Remove the gasket.

8. Remove the caliper bracket bolt and boots (A, **Figure 50**). Carefully remove the bolt to prevent tearing or pinching the boots.

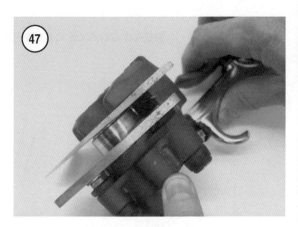

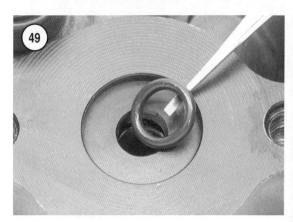

9. Remove the caliper bracket and washer (B, **Figure 50**).

10. Remove the slide pin boot (C, **Figure 50**).

11. Remove the bleeder valve and cap (D, **Figure 50**).

### Brake Caliper Inspection

All models use a floating caliper design, in which the caliper slides or floats on threaded shafts mounted parallel with each other on the caliper and caliper bracket. Rubber boots around each shaft prevent dirt from damaging the shafts. If the shafts are worn or

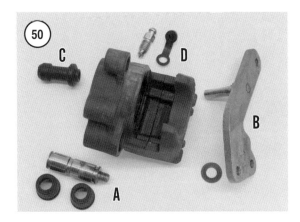

damaged the caliper can move out of alignment on the caliper bracket. This will cause brake drag, uneven pad wear and overheating. Inspect the rubber boots and shafts during caliper inspection as they play a vital role in brake performance.

Refer to **Figure 46** when servicing the rear brake caliper assembly. Replace parts that are out of specification (**Table 1**) or damaged as described in this section.

> *WARNING*
> *Do not allow oil or grease on the brake components. Do not clean the parts with kerosene or other petroleum products. These chemicals cause the rubber brake system components to swell, which may cause brake failure.*

1. Clean and dry the caliper and the other metal parts. Clean the seal grooves carefully. If the contamination is difficult to remove, soak the caliper in a suitable solvent and then reclean. If any of the rubber parts are to be reused, clean them with isopropyl alcohol or new DOT 4 brake fluid. Do not use a petroleum-based solvent.

> *CAUTION*
> *The caliper bore and seal grooves can be difficult to clean, especially if brake*

*fluid was leaking past the seals. Clean the grooves carefully to avoid damaging the grooves and bore surfaces.*

2. Inspect the caliper bracket, shafts and rubber boots as follows:
   a. Inspect the rubber boots for cracks, tearing, weakness or other damage.
   b. Inspect the shafts on the caliper bracket for excessive or uneven wear. If the shaft is damaged, replace the shaft.
3. Check the cylinder bore for corrosion, pitting, deep scratches or other wear.
4. Measure the inside diameter of the caliper bore (**Figure 51**).
5. Check the piston for wear marks, scoring, cracks or other damage.
6. Check the bleeder valve and cap for wear or damage. Make sure air can pass through the bleeder valve.
7. Check the union bolt for wear or damage. Discard the washers.
8. Inspect the brake pads and pad spring as described under *Front Brake Pads* in this chapter.

### Parking Brake Housing Inspection

Refer to **Figure 46** when servicing the parking brake assembly. Internal components of the parking brake housing are not available separately, but only as a parking brake housing unit assembly. The following procedure describes disassembly for inspection purposes.

> *CAUTION*
> *Unless disassembly is required, do not wash the parking brake housing in solvent as this will wash the grease out of the housing.*

1. Remove the spring (13, **Figure 46**) and nut (12).
2. Remove the outer ball race (11, **Figure 46**).
3. Remove the three balls (10, **Figure 46**) and inner ball race (9).
4. Clean all parts with solvent and inspect for excessive wear or damage.
5. Install the inner race so the ball pockets face out and the tab engages the notch (**Figure 52**) in the housing.
6. Apply wheel bearing grease to the balls and bearing races. Install the balls and outer bearing race.
7. Install the spring and nut.

### Assembly

> *NOTE*
> *Use new DOT 4 brake fluid when lubricating parts.*

**14**

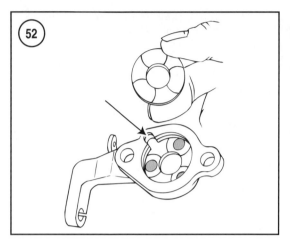

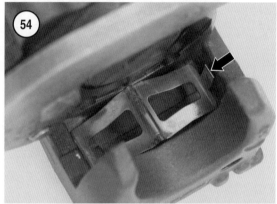

1. Install a new O-ring into the back side of the piston bore (**Figure 49**).

2. Install the piston seal, then the dust seal in the caliper grooves. The piston seal fits in the back groove.

3. Install the piston. Twist the piston past the seals then press the piston to the bottom of the bore.

4. Install the boots and caliper bracket bolt as follows:

   a. Apply lithium-based brake grease to the interior of the boots and to the bracket bolt.

   b. Seat the bracket bolt boots in the caliper grooves and pass the slide pin boot through its bore. If necessary, apply a light coat of grease on the exterior of the boot, to aid in passing it through the caliper.

   c. Carefully twist the bracket bolt through the caliper, then install the boot over the end of the bolt.

5. Install the caliper bracket as follows:

   a. Lubricate the slide pin on the bracket, then install it onto the caliper.

   b. Align the bracket with the caliper bracket bolt. Place the washer over the bolt, then tighten the bracket shaft bolt (**Figure 53**) to 23 N•m (17 ft.-Ib.).

6. Install the bleeder valve and cap.

7. Install the pad spring with the small tabs pointing out (**Figure 54**).

8. Install the inner pad and shim, seating the pad under the caliper bracket and against the piston (**Figure 55**).

9. Install the outer pad.

10. Press down on the pads, then align and install the pad pins. Tighten the pins to 18 N•m (13 ft.-lb.).

11. Bend the lockwasher tabs against the pin heads.

12. Install the parking brake assembly onto the caliper. Apply threadlocking compound to the parking brake housing mounting bolt threads. Tighten the bolts to 23 N•m (17 ft.-lb.).

13. Install the parking brake lever onto the parking brake shaft so the lever centerline is 58 mm (2.28 in.) from the cable bracket as shown in **Figure 56**.

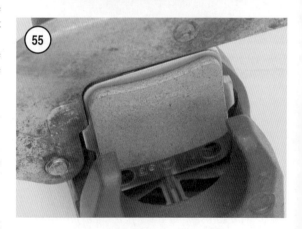

14. Install the adjust bolt (1, **Figure 46**) and locknut (2).

15. Hook the spring between the parking brake lever and cable bracket.

16. Install the brake caliper assembly as described in this section.

## REAR BRAKE CALIPER (2006-ON MODELS)

### Removal/Installation

1. If the caliper will be disassembled, do the following:

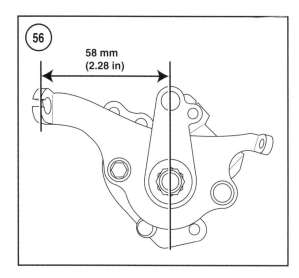

58 mm
(2.28 in)

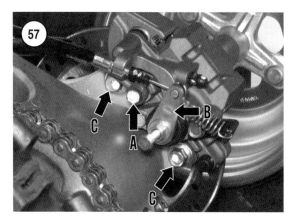

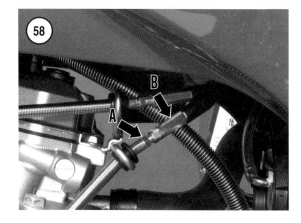

a. Drain the system as described in this chapter.
b. After draining, loosen the brake hose union bolt (A, **Figure 57**) while the caliper is mounted. Leave the bolt finger-tight. It will be removed in a later step.
c. On the parking brake cable, loosen the locknut (A, **Figure 58**) and turn the cable adjuster (B) until there is enough slack in the cable to remove it from the parking brake lever (B, **Figure 57**).

*NOTE*
*If necessary, disengage the upper end of the parking brake cable from the handlebar lever to obtain sufficient cable slack.*

2. Remove the caliper mounting bolts (C, **Figure 57**). Remove the caliper from the disc. Avoid kinking the brake hose.
3A. If the caliper will be left attached to the brake hose, but not disassembled and serviced do the following:
 a. Suspend the caliper with wire. Do not let the caliper hang from the brake hose.
 b. Insert a wood block between the brake pads. This will prevent the caliper piston from extending out of the caliper if the brake lever is operated.
3B. If the caliper will be disassembled, do the following:
 a. Remove the union bolt and seal washers from the brake hose. Have a shop cloth ready to absorb excess brake fluid that drips from the hose.
 b. Tie a plastic bag around the end of the hose to prevent brake fluid from damaging other surfaces.
 c. Drain excess brake fluid from the caliper.
 d. Remove the brake pads as described in this chapter.
 e. Repair the caliper as described in this section.
4. Reverse this procedure to install the caliper while noting the following:
 a. Install and tighten the caliper mounting bolts to 43 N•m (32 ft.-lb.).
 b. If removed, install new seal washers on the union bolt. Position the brake hose fitting so the pin contacts the boss on the caliper (**Figure 59**), then tighten the union bolt to 30 N•m (22 ft.-lb.).
 c. If the caliper was rebuilt, or the brake hose disconnected from the caliper, bleed the brake system as described in this chapter.
5. Operate the brake lever several times to seat the pads.

14

60  **REAR BRAKE CALIPER (2006-ON MODELS)**

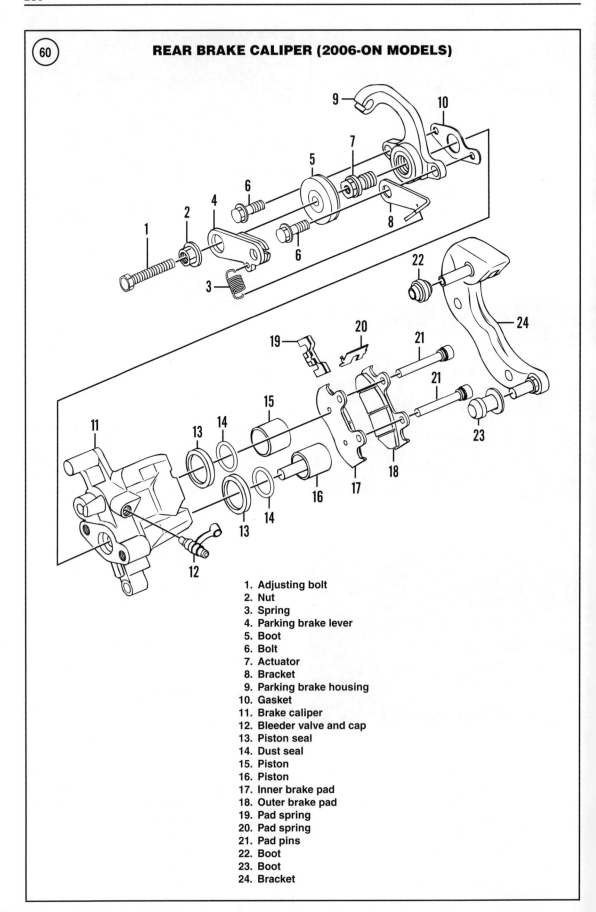

1. Adjusting bolt
2. Nut
3. Spring
4. Parking brake lever
5. Boot
6. Bolt
7. Actuator
8. Bracket
9. Parking brake housing
10. Gasket
11. Brake caliper
12. Bleeder valve and cap
13. Piston seal
14. Dust seal
15. Piston
16. Piston
17. Inner brake pad
18. Outer brake pad
19. Pad spring
20. Pad spring
21. Pad pins
22. Boot
23. Boot
24. Bracket

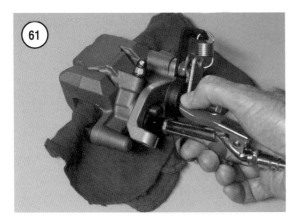

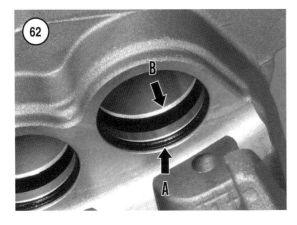

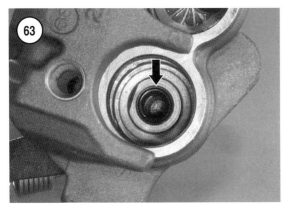

### Removing the piston hydraulically

If the piston and dust seals are in good condition and there are no signs of brake fluid leaking from the bore, it may be possible to remove the pistons hydraulically. However, note that brake fluid will spill from the caliper once the pistons become free.

1. Remove the rear brake caliper as described in this section. Do not loosen or remove the brake hose.
2. Remove the rear brake pads as described in this chapter.
3. Remove the caliper bracket from the caliper. Have a supply of paper towels and a pan available to catch and wipe up spilled brake fluid.
4. Hold the caliper with the pistons facing out and operate the brake pedal to push the pistons out of the caliper bore.
5. Remove the union bolt with an impact gun, if available. Otherwise, hold the caliper and caliper bracket against the swing arm with an adjustable wrench and remove the union bolt with hand tools.
6. Perform the relevant steps in the following section to complete caliper disassembly.

### Removing the piston with compressed air

1. Remove the brake caliper as described in this section.
2. Remove the rear brake pads as described in this chapter.
3. Slide the caliper bracket out of the caliper.

> *WARNING*
> *Wear eye protection when using compressed air to remove the piston. Keep your fingers away from the piston.*

4. Cushion the piston with a shop rag and position the caliper with the piston bore facing down. Apply compressed air through the brake hose port (**Figure 61**) to force out the pistons.
5. Cushion the caliper piston with a shop rag and position the caliper with the piston bores facing down. Apply compressed air through the brake hose port (**Figure 11**, typical) to pop the piston out. If only one piston came out, block its bore opening with a piece of thick rubber (old inner tube), wooden block and clamp as shown in **Figure 12**, typical. Apply compressed air again and remove the remaining piston. Refer to **Figure 13**, typical.
6. Remove the dust (A, **Figure 62**) and piston seals (B) from the caliper bore grooves and discard them.
7. Remove the small O-ring (**Figure 63**) from the inside of the parking brake housing.
8. To remove the rear parking brake assembly, perform the following:
   a. Remove the return spring (A, **Figure 64**).

6. Check the brake fluid reservoir and replenish or remove fluid as described in Chapter Three.
7. If necessary, adjust the parking brake cable (Chapter Three).
8. With the rear wheels raised, check that the disc spins freely and the brake operates properly.

### Disassembly

Refer to **Figure 60**.

> *CAUTION*
> *Do not try to pry out the pistons. This will damage the piston and caliper bore.*

14

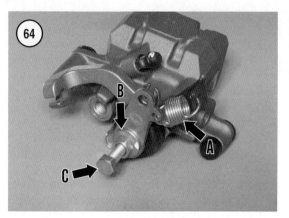

b. Loosen the locknut (B, **Figure 64**) and remove the adjust bolt (C).

c. Remove the parking brake lever (**Figure 65**).

d. Remove the actuator cover (**Figure 66**).

e. Remove the actuator (**Figure 67**).

f. Remove the two bolts (A, **Figure 68**) that hold the parking brake housing to the rear brake caliper. Remove the spring arm (B, **Figure 68**), then remove the parking brake housing (C).

g. Remove the gasket (**Figure 69**).

9. If necessary, remove the boots (A, **Figure 70**) from the brake caliper.

10. If necessary, remove the pad spring on the caliper bracket (A, **Figure 71**).

11. If necessary, remove the shafts (B, **Figure 71**) from the caliper bracket.

12. Remove the bleeder valve and its cover from the caliper.

13. Remove the pad spring from the caliper (B, **Figure 70**).

### Brake Caliper Inspection

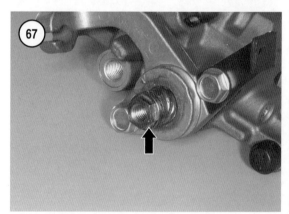

All models use a floating caliper design, in which the caliper slides or floats on threaded shafts mounted parallel with each other on the caliper and caliper bracket. Rubber boots around each shaft prevent dirt from damaging the shafts. If the shafts are worn or damaged the caliper can move out of alignment on the caliper bracket. This will cause brake drag, uneven pad wear and overheating. Inspect the rubber boots and shafts during caliper inspection as they play a vital role in brake performance.

Refer to **Figure 60** when servicing the rear brake caliper assembly. Replace parts that are out of specification (**Table 1**) or damaged as described in this section.

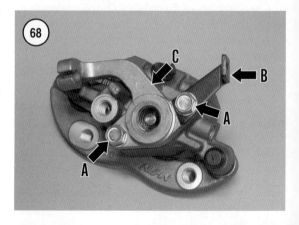

> *WARNING*
> *Do not allow oil or grease on the brake components. Do not clean the parts with kerosene or other petroleum prod-*

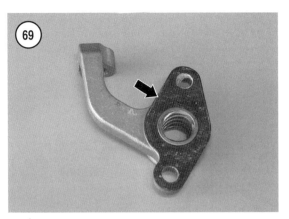

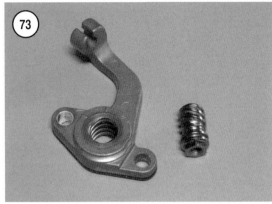

*ucts. These chemicals cause the rubber brake system components to swell, which may cause brake failure.*

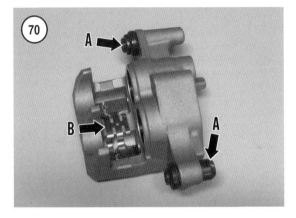

> *CAUTION*
> *The caliper bore and seal grooves can be difficult to clean, especially if brake fluid was leaking past the seals. Clean the grooves carefully to avoid damaging the grooves and bore surfaces.*

1. Clean and dry the caliper and the other metal parts. Clean the seal grooves carefully. If the contamination is difficult to remove, soak the caliper in a suitable solvent and then reclean. If any of the rubber parts are to be reused, clean them with isopropyl alcohol or new DOT 4 brake fluid. Do not use a petroleum-based solvent.

2. Inspect the caliper bracket, shafts and rubber boots as follows:
   a. Inspect the rubber boots for cracks, tearing, weakness or other damage.
   b. Inspect the shafts (B, **Figure 71**) on the caliper bracket for excessive or uneven wear. If the shaft is damaged, replace the shaft.

3. Check each cylinder bore for corrosion, pitting, deep scratches or other wear.

4. Measure the inside diameter of the caliper bore (**Figure 72**).

5. Check the piston for wear marks, scoring, cracks or other damage.

6. Check the bleeder valve and cap for wear or damage. Make sure air can pass through the bleeder valve.

7. Check the union bolt for wear or damage. Discard the washers.

8. Inspect the brake pads and pad spring as described in *Front Brake Pads* in this chapter.

9. Inspect the actuator and parking brake housing (**Figure 73**) for damaged threads, or other damage.

10. Inspect the parking brake actuator cover. Replace if damaged.

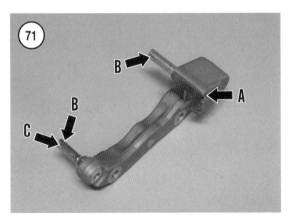

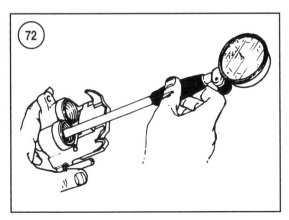

14

## Assembly

*NOTE*
*Use new DOT 4 brake fluid when lubricating parts in the following steps.*

1. Install the bleeder valve and its cover into the caliper.
2. Install the new parking brake O-ring into the groove in the back of the caliper. Refer to **Figure 63**.
3. Soak the new piston and dust seals in brake fluid.
4. Lubricate the cylinder bores with brake fluid.

*NOTE*
*The piston seals are thicker than the dust seals.*

5. Install a new piston seal (A, **Figure 74**) into each rear bore groove.
6. Install a new dust seal (B, **Figure 74**) into each front bore groove.
7. Lubricate the pistons with brake fluid.

*CAUTION*
*The tight piston-to-seal fit can make piston installation difficult. Make sure each seal fits squarely inside its bore groove. Do not install the pistons by pushing them straight in as they may bind in their bores and tear the seals.*

8. With the open side facing out, align a piston with the caliper bore. Rock the piston slightly to center it in the bore while at the same time pushing the lower end past the seals. When the lower end of the piston passes through both seals, push and bottom the piston in the bore (**Figure 75**). After installing the other piston, clean spilled brake fluid from the area in front of the pistons to prevent brake pad contamination.

*CAUTION*
*In the following steps, use only lithium-base grease specified for brake use. Do not use brake fluid to lubricate the rubber boots or fixed shafts.*

9. If removed, install the shafts into the caliper bracket. Note the location of the short shaft (C, **Figure 71**). Tighten the shafts securely.
10. Partially fill the boots (A, **Figure 70**) with lithium-based grease and install them into the caliper.
11. Lubricate the caliper bracket shafts with lithium-based grease.
12. Align and slide the mounting bracket (**Figure 76**) onto the caliper body. Hold the caliper and slide the caliper bracket in and out by hand. Make sure there is no roughness or binding.

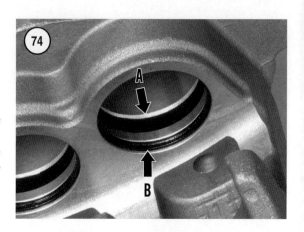

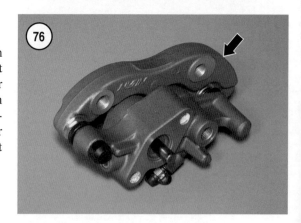

13. If removed, install the parking brake housing as follows:
   a. Install the gasket (**Figure 69**) onto the brake housing.
   b. Place the parking brake housing (C, **Figure 68**) onto the brake caliper, aligning the mounting holes and gasket.
   c. Apply threadlocking compound onto the parking brake housing mounting bolts prior to installation. Install the bolts (A, **Figure 68**), including the spring arm (B). Tighten the bolts to 23 N•m (17 ft.-lb.).

d. Turn in the actuator until it stops. The mark on the actuator (A, **Figure 77**) must be located between the marks (B) on the housing. If not, check for damage or incorrect assembly.

e. Install the actuator cover (**Figure 66**).

f. Install the parking brake lever and spring. The lever centerline must align (A, **Figure 78**) with the punch mark on the actuator (B).

g. Install the adjust bolt (C, **Figure 64**) and locknut (B).

14. Install the brake caliper assembly and brake pads as described in this chapter.

## REAR MASTER CYLINDER

### Removal/Installation

1. Drain the brake system as described in this chapter.

2. Remove the cap and diaphragm and verify that the reservoir is empty.

*CAUTION*
*Have shop cloths ready to absorb excess brake fluid that drips from disconnected hoses. Wrap the hose ends to prevent brake fluid from damaging other surfaces.*

3. Detach the reservoir hose (A, **Figure 79**) from the master cylinder. If necessary, unscrew the reservoir bolt and remove the reservoir.

4. Remove the union bolt and seal washers from the brake hose end (B, **Figure 79**).

5. Remove the cotter pin, washer and clevis pin (**Figure 80**) that secure the master cylinder clevis to the brake pedal.

6. Remove the master cylinder mounting bolts (C, **Figure 79**), then remove the master cylinder (D).

7. Disassemble and inspect the master cylinder as described in this section.

8. Reverse the preceding procedure to install the master cylinder and reservoir. Note the following:

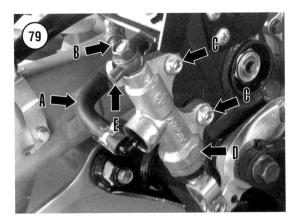

a. Tighten the master cylinder mounting bolts to 20 N•m (15 ft.-lb.).

b. Install new seal washers on the union bolt. Position the brake hose fitting so the pin contacts the boss on the master cylinder (E, **Figure 79**), then tighten the bolt to 30 N•m (22 ft.-lb.).

c. Install a new cotter pin on the clevis pin.

d. Fill the brake fluid reservoir and bleed the brake system as described in this chapter.

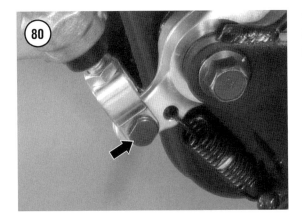

**14**

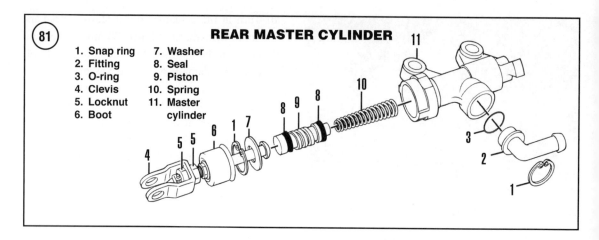

**REAR MASTER CYLINDER**

1. Snap ring
2. Fitting
3. O-ring
4. Clevis
5. Locknut
6. Boot
7. Washer
8. Seal
9. Piston
10. Spring
11. Master cylinder

## Disassembly/Inspection/Reassembly

The piston, seals and spring are only available as a complete assembly. Refer to **Figure 81**.

1. Remove the master cylinder and reservoir as described in this section.

2. Remove the clamp and reservoir hose from the master cylinder input hose fitting (if still installed).

3. Remove the snap ring (A, **Figure 82**) that retains the hose fitting (B) against the master cylinder (C), then remove the fitting and internal O-ring (D).

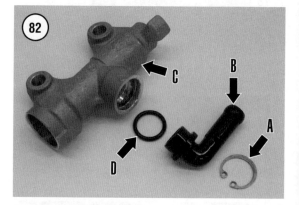

4. Remove the snap ring from the master cylinder (**Figure 83**) as follows:

   a. Unseat the boot from the cylinder bore and fold it toward the clevis. The boot is a friction fit. To avoid damaging the boot on removal, apply penetrating lubricant around the perimeter of the boot. Carefully pull the bottom edge back so the lubricant can loosen the boot.

   b. If desired, lock the cylinder in a vise with soft jaws.

   c. Press and tilt the pushrod to relieve pressure on the snap ring, then remove the snap ring with snap ring pliers.

   d. Slowly relieve the pressure on the piston.

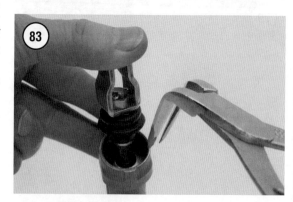

5. Remove the piston and pushrod assembly from the bore (**Figure 84**).

6. Inspect the master cylinder assembly.

   a. Clean all parts with brake fluid or isopropyl alcohol.

   b. Inspect the cylinder bore for wear, pitting or corrosion.

   c. Measure the inside diameter of the cylinder bore (**Figure 85**). Refer to **Table 1** for specifications.

   d. Inspect and clean the threads and orifices in the master cylinder (**Figure 86**). Clean with compressed air.

   e. Inspect the pushrod assembly (**Figure 87**). Check the parts for corrosion and wear. Install a new snap ring on the pushrod, with the sharp edge of the snap ring facing out. Remove/in-

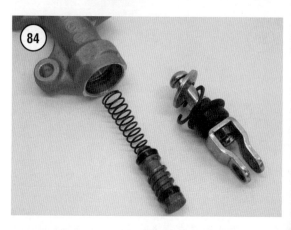

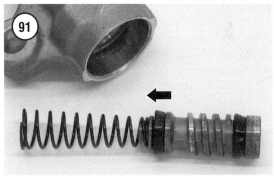

14

stall the old/new snap ring by passing it by the washer as shown in **Figure 88**. Do not expand the new snap ring when installing it on the pushrod.

f. Inspect the clevis pin (A, **Figure 89**), union bolt (B) and mounting hardware (C) for wear or damage.

g. Inspect the reservoir, diaphragm, diaphragm holder and reservoir cap for damage (**Figure 90**).

7. Assemble the piston, seals and spring (**Figure 91**) as follows:

   a. Soak the seals in DOT 4 brake fluid for 15 minutes. This will soften and lubricate the seals.

   b. Apply brake fluid to the piston so the seals can slide over the ends.

c. Mount the seals on the piston. Identify the wide (open) side of both seals. When installed, the wide side of the seals must face in the direction of the arrow (**Figure 91**). Mount the seal with the small hole nearer the spring.

d. Install and seat the spring onto the piston.

8. Install the piston and pushrod assembly into the master cylinder as follows:

a. Lubricate the cylinder bore and piston assembly with brake fluid.

b. Apply a small amount of lithium-based brake grease to the contact area of the pushrod.

c. Insert the piston into the cylinder.

d. If desired, lock the cylinder in a vise with soft jaws. Do not overtighten the vise or cylinder damage could occur.

e. Compress the snap ring with snap ring pliers.

f. Press and tilt the pushrod in the cylinder while guiding the snap ring into position. If the snap ring does not easily seat, release the snap ring and use the tip of the pliers to press it into the groove. Keep the pushrod compressed until the snap ring is seated.

9. Apply lithium-based brake grease to the inside of the boot. Seat the boot into the cylinder (**Figure 92**).

10. Install a new, lubricated O-ring into the master cylinder (**Figure 93**), then lock the hose fitting into the O-ring. Install a new snap ring with the flat side facing out.

11. Attach the reservoir and hose to the fitting, then clamp into place.

12. Install the diaphragm, diaphragm holder and cap onto the reservoir.

13. Install the master cylinder as described in this section.

## REAR BRAKE PEDAL

### Removal/Installation

1. Remove the right foot protector as described in Chapter Fifteen.

2. Detach the brake light switch spring (A, **Figure 94**) from the brake pedal.

3. Remove the master cylinder clevis pin (B, **Figure 94**).

*NOTE*
*The right footrest retains the pedal on the pedal shaft.*

4. Remove the right footrest retaining bolts (**Figure 95**), then remove the footrest.

5. Remove the brake pedal while also detaching the pedal return spring.

6. Clean and inspect the parts for wear and damage.

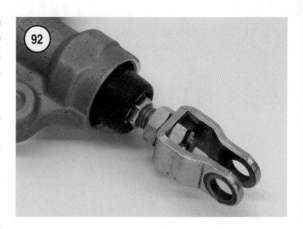

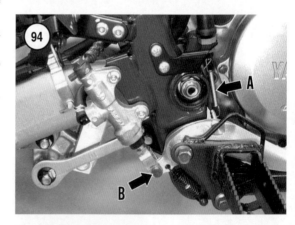

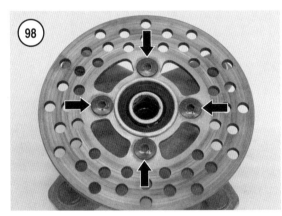

## BRAKE DISC

The front brake discs (**Figure 96**) are mounted on the front hubs. The rear brake disc (A, **Figure 97**) is mounted on a splined hub that is driven by the rear axle.

### Inspection

The brake disc can be inspected while installed. Small marks on the disc are not important, but deep radial scratches that run all the way around the disc surface can reduce braking effectiveness and increase brake pad wear. If these grooves are evident, and the brake pads are wearing rapidly, replace the brake disc.

Do not machine a deeply scored or warped disc. Removing disc material causes the disc to overheat rapidly and warp. Maintain the discs by keeping them clean and corrosion-free. Clean the discs with a non-petroleum solvent.

Refer to **Table 1** for brake disc specifications. Replace the brake disc if not within specification.

1. Measure the thickness at several locations around the disc with a micrometer.

*WARNING*
*Excessive brake disc runout causes the disc to push against the pistons, which pushes the brake pads back into the caliper. This causes brake chatter and increased brake lever or pedal travel when applying the brakes.*

*NOTE*
*Before checking front brake disc runout, make sure the wheel bearings are in good condition and the wheel is running true as described in Chapter Eleven.*

2. Measure the disc runout with a dial indicator.

7. Reverse the preceding steps to install the pedal while noting the following:
   a. Apply waterproof grease to the bore and pedal shaft.
   b. Tighten the footrest bolts to specification (**Table 2**).
   c. Install a new cotter pin in the clevis pin.
   d. Check brake operation.
   e. Check pedal height. If necessary, adjust the pedal (Chapter Three).
   f. Check brake light operation. If necessary, adjust the switch (Chapter Three).

### Removal/Installation

1A. To remove the front brake disc:
   a. Remove the front wheel hub as described in Chapter Twelve.
   b. Remove the bolts (**Figure 98**) securing the brake disc to the wheel hub.
1B. To remove the rear brake disc:
   a. Apply the rear wheel brake.
   b. Loosen, but do not remove, the rear brake disc mounting bolts (B, **Figure 97**).
   c. Remove the right rear wheel hub as described in Chapter Thirteen.

**14**

d. Remove the rear brake caliper as described in this chapter.

e. Remove the brake disc bolts and remove the brake disc.

2. Reverse the removal steps to install the brake disc while noting the following:

a. Apply threadlocking compound to the brake disc mounting bolt threads.

b. Tighten the brake disc mounting bolts to the torque specified in **Table 2**.

## FRONT BRAKE HOSE/ TUBE REMOVAL/INSTALLATION

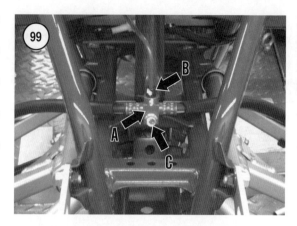

The upper brake hose and center brake tube can be replaced separately. The lower brake hoses must be replaced as an assembly with the tee fitting (A, **Figure 99**).

1. Drain the brake fluid as described in this chapter. Because air has entered the brake lines, not all of the brake fluid will drain out. Have a supply of paper towels and a pan available to catch and wipe up spilled brake fluid.

2. To remove the lower brake hoses, proceed as follows:

a. Remove both front wheels (Chapter Eleven).

b. Remove the brake hose guard (A, **Figure 100**) on each upper control arm.

c. Remove the union bolt and sealing washers (B, **Figure 100**) on each front brake caliper. Hold the open hose end in a container to catch any residual brake fluid.

d. Unscrew the nut (B, **Figure 99**) securing the center brake tube in the tee fitting.

e. Remove the tee fitting mounting bolt (C, **Figure 99**).

f. Note the routing of the brake hose through the frame and the front suspension arms, then remove the hose. Reinstall the hose through the same path to avoid damage to the hose during suspension arm movement when riding.

3. To remove the upper brake hose, proceed as follows:

a. Remove the front fender as described in Chapter Fifteen.

b. Remove the union bolt and sealing washers (**Figure 101**) from the master cylinder.

c. Remove any clamps securing the brake hose.

d. Unscrew the nut (**Figure 102**) securing the center brake tube to the hose fitting.

e. Detach the clip that secures the hose fitting in the bracket. Remove the brake hose.

4. To remove the center brake tube, proceed as follows:

a. Remove the front fender as described in Chapter Fifteen.

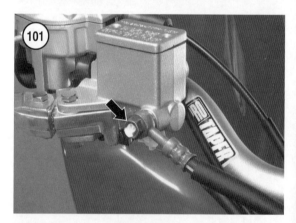

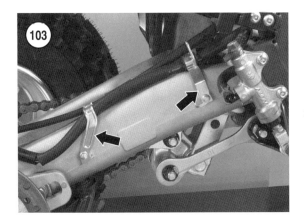

b. Unscrew the nut (B, **Figure 99**) securing the center brake tube in the tee fitting.

c. Unscrew the nut (**Figure 102**) securing the center brake tube to the upper hose fitting.

d. Note the routing of the brake tube, then remove it.

5. Note the following during installation:

a. Install new sealing washers.

b. Position the pin on the brake hose end against the boss on the caliper.

c. Tighten the union bolts to 27 N•m (20 ft.-lb.).

d. Tighten the brake tube nuts to 19 N•m (14 ft.-lb.).

e. Tighten the tee fitting mounting bolt to 10 N•m (88 in.-lb.).

f. Refill the master cylinder with DOT 4 brake fluid. Bleed both front brakes as described in this chapter.

### REAR BRAKE HOSE REMOVAL/ INSTALLATION

1. Drain the brake fluid as described in this chapter. Because air has entered the brake lines, not all of the brake fluid will drain out. Have a supply of paper towels and a pan available to catch and wipe up spilled brake fluid.

2. Remove the clamps securing the brake hose (**Figure 103**).

3. Remove the union bolt and sealing washers on the rear brake caliper and the rear master cylinder. Hold the open hose end in a container to catch any residual brake fluid.

4. Note the routing of the brake hose, then remove it.

5. When installing the brake hose, note the following:

a. Install new sealing washers.

b. On 2004-2005 models, make sure the hose end tube contacts the boss on the caliper (**Figure 104**).

c. On 2006-on models, position the brake hose end so the pin contacts the boss on the caliper (**Figure 105**).

d. Position the brake hose fitting so the pin contacts the boss on the master cylinder (**Figure 106**).

e. Tighten the union bolts to 30 N•m (22 ft.-lb.).

### BRAKE SYSTEM DRAINING

Before disconnecting a brake hose when servicing the brake system, pump as much brake fluid from the system as possible. This prevents brake fluid from leaking from the open lines.

**14**

The brake system can be drained either manually or with a vacuum pump. When draining the system manually, the master cylinder is used as a pump to expel brake fluid from the system. An empty bottle, a length of clear hose that fits tightly onto the caliper bleeder valve and a wrench (**Figure 107**) are required. When using a vacuum to drain the system, a hand-operated vacuum pump (**Figure 108**) is required.

1. Remove the cover and diaphragm from the reservoir.

2A. When draining the system manually, perform the following:

    a. Lift off the cap from the caliper bleeder valve (**Figure 109**), then connect the hose to the bleeder valve. Insert the other end of the hose into a clean bottle.

    b. Apply (do not pump) the brake lever or brake pedal until it stops and then hold in this position.

    c. Open the bleeder valve with a wrench, then apply the brake lever or brake pedal until it reaches the end of its travel. This expels some of the brake fluid from the system.

    d. Hold the lever or pedal in this position and close the bleeder valve, then slowly release the lever or pedal.

    e. Repeat this sequence to remove as much brake fluid as possible.

2B. When using a vacuum pump, perform the following:

    a. Assemble the vacuum pump and connect it to the caliper bleeder valve (**Figure 109**) following the manufacturer's instructions.

    b. Operate the pump lever five to ten times to create a vacuum in the line, then open the bleeder valve with a wrench. Brake fluid will begin to flow into the bottle connected to the vacuum pump.

    c. When the fluid draining from the system begins to slow down and before the gauge on the pump (if so equipped) reads zero, close the bleeder valve.

    d. Repeat this sequence to remove as much brake fluid as possible.

3. Close the bleeder valve and disconnect the hose or vacuum pump.

4. If necessary, use a syringe to remove brake fluid remaining in the bottom of the master cylinder reservoir.

5. Reinstall the diaphragm and cover.

6. Discard the brake fluid removed from the system.

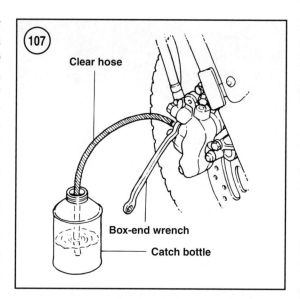

Clear hose

Box-end wrench

Catch bottle

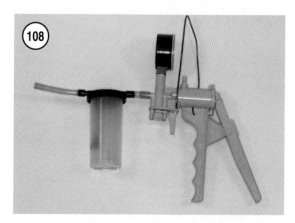

## BRAKE BLEEDING

Whenever air enters the brake system, bleed the system to remove the air. Air can enter the system when the brake fluid level drops too low, after flushing the system or when a union bolt or brake hose is loosened or removed. Air in the brake system will increase lever or pedal travel while causing it to feel spongy and less responsive. Under excessive conditions, it can cause complete loss of the brake pressure.

*NOTE*
*When bleeding the brakes, check the fluid level in the master cylinder frequently. If the reservoir runs dry, air will enter the system.*

Bleed the brakes manually or with a vacuum pump. Both methods are described in this section.

When adding brake fluid during the bleeding process, use new DOT 4 brake fluid. Do not reuse brake fluid drained from the system or use a silicone based DOT 5 brake fluid. Because brake fluid is very harm-

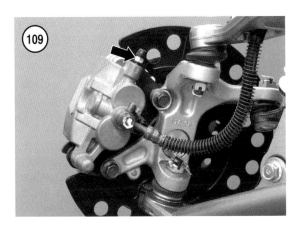

ful to most surfaces, wash spills immediately with soapy water and rinse with plenty of fresh water.

## Manual Bleeding

This procedure describes how to bleed the brake system manually by using the master cylinder as a pump. A catch bottle, length of clear hose and a wrench are required (**Figure 107**).
1. Make sure the brake system union bolts are tight.

*CAUTION*
*Dirt that is left inside the bleeder valve opening can enter the brake system. This could plug the brake hose and contaminate the brake fluid.*

2. Remove the dust cap from the brake bleeder valve and clean the valve and its opening of all dirt and debris. If a dust cap was not used, use a thin screwdriver or similar tool and compressed air to remove all dirt from inside the bleeder valve opening.
3. Connect the clear hose to the bleeder valve (**Figure 109**, typical) on the caliper. Place the other end of the hose into a container filled with enough new brake fluid to keep the hose end submerged. Loop the hose higher than the bleeder valve to prevent air from being drawn into the caliper during bleeding.

*CAUTION*
*Cover all parts that could become damaged by brake fluid. Wash spilled brake fluid from any surface immediately, as it will damage the finish. Use soapy water and rinse completely.*

4. Remove the master cylinder cover and diaphragm. Fill the reservoir to the upper level.
5. Apply the brake lever or brake pedal, and open the bleeder valve. This will force air and brake fluid from the brake system. Close the bleeder valve before the brake lever or pedal reaches its maximum limit or before brake fluid stops flowing from the

bleeder valve. Do not release the brake lever or pedal while the bleeder valve is open. If the system was previously drained or new parts installed, brake fluid will not start draining from the system until after several repeated attempts are made. This is normal.

*NOTE*
*As the brake fluid enters the system, the level will drop in the master cylinder reservoir. Maintain the level at the upper level of the reservoir to prevent air from being drawn into the system.*

6. Repeat the process until the brake fluid exiting the system is clear, with no air bubbles. If the system is difficult to bleed, tap the master cylinder and caliper housing with a soft-faced mallet to dislodge internal air bubbles so they can be released.

*NOTE*
*If the brake lever or pedal feel firm, indicating that air has been bled from the system, yet air bubbles are still visible in the hose connected to the bleeder valve, air may be entering the hose from its connection around the bleeder valve.*

7. The system is bled when the brake lever or pedal feels firm, and there are no air bubbles exiting the system.

*WARNING*
*Do not ride the vehicle until both brakes operate correctly. Make sure the brake lever and pedal travel is not excessive and they do not feel spongy. If either condition exists, repeat the bleeding procedure.*

8. If necessary, add brake fluid to correct the level in the master cylinder reservoir. It must be above the low level line. Tighten the bleeder valve to 6 N•m (53 in.-lb.) and remove the hose.

## Vacuum Bleeding

This procedure describes how to bleed the brake system with a vacuum pump (**Figure 108**).
1. Make sure the brake system union bolts are tight.

*CAUTION*
*Dirt left inside the bleeder valve opening can enter the brake system. This could plug the brake hose and contaminate the brake fluid.*

2. Remove the dust cap from the bleeder valve and clean the valve and its opening of all dirt and other

debris. If a dust cap was not used, use a thin screwdriver or similar tool and compressed air to remove all dirt from inside the bleeder valve opening.

*CAUTION*
*Cover all parts that could be damaged by brake fluid. Wash any spilled brake fluid from any surface immediately, as it will damage the finish. Use soapy water and rinse completely.*

3. Remove the master cylinder cover and diaphragm. Fill the reservoir to the upper level.
4. Assemble the vacuum tool according to the manufacturer's instructions.
5. Attach the pump hose to the bleeder valve.

*NOTE*
*When bleeding the system with a vacuum pump, the brake fluid level in the master cylinder will drop rapidly. This is especially true for the rear reservoir because it contains a small amount of brake fluid. Stop often and check the brake fluid level. Maintain the level at the upper level to prevent air from being drawn into the system.*

6. Operate the pump handle five to ten times to create a vacuum in the line between the pump and caliper.

Then, open the bleeder valve with a wrench. Doing so forces air and brake fluid from the system. Close the bleeder valve before the brake fluid stops flowing from the valve or before the master cylinder reservoir runs empty. If the vacuum pump is equipped with a vacuum gauge, close the bleeder valve before the vacuum reading on the gauge reaches 0 HG of vacuum.

7. Repeat the process until the brake fluid exiting the system is clear, with no air bubbles. If the system is difficult to bleed, tap the master cylinder and caliper housing with a soft-faced mallet to dislodge the internal air bubbles so they can be released.
8. The system is bled when the brake lever or pedal feels firm, and there are no air bubbles exiting the system. Tighten the bleeder valve to 6 N•m (53 in.-lb.) and disconnect the hose.

*WARNING*
*Do not ride the vehicle until both brakes operate correctly. Make sure brake lever and pedal travel is not excessive and they do not feel spongy. If either condition exists, repeat the bleeding procedure.*

9. If necessary, add fluid to correct the level in the master cylinder reservoir. It must be above the low level line.

### Table 1 BRAKE SERVICE SPECIFICATIONS

| | New<br>mm (in.) | Service limit<br>mm (in.) |
|---|---|---|
| **Brake disc thickness** | | |
| Front | 3.5<br>(0.138) | 3.0<br>(0.12) |
| Rear | | |
| 2004-2006 models | 3.6<br>(0.142) | 3.0<br>(0.12) |
| 2007-on models | 4.0<br>(0.160) | – |
| **Brake disc runout** | – | 0.1<br>(0.004) |
| **Brake pad thickness** | | |
| 2004-2005 models | | |
| Front and rear | 4.5<br>(0.177) | 1.0<br>(0.040) |
| 2006-on models | | |
| Front | 4.3<br>(0.169) | 1.0<br>(0.040) |
| Rear | 5.4<br>(0.212) | 1.0<br>(0.040) |
| | (continued) | |

**Table 1 BRAKE SERVICE SPECIFICATIONS (continued)**

| | New mm (in.) | Service limit mm (in.) |
|---|---|---|
| Caliper bore inside diameter | | |
| 2004-2005 models | | |
|   Front | 27.0 (1.063) | – |
|   Rear | 33.96 (1.337) | – |
| 2006-on models | | |
|   Front | 25.4 (1.000) | – |
|   Rear | 25.4 (1.000) | – |
| Master cylinder bore inside diameter (both) | 12.7 (0.5000) | – |

**Table 2 BRAKE TORQUE SPECIFICATIONS**

| Item | N•m | in.-lb. | ft.-lb. |
|---|---|---|---|
| Bleeder valve | 6 | 53 | – |
| Brake tee fitting mounting bolt | 10 | 88 | – |
| Brake tube nuts | 19 | – | 14 |
| Footrest bolts | | | |
|   2004-2005 models | 65 | – | 48 |
|   2006-on models | 73 | – | 53 |
| Front brake disc mounting bolts* | 28 | – | 21 |
| Front caliper mounting bolts | 28 | – | 21 |
| Front caliper pad pins* | 18 | – | 13 |
| Front caliper union bolt | 27 | – | 20 |
| Front master cylinder mounting bracket bolts* | 7 | 62 | – |
| Front master cylinder union bolt* | 27 | – | 20 |
| Parking brake housing mounting bolts* | 23 | – | 17 |
| Rear brake disc mounting bolts* | | | |
|   2004-2005 models | 28 | – | 21 |
|   2006-on models | 33 | – | 24 |
| Rear caliper bracket shaft bolt (2004-2005 models) | 23 | – | 17 |
| Rear caliper mounting bolts | | | |
|   2004-2005 models | 31 | – | 23 |
|   2006-on models | 43 | – | 32 |
| Rear caliper pad pins | | | |
|   2004-2005 models | 18 | – | 13 |
|   2006-on models | 17 | – | 12 |
| Rear caliper union bolt* | 30 | – | 22 |
| Rear master cylinder mounting bolts | 20 | – | 15 |
| Rear master cylinder union bolt | 30 | – | 22 |

*Refer to text.

14

NOTE: Refer to the Supplement at the back of the manual for information unique to 2009-on YFZ450R models.

# CHAPTER FIFTEEN

# BODY

**Table 1** is at the end of this chapter.

## SEAT

### Removal/Installation

The seat latch (**Figure 1**) is located above the tail-light.

1. Push the seat latch button forward and raise the rear of the seat.
2. Pull back on the seat to disengage the prongs from the front mount.
3. To install the seat, align and lock the prongs around the front mount.
4. Slide the seat forward and lock the rear of the seat into place.
5. Lightly lift the rear of the seat to ensure it is locked.

## FUEL TANK COVER

### Removal/Installation

1. Remove the seat as described in this chapter.
2. Remove the fuel tank cap (A, **Figure 2**).
3. Unscrew and lift out the plastic fasteners (B, **Figure 2**).
4. Remove the front retaining bolt (C, **Figure 2**) on each side.

5. Remove the fuel tank cover (D, **Figure 2**) by moving the cover up, then to the rear to disengage the cover hooks from the slots in each side cover.
6. Reverse the removal steps to install the fuel tank cover. Tighten the front retaining bolts securely.

## FUEL TANK SHIELD

### Removal/Installation

1. Remove the fuel tank as described in Chapter Eight.
2. Unscrew and lift out the plastic fasteners (A, **Figure 3**).
3. Disengage the fuel tank shield (B, **Figure 3**) from the frame tubes.
4. Remove the fuel tank shield.
5. Reverse the removal steps to install the fuel tank shield.

## SIDE COVERS

### Removal/Installation

1. Remove the fuel tank cover as described in this chapter.
2. Remove the front retaining bolts (**Figure 4**).
3. Remove the rear retaining bolt and collar (**Figure 5**).

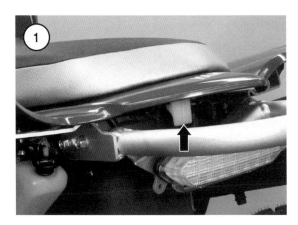

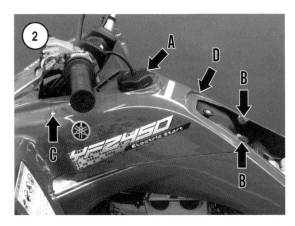

4. Remove the side cover by moving it forward out the front of the ATV.

5. Repeat for the other side.

6. Reverse the removal steps to install the side covers. Tighten the retaining bolts to 7 N•m (62 in.-lb.).

## FRONT FENDER

### Removal/Installation

1. Remove both side covers as described in this chapter.

2. Remove both headlight units as described in Chapter Nine.

3. Disconnect the ignition switch connector (A, **Figure 6**).

4. Remove the lower fender mounting bolt on each side (**Figure 7**).

5. Remove the front fender mounting bolts and grommets (B, **Figure 6**) on each side of the fender.

6. Remove the front fender.

7. Reverse the removal steps to install the front fender. Tighten the mounting bolts (B, **Figure 6**) to 7 N•m (62 in.-lb.).

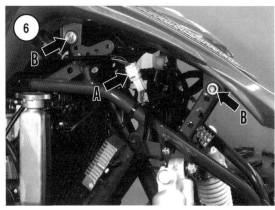

**15**

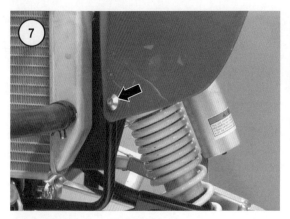

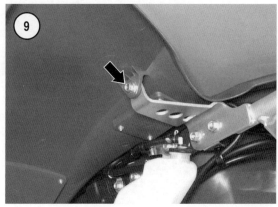

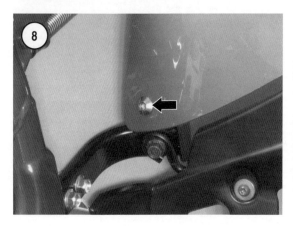

## REAR FENDER

### Removal/Installation

1. Remove the battery as described in Chapter Nine.
2. Remove the air box as described in Chapter Eight.
3. Remove both side covers as described in this chapter.
4. Remove the front mounting bolt on each side (**Figure 8**).
5. Remove the rear mounting bolt on each side (**Figure 9**).
6. Remove the upper retaining bolt (**Figure 10**).
7. Remove the rear fender.
8. Reverse the removal steps to install the rear fender. Tighten the mounting bolts to 7 N•m (62 in.-lb.).

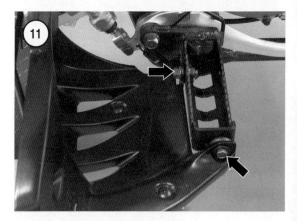

## FOOT PROTECTORS

### Removal/Installation

1. Remove the bolts securing the foot protector to the foorest (**Figure 11**).
2. Remove the rear retaining bolt (**Figure 12**).
3. Remove the foot protector.
4. Reverse the removal steps to install the foot protector.

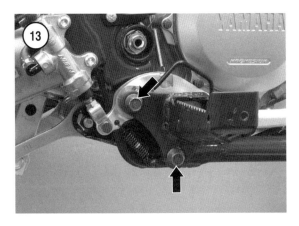

## FOOTRESTS

### Removal/Installation

1. Remove the foot protector as described in this chapter.

> *NOTE*
> *The right footrest holds the rear brake pedal in place. If brake pedal service is necessary refer to Chapter Fourteen.*

2. Remove the footrest retaining bolts (**Figure 13**).
3. Remove the footrest.

4. Reverse the removal steps to install the footrest. Tighten the footrest to specification (**Table 1**).

## ENGINE SKIDPLATE

### Removal/Installation

1. Remove the bolts securing the skidplate (**Figure 14**) to the frame.
2. Remove the skidplate.
3. Reverse the removal steps to install the skidplate. Apply threadlocking compound to the bolt threads. Tighten the bolts to 7 N•m (62 in.-lb.).

**Table 1 BODY TORQUE SPECIFICATIONS**

|  | N•m | in.-lb. | ft.-lb. |
|---|---|---|---|
| Footrest bolts |  |  |  |
| 2004-2005 models | 65 | – | 48 |
| 2006-on models | 73 | – | 53 |
| Front fender mounting bolts | 7 | 62 | – |
| Rear fender mounting bolts | 7 | 62 | – |
| Side cover mounting bolts | 7 | 62 | – |
| Skidplate mounting bolts* | 7 | 62 | – |
| *Refer to text. |  |  |  |

15

**SUPPLEMENT**

# 2009-ON YFZ450R INFORMATION

This supplement contains all procedures and specifications unique to the 2009 and later YFZ450R models. If a procedure or specification is not included in this supplement, refer to the procedure in the appropriate chapter of the manual.

This supplement is divided into sections that correspond to the chapters in this manual. Refer to the table of contents at the front of the manual if necessary. When required, tables are located at the end of the appropriate section in this supplement.

## CHAPTER ONE

# GENERAL INFORMATION

**Table 1 GENERAL MOTORCYCLE DIMENSIONS AND WEIGHT**

|  | mm | in. |
|---|---|---|
| Ground clearance | 235 | 9.25 |
| Overall height | 1065 | 41.9 |
| Overall length | 1795 | 70.7 |
| Overall width | 1240 | 48.8 |
| Turning radius | 3600 | 142 |
| Wheelbase | 1270 | 50 |
| Weight (with oil and fuel) | 184 kg | 406 lb. |

**Table 2 FUEL TANK CAPACITY**

| Total (including reserve) | 10 L (2.64 U.S. gal.) |
|---|---|
| Reserve capacity | 3.4 L (0.9 U.S. gal.) |

## CHAPTER TWO

# TROUBLESHOOTING

### ELECTRONIC DIAGNOSTIC SYSTEM

The fuel-injected YFZ450R uses an electronic diagnostic system to monitor and control the fuel-injection and ignition systems. Refer to **Figure 1** for system components.

The engine control unit (ECU) detects errors and stores this information. If a fault is detected, the diagnostic system displays either a continuous or flashing light (**Figure 2**) on the warning light display when the machine is switched on. If no fault is detected,

neither warning will be displayed by the diagnostic system when the engine is started.

Two different types of warnings (**Table 4**) are indicated by the diagnostic system using the meter display:

1. A steady warning light indicates a relatively minor fault. Troubleshoot the fault as described in the tables found at the end of this section.

2. A flashing light occurs if the machine will not start and indicates a problem with the crankshaft position sensor, the lean angle sensor, or the ECU.

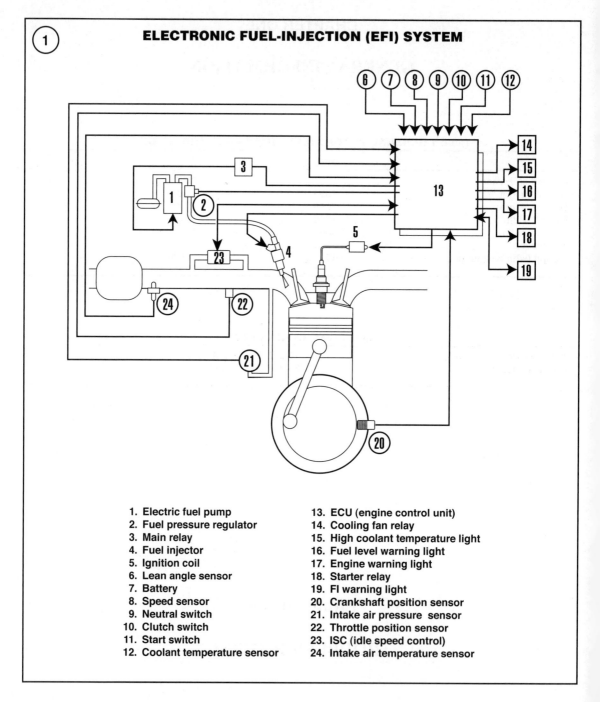

**ELECTRONIC FUEL-INJECTION (EFI) SYSTEM**

1. Electric fuel pump
2. Fuel pressure regulator
3. Main relay
4. Fuel injector
5. Ignition coil
6. Lean angle sensor
7. Battery
8. Speed sensor
9. Neutral switch
10. Clutch switch
11. Start switch
12. Coolant temperature sensor
13. ECU (engine control unit)
14. Cooling fan relay
15. High coolant temperature light
16. Fuel level warning light
17. Engine warning light
18. Starter relay
19. FI warning light
20. Crankshaft position sensor
21. Intake air pressure sensor
22. Throttle position sensor
23. ISC (idle speed control)
24. Intake air temperature sensor

## Reading Trouble and Diagnostic Codes

Unlike late-model street bikes, the electronic diagnostic system will not display an actual numerical code. These codes can only viewed and cleared with the fuel-injection (FI) diagnostic tool (Yamaha part No. 90890-03182/YU-03182), or its equivalent.

## Fail-Safe Operation

When the ECU detects a fault with a sensor or actuator, it compares the signal with a programmed range of signals, based on the inputs it receives from the other control system components. It will then either prevent the machine from running, allow the machine to run at a reduced power level (limp-home mode), or take no action all. For example, trouble code No. 12, which relates to the crankshaft position sensor, prevents the engine from starting while trouble code No. 13, which relates to the signal from the intake air pressure sensor, will permit starting of the engine and allow limited operation of the machine.

A continuous engine warning light indicates the machine has stored a trouble code (**Table 4**).

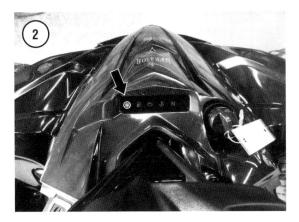

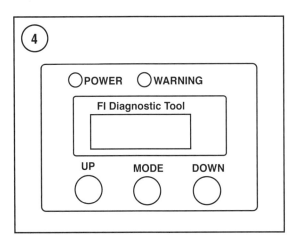

POWER WARNING

FI Diagnostic Tool

UP MODE DOWN

Depending on the code stored, the machine may or may not start.

A flashing warning light, on the other hand, indicates the engine will not start due to a trouble code that must be resolved. Codes related to a flashing warning light include:

1. No. 12: Crankshaft position sensor signal.

2. No. 30: Lean angle sensor signal (latch-up detected).

3. No. 33: Fault in the primary wire of the ignition coil.

4. No. 39: Fuel injector (open circuit).

5. No. 41: Lean angle sensor (open or short circuit).

6. No. 50: ECU internal error (memory check error).

If a code reader such as the FI diagnostic tool (Yamaha part No. 90890-03182/YU-03182), or its equivalent, is not available, eliminate these six items as the cause of the fault by testing each component as described in the *Electrical System* section of this supplement.

**Troubleshooting with FI Diagnostic Tool**

*Engine not running normally warning light is on*

1. Remove the seat. Remove the cover from the diagnostic plug (**Figure 3**) and connect the FI diagnostic tool.

2. Turn on the switch without starting the engine.

3. Note if there is a numerical trouble code on the FI diagnostic tool display (**Figure 4**). Refer to **Table 5** at the end of this section of the supplement. Note which diagnostic code is listed and refer to **Table 6** for more fault information.

4. Repair the faulty componenet as described in **Tables 7-24**. Follow the instructions for the method of reinstatement.

5. Reset the ECU by turning the switch off, and then back on, to verify the code has cleared. However, if the root cause of the fault is mechanical, refer to the appropriate chapter and repair or replace the damaged mechanical component(s).

*Engine not running normally warning light is off*

1. With the FI diagnostic tool in the diagnostic (DIAG) mode, check the operation of the following sensors and actuators as indicated in **Table 6**:

  a. Diagnostic code 01: Throttle Position Sensor (TPS angle)

  b. Diagnostic code 30: Ignition coil

  c. Diagnostic code 36: Injector

2. Repair or replace as recommended. If the cause of the fault is mechanical, refer to the appropriate chapter and repair or replace the damaged mechanical component(s).

**Selecting FI Diagnostic Tool Operating Mode**

*NOTE*
*Except for the warning lights described in this section, all sensors and actuators may be checked with the FI di-*

*agnostic tool in either the normal or
diagnostic (DIAG) mode.*

*Normal mode*

> *NOTE*
> *Trouble codes for engine speed, and
> coolant temperature are displayed in
> the normal mode with the tool connect-
> ed to the machine.*

1. Remove the seat. Then remove the cover from the
diagnostic plug (**Figure 3**).
2. Turn the ignition switch off and the handle bar
mounted engine stop switch on.
3. Connect the FI tool to the diagnostic plug.
4. Start the engine and observe the FI tool display.
Engine speed and the coolant temperature measurement will appear, along with the green POWER
light. If a fault is detected, the orange WARNING
light will switch on. However, no codes will appear
with the engine running.
5. Stop the engine and note if a trouble code regis-
ters on the display, along with the orange WARNING
light.
6A. If the orange WARNING light appears, follow
the troubleshooting instructions in the respective
table for the code shown.
6B. If the orange WARNING light does not appear,
turn the ignition switch off to cancel the normal
mode, and then disconnect the tool.

7. Install the diagnostic plug cover to prevent contamination and corrosion within the connector.
8. Install the seat.

*Diagnostic monitoring mode*

1. Remove the seat. Then remove the cover from the
diagnostic plug (**Figure 3**).
2. Turn the ignition switch off and the engine stop
switch on before attaching the FI diagnostic tool.
3. While pressing the mode switch on the face of the
FI diagnostic tool, turn the ignition switch on. DIAG
will appear in the display of the FI diagnostic tool,
and the green POWER light will show.
4. Continue pressing the UP button to scroll past
the CO adjustment mode to the diagnostic (DIAG)
mode.
5. Press MODE and select the code that applies to
the component associated with the fault code. This is
done by pressing either the UP or DOWN buttons.
6A. Sensor operating data is displayed on the FI diagnostic tool screen.
6B. Actuator operation is verified by pressing the
MODE button.
7. Turn the ignition switch off to cancel the diagnostic mode, and then disconnect the tool.
8. Install the diagnostic plug cover to prevent contamination and corrosion within the connector.
9. Install the seat assembly.

**Table 3 TECHNICAL ABBREVIATIONS**

| | |
|---|---|
| ECU | Engine control unit |
| TPS | Throttle position sensor |
| ISC | Idle speed control |
| FI | Fuel injection |
| EEPROM | Electrically erasable programmable read only memory |
| IAP | Intake air pressure sensor |

## Table 4 INITIAL SELF DIAGNOSTIC WARNING INDICATORS-NO CODE READER USED

| Warning light on | Operation of engine control unit | Operation of fuel injection system | Limitations to vehicle operation |
|---|---|---|---|
| Flashes to alert the rider to a possible problem with:<br>crank-shaft position sensor (12)<br>lean angle sensor-machine tilted too far (30)<br>electrical fault with the lean angle sensor (41)<br>ECU (50) | ECU sends the flashing light warning when the engine will not start | Fuel injection system operation is stopped | Engine will not start |
| Light stays on | Malfunction is detected | Limited operation of the machine may be possible, depending on the fault detected | Engine may or may not start and/or limited speed operation may be possible |

## Table 5 TROUBLE CODES

| Trouble code number | System and/or operational malfunctions | Likely cause-items to check-order of procedures | Diagnostic code number |
|---|---|---|---|
| 12 | No crank position sensor signal reaching the ECU | -Poorly installed sensor<br>-Faulty sensor<br>-Faulty pick-up rotor<br>-Shorted or open circuit in the harness or circuit connections<br>-Check the blue/yellow and black/blue wires<br>-Check connectors for bent or damaged pins/ sockets<br>-Make sure connectors snap together securely<br>-Faulty engine control unit (ECU) | None |
| 13 | No intake air pressure signal reaching the ECU due to a sensor or electrical malfunction | -Poorly installed sensor<br>-Faulty sensor<br>-Shorted or open circuit in the harness or circuit connections<br>-Check the pink/blue, black/blue, and blue wires<br>-Check connectors for bent or damaged pins/ sockets<br>-Make sure the connectors snap together securely | D03 |
| 14 | No intake air pressure | -Verify that sensor | D03 |

(continued)

Table 5 TROUBLE CODES (continued)

| Trouble code number | System and/or operational malfunctions | Likely cause-items to check-order of procedures | Diagnostic code number |
|---|---|---|---|
| 14 (continued) | signal reaching the ECU due to a sensor or electrical malfunction | hose is intact and is connected<br>-If sensor is defective, replace | D03 |
| 15 | No throttle position signal reaching the ECU due to a faulty sensor or electrical malfunction | -Wiring to the sensor is damaged or disconnected, resulting in a short or open circuit<br>-Sensor is faulty<br>-Sensor is installed wrong<br>-ECU is faulty | D01 |
| 16 | No throttle position signal reaching the ECU due to a mechanical or electrical malfunction | -Sensor stuck in one position or will not move the full range it should<br>-Sensor may be faulty sensor installed wrong | D01 |
| 21 | No coolant temperature signal reaching the ECU due to a sensor or electrical malfunction | -Check the coolant level. Coolant sensor will not send a signal unless in contact with coolant<br>-Wiring to sensor disconnected or shorted<br>-Sensor may be damaged<br>-Sensor may be installed wrong<br>-ECU may be faulty | D06 |
| 22 | No intake air temperature signal reaching the ECU due to a sensor or electrical malfunction | -Wiring to sensor disconnected or shorted<br>-Sensor may be damaged<br>-Sensor may be installed wrong<br>-ECU may be faulty | D05 |
| 30 | Signal from lean angle sensor shows the machine is tipping over when it is not | -Machine is overturned<br>-Wires to sensor may be in continuity with each other due to faulty insulation<br>-Faulty installation of sensor<br>-ECU may be faulty | D08 |
| 33 | Poor or non-existent signal to ECU from the primary side of the ignition coil | -Ignition primary wires may be open or shorted<br>-Ignition coil may be faulty<br>-Coil wire terminals may be loose or badly corroded<br>-ECU may be faulty | D30 |
| 37 | Low engine idle speed | -Defective mechanical | D54 |

(continued)

**Table 5 TROUBLE CODES (continued)**

| Trouble code number | System and/or operational malfunctions | Likely cause-items to check-order of procedures | Diagnostic code number |
|---|---|---|---|
| 37 (continued) | is higher than it should be | throttle components, such as the cable<br>-Loose or missing hose on throttle body<br>-Wires to sensor are shorted or open<br>-Speed sensor is damaged<br>-Moving parts in throttle body in a bind<br>-Faulty idle speed control (ISC) valve<br>-Intake air leak between air cleaner and throttle body<br>-Faulty ECU | |
| 39 | Code indicates the circuit to injector open or shorted | -Wires may be open or shorted<br>-Faulty installation of injector<br>-Damaged injector<br>-Faulty ECU | D36 |
| 41 | Code indicates the circuit to the lean angle sensor is open or shorted | -Wires may be open or shorted<br>-Faulty installation of lean angle sensor<br>-Damaged sensor<br>-Faulty ECU | D08 |
| 42 | Code indicates no signals are coming from the speed sensor | -Wires may be open or shorted<br>-Faulty installation of speed sensor<br>-Damaged sensor<br>-Faulty ECU | D07 |
| 43 | Code indicates low voltage or no voltage to fuel system | -Wires may be open or shorted<br>-Faulty, corroded, or loose terminals in circuit<br>-Faulty ECU | D50 |
| 44 | This is internal to the engine control unit (ECU) | This is the data the ECU stores, related to exhaust CO levels | D60 |
| 46 | Code indicates a problem with the power supply | This is caused by a malfunction of the charging system | – |
| 50 | Code indicates faulty ECU memory Fault may also prevent code from showing | Fault in the ECU | – |
| Waiting | Signals are not being | -Open or short | – |

*(continued)*

## Table 5 TROUBLE CODES (continued)

| Trouble code number | System and/or operational malfunctions | Likely cause-items to check-order of procedures | Diagnostic code number |
|---|---|---|---|
| Waiting (continued) | received from the ECU | circuit in circuit wiring<br>-Faulty FI diagnostic tool, or faulty ECU | |
| Er-4 | FI tool signal to ECU not recognizable | -Open or short circuit in circuit wiring<br>-Faulty FI diagnostic tool, or faulty ECU | – |

## Table 6 DIAGNOSTIC CODES (2009-2013 models)

| Diagnostic Code | Component | FI tool display/action | How to check |
|---|---|---|---|
| D01 | Throttle is either fully open or fully closed | N/A<br>12-22 | 1-open throttle fully<br>2-close throttle fully |
| D03 | Varying intake air pressure | Intake air pressure | Engage the engine stop switch and turn the throttle while cranking the engine. Changing readings on the display indicates good performance |
| D05 | Intake air temperature | Intake air temperature | With a thermometer compare the temperature reading of the intake or ambient air to the value shown on the FI tool |
| D06 | Coolant temperature | Coolant temperature | With a thermometer compare the temperature reading of the coolant to the value shown on the FI tool |
| D07 | Signal of vehicle speed as shown by rear wheel rotation | 0-999 | Verify that the number increases when the wheel is turned. Repeated starts and stops of the wheel should increase the number shown. Number will not return to zero when the wheel stops |
| D08 | Code means lean angle is either safe or extreme | 0.4 to 1.4 when upright (safe)<br>3.8 to 4.2 when angle is extreme (unsafe) | Holding the sensor by hand, rotate it and watch the value change |
| D09 | Voltage supply to fuel system | 12 volts | Compare with measured battery voltage |
| D21 | Transmission neutral switch | Will be on or off | Shift the transmission in and out of neutral |
| D30 | Ignition coil | Actuates the ignition coil five times at one-second intervals | With a spark tester, check for spark |

(continued)

## Table 6 DIAGNOSTIC CODES (continued)

| Diagnostic Code | Component | FI tool display/action | How to check |
|---|---|---|---|
| D36 | Injector | Actuates the injector five times at one-second intervals | Listen for the injector to operate five times |
| D50 | Main relay | Actuates the main relay five times at one-second intervals. | Listen for the main relay to click five times |
| D51 | Radiator fan motor relay | Actuates the radiator fan relay for five cycles every five seconds. (On 2 seconds, off 3 seconds) | Listen for the radiator fan relay to click five times |
| D54 | ISC (idle speed control) unit | Actuates and fully closes the ISC valve, then opens it to the standby opening position when the engine is started. This operation takes approximately 3 seconds until it is completed | ISC unit vibrates when operating |
| D60 | EEPROM fault code showing either no fault, or that a fault is detected | 00 = No fault 01 = Detecting Carbon Monoxide (CO) adjustment value Shows trouble with data from EEPROM (fault code 44) | Not checked |
| D61 | History of malfunction codes showing: no history, or existing history | 00 = no history 12-50 is the fault detection code When more than one code is present, the display shows a different one every two seconds and continues repeating them | Not checked |
| D62 | Erasure of malfunction code history | 00 = no history  When history is present, the number of fault codes since last erasure are shown | Not checked, to erase press the FI tool MODE button |
| D70 | Control Number | 00-254 | Not checked |

S

## Table 7 DIAGNOSTIC CODES

| Diagnostic Code | Component | FI tool display/action | How to check |
|---|---|---|---|
| D01 | Throttle position sensor | Displays the throttle angle.<br>- 14-20 | Check when throttle fully closed. |
| D03 | Intake air pressure sensor | Displays intake air pressure.<br>0-126 kPa | Check by turning the main switch to start.<br>- When the engine is cranking, the displayed values should change.<br>- When the engine is stopped, the display should indicate the following at the given altitude:<br>- - Sea level: approx 101 kPa.<br>- - 1000 meters above sea level: approx 90 kPa<br>- - 2000 meters above sea level: approx 80 kPa<br>- - 3000 meters above sea level: approx 70 kPa |
| D05 | Intake air temperature sensor | Displays temperature of the air in the intake manifold and air filter case.<br>-30 to 120 degrees C (-22 to 248 degrees F) | - When engine is cold, the displayed temperature is close to ambient air temp.<br>- When engine is warm, the displayed temperature equals ambient air temp plus approx. 20 degrees C to account for radiant heat. |
| D06 | Coolant temperature sensor | Displays coolant temperature.<br>-30 to 120 degrees C (-22 to 248 degrees F) | - When engine is cold, the displayed temperature is close to ambient air temp.<br>- When engine is warm, the display temperature equals ambient air temp plus approx. 20 degrees C to account for radiant heat. |
| D07 | Speed sensor | Displays cumulative number of speed pulses.<br>0-999 pulses | - Pulse number should not vary when rear wheel is stopped.<br>- The display should increase when the rear wheel is manually rotated. |
| D08 | Lean angle sensor | Displays the output voltage of the lean angle sensor.<br>0-5.0 volts | Remove the sensor. Manually rotate it and watch the displayed values change.<br>- When the motorcycle is upright: 3.5-4.5 volts.<br>- When the motorcycle is overturned: 0.6-1.4 volts |
| D09 | Monitor voltage | Displays the voltage of the fuel system.<br>0-18.7 volts | Standard value: approx. 12 volts. |

(continued)

**Table 7 DIAGNOSTIC CODES (continued)**

| Diagnostic Code | Component | FI tool display/action | How to check |
|---|---|---|---|
| D21 | Neutral switch and clutch switch | Displays the working condition of the neutral and clutch switches. | - When the transmission is shifted into Neutral: ON is displayed.<br>- When the transmission is shifted into any gear other than neutral and the clutch is disengaged: OFF is displayed. |
| D30 | Ignition coil | Actuates the ignition coil five times at one-second intervals. | The WARNING LED on the diagnostic tool turns ON each time the coil is actuated.<br>- Use a spark tester to confirm that a spark is being generated. |
| D36 | Fuel injector | Actuates the fuel injector fives times at one-second intervals. - Disconnect the fuel pump electrical connector before checking the injector. | The WARNING LED on the diagnostic tool turns ON each time the injector is actuated.<br>- Listen for injector operation each time it's actuated. |
| D48 | Air-induction-system solenoid | Actuates the air-induction-system solenoid fives times at one-second intervals. | The WARNING LED on the diagnostic tool turns ON each time the air-induction-system solenoid is actuated.<br>- Confirm the solenoid's operation by listening for its click each time it's actuated. |
| D50 | Main relay | Actuates the main relay fives times at one-second intervals. | The WARNING LED on the diagnostic tool turns ON each time the main relay is actuated.<br>- Confirm the relay's operation by listening for its click each time it's actuated. |
| D51 | Radiator-fan-motor relay | Actuates the radiator-fan-motor relay fives times at one-second intervals. | The WARNING LED on the diagnostic tool turns ON each time the radiator-fan-motor relay is actuated.<br>- Confirm the relay's operation by listening for its click each time it's actuated. |
| D54 | ISC Valve (idle speed control valve) | Actuates and fully closes the ISC valve, and then opens it to the standby opening position when the engine is started. It takes approximately three seconds to complete this operation. | The WARNING LED on the diagnostic tool turns ON each time the ISC valve is actuated.<br>- Confirm the valve's status by listening for its operation each time it is actuated. |
| D60 | EEPROM fault code | Displays the location of the abnormal portion of the EEPROM data that has detected a trouble code 44 (ECU malfunction). If more than one code has been detected, the display alternates every two seconds. | 00 = No fault. If code 44 is displayed, the ECU is faulty.<br>01 = Detecting carbon monoxide adjustment value. |

(continued)

## Table 7 DIAGNOSTIC CODES (continued)

| Diagnostic Code | Component | FI tool display/action | How to check |
|---|---|---|---|
| D61 | Malfunction history code | Displays the trouble codes stored in the malfunction history. If more than one code is stored, the display changes every two seconds until all codes are displayed. | 00 = no malfunction history 12-50 = the individual trouble code(s) that are stored in the malfunction history. |
| D62 | Malfunction history erasure code | Erases the entire malfunction code history, and displays the total number of trouble codes that have been stored in the malfunction history since the last erasure. | 00 = no history. |
| D70 | Program version number | Check the version number of the program. | 00-254. |

## Table 8 TROUBLE CODE 12: NORMAL SIGNALS ARE NOT RECEIVED FROM THE CRANSHAFT POSITION SENSOR

| Possible cause | Inspect, test and repair or replace |
|---|---|
| Sensor installation | Check installation of sensor and routing of wiring harness |
| Open or short circuit in the wiring harness | Verify continuity through the sensor blue/yellow and black/blue wires |
| Poor electrical connections | Check all connector terminal pins |
| Faulty crankshaft position sensor | Test the sensor as outlined in this Supplement |
| Faulty ECU | Replace the ECU as outlined in this Supplement |
| To reinstate after problem correction | Crank the engine |

## Table 9 TROUBLE CODE 13: OPEN OR SHORT CIRCUIT IN THE INTAKE AIR PRESSURE SENSOR (DIAGNOSTIC CODE 03)

| Possible cause | Inspect, test and repair or replace |
|---|---|
| Faulty sensor installation | Check installation of sensor and routing of harness |
| Open or short circuit found in the wiring harness | Verify continuity in the sensor pink/blue, black/blue, and blue wires |
| Faulty electrical connectors | Check condition of connectors and pins |
| Faulty sensor | Test the sensor as outlined this Supplement |
| Faulty ECU | Replace the ECU as described in this Supplement |
| To reinstate after problem is corrected | Turn the ignition switch on |

### Table 10 TROUBLE CODE 14: PLUGGED, KINKED OR DISCONNECTED HOSE TO THE INTAKE AIR PRESSURE SENSOR (DIAGNOSTIC CODE 03)

| Possible cause | Inspect, test and repair or replace |
|---|---|
| Faulty sensor installation | Check sensor installation and routing of harness |
| Plugged or detached hose to sensor | Repair or replace hose |
| Faulty sensor | Test the sensor as outlined in this Supplement |
| Poor reinstatement after problem is corrected | Start engine and let it run at idle speed |

### Table 11 TROUBLE CODE 15: OPEN OR SHORT CIRCUIT IN THE THROTTLE POSITION SENSOR (DIAGNOSTIC CODE 01)

| Possible cause | Inspect, test and repair or replace |
|---|---|
| Faulty sensor installation | Check installation of sensor and routing of harness |
| Open or short circuit found in the wiring harness | Verify continuity in the sensor black/blue, yellow, and blue wires |
| Faulty electrical connectors | Check condition of connectors and pins |
| Faulty sensor | Test the sensor as outlined in this Supplement |
| Faulty ECU | Replace the ECU as described in this Supplement |
| To reinstate after correction | Turn the ignition switch on |

### Table 12 TROUBLE CODE 16: THROTTLE POSITION SENSOR MECHANISM WILL NOT MOVE (DIAGNOSTIC CODE 01)

| Possible cause | Inspect, test and repair or replace |
|---|---|
| Faulty sensor installation | Check installation of sensor and routing of harness |
| Faulty throttle position sensor | Activate diagnostic monitoring (diagnostic code 01). Replace sensor if defective. |
| Faulty ECU | Replace the ECU as described in this Supplement. Replace the sensor as needed |
| Reinstatement method | Start engine and let idle. Then rev engine |

### Table 13 TROUBLE CODE 21: FAULTY COOLANT TEMPERATURE SENSOR CIRCUIT (DIAGNOSTIC CODE 06)

| Possible cause | Inspect, test and repair or replace |
|---|---|
| Faulty sensor installation | Check installation of sensor and routing of harness |
| Open or short circuit found in the wiring harness | Verify the continuity in the black/yellow and black/blue wires |
| Faulty electrical connectors | Check the condition of the connectors and pins |
| Faulty sensor | Execute diagnostic monitoring (diagnostic code 06). Replace the sensor as needed. |
| Faulty ECU | Replace the ECU as described in this Supplement. |
| Reinstatement method | Turn the ignition switch on |

**Table 14 TROUBLE CODE 22: FAULTY INTAKE AIR**
**TEMPERATURE SENSOR CIRCUIT (DIAGNOSTIC CODE 05)**

| Possible cause | Inspect, test and repair or replace |
|---|---|
| Faulty sensor installation | Check sensor for loose fasteners or for faulty installation and sensor positioning |
| Open or short circuit found in the wiring harness | Verify the continuity in the black/blue wire (2009-2013 models only), brown wire and black wire |
| Faulty electrical connectors | Check connectors for damage and loose pins |
| Damaged or faulty sensor | Execute diagnostic monitoring (diagnostic code 05). Test the sensor as described in this Supplement |
| ECU malfunction | Replace as outlined in this Supplement |
| Reinstatement method | Turn ignition switch on |

**Table 15 TROUBLE CODE 30: VEHICLE HAS**
**LEANED AT AN EXTREME ANGLE (DIAGNOSTIC CODE 08)**

| Possible cause | Inspect, test and repair or replace |
|---|---|
| The vehicle has overturned | Turn the machine upright |
| Faulty sensor installation | Check sensor for loose fasteners or for faulty installation and sensor positioning |
| Faulty lean angle sensor | Execute diagnostic monitoring (diagnostic code 08). Test the sensor as described in this Supplement. Replace the sensor as needed. |
| Faulty electrical connector | Verify the wiring harness connector is secured |
| Faulty ECU | Replace the ECU as described in this Supplement. |
| Reinstatement method | Turn the ignition switch on after first turning the switch off |

**Table 16 TROUBLE CODE 33: MALFUNCTION IN**
**IGNITION COIL PRIMARY CIRCUIT (DIAGNOSTIC CODE 30)**

| Possible cause | Inspect, test and repair or replace |
|---|---|
| Ignition coil Installation | Inspect coil installation and the routing of the wiring harness |
| Open or short detected in the individual wires or connectors | Check the orange wire between the ignition coil and ECU connectors |
| Faulty electrical connectors | Check connectors for damage and loose pins |
| Damaged ignition coil | Execute diagnostic monitoring (diagnostic code 30). Test the continuity of the primary and secondary coils as described in this supplement. Replace the ignition coil as needed. |
| Reinstatement method | Start the engine and let it idle. |

**Table 17 TROUBLE CODE 37: ENGINE IDLE SPEED IS TOO HIGH (DIAGNOSTIC CODE 54)**

| Possible cause | Inspect, test and repair or replace |
|---|---|
| Faulty speed sensor signal | Refer to Table 20 (Trouble code 42) and check the condition of the speed sensor circuit. Test the speed sensor as described in this supplement |
| Throttle valve does not fully close | Inspect the throttle body for damage; clean if needed. |
| Throttle cable damage | Inspect and adjust the throttle cable (Chapter Three) |
| Faulty ISC valve (idle speed control valve) installation | Inspect the ISC valve installation and the routing of its wiring harness |
| Faulty ISC valve operation | Check operation of the ISC valve. It should vibrate when the engine is running. |
| Faulty connector | Check the condition of the ISC valve connectors and pins |
| Open or short circuit in wiring or connectors | Check the continuity of the red, red/green, pink, white/yellow and brown/blue ISC valve wiring |
| Faulty ECU | Replace the ECU as described in this Supplement. |
| To reinstate after problem is corrected | Start the engine and let it idle. |

**Table 18 TROUBLE CODE 39: FAULTY FUEL INJECTOR CIRCUIT (DIAGNOSTIC CODE 36)**

| Possible cause | Inspect, test and replace or repair |
|---|---|
| Connector to injector poorly seated or coupler damaged | Inspect the electrical connector/pins and wiring to the injector |
| Damaged wires to injector | Inspect the red/black and red/blue wires |
| Faulty injector | Replace if needed |
| Reinstatement method | Replace injector |

**Table 19 TROUBLE CODE 41: FAULTY LEAN ANGLE SENSOR CIRCUIT (DIAGNOSTIC CODE 08)**

| Possible cause | Inspect, test and repair or replace |
|---|---|
| Faulty electrical connectors | Check sensor connector for damage or loose pins |
| Damaged wires between sensor connector and ECU connector | Check the continuity of the black/blue, yellow/green and blue wires between the connectors |
| Faulty sensor | Replace the lean angle sensor as described in this Supplement |
| Faulty ECU | Replace the ECU |
| Reinstatement method | Turn the ignition switch on |

S

### Table 20 TROUBLE CODE 42: FAULTY SPEED SENSOR CIRCUIT (DIAGNOSTIC CODE 07)

| Possible cause | Inspect, test and replace or repair |
|---|---|
| Poor connection of wiring harness to speed sensor | Check the connector/pins and make sure the connector is secure |
| Open circuit or short in wiring between sensor and ECU | Check the blue, white, and black/blue wires |
| Broken gear tooth prevents correct signal from sensor | Replace gear if needed |
| Faulty speed sensor | Activate diagnostic monitoring for code 07 |
| Reinstatement method | Start the engine and drive the machine a short distance |

### TABLE 21 TROUBLE CODE 43: LOW OR INCONSISTENT BATTERY VOLTAGE READING (DIAGNOSTIC CODE 09 (2014-ON MODELS), 50 (ALL MODELS)

| Possible cause | Inspect, test and repair or replace |
|---|---|
| Faulty electrical connectors | Check the electrical connector/pins of the main relay. Make sure the connector is secure |
| Faulty main relay | Replace the relay. Activate diagnostic monitoring for diagnostic codes 09 (2014-on models) and/or 50. |
| An open or short circuit in the wiring harness | - Check the red/blue, yellow/red, red, and red/black wires between the main relay and the ECU<br>- Check the red wire between the main relay and the starter relay<br>- Check the brown wire between the main relay and the handlebar switch |
| Reinstatement method | Start the engine and let it idle |

### Table 22 TROUBLE CODE 44: ERROR CODE DETECTED WHILE READING OR WRITING TO EEPROM (DIAGNOSTIC CODE 60)

| Possible cause | Inspect, test and repair or replace |
|---|---|
| Faulty ECU | Execute diagnostic monitoring (diagnostic code 60)<br>- If the Yamaha diagnostic tool (2014-on models) displays code 01, readjust the CO setting<br>- Replace ECU if faulty |
| Reinstatement method | Turn ignition switch on |

**Table 23 TROUBLE CODE 46: ABNORMAL VOLTAGE SUPPLY TO ECU
(NO DIAGNOSTIC CODE)**

| Possible cause | Inspect, test and replace or repair |
| --- | --- |
| Poor connection or open circuit through main wire harness or connector | Check the electrical connector/pins and make sure the connector is secure<br>Check the brown wire to the ECU from the main switch<br>Check the red wire from the battery to the main switch |
| Non-functional battery | Replace battery |
| Faulty rectifier/regulator assembly | Replace faulty assembly |
| Reinstatement method | Start the engine and let it idle |

**Table 24 TROUBLE CODE 50: FAULTY ECU MEMORY (NO DIAGNOSTIC CODE)**

| Possible cause | Inspect, test and replace or repair |
| --- | --- |
| Faulty ECU | Replace if needed as described in this Supplement |
| Reinstatement method | Turn ignition switch on |

**Table 25 TROUBLE CODE: WAITING FOR CONNECTION,
NO SIGNALS ARE RECEIVED FROM THE ECU (NO DIAGNOSTIC CODE)**

| Possible cause | Inspect, test and repair or replace |
| --- | --- |
| Poor or faulty electrical connectors | Inspect the ECU connector and the diagnostic connector (FI tool connector on 2009-2013 models; Yamaha diagnostic tool connector on 2014 and later models). Check each connector for loose or missing pins. Make sure each connector properly engages its mate. Repair a connector as needed |
| Open or short circuit found in wiring harness | Inspect and test the yellow/blue wire between the ECU and the diagnostic connector |
| Faulty ECU or diagnostic tool | Replace the ECU or diagnostic tool as needed |
| Reinstatement method | Turn the ignition switch on |

S

**Table 26 TROUBLE CODE: ER-4, UNABLE TO RECEIVE CORRECT DATA (NO DIAGNOSTIC CODE)**

| Possible cause | Inspect, test and repair or replace |
|---|---|
| Poor or faulty electrical connectors | Inspect the ECU connector and the diagnostic connector (FI tool connector on 2009-2013 models; Yamaha diagnostic tool connector on 2014 and later models). Check each connector for loose or missing pins. Make sure each connector properly engages its mate. Repair a connector as needed |
| Open or short circuit found in wiring harness | Inspect and test the yellow/blue wire between the ECU and the diagnostic connector |
| Faulty ECU or diagnostic tool | Replace the ECU or diagnostic tool as needed |
| Reinstatement method | Turn the ignition switch on |

# CHAPTER THREE

# LUBRICATION AND MAINTENANCE

### ENGINE OIL

#### Engine Oil and Filter Change

The cylinder head and crankcase have been redesigned to incorporate the oil tank and oil lines. The new design still uses a dipstick and a drain plug. The oil change procedure is unchanged.

The engine oil gallery bolt on earlier models has been replaced on YFZ450R models with an oil check bolt. The check bolt is located at the rear of the cylinder. Its function is identical to the oil gallery bolt.

### IDLE SPEED ADJUSTMENT

The idle speed is adjusted automatically by the ECU.

### SPARK PLUG

#### Removal

To remove the spark plug on YFZ450R models, coil removal is not required.

### EXHAUST SYSTEM

#### Spark Arrestor Cleaning (2014-on models)

1. Turn out the muffler cap bolts (A, **Figure 5**), and pull the cap (B) from the end of the muffler.

2. Remove the muffler-cap bracket bolts (A, **Figure 6**), and lower the muffler-cap bracket (B) from the muffler.

3. Grasp the tailpipe (C, **Figure 6**), and pull the tailpipe/spark arrestor assembly from the end of the muffler. Remove the gasket behind the assembly.

4. Using a soft-face mallet, lightly tap the tailpipe to dislodge any loose carbon deposits from the assembly. Use a wire brush to remove carbon deposits from the spark arrestor portion of the assembly (**Figure 7**).

5. Installation is the reverse of removal.

   a. Seat the gasket in the muffler, and then install the tailpipe/spark arrestor assembly.

   b. Torque the muffler-cap bracket bolts to 10 Nm (88 in.-lb.), and torque the muffler cap bolts to 8 Nm (71 in.-lb.).

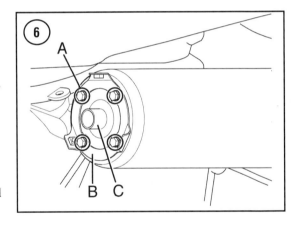

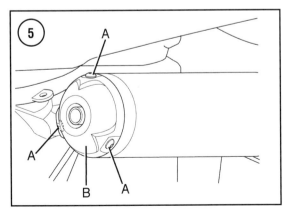

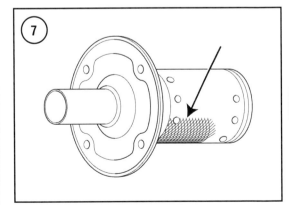

**Table 27 MAINTENANCE AND TUNE-UP SPECIFICATIONS**

| | |
|---|---|
| Idle speed | 1950-2050 rpm |
| Ignition timing | 7.5° BTDC @ 2000 rpm |
| Shift pedal height | 48.0 mm (1.9 in.) |

### Table 28 RECOMMMENDED LUBRICANTS, FLUIDS AND CAPACITIES

| | |
|---|---|
| Coolant capacity | |
| Radiator and engine | 1.25 L (1.32 qt.) |
| Reservoir | 0.25 L (0.26 qt.) |
| Engine oil | |
| Grade | Yamalube 4 or 4-wc (cold weather), API SG or higher, JASO MA |
| Viscosity | |
| 2009-2013 models | SAE 5W-30, 10W-40, 20W-50 or 5w-30 (cold weather) |
| 2014-on models | SAE 5W-30, 10W-30, 10W-40, 15W-40, 20W-40 or 20W-50 |
| Capacity | |
| Oil change only | 1.40 L (1.48 qt.) |
| Oil and filter change | 1.45 L (1.53 qt.) |
| After disassembly (engine dry) | 1.65 L (1.74 qt.) |
| Fuel tank | |
| Total (including reserve) | 10 L (2.64 U.S. gal.) |
| Reserve capacity | 3.4 L (0.9 U.S. gal.) |

### Table 29 FRONT SUSPENSION SPECIFICATIONS

| Item | Specifications |
|---|---|
| Front shock absorber spring preload | |
| 2009-2013 models | |
| Minimum length | 279.8 mm (11.0 in.) |
| Standard length | 289.8 mm (11.4 in.) |
| Maximum length | 299.8 mm (11.8 in.) |
| 2014-on models | |
| Minimum length | 283.5 mm (11.16 in.) |
| Standard length | 293.0 mm (11.54 in.) |
| Maximum length | 303.5 mm (11.95 in.) |
| Front shock rebound damping adjusting positions* | |
| 2009-2013 models | |
| Minimum | 20 clicks out |
| Standard | 12 clicks out |
| Maximum | 1 click out |
| 2014-on models | |
| Minimum | 30 clicks out |
| Standard | 16 clicks out |
| Maximum | 1 click out |
| Front shock compression damping adjusting positions* | |
| High-speed compression damping | |
| Minimum | 2 turns out |
| Standard | 1 turn out |
| Maximum | Fully turned in |

**Table 29 FRONT SUSPENSION SPECIFICATIONS (continued)**

| Item | Specifications |
|------|----------------|
| Low-speed compression damping | |
| 2009-2013 models | |
| Minimum | 18 clicks out |
| Standard | 10 clicks out |
| Maximum | 1 click out |
| 2014-on models | |
| Minimum | 20 clicks out |
| Standard | 7 clicks out |
| Maximum | 1 click out |

*From the fully turned-in position

**Table 30 REAR SUSPENSION SPECIFICATIONS**

| Item | Specifications |
|------|----------------|
| Rear shock absorber spring preload | |
| 2009-2013 models | |
| Minimum length | 253.5 mm (10.0 in.) |
| Standard length | 265.0 mm (10.4 in.) |
| Maximum length | 273.5 mm (10.8 in.) |
| 2014-on models | |
| Minimum length | 269.5 mm (10.61 in.) |
| Standard length | 278.0 mm (10.94 in.) |
| Maximum length | 289.5 mm (11.40 in.) |
| Rear shock rebound damping adjusting positions* | |
| 2009-2013 models | |
| Minimum | 20 clicks out |
| Standard | 11 clicks out |
| Maximum | 1 click out |
| 2014-on models | |
| Minimum | 30 clicks out |
| Standard | 15 clicks out |
| Maximum | 1 click out |
| Rear shock compression damping adjusting positions* | |
| High-speed compression damping | |
| Minimum | 2 turns out |
| Standard | 1 turn out |
| Maximum | Fully turned in |
| Low-speed compression damping | |
| 2009-2013 models | |
| Minimum | 18 clicks out |
| Standard | 8 clicks out |
| Maximum | 1 click out |
| 2014-on models | |
| Minimum | 20 clicks out |
| Standard | 8 clicks out |
| Maximum | 1 click out |

*From the fully turned-in position

**Table 31 MAINTENANCE TORQUE SPECIFICATIONS**

| Item | NM | in.-lb. | ft.-lb. |
|------|-----|---------|---------|
| Camshaft cap bolt (2014-on models | 10 | 88 | - |
| Drive sprocket nut | 100 | - | 72 |
| Muffler cap bolts | 8 | 71 | - |
| Muffler-cap bracket bolts | 10 | 88 | - |
| Oil check bolt | 7 | 62 | - |
| Oil tank drain bolt | 20 | - | 15 |
| Shock absorber spring locknut (front) | 50 | - | 36 |
| Wheel lugnut | 45 | - | 33 |

# CHAPTER FOUR

# ENGINE TOP END

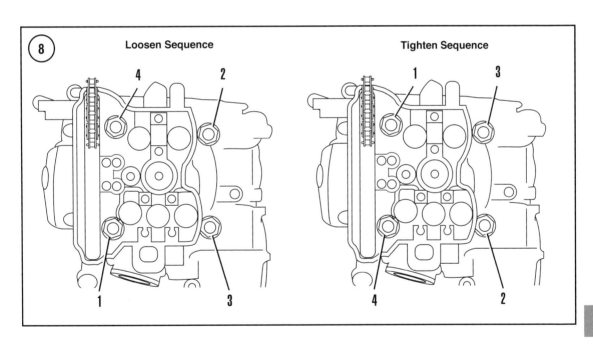

## CYLINDER HEAD

The cylinder head and crankcase incorporate an oil tank and oil lines.

The two nuts that secure the cylinder head to the cylinder (Chapter Four, **Figure 41**), are now bolts.

The cylinder head bolt removal and tightening sequence was revised as shown in **Figure 8**. Loosen the bolts 1/4 turn at a time until all bolts are loose. Tighten the bolts as described in Chapter Four.

## Cylinder Head Removal/Installation (2014-on models)

1. When removing the cylinder head on later models, remove the air induction pipe from the cylinder head by performing the following:

    a. Remove the air cut-off valve and the reed valve as described in AIR INDUCTION SYSTEM in this Supplement.

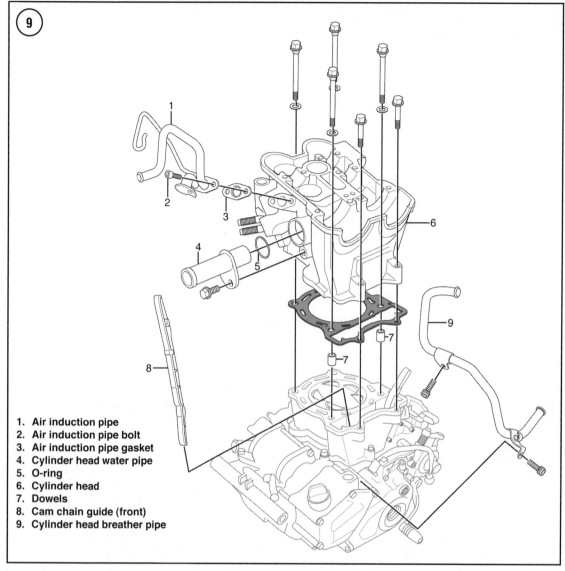

1. Air induction pipe
2. Air induction pipe bolt
3. Air induction pipe gasket
4. Cylinder head water pipe
5. O-ring
6. Cylinder head
7. Dowels
8. Cam chain guide (front)
9. Cylinder head breather pipe

b. Release the clamp, and detach air induction hose 3 from the air induction pipe (**Figure 9**).

c. Turn out the air induction pipe bolts, and remove the air induction pipe from the cylinder head.

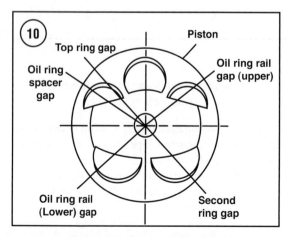

d. Discard the air induction pipe gasket. A new one must be installed during cylinder head installation.

2. During cylinder head installation, install a new cylinder head gasket so its 3 mark faces up.

3. Attach the air induction pipe to the head by performing the following:

a. Fit a new gasket onto the air induction pipe fitting, and set the pipe onto the cylinder head.

b. Torque the air induction pipe bolts to 10 Nm (88 in.-lb.).

c. Connect air induction hose 3 to the air induction pipe.

d. Install the reed valve and air cut-off valve as described in this Supplement.

## PISTON AND PISTON RINGS

Stagger the piston ring gaps as shown in **Figure 10**.

## CAMSHAFTS

### Camshaft Cap Bolt Tightening (2014-on models)

1. Apply molybdenum disulfide oil to the threads of the camshaft cap bolts, and loosely turn the bolts into place.

2. Evenly tighten the bolts in two-to-three stages in the sequence shown in **Figure 11**.

3. Torque the camshaft cap bolts – in sequence – to 10 Nm (88 in-lb.).

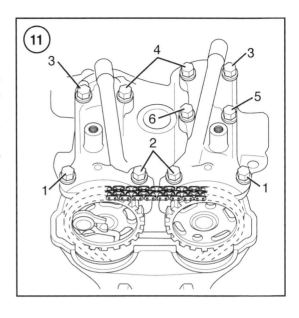

#### Table 32 GENERAL ENGINE SPECIFICATIONS

| Item | Specifications |
|---|---|
| Compression ratio | |
| 2009-2013 models | 11.6:1 |
| 2014-on models | 11.8:1 |
| Ignition timing | 7.5° BTDC @ 2000 rpm |

#### Table 33 CAMSHAFT SPECIFICATIONS

| Item | Standard mm (in.) | Service limit mm (in.) |
|---|---|---|
| Cam base circle diameter | | |
| Intake | 22.450-22.550 (0.8839-0.8878) | 22.350 (0.8799) |
| Cam lobe height | | |
| Intake | 30.100-30.200 (1.1850-1.1890) | 30.0 (1.1811) |

#### Table 34 CYLINDER HEAD SPECIFICATIONS

| Item | Standard mm (in.) | Service limit mm (in.) |
|---|---|---|
| Valve spring free length | | |
| 2009-2013 models | | |
| Intake | 39.46 (1.55) | 38.46 (1.51) |
| Exhaust | 37.68 (1.483) | 36.68 (1.44) |
| 20014-on models | | |
| Intake | 39.46 (1.55) | 37.49 (1.486) |
| Exhaust | 37.61 (1.481) | 35.73 (1.41) |
| Valve spring pressure (installed) | | |
| Intake | 130.20-149.80 N (29.28-33.68 lbf) | - |
| Exhaust (2014-on models) | 123.10-141.80 N (27.67-31.85 lbf) | - |

(continued)

**Table 34 CYLINDER HEAD SPECIFICATIONS (continued)**

| Item | Standard mm (in.) | Service limit mm (in.) |
|---|---|---|
| Valve spring tilt | | |
| 2009-2013 models | - | 1.70 (0.067) |
| 2014-on models | | |
| Intake | - | 1.7 (0.067) |
| Exhaust | - | 1.6 (0.063) |
| Piston rings (2014-on models) | | |
| Ring-to-groove clearance | | |
| Top | 0.030-0.070 (0.0012-0.0028) | 0.12 (0.047) |
| Top | 0.030-0.070 (0.0012-0.0028) | 0.12 (0.047) |
| Oil ring | 0.040-0.140 (0.0016-0.0055) | - |
| Ring end gap (installed) | | |
| Oil ring | 0.02-0.05 (0.01-0.02) | - |

**Table 35 ENGINE TOP END TORQUE SPECIFICATIONS**

| Item | NM | in-lb. |
|---|---|---|
| Air induction pipe bolts (2014-on models) | 10 | 88 |
| Camshaft cap bolts (2014-on models) | 10 | 88 |
| Exhaust pipe nuts | 20 | - |
| Muffler clamp bolt (2014-on models) | 20 | - |

# CHAPTER FIVE

# ENGINE LOWER END

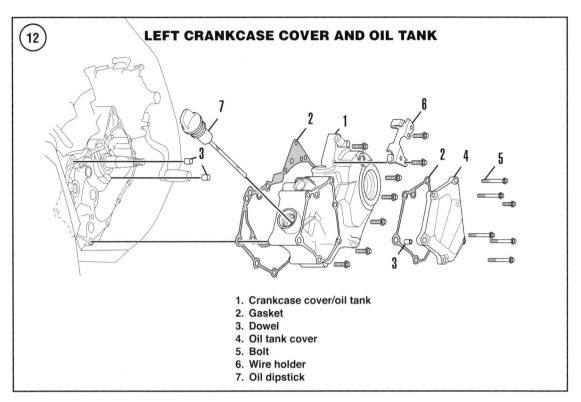

**LEFT CRANKCASE COVER AND OIL TANK**

1. Crankcase cover/oil tank
2. Gasket
3. Dowel
4. Oil tank cover
5. Bolt
6. Wire holder
7. Oil dipstick

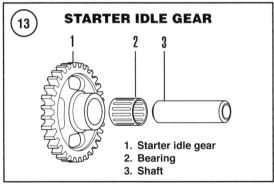

**STARTER IDLE GEAR**

1. Starter idle gear
2. Bearing
3. Shaft

## TORQUE LIMITER

The torque limiter is located behind the left crankcase cover.

## LEFT CRANKCASE COVER

The cylinder head and crankcase incorporate an oil tank and oil lines (**Figure 12**).

## STARTER IDLE GEAR

Refer to **Figure 13** for the starter idle gear assembly.

## CRANKCASE

### Disassembly/assembly tools (2014-on models)

1. The Yamaha crankcase separator: part No. YU-A9642 (90890-04152) is needed to remove the crankshaft during disassembly.

2. The following Yamaha special tools are needed to pull the crankshaft into the bearing during assembly.
   a. Crankshaft installer pot: part No. YU-90058/ YU-90059 (90890-01274)
   b. Bolt: part No. YU-90060 (90890-01275)
   c. Adapter #3: part No. YU-90063 (90890-01278)
   d. Pot spacer: part No. YM-91044 90890-04081)

### Crankshaft bearing retainer screws

When replacing the crankshaft bearings, torque the bearing retainer screws to 22 Nm (16 ft-lb). Lock the screws in place by using a punch to drive the edge of each screw head into the depression in the bearing retainer. See **Figure 129** in Chapter Five.

### Table 36 ENGINE LOWER END SPECIFICATIONS

| Item | Standard mm (in.) | Service limit mm (in.) |
|---|---|---|
| Crankshaft width | 63.95-64.00 (2.518-2.520) | - |
| Oil pump (2014-on models) | | |
|   Tip clearance (feed pump and scavenging pump sides) | 0.00-0.12 (0.0000-0.0047) | 0.20 (0.0079) |
|   Oil pump housing clearance (scavenging pump side) | 0.030-0.100 (0.0012-0.0039) | 0.170 (0.0067) |

### Table 37 MAINTENANCE TORQUE SPECIFICATIONS

| Item | N•m | in.-lb. | ft.-lb. |
|---|---|---|---|
| Crankshaft bearing retainer screw* | 22 | - | 16 |
| Front engine mounting bracket bolts | 48 | - | 35 |
| Left crankcase cover bolts (2014-on models) | 10 | 88 | - |
| Neutral switch (2014-on models) | 17 | 144 | - |
| Oil tank cover bolts (2014-on models) | 10 | 88 | - |
| Primary gear nut | 110 | - | 80 |

*Refer to text in Chapter Five

# CHAPTER SIX

# CLUTCH AND EXTERNAL SHIFT MECHANISM

## CLUTCH (2009 and 2013 models)

The clutch assembly uses two special friction plates that must be the first and last friction plates installed (12, **Figure 14**). These plates are identified as friction plates No. 1. They can be identified by their inside diameter, which is larger than the inside diameter of friction plates No. 2.

Note in the procedures in Chapter Six (using the manufacturer's indentification) these friction plates use the opposite names. What is now a friction plate No. 1, was friction plate No. 2 on earlier models.

What is now a friction plate No. 2, was a friction plate No.1 on earlier models.

The other change to the clutch assembly is the clutch release mechanism. The bolt and plate at the base of the assembly on earlier models has been replaced with a snap ring on YFZ450R models.

## CLUTCH (2014-ON MODELS)

The clutch assembly on these models uses eight friction plates: five friction plates No. 1 and three friction plates No. 2 (14, **Figure 15**). During assem-

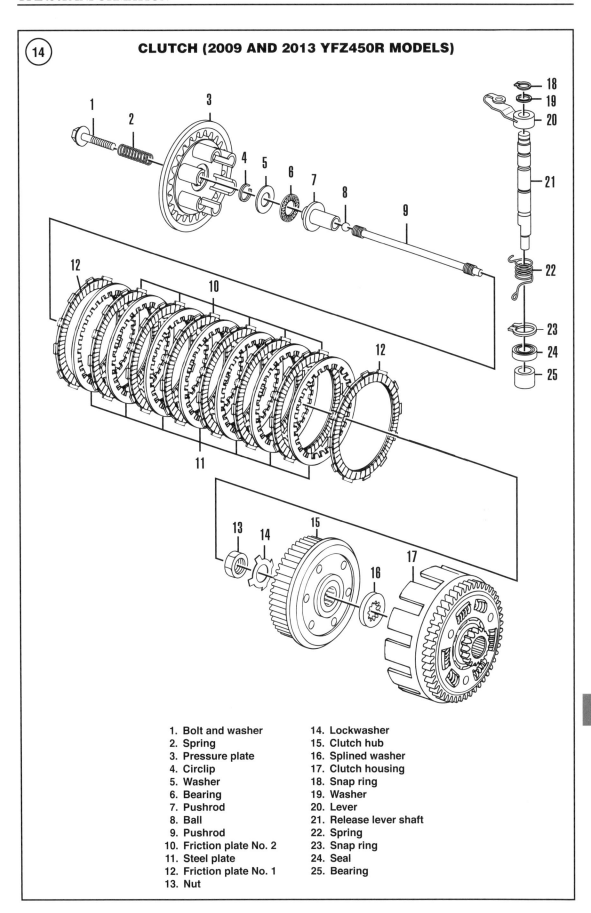

**CLUTCH (2009 AND 2013 YFZ450R MODELS)**

1. Bolt and washer
2. Spring
3. Pressure plate
4. Circlip
5. Washer
6. Bearing
7. Pushrod
8. Ball
9. Pushrod
10. Friction plate No. 2
11. Steel plate
12. Friction plate No. 1
13. Nut
14. Lockwasher
15. Clutch hub
16. Splined washer
17. Clutch housing
18. Snap ring
19. Washer
20. Lever
21. Release lever shaft
22. Spring
23. Snap ring
24. Seal
25. Bearing

S

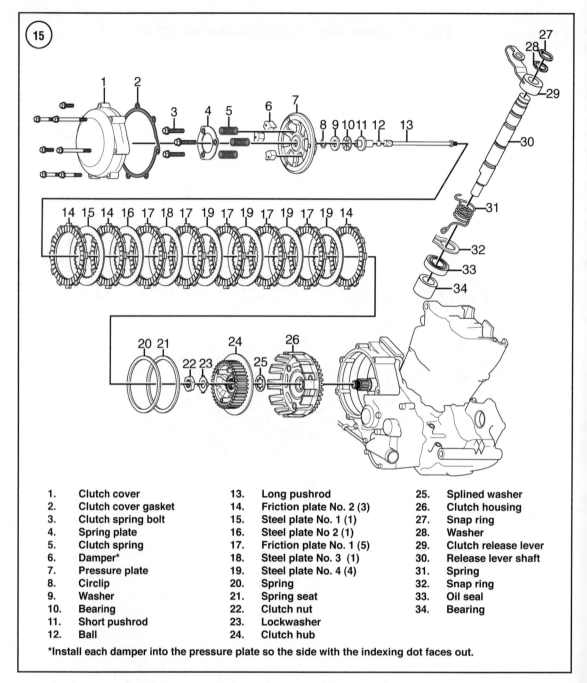

| 1. | Clutch cover | 13. | Long pushrod | 25. | Splined washer |
|----|--------------|-----|--------------|-----|----------------|
| 2. | Clutch cover gasket | 14. | Friction plate No. 2 (3) | 26. | Clutch housing |
| 3. | Clutch spring bolt | 15. | Steel plate No. 1 (1) | 27. | Snap ring |
| 4. | Spring plate | 16. | Steel plate No 2 (1) | 28. | Washer |
| 5. | Clutch spring | 17. | Friction plate No. 1 (5) | 29. | Clutch release lever |
| 6. | Damper* | 18. | Steel plate No. 3 (1) | 30. | Release lever shaft |
| 7. | Pressure plate | 19. | Steel plate No. 4 (4) | 31. | Spring |
| 8. | Circlip | 20. | Spring | 32. | Snap ring |
| 9. | Washer | 21. | Spring seat | 33. | Oil seal |
| 10. | Bearing | 22. | Clutch nut | 34. | Bearing |
| 11. | Short pushrod | 23. | Lockwasher | | |
| 12. | Ball | 24. | Clutch hub | | |

*Install each damper into the pressure plate so the side with the indexing dot faces out.

bly, a friction plate No 2 must be the first, second-to-last and the last friction plate installed in the clutch housing. Each friction plate No 2 can be identified by its inside diameter, which is larger than the inside diameter of the five friction plates No. 1 (see **Figure 29** in Chapter Six of this manual's main body). Each friction plate No. 1 can be identified by the purple paint mark on the plate.

This clutch also use four different steel plates: a single steel plate No. 1 (15, **Figure 15**), single steel plate No. 2 (16), single steel plate No. 3 (18) and four steel plates No 4 (19). Steel plates are identified by their positions in the stack.

During disassembly, stack the clutch plates in the order in which they are removed. If these plates will be reused, each must be reinstalled in its original position in the stack.

## CLUTCH-PLATE-ASSEMBLY WIDTH

Whenever all the clutch plates are replaced, the friction and steel plates must be assembled in the correct order so the clutch-plate-assembly width can be measured. This measurement can be made when the clutch plates have been assembled in the clutch housing or when the friction and steel plates have been stacked in the proper order on the bench (A, **Figure 16**). If the measured width is outside the range specified in Table 38, the assembly width must be adjusted.

This is accomplished by replacing steel plates No 2 (B, **Figure 16**) and No 3 (C) with one of the replacement plates listed in Table 38. Refer to the table, and select the replacement plate with the thickness that will most likely bring the clutch-plate-assembly width into specification. Remove the existing steel plate No 2 from the stack, and replace it with the selected replacement. Measure the assembly with the replacement plate in place. If the measurement is still out of specification, select a replacement plate for steel plate No. 3.

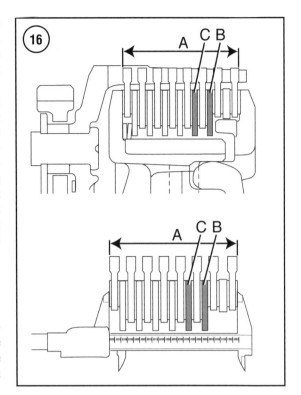

### CLUTCH CABLE LENGTH ADJUSTMENT

1. At the clutch release mechanism, measure the distance from the center of the clutch cable end to the edge of the clutch cable bracket (A, **Figure 17**). The measurement should be within the range specified in Table 38.
2. If necessary, loosen the negative battery terminal bolt, which also secures the clutch cable bracket in place (see A, **Figure 1** in Chapter Six of this manual's main body). Adjust the bracket as needed to bring the cable length within specification.
3. Tighten the negative battery terminal bolt to 10 Nm (88 in.-lb.)

### EXTERNAL SHIFT MECHANISM

A washer is now installed between the stopper lever and torsion spring. Note that the stopper lever is installed with the roller on the lever facing inward.

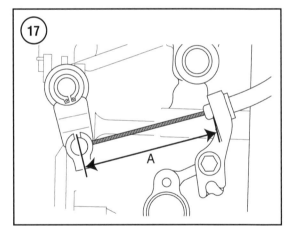

| Table 38 CLUTCH SPECIFICATIONS (2014-ON MODELS) | | |
|---|---|---|
| **Item** | **Standard mm (in.)** | **Service limit mm (in.)** |
| Clutch cable length | 66.5-73.6 (2.62-2.90) | |
| Clutch housing radial clearance | 0.020-0.066 (0.0008-0.0026) | |
| Clutch housing thrust clearance | 0.100-0.110 (0.0039-0.0043) | |
| Clutch-plate-assembly width | 35.5-36.3 (1.40-1.43) | - |
| Cutch spring free length | 44.1 (1.74) | 42.3 (1.67) |
| Friction plate thickness (Friction plates Nos. 1 & 2) | 2.92-3.08 (0.11-0.12) | 2.80 (0.1102) |

(continued)

**Table 38 CLUTCH SPECIFICATIONS (2014-ON MODELS) (continued)**

| Item | Standard mm (in.) | Service limit mm (in.) |
|---|---|---|
| Steel plate thickness | | |
|   Steel plate No. 1 | 2.20-2.40 (0.087-0.094) | - |
|   Steel plates Nos. 2 & 3* | 1.50-1.70 (0.06-0.07) | 0.20 (0.0079 |
|   Steel plate No. 4 | 1.50-1.70 (0.06-0.07) | 0.20 (0.0079) |
|   Replacement steel plates | | |
|     Part No. 5JG-16325-00 | 1.2 (0.047) | - |
|     Part No. 4X7-16325-00 (standard) | 1.6 (0.063) | - |
|     Part No. 1TA-16325-00 | 2.0 (0.079) | |
| Steel plate warp | - | 0.20 (0.0079) |
| Shift pedal height | 48.0 (1.89) | - |

*The thickness specification for steel plates Nos 2 & 3 only applies to plates with a standard thickness. If steel plate No. 2 or No. 3 has been replaced with a non-standard plate, consider 1.50-1.70 mm (0.059-0.067 in.) or 2.50-2.70 mm (0.098-0.106 in.) to be a plate's specified thickness when inspecting the clutch plates during maintenance.

**Table 39 CLUTCH TORQUE SPECIFICATIONS (2014-ON MODELS)**

| Item | N•m | in.-lb. | ft.-lb. |
|---|---|---|---|
| Clutch spring bolts | 10 | 88 | - |

# Notes

S

# CHAPTER SEVEN

# TRANSMISSION AND INTERNAL GEARSHIFT MECHANISM

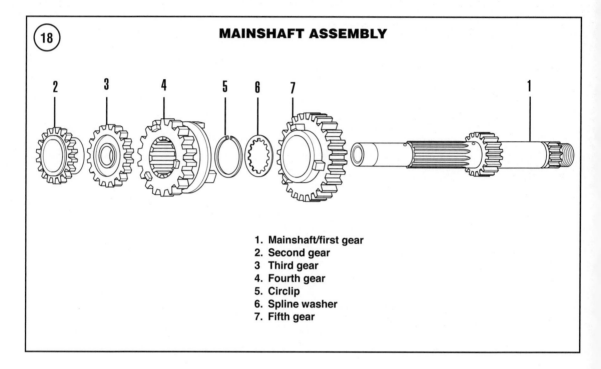

**MAINSHAFT ASSEMBLY**

18

1. Mainshaft/first gear
2. Second gear
3  Third gear
4. Fourth gear
5. Circlip
6. Spline washer
7. Fifth gear

Refer to **Table 38** for the gear ratios.

### TRANSMISSION MAINSHAFT

Refer to **Figure 18** for the mainshaft assembly.
When assembling the mainshaft, press second gear onto the shaft until the distance between first and second gear is as shown in **Figure 19**.

### TRANSMISSION COUNTERSHAFT

Refer to **Figure 20** for the countershaft assembly.

### SHIFT FORKS

Refer to **Figure 21** for the shift fork assembly.

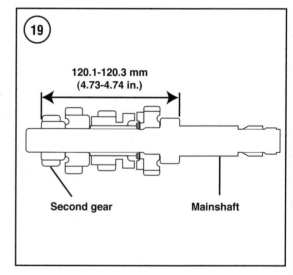

19

120.1-120.3 mm
(4.73-4.74 in.)

Second gear                    Mainshaft

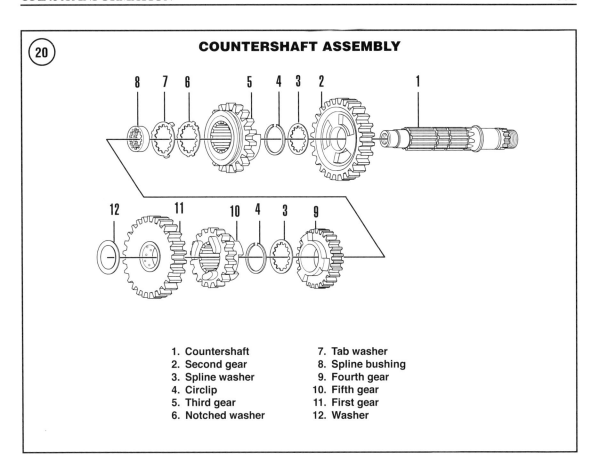

## COUNTERSHAFT ASSEMBLY

1. Countershaft
2. Second gear
3. Spline washer
4. Circlip
5. Third gear
6. Notched washer
7. Tab washer
8. Spline bushing
9. Fourth gear
10. Fifth gear
11. First gear
12. Washer

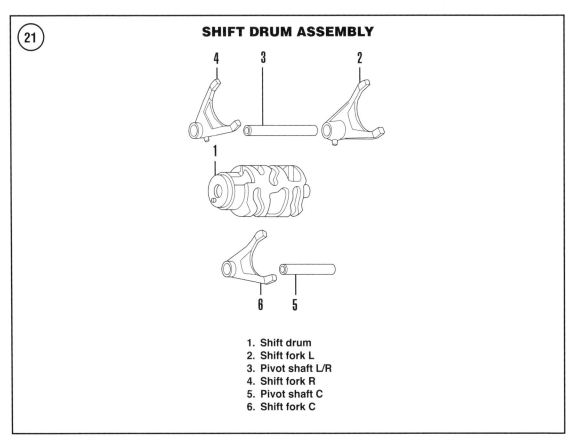

## SHIFT DRUM ASSEMBLY

1. Shift drum
2. Shift fork L
3. Pivot shaft L/R
4. Shift fork R
5. Pivot shaft C
6. Shift fork C

S

**Table 40 TRANSMISSION SPECIFICATIONS**

| Transmission | Constant mesh, 5-speed |
|---|---|
| Primary reduction ratio | 2.652 (61/23) |
| Transmission gear ratios | |
|   First | 2.500 (35/14) |
|   Second | 2.000 (30/15) |
|   Third | 1.632 (31/19) |
|   Fourth | 1.333 (28/21) |
|   Fifth | 1.095 (23/21) |

**Table 41 TRANSMISSION SERVICE SPECIFICATIONS**

| Item | Standard mm (in.) | Service limit mm (in.) |
|---|---|---|
| Mainshaft second gear position | 120.1-120.3 (4.73-4.74) | - |
| Shift fork thickness | 4.85 (0.1909) | - |
| Shift-fork pivot-shaft bending limit | - | 0.05 (0.0020) |

# CHAPTER EIGHT

# FUEL INJECTION SYSTEM

Observe all safety precautions (Chapter One).

The fuel injection system includes the fuel tank, electric pump, fuel level sensor, fuel injector, throttle body, throttle lever and cable, the fuel supply hoses, fuse, and wiring. Refer to **Figure 22** for the component's location.

## SYSTEM OPERATION

When the rider presses the throttle lever to accelerate, the engine control unit (ECU) verifies, for example, that the engine is not overheating and that the machine is upright and not leaning dangerously, among other parameters. When all programmed parameters are met the control system signals the throttle body injector to spray more fuel into the air flowing through the throttle body. If the parameters cannot be met due to a malfunction, the ECU generates an error code as described in this supplement, and may also reduce the available power or stop the engine altogether.

## Engine Control Unit (ECU) and Sensors

The ECU is located beneath the seat. It is a microprocessor with three parts: Inputs (sensing), information processing (computing) and outputs (actions). Actions performed by the ECU result from information provided by the following system sensors:

1. The throttle position sensor (TPS) is mounted directly to the left side of the throttle body above the idle speed control, and is actuated by the throttle plate shaft. The sensor signals the position of the throttle to the ECU.

2. The intake air pressure sensor reports the barometric pressure to the ECU. This is important to maintain performance as the machine changes altitude, or if the air filter should become partially plugged.

3. The intake air temperature sensor provides a measurement of intake air temperature to the ECU, further enabling precise air-fuel-ratio control.

4. The lean angle sensor, located in the battery compartment, signals the ECU when the machine begins to lean so far as to become unstable, and then shuts off the engine.

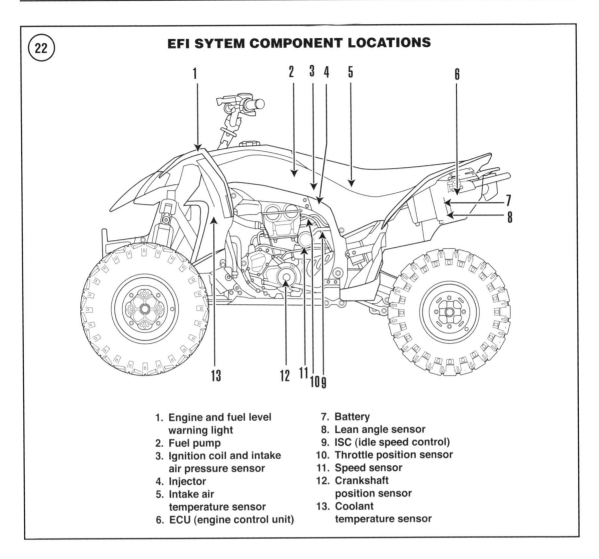

㉒ **EFI SYTEM COMPONENT LOCATIONS**

1. Engine and fuel level warning light
2. Fuel pump
3. Ignition coil and intake air pressure sensor
4. Injector
5. Intake air temperature sensor
6. ECU (engine control unit)
7. Battery
8. Lean angle sensor
9. ISC (idle speed control)
10. Throttle position sensor
11. Speed sensor
12. Crankshaft position sensor
13. Coolant temperature sensor

5. The speed sensor is mounted on top of the transmission housing behind the engine, and tells the ECM the speed of the rear wheels.

6. The crankshaft position sensor is mounted next to the alternator stator, and signals the ECU when the piston is rising on the compression stroke. This matches the spark timing with the fuel injection.

7. The coolant temperature sensor provides the ECU with the engine coolant temperature. When the temperature is too high the ECU will activate the warning light, and also reduce engine power. The ECU will allow the machine to run at a lower power level.

**Fuel Delivery System**

*Fuel pump*

The fuel pump is located inside the fuel tank. The electrical connection is on the left and the fuel connection is on the right (**Figure 23**).

*Fuel pressure regulator*

The throttle-body-mounted fuel pressure regulator maintains fuel pressure at 324 kPa (47 psi).

### Throttle body fuel injector

The constant pressure, multiple-orifice injector is mounted in the top of the throttle body assembly.

### Throttle body assembly

The throttle body assembly (**Figure 24**) houses the injector, throttle position sensor and the idle speed control.

### Fuel injection system fuse

The 20-amp main fuse protects all circuits in the ATV including the fuel injection system. Refer to the *Electrical System* section of this supplement for fuse test procedures.

### FUEL DELIVERY SYSTEM TESTS

*WARNING*
*Be sure the main switch is off before working on the fuel system. After operating the engine, allow 10 minutes for the fuel system pressure to dissipate before disconnecting fuel hose clamps and fittings.*

*WARNING*
*Never start the engine if there is a fuel leak.*

*WARNING*
*Perform all fuel system work in a no smoking area free of sparks and open flames. Gasoline is extremely flammable and explosive.*

*WARNING*
*Wear skin and eye protection when working with the fuel system.*

### Fuel Pump Operation Test

Verify that the electrical system, including battery, main ignition switch and the engine stop switch are all working correctly.

1. Turn on the main ignition switch and listen for the sound of the fuel pump.

2. If the pump cannot be heard, check the fuel injection system fuse as described in the *Electrical System* section of this supplement.

3. If the fuse is operational, check the main relay as described in this section of the supplement. If the re-

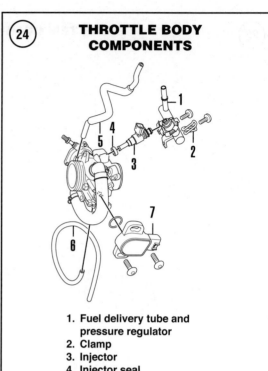

**THROTTLE BODY COMPONENTS**

24

1. Fuel delivery tube and pressure regulator
2. Clamp
3. Injector
4. Injector seal
5. Intake pressure sensor hose
6. TPS drain hose
7. Throttle position sensor

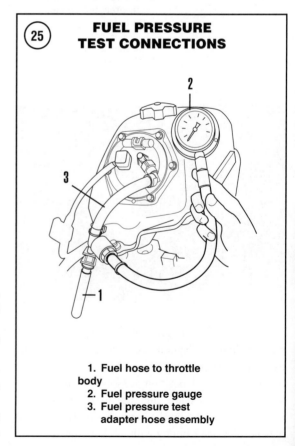

**FUEL PRESSURE TEST CONNECTIONS**

25

1. Fuel hose to throttle body
2. Fuel pressure gauge
3. Fuel pressure test adapter hose assembly

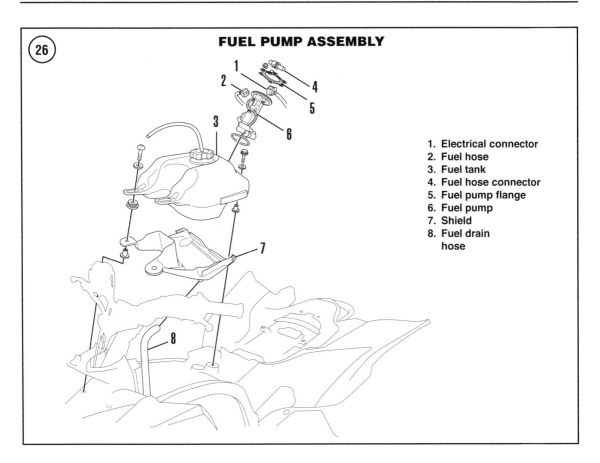

**FUEL PUMP ASSEMBLY**

1. Electrical connector
2. Fuel hose
3. Fuel tank
4. Fuel hose connector
5. Fuel pump flange
6. Fuel pump
7. Shield
8. Fuel drain hose

lay is good, check the lean angle sensor as described in the *Electrical System* section of this Supplement.

4. Check continuity of the fuel pump wiring harness, and then continuity of the fuel pump windings. Check to see if there is continuity between the pump motor windings and the electrical ground. If so replace the pump.

5. If all the above items test good, replace the ECU.

**Fuel Pressure test**

This test requires a fuel pressure gauge (Yamaha part No. 90890-03153/ YU-31533) and test adapter hose assembly (Yamaha part No. 90890-03186/YU-03186), or their equivalents. This test is done with the tank in place (**Figure 25**).

1. Remove the seat.
2. Prepare to remove the fuel line from the tanks:
   a. Wrap an absorbent shop towel around the tank end of the fuel line to catch any fuel dripping from the line upon disconnection.
   b. Slide the fuel hose lock into the release position and disconnect it from the tank fitting.
3. Connect the fuel pressure T-adapter test assembly.
4. Connect the fuel pressure gauge to the test hose assembly.

5. Start the engine and operate at idle speed and note the fuel pressure level.

6. If the pressure is too high replace the fuel pressure regulator.

7. If the fuel pressure is low check for an external leak or kinking of the fuel hose. If neither of these problems is found, replace the fuel pump.

8. To remove the fuel pressure test gauge, again place an absorbent towel under the fuel line and remove the test assembly before reconnecting the original fuel line in the reverse order of disassembly.

9. Turn on the ignition switch. The self-bleeding fuel system will purge air from the fuel line for starting.

**FUEL PUMP**

**Removal/Installation**

1. Place the machine in a spark-free area with good ventilation. The pump may be removed with the tank in place.

2. Pump the fuel from the tank through its fill opening and safely dispose of the fuel.

3. Slide up the hose connector cover to expose the release button on each side of the fuel hose connector. Press the two buttons, disconnect the fuel line from the pump fitting, and plug the fuel line openings.

4. Remove the fuel pump nuts, and lift the fuel pump and its flange from the fuel tank (**Figure 26**). Protect the pump assembly from damage during handling, especially the sender area.

5. Installation is the reverse of removal. Note the following.

   a. Install the fuel pump flange seal with the lip facing upward.

   b. Seat the fuel pump flange so its two holes engage the two small barbs on the top of the fuel pump (A, **Figure 27**).

   c. Make sure slot of the fuel pump flange faces forward. Also align the rear hole of the fuel pump flange with the small barb on the fuel tank (B).

   d. Following the sequence shown in **Figure 27**, tighten the fuel pump nuts to 7 Nm (62 in.-lb.). Refill the tank with clean fuel. The fuel system is self-priming and will clear the line of air when the keyed switch is turned on and the starter engages.

## MAIN (FUEL SYSTEM) RELAY

The main relay is located behind the ECU, beneath the seat assembly. Refer to the *Electrical System* section of this supplement for location, testing and removal instructions.

## THROTTLE BODY

### Removal/Installation

*WARNNG*
*Wear nitrile gloves to protect the skin from contact with fuel.*

*CAUTION*
*When working with the throttle body, do not disturb the mounting of the idle speed control (ISC) or its retaining screws, as the ISC positioning is preset by the manufacturer.*

*CAUTION*
*The throttle stop screw is preset by the manufacturer and should not be adjusted.*

*NOTE*
*The throttle body assembly includes the throttle position sensor (A, Figure 28) and the idle speed control (B).*

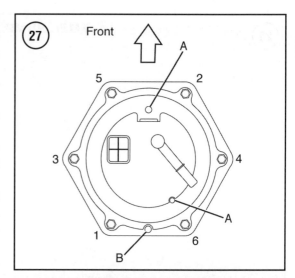

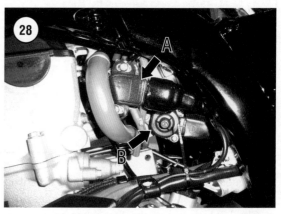

1. Remove the throttle cable, throttle position sensor, and the idle speed control electrical coupler from the throttle body. Leave the idle speed control attached to the throttle body. Refer to **Figure 22** for component locations.

2. Disconnect the throttle position sensor (TPS) connector.

3. Wrap a shop towel around the fuel hose to absorb the fuel in the hose as it is disconnected. Remove the fuel hose.

4. After removal of the hose, plug or cover all openings to prevent contamination.

5. Loosen the throttle body clamp screw, and remove the throttle body from the throttle body joint. Cover the joint to prevent contamination.

6. Clean and inspect the throttle body. Installation is the reverse of removal.

   a. If removed, tighten the throttle body joint screws to 10 Nm (88 in.-lb.). Install the throttle body joint so its 18P mark faces up.

   b. Make sure the slot in the throttle-body-joint clamp engages the notch in the throttle body joint.

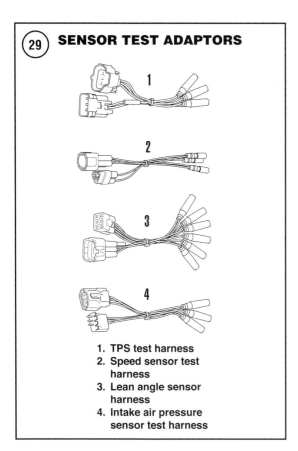

**29** **SENSOR TEST ADAPTORS**

1. TPS test harness
2. Speed sensor test harness
3. Lean angle sensor harness
4. Intake air pressure sensor test harness

c. Seat the throttle body onto the throttle body joint so the tab on the throttle body engages the slot in the joint. Torque the throttle-body-joint clamp screw to 3.3 Nm (29 in.-lb.).

## Cleaning and Inspection

1. Remove the injector and perform a visual inspection of the injector and throttle body.
2. Do not immerse the injector in solvent or detergent, but rather spray it with carburetor cleaner and blown dry after lightly brushing it with a nylon or brass brush. Replace the O-ring seal before installation.
3. Similarly, the throttle body will require a visual inspection and may be cleaned in solvent, and then blown dry with low-pressure compressed air. It is assembled/installed in the reverse order of disassembly
4. Line up the tab on the throttle body with the notch on the throttle body joint clamp, and tighten the clamp bolt.

### THROTTLE POSITION SENSOR (TPS)

The throttle position sensor (TPS) (**Figure 24**) has a a shaft that rotates, when pulled by the throttle cable. This sensor is spring-loaded to return to idle speed.

## Adjustment

*CAUTION*
*The throttle stop screw is preset by the manufacturer and should not be adjusted.*

1. Test the TPS after removal from the throttle body by performing an electrical resistance test.
2. Connect a digital ohmmeter's positive test probe to the sensor's blue terminal, and connect the negative test probe to the sensor's black/blue terminal. Verify the sensor has a maximum resistance of 2.64-6.16k ohms. If not, replace the sensor.
3. To adjust the throttle position sensor after testing and installation, leave the retaining screws slightly loose to allow adjustment.
4. Attach the TPS test harness (**Figure 29**) (Yamaha part No. 90890-03204/YU-03204) or its equivalent inline between the sensor and the sensor's harness connector. Connect a digital voltmeter's positive test probe to the yellow test port in the test harness. Connect the negative test probe to the black/blue test port. Slowly rotate the sensor until the output voltage is 0.679-0.681 volts.
5. Tighten the retaining screws to 3.5 Nm (31 in.-lb.).

*NOTE*
*New machines have a white mark on the mounting bolt slot to show the pre-set positioning.*

## Removal/Installation

*WARNING*
*Nitrile gloves and safety glasses must be worn to keep fuel from the skin and eyes to ensure technician safety.*

1. Disconnect the 3-pin connector from the throttle position sensor.
2. Disconnect the TPS drain hose from the throttle body fitting beneath the sensor. Note how the hose is routed over the top of the throttle body. The hose must be rerouted along the same path during installation.
3. Turn out the TPS screws, and remove the sensor from the throttle body. Remove and discard the O-ring behind the sensor. A new O-ring must be installed during installation.
4. Installation is the reverse of removal. Install a new TPS O-ring, and torque the TPS screws to 3.5 Nm (31 in.-lb.).

## ENGINE CONTROL UNIT (ECU)

### Testing

Test specifications are not available for the ECU. Throroughly troubleshoot and eliminate all other possible causes before considering replacement of the ECU.

### Removal/Installation

1. Remove the seat.
2. Disconnect the ECU (**Figure 30**) electrical connector.
3. Remove both bolts and lift out the ECU.
4. Installation is the reverse of removal. Make sure the connector is secure. On 2014-on models, tighten the engine control unit bolts to 7 Nm (62 in.-lb.).

## INTAKE AIR PRESSURE (IAP) SENSOR

### Removal/Installation

1. Remove the seat.
2. Disconnect the sensor electrical connector.
3. Remove the fastener from the sensor (A, **Figure 31**) and lift it out of position.
4. Remove the sensing hose from the bottom of the sensor.
5. Reverse this procedure to install the parts.

### Output Voltage Test

1. Disconnect the electrical connector from the IAP sensor.
2. Attach the intake air pressure sensor test harness (**Figure 29**) (Yamaha part No. 90890-03211/YU-03211), or its equivalent, inline between the IAP sensor and the sensor's harness connector.
3. Connect the positive test probe of a digital voltmeter to the pink/blue test port in the test harness. Connect the negative test probe to the black/blue test port.
4. Turn the main switch on, and measure the output voltage. Replace the sensor if its output voltage is out of specifications. On 2009-2013 models, output voltage should be 3.594-3.684 volts @101.32 kPa (14.7 psi); on 2014-on models, output voltage should be 3.58-3.70 volts

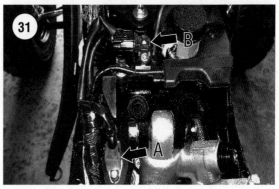

## INTAKE AIR TEMPERATURE (IAP) SENSOR

> *CAUTION*
> *The intake air temperature sensor can easily be damaged by shock. Use care when handling this sensor, and replace if it is accidentally dropped.*

The intake air temperature sensor (B, **Figure 31**) is mounted under the seat and provides a measurement of intake air temperature to the ECM, ensuring precise air-fuel-ratio control.

### Removal/Installation

1. Remove the seat.
2. Disconnect the sensor electrical connector.
3. Remove the fastener from the sensor and lift it out of position.
4. Reverse this procedure to install the parts. On 2014-on models, torque the IAT sensor screw to 1.5 Nm (13 in.-lb.).

### Resistance Test

1. Immerse the sensor, except the terminals, in ice water 0° C (32° F). The resistance at this temperature should be 5.4-6.6k ohms.

2. Warm the water to 80° C (176° F). The resistance should be 290-390 ohms.
3. Replace the sensor if it fails either test.

## COOLANT TEMPERATURE SENSOR

### Removal/Installation

*CAUTION*
*The coolant temperature sensor can easily be damaged by shock. Use care when handling this sensor, and replace it if accidentally dropped.*

1. Drain the coolant from the radiator and engine.
2. Disconnect the temperature sensor (**Figure 32**).
3. Turn the sensor counter-clockwise to remove it from the radiator.
4. Install a new sealing washer.
5. Reverse this procedure to install the parts. Tighten the sensor to 18 N•m (13 ft.-lb.).
6. Refill the cooling system.

### Resistance test

*CAUTION*
*Keep the ohmmeter leads from excess heat when heating water and performing this test.*

The coolant temperature sensor provides the ECM with the engine coolant temperature. When the temperature is too high the ECM will energize a warning light, while also reducing engine power.
1. Select the resistance range on the meter.
2. Immerse the sensor, except the terminals, in ice water 0° C (32° F). The resistance should be 5.21-6.37k ohms.

3. Warm the water to 20°C (68° F) and check the resistance. It should be is 2.45k ohms.
4. Warm the water to 80° C (176° F) and check the resistance. It should be 290-354 ohms.
5. Replace the sensor if it fails any test.

## RADIATOR FAN THERMOSWITCH

Refer to the Electrical System section in this supplement for removal, installation and testing procedures.

## CRANKSHAFT POSITION SENSOR

Refer to the *Electrical System* section in this supplement for removal, installation and testing procedures.

## LEAN-ANGLE SENSOR

Refer to the *Electrical System* section in this Supplement for removal, installation and testing procedures. Testing requires use of the lean angle sensor test harness (C, **Figure 29**) (Yamaha part No. 90890-03209/YU-03209 ), or its equivalent.

## AIR INDUCTION SYSTEM
## (2014-ON MODELS)

### Removal/Installation

The air induction system injects secondary air into the exhaust port so unburned exhaust gases can be burned instead of being released into the atmosphere.
1. Remove the seat, fuel tank cover, left side cover and the right side cover as described in Chapter Fifteen.
2. Remove the air box (Chapter Eight).
3. Disconnect the electrical connector from the air cut-off valve (see **Figure 33**).
4. Turn out the reed valve bracket screws, and lower the reed valve bracket from the frame.
5. Disconnect air cut-off hose 1 from its fitting on the air cut-off valve.
6. Disconnect air cut-off hose 3 from its fitting on the reed valve. If necessary, disconnect the other end of hose 3 from the air induction pipe on the cylinder head.
7. Disconnect air cut-off hose 2 from the reed valve and from the air cut-off valve, and remove each valve.

S

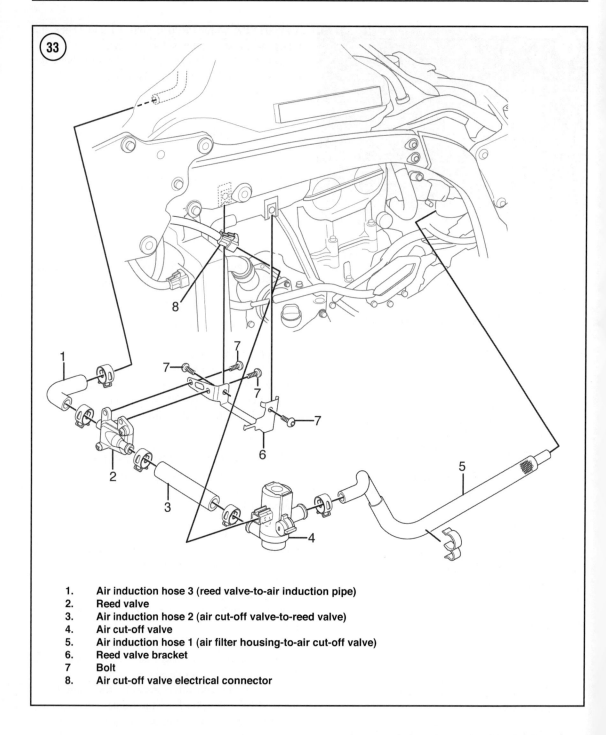

1.   Air induction hose 3 (reed valve-to-air induction pipe)
2.   Reed valve
3.   Air induction hose 2 (air cut-off valve-to-reed valve)
4.   Air cut-off valve
5.   Air induction hose 1 (air filter housing-to-air cut-off valve)
6.   Reed valve bracket
7    Bolt
8.   Air cut-off valve electrical connector

8. Installation is the reverse of removal.
  a. Make sure each hose is connected to the correct
     fitting and secured in place with a clamp.
  b. Tighten the reed valve bracket screws to 7 Nm
     (62 in.-lb.).

## AIR-CUT-OFF VALVE SOLENOID TEST

1. Remove the electrical connector from the solenoid
on the air-cut-off valve.

2. Connect the positive test probe of a digital ohmmeter to the solenoid's brown/red terminal. Connect
the meter's negative test probe to the red/black terminal in the solenoid, and measure the resistance.
3. The solenoid resistance should equal 20.0-24.0
ohms Replace the air-cut-off valve is the resistance
is out of specification.

### Table 40 FUEL INJECTION SYSTEM SPECIFICATIONS

| Item | Specifications |
|------|----------------|
| Air cut-off valve solenoid resistance (2014-on models) | 20.0-24.0 ohms |
| Coolant temperature sensor resistance | |
| 2009-2013 models | 5.21-6.3k ohms @ 0° C (32° F) |
| 2009-2013 models | 2.45k ohms @ 20° C (68° F) |
| 2009-on models | 290-354 ohms @ 80° C (176° F) |
| Fuel pump pressure | 324 kPa (47 psi) |
| Intake air pressure sensor output voltage | |
| 2009-2013 models | 3.594-3.684 volts @101.32 kPa (14.7 psi) |
| 2014-on models | 3.58-3.70 volts |
| Intake air temperature sensor resistance | |
| | 5.4-6.6k ohms @ 0° C (32° F) |
| | 290-390 ohms @ 80° C (176° F) |
| Throttle body | |
| Type | 42EHS |
| ID mark | |
| 2009-2013 models | 18P100 |
| 2014-on models | 1TD1 00 |
| Throttle position sensor | |
| Output voltage | 0.679-0.681 volts |
| Maximum resistance | 2.64-6.16K ohms |

### Table 41 FUEL INJECTION SYSTEM TORQUE SPECIFICATIONS

| Item | N•m | in.-lb. | ft.-lb. |
|------|-----|---------|---------|
| Coolant temperature sensor | 18 | - | 13 |
| Engine control unit bolts (2014-on models) | 7 | 62 | - |
| Fuel pump nuts | 7 | 62 | - |
| Intake air pressure sensor | 7 | 62 | - |
| Intake air temperature sensor screw (2014-on models) | 1.5 | 13 | - |
| Reed valve bracket screws | 7 | 62 | - |
| Throttle body joint screw | 10 | 88 | - |
| Throttle-body-joint clamp screw | 3.3 | 29 | - |
| Throttle position sensor screw | 3.5 | 31 | - |

S

# CHAPTER NINE

# ELECTRICAL SYSTEM

This section provides test procedures for the electrical system.

## CRANKSHAFT POSITION SENSOR

The crankshaft position sensor is located in the left crankcase cover. Test the sensor with the cover in place by locating the wiring connectors to the sensor. The sensor is mounted next to the alternator stator (**Figure 34**). The sensor signals the ECM when the piston is rising on its compression stroke.

## Testing

1. Disconnect the CPS sensor wire connector from the wiring harness.
2. The color combination of the first wire is blue/yellow and the second wire is black/blue.
3. Test by measuring the resistance through the sensor. If not in the normal range of 248-372 ohms

at 20° C (68° F), replace the assembly. Reconnect the electrical connector after testing.

*NOTE*
*If the sensor must be replaced, first block the machine securely.*

## Removal/Installation

1. Have a new oil tank gasket and the left crankcase cover gasket on hand for reassembly.
2. Drain the oil tank and remove the tank cover bolts, the oil tank cover and the electrical lead holder.

*NOTE*
*Most of the oil tank cover bolts also protrude through the crankcase cover. Make a cardboard template with an outline of the bolt pattern on it. Insert each bolt into its position on the card as it is removed. This ensures proper bolt location during assembly.*

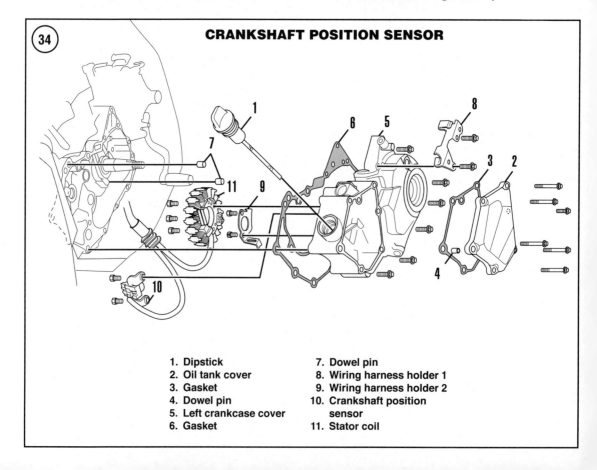

**CRANKSHAFT POSITION SENSOR**

1. Dipstick
2. Oil tank cover
3. Gasket
4. Dowel pin
5. Left crankcase cover
6. Gasket
7. Dowel pin
8. Wiring harness holder 1
9. Wiring harness holder 2
10. Crankshaft position sensor
11. Stator coil

3. Remove the remaining crankcase cover bolts and slide the cover away from the engine.

4. The crankshaft position sensor is inside the left crankcase cover, attached by two bolts. Remove the sensor electrical connector and both attachment bolts.

5. Reverse this procedure to install the sensor and note:

    a. Tighten all fasteners to 10 N•m (88 in.-lb.).

    b. Refill the oil tank.

    c. Start the engine and check for leaks.

## IGNITION SYSTEM

The YFZ450R models use a spark plug wire to connect the ignition coil to the spark plug.

## IGNITION COIL

The single ignition coil is mounted on the left side of the engine, near the spark plug.

### Testing

The coil may be tested on the engine.

1. Check the primary circuit resistance (A, **Figure 35**) of the coil after locating and disconnecting the primary wires. The specification is 2.16-2.64 ohms at 20° C (68° F).

2. Check the secondary circuit resistance (B, **Figure 35**) of the coil after locating and disconnecting the secondary circuit wires. The specification is 8.64-12.96k ohms at 20° C (68° F).

3. Reconnect all electrical terminals.

### Removal/Installation

1. Disconnect the spark plug wire from the plug.

2. Disconnect the primary wires from the coil and label them if needed, for later connection.

3. Remove the fasteners that hold the coil assembly in place.

4. Reverse this procedure to install the coil.

5. Lubricate the cap boot with dielectric grease and install on the spark plug.

## SPARK PLUG CAP

### Testing

1. Remove the cap from the ignition wire.

2. Check the resistance of the cap (**Figure 36**). It should be 10k ohms. Replace the cap if necessary.

3. Install the cap onto the ignition wire.

4. Lubricate the cap boot with dielectric grease and install on the spark plug.

## ENGINE CONTROL UNIT (ECU)

The ECU controls both ignition timing and the electronic fuel injection system. Refer to *Fuel Injection System* in this Supplement for removal, installation and testing procedures.

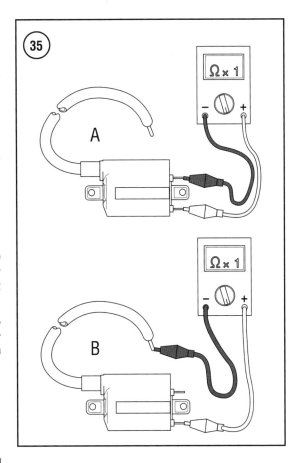

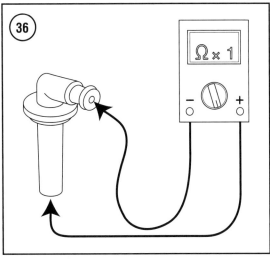

## ⟨37⟩ ELECTRICAL SYSTEM COMPONENT LOCATIONS

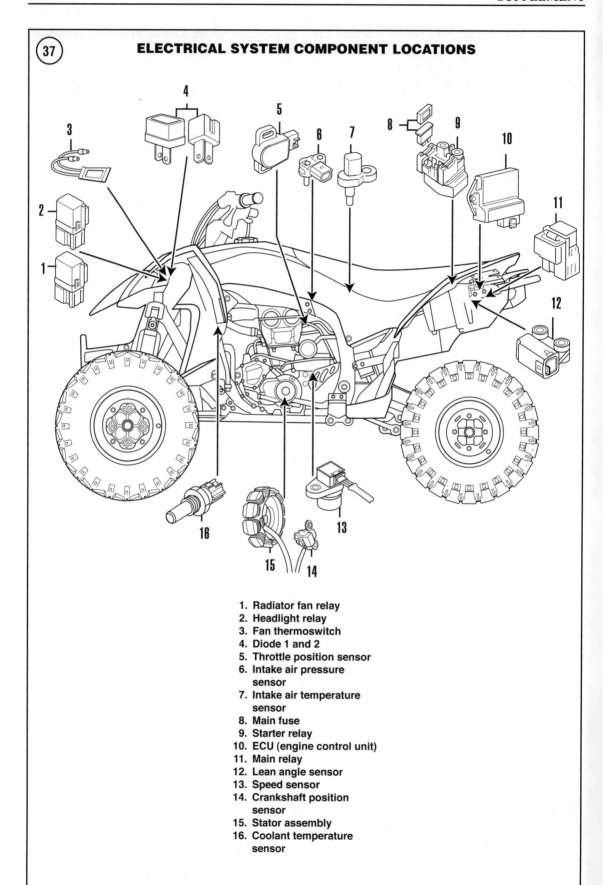

1. Radiator fan relay
2. Headlight relay
3. Fan thermoswitch
4. Diode 1 and 2
5. Throttle position sensor
6. Intake air pressure
   sensor
7. Intake air temperature
   sensor
8. Main fuse
9. Starter relay
10. ECU (engine control unit)
11. Main relay
12. Lean angle sensor
13. Speed sensor
14. Crankshaft position
    sensor
15. Stator assembly
16. Coolant temperature
    sensor

## RADIATOR FAN THERMOSWITCH

The radiator fan thermoswitch (**Figure 37**) controls current to the fan relay. The relay turns on the fan when coolant temperatures are high, and turns off the fan when coolant temperatures are low.

### Testing

> *CAUTION*
> *The radiator fan thermoswitch is fragile and must be handled carefully.*

Refer to Chapter Nine in the main body of this manual for testing. Refer to **Table 47** in this Supplement for the test specifications.

## FUEL SENDING UNIT

The fuel sending unit is located on the fuel pump. Remove the fuel pump as described in this Supplement.

### Testing

1. Use an ohmmeter and measure the sending unit resistance at the harness.
2. Measure the resistance with the unit in the full position. The resistance should be 10 ohms.
3. Measure the resistance with the unit in the empty position. The resistance should be 216 ohms.
4. If the test results are out of specification replace the sending unit.

## SPEED SENSOR

The wheel speed sensor is mounted on the transmission housing (**Figure 38**) and signals rear wheel speed to the ECM.

### Testing

1. To verify the voltage output range, disconnect the speed sensor connector. Connect the speed sensor test harness (**Figure 39**) (Yamaha part No 90890-03208/YU-03208), or its equivalent, inline between the halves of the speed sensor connector.
2. Raise the rear wheel and securely block-up the machine.
3. Connect the positive test probe of a digital voltmeter to the white test port in the test harness; connect negative test probe to the black/blue test port.
4. Turn the main switch on and slowly rotate the rear wheel while measuring voltage at the sensor.

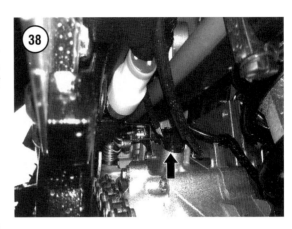

5. During each complete rotation of the wheel the voltage should cycle from 0.6 volt to 4.8 volts to 0.6 volt, to repeat the cycle.
6. If the test results are out of specification replace the sensor.

### Removal/Installation

1. To replace the sensor disconnect the electrical connector and remove the fastener.
2. Remove the sensor.
3. Cover the opening to avoid contamination.
4. Install a new oil seal on the sensor and lubricate with engine oil before installing.
5. Install the fastener and tighten to 10 N•m (88 in.-lb.).
6. Connect the wiring harness coupling.

## MAIN FUSE

The 20-amp main fuse protects all the circuits on the ATV. The main fuse and a spare fuse are found on the starter relay under the seat. To test the fuse, remove it from the starter relay and verify that there is continuity through the fuse.

S

## MAIN (FUEL SYSTEM) RELAY

The main relay is located behind the ECU (**Figure 40**) and secured by a plastic clip.

### Testing

1. Disconnect the electrical coupler from the wiring harness.
2. Detach the relay from its position.
3. Use a spare 12-volt battery to energize the two pull-in windings of the relay. Connect the positive

terminal of the test battery to the red/blue terminal in the main relay. Connect the battery negative terminal to the relay's yellow/red terminal.

4. While the pull-in windings are energized, check for continuity through the load terminals of the relay. Connect an ohmmeter's positive test probe to the red terminal in the relay; connect the negative test probe to the relay's red/blue terminal.

5. If there is no continuity, replace the relay.

## LEAN ANGLE SENSOR

The lean angle sensor (**Figure 41**) sends a signal to the ECU when the machine begins to lean so far as to become unstable. The engine then shuts off.

### Testing

1. Remove the lean angle sensor from beneath the battery case. Connect the lean-angle-sensor test harness (**Figure 29**) (Yamaha part No. 90890-03209/YU/03209) inline between the sensor and its main harness connector.
2. Connect a voltmeter's positive test probe to the yellow/green test port on the test harness; connect the negative test probe to the black/blue test port.
3. Turn the main switch on, and note the voltage reading while rolling the sensor 65 degrees back and forth. Output voltage should be 0.40-1.40 volts when the sensor is held at less than a 65-degree angle. When the sensor's angle exceeds 65 degrees, output voltage should increase to 3.70-4.40 volts.
4. Replace the sensor if any reading is out of specification.

## STARTER

Refer to **Figure 42** for the starter assembly.

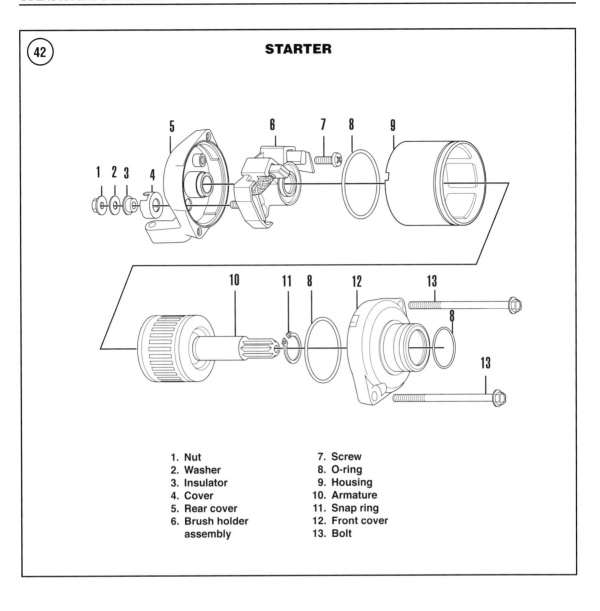

42 STARTER

1. Nut
2. Washer
3. Insulator
4. Cover
5. Rear cover
6. Brush holder
   assembly
7. Screw
8. O-ring
9. Housing
10. Armature
11. Snap ring
12. Front cover
13. Bolt

**Table 44 BATTERY SPECIFICATIONS**

| Type | YTZ-7S |
|---|---|
| Voltage @ 20° C (68° F) | 12 volt 6.0 amp hour |

**Table 45 ALTERNATOR AND CHARGING SYSTEM SPECIFICATIONS**

| Item | Specifications |
|---|---|
| Alternator | |
|   Normal output | 14.0 volts/265 watts @ 5000 rpm |
|   Stator coil resistance | 0.32-0.48 ohms |
| Rectifier | |
|   Input voltage | Above 14 volts @ 5000 rpm |
|   Output voltage | 14.1-14.9 volts |
|   Capacity | 18.0 amps |

S

### Table 46 IGNITION SYSTEM SPECIFICATIONS

| | |
|---|---|
| Ignition coil | |
|   Primary resistance | 2.16-2.64 ohms @ 20° C (68° F) |
|   Secondary resistance | 8.64-12.96k ohms @ 20° C (68° F) |
| Ignition timing | 7.5° BTDC @ 2000 rpm |
| Spark plug cap resistance | 10k ohms |

### Table 47 STARTER SPECIFICATIONS

| Item | New mm (in.) | Service limit mm (in.) |
|---|---|---|
| Starter brush length | 12 (0.47) | 6.5 (0.26) |

### Table 48 BULB SPECIFICATIONS

| Item | Type |
|---|---|
| Coolant temperature warning light | LED |
| Engine trouble warning light | LED |
| Fuel level warning light | LED |
| Neutral indicator light | LED |
| Tail/brake light | LED |

### Table 49 SENSOR, SWITCH AND RESISTOR TEST READINGS

| Item | Test readings |
|---|---|
| Crankshaft position sensor resistance | 248-372 ohms @ 20° C (68° F) |
| Fuel sending unit resistance | |
|   Empty | 216 ohms |
|   Full | 10 ohms |
| Lean angle sensor output voltage | |
|   Less than 65° | 0.40-1.40 volts |
|   More than 65° | 3.70-4.40 volts |
| Radiator fan thermoswitch | |
|   Heating phase | |
|     Less than 115-125° C (207-289°F) | Continuity |
|     More than 115-125° C (207-289°F) | No continuity |
|   Cooling phase | |
|     More than 80-110° C (144-262°F) | No continuity |
|     Less than 80-110° C (144-262°F) | Continuity |
| Speed sensor voltage cycle | 0.6 volt to 4.8 volts to 0.6 volt |

### Table 50 ELECTRICAL SYSTEM TORQUE SPECIFICATIONS

| Item | N•m | in.-lb. | ft.-lb. |
|---|---|---|---|
| Neutral switch | 17 | – | 12 |
| Stator coil mounting bolts | 10 | 88 | – |
| Speed sensor fastener | 10 | 88 | – |
| Crankshaft position sensor bolts | 10 | 88 | – |

# CHAPTER TEN

# COOLING SYSTEM

## COOLANT TEMPERATURE SENSOR

The coolant temperature sensor is located on the front of the radiator (**Figure 43**).

Refer to the *Fuel Injection System* section of this Supplement for procedures.

## WATER PUMP

Refer to **Figure 44** for the water pump assembly.

### Bearing and Seal Removal/Installation

Refer to **Figure 34** when disassembling and assembling the water pump. Refer to Chapter One and Chapter Ten in the manual for bearing and seal removal and installation techniques. Note the following when replacing the seals and bearing.

1. Remove the right crankcase cover and impeller shaft as described in Chapter Ten.

2. From the back of the crankcase cover, carefully drive out the mechanical seal with a punch and hammer.

3. From the front of the crankcase cover, drive out the seal and bearing with an appropriately sized driver.

4. During assembly, install the oil seal and bearing before installing the mechanical seal.

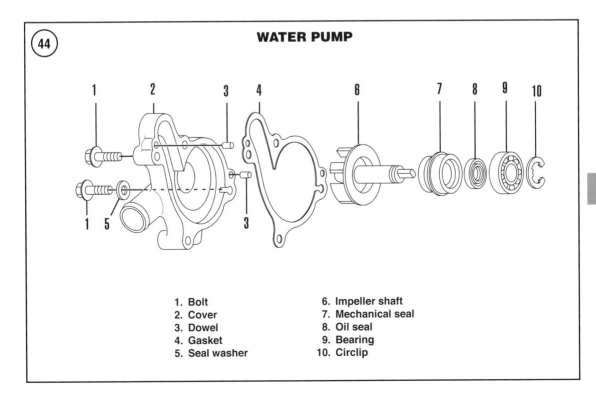

**WATER PUMP**

1. Bolt
2. Cover
3. Dowel
4. Gasket
5. Seal washer
6. Impeller shaft
7. Mechanical seal
8. Oil seal
9. Bearing
10. Circlip

### Table 51 COOLING SYSTEM SPECIFICATIONS

| Item | Specifications |
|---|---|
| Coolant capacity | |
|   Radiator and engine | 1.25 L (1.32 qt.) |
|   Reservoir | 0.25 L (0.26) |
| Radiator fan thermoswitch continuity (2014-on models) | |
| Coolant temp less than 120 ± 5° C (248 ± 41° F) | yes |
| Coolant temp more than 120 ± 5 ° C (248 ± 41° F) | no |
| Coolant temp more than 95 ± 15° C (203 ± 59° F) | no |
| Coolant temp less than 95 ± 15° C (203 ± 59° F) | yes |

# CHAPTER ELEVEN

# WHEELS, TIRES AND DRIVE CHAIN

### Table 52 TIRE AND WHEEL SPECIFICATIONS

| Item | Specifications |
|---|---|
| Tires | |
|   Type | |
|     Front | |
|       2009-2013 models | Dunlop KT351 |
|       2014-on models | MAXXIS/MS21 |
|     Rear | |
|       2009-2013 models | Dunlop KT356 |
|       2014-on models | MAXXIS/MS22 |
|   Size (2014-on models) | |
|     Front | AT21 x 7R10 |
|     Rear | AT20 x 10R9 |
|   Wear limit, front and rear (2014-on models) | 3.0 mm (0.12 in.) |
|   Inflation pressure* (2014-on models) | |
|     Recommended, front and rear | 5.1 psi (35.0 kPa) |
|     Minimum, front and rear | 4.6 psi (32.0 kPa) |
| Wheel (2014-on models) | |
|   Rim size | |
|     Front | 10 x 5.5 AT |
|     Rear | 9 x 8.0 AT |

*Tire inflation pressure is for original equipment tires. Aftermarket tires may require different inflation pressure.

### Table 53 DRIVE CHAIN SPECIFICATIONS

| | |
|---|---|
| Number of links | 98 |
|   Length limit for 15 links | 239.3 mm (9.42 in.) |

### Table 54 TIRE AND WHEEL SPECIFICATIONS

| Item | N•m | in.-lb. | ft.-lb. |
|---|---|---|---|
| Drive sprocket cover screw | 10 | 88 | - |
| Drive sprocket nut | 100 | - | 72 |

# CHAPTER TWELVE

# FRONT SUSPENSION AND STEERING

## HANDLEBAR HOLDERS

### Handlebar Position Adjustment

The steering shaft on these models has two sets of mounting holes for the lower handlebar holders (**Figure 45**). The handlebar position can be adjusted forward or rearward by moving the lower handlebar holders to a different set of mounting holes and/or by changing the front-to-back orientation of the lower handlebar holders.

The handlebar is in the standard position when the lower handlebar holders are mounted in the rear set of steering-shaft holes and the long-arc side of each lower holder faces forward as shown in **Figure 45**. With the lower handlebar holders still mounted in the rear holes, rotating the holders 180 degrees so their long-arc sides face rearward moves the handlebar 10 mm (0.39 in) to the rear of the standard position.

If the lower handlebar holders are mounted in the forward set of holes and the long-arc sides of the lower holders face rearward, the handlebar is moved 10 mm (0.39 in.) forward of the standard position. When the lower holders are in the forward set of holes and the long-arc side of each lower

holder faces forward, the handlebar is now 20 mm (0.079 in.) in front of the standard position.

When installing the upper handlebar holders on these models, make sure the indexing mark on the side of each upper holder (A, **Figure 46**) aligns with the center mark (B) on each handlebar angle scale (C).

### Handlebar Angle Adjustment

The handlebar angle scale (C, **Figure 46**) is also used to adjust the handlebar ends upward or downward within an acceptable range. To adjust the handlebar angle, loosen the handlebar holder bolts and tilt the handlebar to the desired position. Make sure the indexing marks (A) on the upper holders align with the same mark on each corresponding angle scale, and then torque the handlebar holder bolts to 23 Nm (17 ft.-lob.). Do not tilt the handlebar so far that upper holder indexing marks sit outside the handlebar angle scale.

## STEERING SHAFT

The steering shaft seats into a bearing, two collars and two seals that are located in the frame. The upper collar is shouldered and the lower collar is straight.

## BALL JOINT REPLACEMENT

The ball joint can be replaced on both the upper and lower control arms on 2009-on models. Follow the procedure for *Lower Control Arm Ball Joint Removal/Installation* in the main body of this manual.

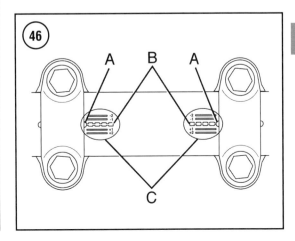

**HANDLEBAR HOLDERS**

45

1. Bolt
2. Upper holder
3. Lower holder
4. Washer
5. Nut

46

**Table 55 STEERING AND FRONT SUSPENSION SPECIFICATIONS**

| Item | Specifications |
|---|---|
| Front shock absorber | |
| Travel | 128 mm (5.04 in.) |
| Spring free length | 304 mm (12 in.) |
| Spring installed length | |
| 2009-2013 models | 289.8 mm (11.4 in.) |
| 2014-on models | 293.0 mm (11.54 in.) |
| Spring rate K1 | 10 N/mm (57 lb.-in.) |
| Spring rate K2 | 30 N/mm (171 lb.-in.) |
| Front wheel travel | 250 mm (9.9 in.) |

**Table 56 FRONT SUSPENSION TORQUE SPECIFICATIONS**

| Item | N•m | in.-lb. | ft.-lb. |
|---|---|---|---|
| Lower handlebar holder nuts | 64 | - | 46 |
| Shock absorber retainer bolt, (2014-on models) | | | |
| Lower bolt | 55 | - | 40 |
| Upper bolt | 40 | - | 29 |
| Tie rod nut | | | |
| 2009-2013 models | 18 | - | 13 |
| 2014-on models | 25 | - | 18 |
| Upper control arm bolt (2014-on models) | 40 | - | 29 |

## CHAPTER THIRTEEN

# REAR AXLE AND SUSPENSION

### REAR AXLE HUB

Before removing the rear axle hub from the end of the swing arm, note that the indexing mark on the swing arm (A, **Figure 47**) sits within the edges of the raised flat (B) on the rear axle hub. During installation, the rear axle hub must be positioned so the swing arm indexing mark sits within this flat.

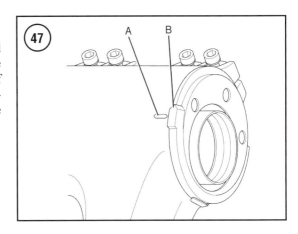

**Table 57 REAR SUSPENSION SPECIFICATIONS**

| Item | Specifications |
|---|---|
| Rear shock absorber | |
|   Travel | 132.5 mm (5.2 in.) |
|   Spring free length | |
|     2009-2013 models | 275 mm (10.8 in.) |
|     2014-on models | 288 mm (11.34 in.) |
|   Spring installed length | |
|     2009-2013 models | 265 mm (10.4 in.) |
|     2014-on models | 278 mm (10.94 in.) |
|   Spring rate | 35 N/mm (200 lb.-in.) |
| Rear wheel travel | 280 mm (11 in.) |
| Shock linkage assembly | |
|   Bearing installed depth | |
|     Connecting-arm-pivot | 4.0 mm (0.16 in.) |
|     Connecting arm-to-relay arm pivot | 7.0 mm (0.28 in.) |
|     Swing arm-to-relay arm pivot | 4.0 mm (0.16 in.) |
|   Oil seal installed depth | |
|     Swing arm-to-relay arm pivot | 1.0 mm (0.04 in.) |
| Swing arm bearing installed depth | |
|   Left swing arm bearing | 15 mm (0.59 in.) |
|   Right swing arm bearing | 5 mm (0.20 in.) |
| Swing arm bushing installed depth | 8 mm (0.31) |

**Table 58 REAR SUSPENSION TORQUE SPECIFICATIONS**

| Item | N•m | in.-lb. | ft.-lb. |
|---|---|---|---|
| Axle nut | 250 | - | 184 |
| Axle nut set screws | 7 | 62 | - |
| Rear shock absorber | | | |
|   Upper and lower bolt/nut | 55 | - | 40 |

# CHAPTER FOURTEEN

# BRAKES

## REAR MASTER CYLINDER

On 2009-on models, a screw secures the hose fitting to the input port on the rear master cylinder. During assembly, torque the hose fitting screw to the specification in Table 60.

## REAR BRAKE PEDAL

### Removal/Installation

A rear-brake-pedal pivot bolt secures the brake pedal to a frame tab (**Figure 48**).
1. Remove the hitch clip from the inboard end of the pivot bolt.
2. Turn out the pivot bolt, detach the pedal return spring, and lower the brake pedal from the frame tab
3. Installation is the reverse of removal. Lubricate the non-threaded shaft of the pivot bolt with lithium grease, and torque the rear-brake-pedal pivot bolt to 26 Nm (19 ft.-lb.).

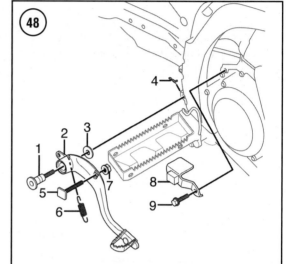

| 1. | Rear-brake-pedal pivot bolt |
| 2. | Rear brake pedal |
| 3. | Washer |
| 4. | Hitch clip |
| 5. | Square head bolt |
| 6. | Pedal return spring |
| 7. | Nut |
| 8. | Rear-brake-light switch cover |
| 9. | Bolt |

### Table 59 BRAKE SERVICE SPECIFICATIONS

| Item | New mm (in.) | Service limit mm (in.) |
|------|--------------|------------------------|
| Brake disc thickness, rear | 4.0 (0.160) | 3.5 (0.138) |

### Table 60 BRAKE TORQUE SPECIFICATIONS

| Item | N•m | in.-lb. | ft.-lb. |
|------|-----|---------|---------|
| Front caliper pad pins | 17 | - | 12 |
| Front caliper mounting bolts (2014) on models | 30 | - | 22 |
| Parking brake housing mounting bolts | 22 | - | 16 |
| Rear-brake-pedal pivot bolt | 26 | - | 19 |
| Rear-master-cylinder reservoir bolt | 4.0 | 35 | - |
| Hose fitting screw | | | |
|   2009-2013 models | 2 | 17.7 | - |
|   2014-on models | 1.5 | 13 | - |

# CHAPTER FIFTEEN

# BODY

The YFZ450R bodywork differs in appearance from earlier models. The attachment of the components essentially remains unchanged. Carefully note the fastener type and size during removal.

## FUEL TANK SHIELD (2014-ON MODELS)

A fuel tank shield bolt secures each side of the fuel tank shield to the frame. During installation, torque the fuel tank shield bolts to 7 Nm (62 in.-lb.).

## FOOT PROTECTORS

### Removal/Installation

The foot protectors on 2009-on models mount onto protector stays, which are secured to the chassis (**Figure 49**). During removal, note the location of any bolt that uses a washer. Washers must be reinstalled on these bolts during assembly.

1. Turn out the foot protector bolts and remove the foot protector from its mounting stay.
2. Remove the stay-to-footrest fasteners and the stay-to-frame fastener. Lower the stay from the frame.
3. If necessary, remove the stay-to-stay fastener and separate stay 1 from stay 2.
4. Installation is the reverse of removal. Torque the fasteners to the specifications in Table 61.

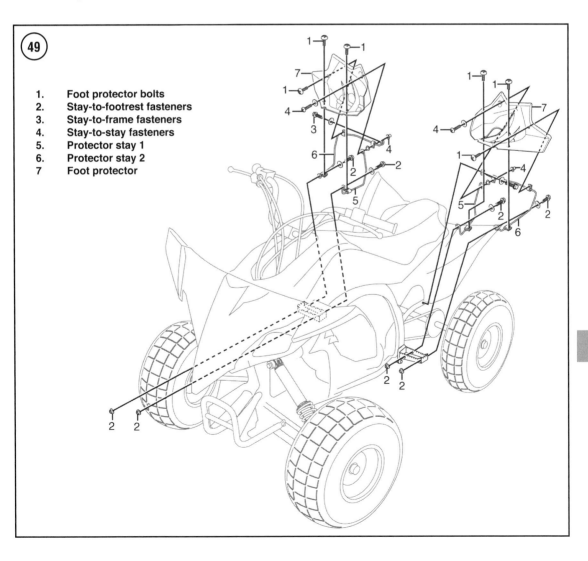

**49**

1. Foot protector bolts
2. Stay-to-footrest fasteners
3. Stay-to-frame fasteners
4. Stay-to-stay fasteners
5. Protector stay 1
6. Protector stay 2
7. Foot protector

## Table 61 Body TORQUE SPECIFICATIONS

| Item | N•m | in.-lb. | ft.-lb. |
|------|-----|---------|---------|
| Footrest bolts | 78 | - | 56 |
| Front bumper bolts | 23 | - | 17 |
| Fuel tank shield bolt (2014-on models) | 7 | 61 | - |
| Foot protector bolts | 6 | 53 | - |
| Protector stay fasteners | | | |
|   Stay-to-footrest fasteners | 17 | 144 | - |
|   Stay-to-frame fasteners | | | |
|     2009-2013 models | 16 | 142 | - |
|     2014-on models | 19 | - | 14 |
|   Stay-to-stay fasteners | 12 | 106 | - |

# INDEX

I

# WIRING
# DIAGRAMS

## 2004-2005 YZF450 MODELS

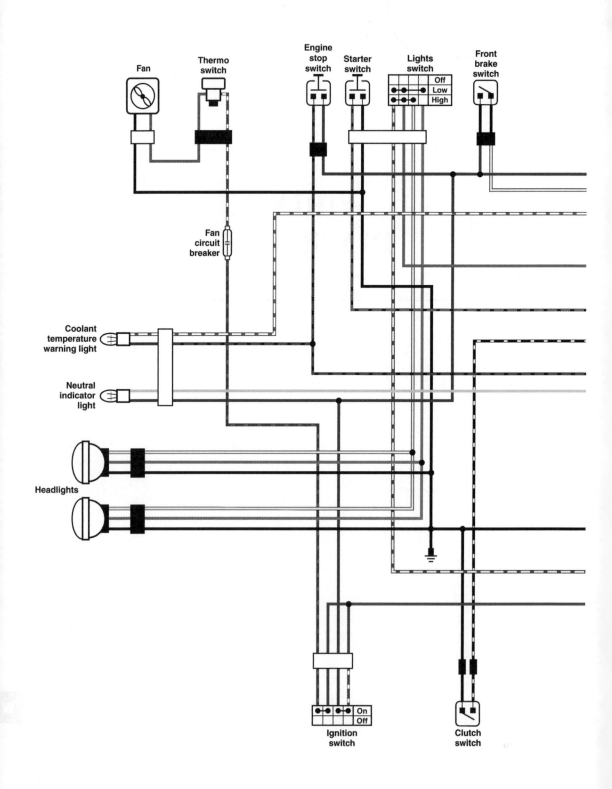

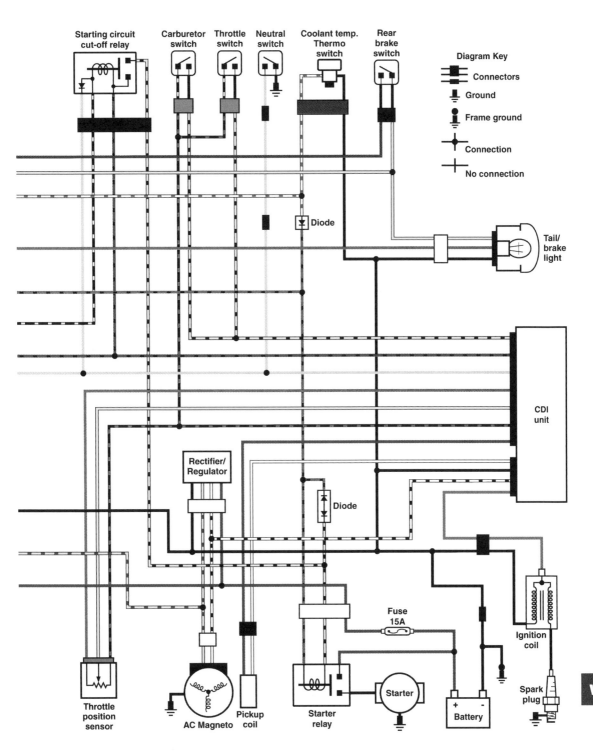

Starting circuit cut-off relay
Carburetor switch
Throttle switch
Neutral switch
Coolant temp. Thermo switch
Rear brake switch

Diagram Key
Connectors
Ground
Frame ground
Connection
No connection

Diode

Tail/ brake light

CDI unit

Rectifier/ Regulator

Diode

Fuse 15A

Ignition coil

Throttle position sensor

AC Magneto

Pickup coil

Starter relay

Starter

+ Battery -

Spark plug

W

## 2006-2009 YZF450 MODELS

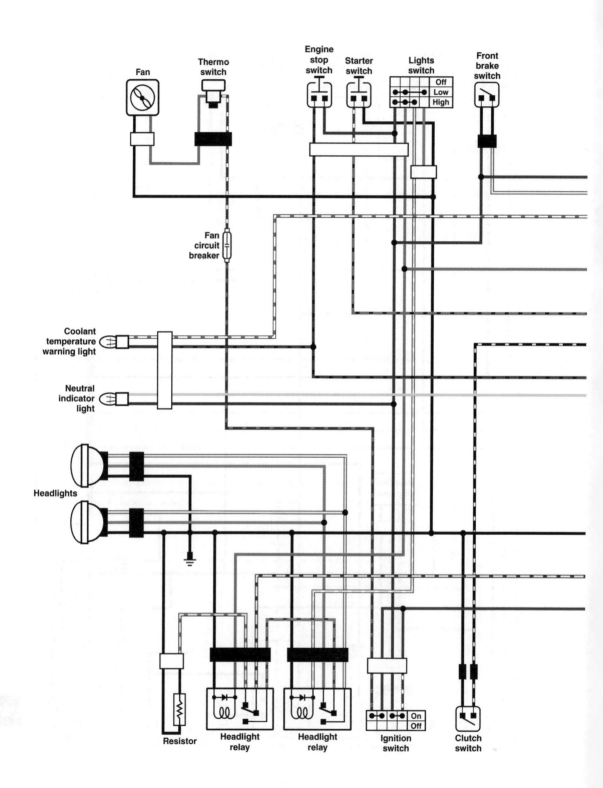

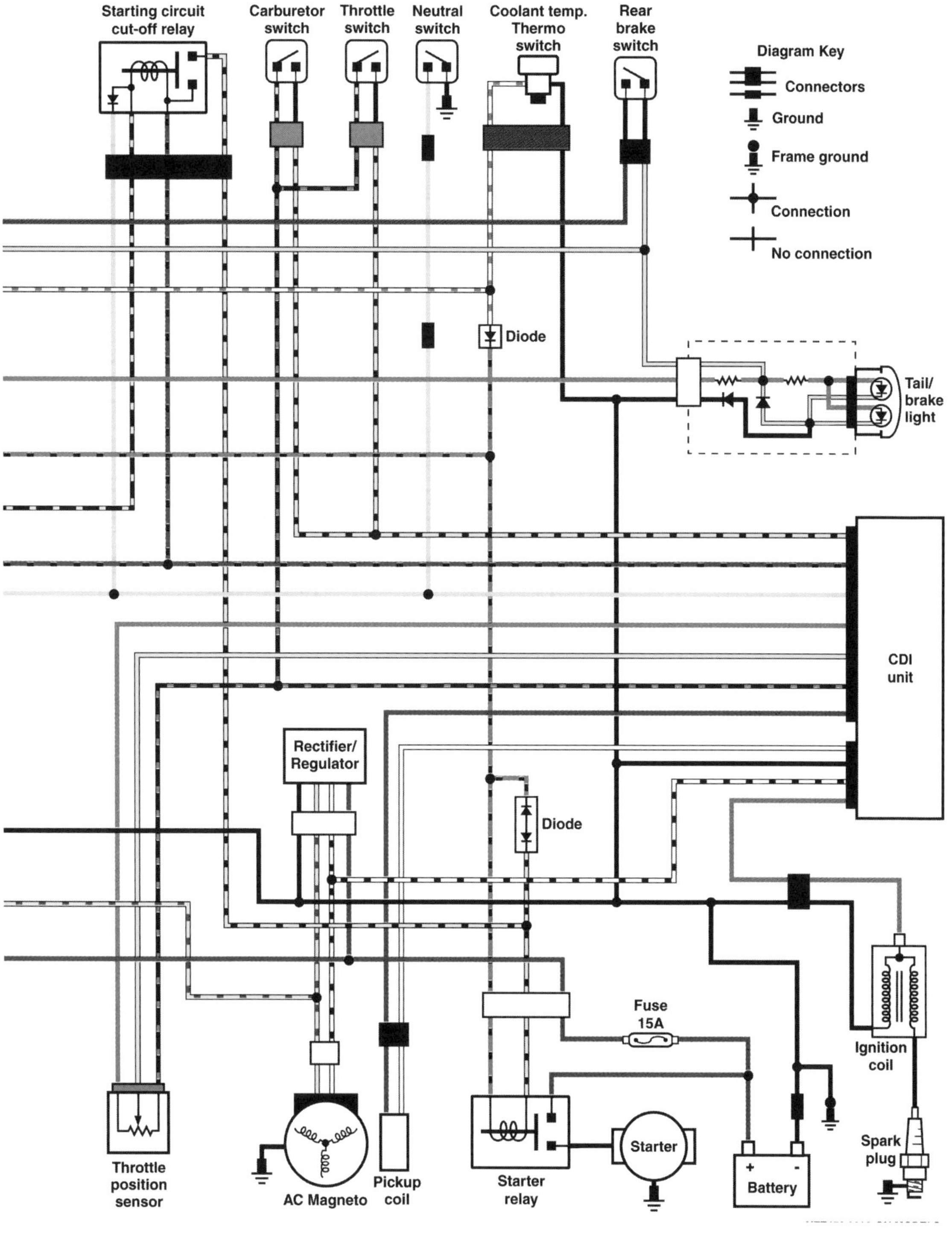

**Starting circuit cut-off relay**

**Carburetor switch**

**Throttle switch**

**Neutral switch**

**Coolant temp. Thermo switch**

**Rear brake switch**

**Diagram Key**

Connectors

Ground

Frame ground

Connection

No connection

Diode

Tail/ brake light

**CDI unit**

**Rectifier/ Regulator**

Diode

**Fuse 15A**

**Ignition coil**

**Throttle position sensor**

**AC Magneto**

**Pickup coil**

**Starter relay**

**Starter**

**Battery**

**Spark plug**

**W**

## YFZ450R 2009-ON MODELS

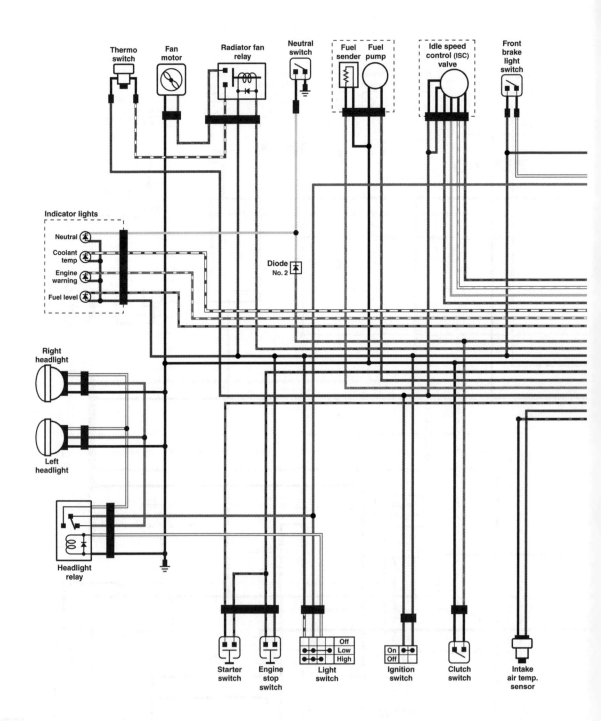

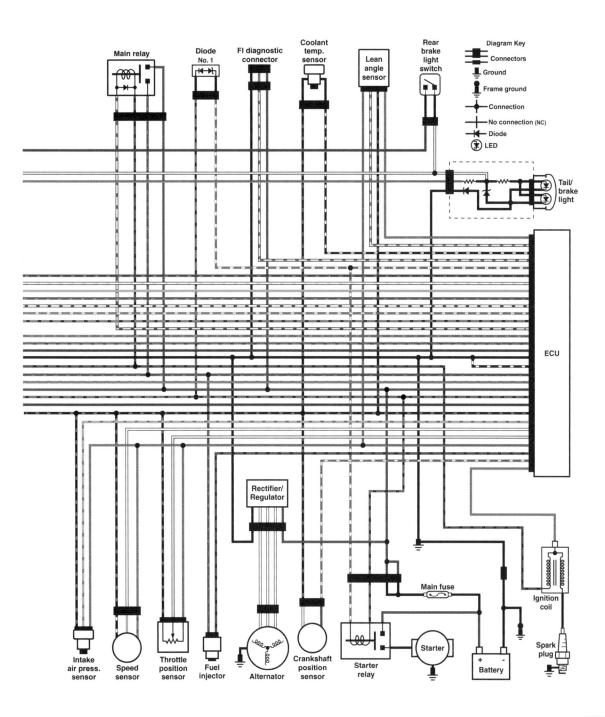

# Check out *clymer.com* for our full line of powersport repair manuals.